UTILIZATION–FOCUSED EVALUATION

Second Edition

Michael Quinn Patton

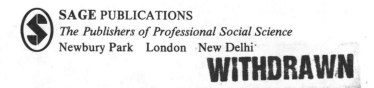

SAGE PUBLICATIONS
The Publishers of Professional Social Science
Newbury Park   London   New Delhi

WITHDRAWN

For information address:

 SAGE Publications, Inc.
2111 West Hillcrest Drive
Newbury Park, California 91320

SAGE Publications Ltd.
28 Banner Street
London EC1Y 8QE
England

SAGE Publications India Pvt. Ltd.
M-32 Market
Greater Kailash I
New Delhi 110 048 India

Printed in the United States of America

Library of Congress Cataloging-in-Publication Data

Patton, Michael Quinn.
    Utilization-focused evaluation (second edition).

    Bibliography: p.
    Includes index.
    1. Evaluation research (Social science programs)—
United States.   I. Title.
H62.5.U5P37   1986   361.6'1'068   85-27817
ISBN 0-8039-2779-7
ISBN 0-8039-2566-2 (pbk.)

FIFTH PRINTING, 1989

CONTENTS

Preface   5

Part I: Toward More Useful Evaluations   9

   1.   The Emergence of Program Evaluation
      and the Utilization Crisis   10

   2.   Utilization in Practice: An Empirical Perspective   29

   3.   The Personal Factor: Fostering Intended Use
      for Intended Users   40

**Part II: Difficult Choices and Multiple Options:
Deciding What to Evaluate**   59

   4.   Focusing Evaluation Questions   61

   5.   Beyond the Goals Clarification Game   83

   6.   Implementation Evaluation:
      What Happened in the Program?   122

   7.   The Program's Theory of Action: Conceptualizing
      Causal Linkages   150

Part III: Appropriate Methods   175

   8.   The Methodology Dragon: The Paradigms Debate
      in Perspective   177

   9.   Evaluations Worth Using: Utilization-Focused
      Methods Decisions   219

  10.   The Meanings of Evaluation Data: Analysis,
      Interpretation, and Reporting   245

Part IV: Utilization: Theory and Practice   281

  11.   Situational Responsiveness and
      the Power of Evaluation   283

  12.   Utilization-Focused Evaluation   322

Appendix I   340

Appendix II   345

References   348

Index   364

About the Author   368

TO VITO PERRONE

PREFACE

Sufi stories are tales used to pass on ancient wisdom. One such story is about a noted Sufi teacher, Mulla Nasrudin. Nasrudin was once asked to return to his home village to share his wisdom with the people there. He mounted a platform in the village square and asked rhetorically, "O my people, do you know what I am about to tell you?"

Some local rowdies, deciding to amuse themselves, shouted rhythmically, "NO. . . ! NO. . . ! NO. . . ! NO. . . !"

"In that case," said Mulla Nasrudin with dignity, "I shall abstain from trying to instruct such an ignorant community," and he stepped down from the platform.

The following week, having obtained an assurance from the hooligans that they would not repeat their harassment, the elders of the village again prevailed upon Nasrudin to address them. "O my people," he began again, "do you know what I am about to say to you?"

Some of the people, uncertain as to how to react, for he was gazing at them fiercely, muttered, "Yes."

"In that case," retorted Nasrudin, "there is no need for me to say more." He then left the village square.

On the third occasion, after a deputation of elders had again visited him and implored him to make one further effort, he stood before the people: "O my people! Do you know what I am about to say?"

Since he seemed to demand a reply, the villagers shouted, "Some of us do, and some of us do not."

"In that case," said Nasrudin as he withdrew, "let those who know teach those who do not" (adapted from Shah, 1964: 80-81).

This book records the things that I have learned about doing program evaluation from those who know. The pages that follow represent an accu-

[5]

mulation of wisdom from many sources: from interviews with 40 federal decision makers and evaluators who participated in a study of the use of federal health evaluation research; from conversations with local program staffs about their evaluation experiences; from colleagues who are professional evaluators; from participants in my evaluation workshops and university classes who are struggling to conduct useful evaluations; and from 15 years of conducting and consulting on evaluations.

The field of evaluation has changed dramatically since the first edition of this book was written in 1977. The practice of evaluation has emerged as an important, recognized profession. Standards have been developed to guide professional practice. Our understanding of how to appropriately adapt social science methods to evaluation problems has increased significantly. Yet, despite these and other developments in evaluation practice and theory, the central issue remains utilization—*doing evaluations that are useful and actually used!*

While I have learned from many people, the personal and professional support of a few special people has been especially important to me in recent years, particularly during the writing of this second edition. Marv Alkin is the scholar and colleague whose evaluation research interests most closely parallel my own. Marv's influence is reflected throughout this book. But perhaps the best indication of my respect for and trust in Marv is that when I moved from being an evaluator to a program administrator, it was to Marv Alkin that I turned to lead the external evaluation of the project for which I was responsible. Kay Adams, now successfully moved from academia to the world of a multinational corporation, was also an important member of that evaluation team. The work of Marv and Kay on that project exemplified and confirmed the principles and practices of *Utilization-Focused Evaluation*. I count them both as close colleagues and, more importantly, as friends.

This edition of *Utilization-Focused Evaluation* has been influenced by my recent work with Cooperative Extension Services in the United States. The premises of utilization-focused evaluation parallel the premises of effective extension work (Patton, 1983). Richard Krueger of the Minnesota Agricultural Extension Service is an internal extension evaluator whose commitment to and skill in both extension and evaluation have taught me a great deal about frontline and grassroots applications of utilization-focused evaluation. Pat Borich, Director of the Minnesota Agricultural Extension Service, and Doris Smith and Susan Laughlin, senior administrators in the California Cooperative Extension Service, have demonstrated to me the difference evaluation can make when it has strong and wise administrative support.

My Caribbean extension colleagues, Tom Henderson and P. I. Gomes, have been important sources of knowledge and experience in international applications of evaluation. Twig Johnson has also helped me understand the relevance of utilization-focused evaluation to evaluations of international projects. An important addition to this book is an international perspective on evaluation, reflecting the fact that a great deal of important evaluation work has been and is being done outside the unusually parochial boundaries of the United States. Delane Welsch, Director of International Agricultural Programs at the University of Minnesota, has been an important source of personal and professional support during the writing of this book. Joan Valasquez and Gene Lyle of Ramsey County Community Human Services have helped me understand how utilization-focused evaluation can work for internal evaluators.

Jeanne Campbell has been editor, critic, collaborator, and consultant. Most of all, she has been a source of power through her unwavering belief that the book would happen. That it did happen owes much to her caring, belief, and support. She helped me make smooth transitions between our family life, writing, consulting, and international travel—while somehow integrating them all in a rich life together with our children.

Patricia Davidson typed the entire manuscript and cut and pasted the few untouched sections of the first edition into this new book. Jeanne Campbell and Patti were the final arbiters of whether some of my more outlandish stories stayed in the book. If they liked them, they stayed. My special thanks for Patti's skill and devotion to high-quality work.

Kathy Manger did the final proofreading with an eye for detail that is extraordinary.

* * *

This book is both practical and theoretical. It tells readers how to conduct program evaluations and why to conduct them in the manner prescribed. Each chapter contains both a review of the relevant literature and actual case examples to illustrate major points. Finally, the book is written in an advocacy style; a definite point of view is offered. The approach presented here is derived from the observation that much of what passes for program evaluation is not very useful; *that evaluation ought to be useful*; and therefore that something different must be done if evaluation *is* to be useful. This book suggests what it is that should be done differently, and how it should be done.

Saint Paul, Minnesota   *Michael Quinn Patton*

PART I

TOWARD MORE USEFUL EVALUATIONS

In the beginning God created the heaven and the earth.

And God saw everything that He made. "Behold," God said, "it is very good." And the evening and the morning were the sixth day.

And on the seventh day God rested from all His work. His archangel came then unto Him asking, "God, how do you know that what you have created is 'very good'? What are your criteria? On what data do you base your judgment? Aren't you a little close to the situation to make a fair and unbiased evaluation?"

God thought about these questions all that day and His rest was greatly disturbed. On the eighth day God said, "Lucifer, go to hell."

Thus was evaluation born in a blaze of glory . . . a legacy under which we continue to operate.

From Halcolm's
The Real Story of Paradise Lost

Chapter 1

THE EMERGENCE OF PROGRAM EVALUATION AND THE UTILIZATION CRISIS

When I was a child, I spake as a child, I understood as a child, I thought as a child: but when I became an adult, I put away childish things. I became an evaluator. And I didn't have the foggiest idea what I was getting into.

—Halcolm

A Setting

It is early morning on a cold November day in Minnesota. Some 15 people in various states of wakefulness have gathered to discuss a county evaluation program. They constitute the Evaluation Advisory Board for a county human service agency. The internal evaluation staff is there; the citizen evaluation advisory board representatives are present; the county board and state representatives have arrived; and I represent the professional evaluation community. We are assembled at this early hour to review the past year's evaluation efforts.

The internal evaluator explains what her staff has done during the year; the problems with getting started (fuzzy program goals, uncertain funding);

[10]

the data collection problems (lack of staff, little program cooperation, inconsistent state and county data processing systems); the management problems (unclear decision-making hierarchies, political undercurrents, trying to do too much); and the findings despite it all ("tentative to be sure, but more than we knew a year ago and some solid recommendations").

Then the advisory board explains its frustration with the disappointing results of the evaluation ("data just aren't solid enough"). The county board representatives explain why their decisions are contrary to evaluation recommendations ("we didn't really get the information we needed when we wanted it and it wasn't what we wanted when we got it"). The room is filled with disappointment, frustration, defensiveness, cynicism, and more than a little anger. There are charges, countercharges, budget threats, moments of planning, and longer moments of explaining away problems. Then the advisory board chairperson turns to me in exasperation and asks, "Tell us, what do we have to do to get useful evaluations that are actually used?"

The Issue of Utilization

This book is an outgrowth of that question. If the scene I have described were unique, it would merely represent a frustrating professional problem for the people involved. But if that scene is repeated over and over on many mornings, with many advisory boards, and if the question of how to produce good evaluations that are used is asked by many people in many settings, then the question of evaluation use would become what sociologist C. Wright Mills (1959: 8-9) called a critical public issue:

> *Issues* have to do with matters that transcend these local environments of the individual and the range of his inner life. They have to do with the organization of many such milieux into the institutions of an historical society as a whole. . . . An issue, in fact, often involves a crisis in institutional arrangements.

In my judgment, the issue of using evaluation in appropriate and meaningful ways represents such a crisis in institutional arrangements. This issue of utilization has emerged at the interface between science and government. It has to do with our fundamental assumptions about human rationality, progress, and science applied to the creation of a better world. The evaluation use issue concerns the spending of billions of dollars in private and public funds to fight problems of poverty, disease, ignorance, joblessness, mental anguish, crime, hunger, and inequality. How are programs to combat these societal ills to be judged? How does one distinguish effective from ineffective programs?

To understand a critical public issue or crisis, C. Wright Mills advised us to begin with the historical context out of which the issue emerged. The emergence of evaluation research is quite recent. To establish a context for understanding the utilization crisis in program evaluation, it is helpful to briefly review the historical emergence of program evaluation. Although the "Paradise Lost" story that opened this book suggests that evaluation, or at least making judgments, is intrinsic to the nature of both humans and deities, the formal establishment of evaluation as a profession is relatively recent— as recent as the mid-1970s and the founding of the Evaluation Research Society and Evaluation Network (now merged as the American Evaluation Association). This chapter is a thumbnail sketch of how evaluation got from Genesis to the Information Age with utilization emerging along the way as a symbol of one of the major public issues of our times: using information for decision making.

Using Information in the Information Age

Looking back it is worth taking a moment to reflect on what a short time we have been doing much of what we are currently doing in modern society, especially research and evaluation. Physical anthropologists tell us that humans have been on the Earth as a species for something like three to five million years, give or take a million. The standard deviation is slightly large in these calculations, but the point is that it has been a long time. During most of that time we were organized in small hunting and gathering societies, concerned primarily about food, tribe, and territory.

It was only about 10,000 years ago that our forebears developed sedentary agriculture, which made possible the emergence of some of the great civilizations of ancient times. The Industrial Revolution is only about 200 years old. Industrialization meant a major change in the means and organization of production. Now social scientists tell us that in the last 25-30 years we have moved into "Postindustrial Society," "the Age of Electronic Technology," or more simply, *the Information Age*.

Each epoch of human history has its special achievements and its special problems. The great achievements of hunting and gathering societies were strong kinship and tribal systems. The great achievement of agricultural society was increased food production and trade. The great achievement of the Industrial Revolution was the substitution of capital for labor, with tremendous increases in human productivity. The great achievement of our age is the capacity to generate, store, retrieve, transmit, and instantaneously communicate information. The great problem of our age is keeping up with, sorting out, absorbing, and *using* information.

The challenge of the information age is *not* figuring out how to produce, store, or transmit information. The challenge is figuring out what is really worth knowing and then getting people to actually use what is known. Our technological capabilities to gather and computerize information now far exceed our human ability to process and make sense out of what is gathered and computerized. In the 3-5 million years of human history technology has changed tremendously, but the human being as an organism has changed relatively little. Neurological, psychological, social, and political barriers come to the fore with the issue of information use. Getting people to use what is known is a critical concern across the different knowledge sectors of society. A major specialty in medicine (compliance research) is concerned with trying to understand why so many people don't follow the doctor's orders. There is a common, underlying problem of information use in trying to get people to use seatbelts, stop smoking, exercise, eat properly, and pay attention to evaluation findings. In the fields of nutrition, energy conservation, education, criminal justice, financial investment, human services, corporate management, international development—the list could go on and on—a central problem, often *the* central problem, is getting people to use information. In agriculture the major activity of extension services is trying to get farmers, homemakers, young people, and community leaders to apply scientific knowledge.

An oft-told agricultural extension story is of the young agent who visits a farmer to tell him about the latest food production techniques. As the young extension agent begins to offer advice the farmer interrupts him and says, "No sense in telling me all those new ideas about what to do, young man. I'm not doing half of what I know I should be doing now."

A concrete research example may help illustrate the nature of the problem. Adolescent health specialist Michael Resnik (1984) reports that teenage pregnancies have gone up 13% in the last decade. In studying teenage girls who become pregnant, he found very few cases in which the problem was a lack of information about contraception, about pregnancy, or about how to avoid pregnancies. The problem was *not* a lack of information. The problem was not confusion about what to do to prevent pregnancies. *The problem was in not doing it, in not applying known information.*

There is an incredible gap between the knowledge and the application of that knowledge. In so many instances it's heartbreaking—they have the knowledge, the awareness, and the understanding, but somehow it doesn't apply to them [Resnik, 1984: 15].

* * *

This book is about narrowing the gap between generating evaluation information and actually applying evaluation information for program decision making and improvement. Although the problem of information use remains central to our age, we are not without knowledge about what to do. Over the past 3-5 million years we've learned a few things about overcoming our human resistance to new knowledge, and over the last 10 years of active evaluation practice, we've learned a great deal about how to increase evaluation use. To set the stage for presenting what we've learned, it will be helpful to clarify what I mean by program evaluation.

What Is Program Evaluation?

Program evaluation is the systematic collection of information about the activities, characteristics, and outcomes of programs for use by specific people to reduce uncertainties, improve effectiveness, and make decisions with regard to what those programs are doing and affecting. This definition of evaluation emphasizes (1) the systematic collection of information about (2) a broad range of topics (3) for use by specific people (4) for a variety of purposes. This broad definition focuses on gathering data that are meant to be, and actually are, used for program improvement and decision making.

Program evaluation uses research methods to gather information, but evaluation differs fundamentally from basic research in the purpose of data collection. Basic scientific research is undertaken to discover new knowledge, test theories, establish truth, and generalize across time and space. Program evaluation is undertaken to inform decisions, clarify options, reduce uncertainties, and provide information about programs and policies within contextual boundaries of time, place, values, and politics. The difference between research and evaluation has been called by Cronbach and Suppes (1969) the difference between conclusion-oriented and decision-oriented inquiry. Research is aimed at truth. Evaluation is aimed at action.

Hemphill has suggested that evaluation is most clearly differentiated from research by the relative emphasis on utilitarianism in evaluation:

> The implications of the primacy of utility in evaluation studies and the relative unimportance of such considerations in research are profound [quoted in Johnson, 1970: 12].

Stake (1981) has emphasized that evaluation differs from research in the relative importance attached to making generalizations. The greater the focus on evaluative information that is highly relevant to the specific developments of a particular program and the special concerns of individual decision makers, the less one will make methods decisions with an eye to the research generalizability of findings. Cronbach articulated this perspective quite dramatically:

> Results of a program evaluation are so dependent on the setting that replication is only a figure of speech; the evaluator is essentially an historian [Cronbach et al., 1980: 7].

In any data collection effort the extent to which there is concern about utility, generalizability, scientific rigor, and relevance of the data to specific information users will vary. Each of these dimensions is a continuum. This book emphasizes utility, relevance, practicality, and meeting the information needs of specific decision makers, thus the focus on program *evaluation*. The term "evaluation *research*" will be used to refer to studies of program outcomes and effects where there is relatively greater emphasis on generalizability, causality, and credibility within the research community.

Later chapters will explore the design and methods implications of viewing program evaluation as distinct from research. At this point it is important to emphasize that both program evaluation and evaluation research bring an empirical perspective to questions of policy and program effectiveness. Both program evaluation and evaluation research are concerned with data accuracy, validity, and reliability. This data-based approach to evaluation stands in contrast to two alternative and competing ways of approaching program assessment. In the past, the use of empirical information for evaluating programs was constrained by these two competing perspectives: the charity orientation and pure pork barrel politics.

The Charity Orientation

> And now abideth faith, hope, charity, these three; but the greatest of these *is* charity.
>
> > —Paul's First Letter
> > to the Corinthians

In the past a charity orientation has dominated the delivery of health, education, and welfare services. From a charity perspective, the main criterion for evaluation of programs is the sincerity of funders and program staff; the primary measure of program worth is that the program organizers care enough to try their very best to help the less fortunate. The charities are modern manifestations and adaptations of the Good Samaritan example; and, from this perspective, as God mandated helping the less fortunate, so God alone will judge the outcomes and effectiveness of these charitable efforts. God clearly needs no assistance from the likes of social scientists, with their impersonal statistics and objective analyses of human suffering.

The charity orientation is still often the predominant approach to the evaluation of many philanthropic, privately funded human service programs, such as United Way efforts, foundation-supported programs, and church-related social service activities. As a director of a local service agency explained to me after a two-day evaluation workshop,

> This scientific evaluation stuff is all very interesting, and I suppose it's something we're going to have to do for funds. But when it comes right down to it, my program is evaluated every night when I get down on my knees and ask God to look into my heart and judge what I do by His criteria. And, by God, so long as His evaluation is positive, we'll keep on serving and helping people.

Or, as another agency director told me after a measurement session, "All I want to know is whether or not my staff are trying their best. When you've got a valid and reliable and all-that-other-stuff measuring instrument for love and sincerity, you can come back and see me."

Social scientists as evaluators have little to offer those who are fully ensconced in a pure charity orientation. Others, however (and their numbers are increasing), have come to believe that, even for the sincere, indeed *especially* for the sincere and caring, empirically based program evaluations can be valuable. After all, sincerity and caring mean that one wants to do a good job, wants to be effective, and wants to make a difference. The purpose of program evaluation is precisely that—to increase effectiveness and provide information on the extent to which what ought to be accomplished is being accomplished. *People who really care about their work are precisely the people who can benefit most from utilization-focused program evaluation.*

A major reason for evaluating policies and programs is to make sure that what we want to have happen actually happens. In 1914, Thomas Edison commented on this problem in his diary when he observed,

> Spencer traced 32 acts of Parliament and discovered that 29 produced effects contrary to those intended [Edison, 1983: I, 5, 1914].

It is also worth noting that many of the pioneers of charitable services were interested in data that would help them in serving the needy. The history of earlier charities that led to modern welfare departments and social service programs has often included attention to empirical information. The first state Board of Charity in the United States was developed in Massachusetts in 1863, just 120 some years ago. There were six others by 1870, although such boards were largely supervisory and administrative until 1917, when Illinois became the first state to develop a modern welfare department. On the research side, charity societies have been doing surveys since the late 1800s. The renowned Hull House and East End House in Boston were early pioneers in using surveys to find out what was going on in the areas they served. That led to more extensive surveys in Washington, D.C., in 1905, Pittsburgh in 1907 and 1908, and Springfield in 1914. There followed creation of the Department of Surveys and Exhibits at the Sage Foundation and work at the University of Chicago in the 1920s. These early research efforts led to what we now know as human service research and evaluation. The roots of modern human services evaluation can be found in those early surveys—what we would now call needs assessments.

Program evaluation, then, need not call into question a staff's faith, hope, and charity. Rather, it is a mechanism for determining the extent to which staff energies and charitable resources are being expended effectively. Negative findings should not be construed as an attack on staff motivations but, rather, as a means of determining the fruitfulness of the specific actions that spring from those motivations. Caring about evaluation findings and caring about helping people can be, and ought to be, complementary.

The Pork Barrel Approach

A second historically important approach to evaluating programs has been pork barrel politics, which takes as its main criterion the political leverage of a program's constituency. The issue in this case is not one of program effectiveness but, rather, one of political efficacy. If powerful constituents want the program, or if more is to be gained politically by support for rather than opposition to the program, then the program is judged worthwhile; no other evidence of program effectiveness is relevant. This is the reason it is so difficult to terminate programs and agencies once they are created by government bodies. Programs rapidly develop constituencies whose vested interests lie in program continuation. The driving force of the pork barrel approach is to give out money where it counts politically, not where it will be used most effectively.

The pork barrel approach is not unique to elected politicians and governmental bodies. The funding boards of philanthropic foundations, corporate boards, and service agencies have their own constituencies to please. There are political debts to be paid and political debts to be incurred. The inter-locking directorates of philanthropic funding bodies make for some interest-ing politics. Under these conditions, program effectiveness is not judged in terms of demonstrable attainment of stated objectives; on the contrary, the issue is how parochial and partisan interests can be served by funding certain programs. Those programs are effective which enhance and serve vested interests. Empirical evaluation findings are of interest only insofar as they can be manipulated for political and public relations purposes. While pork barrel traditions remain an important influence, the emergence of data-based evaluation possibilities has complicated the exercise of *pure* politics in at least some decision-making arenas. (Chapter 11 will address in more depth the relationship, often healthy when properly approached, between politics and evaluation.)

The Emergence of Empirical Program Evaluation

An empirical approach to program evaluation means using reasonably valid and reliable data to assess what is happening in a program and the pro-gram's effects on the people it is intended to serve. The idea of systemati-cally and scientifically evaluating government programs for decision making is relatively new. When the federal government of the United States began to take a major role in human service programs during the Depression and the New Deal, the closest thing to evaluation was the employment of a few jobless academics to write program histories. It was not until the mas-sive federal expenditures on an awesome assortment of programs during the 1960s and 1970s that accountability began to mean more than assessing staff sincerity or political head counts of opponents and proponents. A number of events converged to create a demand for systematic empirical evaluation of the effectiveness of government programs. There is space here to men-tion only a few of the more important forces that led to the emergence of evaluation.

Beginning with education, there was a growing critique of American schools after the Soviets launched Sputnik in 1957, a critique born of fear that the education gap was even larger than the "missile gap." There was also the growing realization that, ten years after the 1954 Supreme Court Brown decision on racial integration in schools, "separate and unequal" was still the norm rather than the exception. There was enormous pressure on schools as the focus of parents' upward mobility dreams for their chil-dren. As sociologists Blau and Duncan (1967) explained, education had be-come the major mechanism for social mobility in modern society. Parents wanted effective schools.

Although educational evaluation can trace its beginnings back to Joseph Rue's comparative study of spelling performance by 33,000 students in

1897, the field of educational evaluation has been dominated by fairly narrow concerns with testing and measurement. From its roots in the work of Tyler (1950), educational evaluation remained quite limited in scope, conceptualization, and impact until the passage of the U.S. Elementary and Secondary Education Act in 1965—"by far the most comprehensive and ambitious educational legislation ever envisioned by the federal government" (Worthen and Sanders, 1973: 5). This legislation grew out of severe and widespread criticisms of American education. The critiques of schools gave rise to a massive influx of federal money aimed at desegregation, innovation, compensatory education, greater equality of opportunity, teacher training, and higher student achievement. Evaluation data were called for to assess the effects of the many programmatic changes being inflicted on the nation's children. To what extent did these changes really make an educational difference?

But education was only one arena in the War on Poverty of the 1960s. Great Society programs from the Office of Economic Opportunity were aimed at nothing less than the elimination of poverty, if not before we landed on the moon, then certainly shortly thereafter. The nation's health delivery systems were found to be highly effective at ignoring the needs of the poor and elderly, although there was debate over which had been most ignored—physical health needs or mental health needs. The creation of large-scale federal health programs, including community mental health centers, was coupled with a mandate for evaluation, often at a level of 1% to 3% of program budgets.

Other major programs were created in housing, manpower, services integration, community planning, urban renewal, welfare, and so on—the whole of which came to be referred to as "butter" (as opposed to "guns") expenditures. In the 1970s, these Great Society programs collided head on with the Vietnam War, rising inflation, increasing taxes, and the fall from glory of Keynesian economics. All in all, it was what sociologists and social historians, with a penchant for understatement, would characterize as "as a period of rapid social and economic change."

From all the turmoil of that period, something called "evaluation" emerged as an alternative to the charity and pork barrel approaches to assessing program effectiveness. By the early 1970s, evaluations were being regularly required as part of health, education, and welfare programs. Although the requirement for evaluation was a political response to the public demand for increased governmental accountability, the empirical evaluation approach to accountability is quite different from a purely cynical pork barrel approach to program assessment.

Program evaluation as an empirical approach to judging programs was born of two lessons from this period of large-scale social experimentation and government intervention: first, the realization that there is not enough money to do all the things that need doing; and, second, the realization that even if there were enough money, it takes more than money to solve complex human and social problems.

Although there is still debate about whether or not Great Society programs in the United States were ever really sufficiently funded and implemented to test their effectiveness, there is now considerably more humility among experienced social activists about our ability to quickly eliminate long-standing social and economic injustices. The demands for government programs far outstrip the ability of even the most liberal legislative body to meet everyone's needs and demands. Expectations and human wants have an uncanny ability to stay well ahead of institutional response capacities. Even if we manage to provide minimum levels of support to all families so as to eliminate poverty in an absolute sense, we can be assured that feelings of relative deprivation will keep the need for new social programs alive and well for the foreseeable future.

As not everything can be done, there must be a basis for deciding which things will be done. Although evaluation and policy analysis are not about to replace politics in that decision-making process, gathering data about actual effects is one important mechanism for facilitating the making of difficult decisions in an attempt to get as much as possible from the money that is spent. Evaluation findings cannot only take the heat off decision makers by providing data (reasons) for making unpopular decisions in a world where everything you do makes someone unhappy; evaluation is also good politics in its own right: If we do not have enough money to do everything and please everyone, we can at least increase the odds of doing something and pleasing someone by funding demonstrably effective programs.

The Great Society programs throughout America clearly demonstrated that money is not enough even when it is abundant. Not all the failures of the American War on Poverty can be attributed to inadequate funds. Some of those failures were due to too much funding too quickly. There were management problems, cultural issues, and enormously complex psychological dimensions to poverty programs. Wanting to help is not the same as knowing how to help; likewise, having the money to help is not the same as knowing how to spend money in a helpful way. Poverty programs turned out to be patronizing, controlling, dependency generating, insulting, inadequate, misguided, overpromised, and mismanaged. If money alone is not the answer, then some mechanism must be found for identifying what combination of factors will work in a specific situation. Some poverty programs were enormously effective; others were awesome disasters. How do we know which ones were which—and how do we find out what made the difference? Program evaluation and policy analysis offer at least a partial solution.

Faith, hope, and charity tell us to do something, but do not tell us what to do. The pork barrel approach to evaluation works best when program constituents are easily identified as more or less important. But in a world where every group is highly politicized, funds are limited, and every decision to do something means a corresponding decision not to do something else, legislators, government officials, and foundation trustees have reason to take seriously evaluation findings on program effectiveness before making their decisions.

Worldwide Demand for Evaluation

Interest in empirically assessing policies and programs has by no means been limited to the United States. The federal government of Canada, especially the Auditor General's Office, has demonstrated a major commitment to conducting program evaluations at both national and provincial levels (Rutman and Mayne, 1985). The Canadian Evaluation Society is active in promoting the appropriate practice and use of program evaluations throughout Canada. European governments are routinely using evaluation and policy analysis tools, although the nature, location, and results of evaluation efforts vary from country to country (see, for example, Hoogerwerf, 1985; Patton, 1985). International agencies have also begun using evaluation to assess the full range of development efforts under way in Third World countries. The World Bank, UNICEF, the Australian Development Assistance Bureau (1982), and the U.S. Agency for International Development are examples of international development organizations with significant and active evaluation offices. The annual meetings of the American Evaluation Association have become an international event, with participants representing evaluation experiences from throughout the world.

Clearly, then, program evaluation is an effort being undertaken by many people, in many different places, on a wide variety of activities. While international evaluators can trace their roots to ancient Babylon (Patton, 1981: 196), China, and Greece (Worthen and Sanders, 1973: 2), evaluations of all kinds of programs and policies are now carried out in all parts of the world—in agriculture, energy conservation, economic development, mental health, housing, environmental protection, integration, and criminal justice, to name but a few of the many arenas in which human beings are engaged in collective action aimed at attaining a grand panorama of goals.

But what difference does all this evaluation activity make? Are the findings actually used? These and related questions of utilization have become the central issues in applied social science generally, and evaluation specifically. Program evaluation is emblematic of the Information Age. The concern with use in evaluation is part of the larger problem of information utilization in postindustrial society.

Using Empirical Data for Decision Making: The Emergent Crisis

Concomitant with the optimism of the early 1960s that we could eliminate poverty was a new optimism about the role scientists could play in efforts to improve society. Edward Suchman (1967: 1) began his seminal
textbook on evaluation research by quoting Hans Zetterberg to the effect that
"one of the most appealing ideas of our century is the notion that science can
be put to work to provide solutions to social problems." Social and behavioral science embodied the hope of finally applying human rationality to the
improvement of society. By the early 1960s, Zetterberg's "appealing idea"
was becoming a reality. Scientists were welcomed to the White House by
President Kennedy as never before. Scientific perspectives were taken into
account in the writing of new social legislation. Economists, historians,
psychologists, political scientists, and sociologists were all welcomed into
the public arena to share in the reshaping of modern postindustrial society.
Thus, concurrent with the elimination of poverty, the American Great Society programs foretold a new order of rationality in government—a rationality undergirded by social scientists who, if not philosopher-kings
themselves, were at least ministers to philosopher-kings. Carol Weiss
(1977: 4) recalls the optimism of that period:

> There was much hoopla about the rationality that social science would bring
> to the untidy world of government. It would provide hard data for planning,
> evidence of need and of resources. It would give cause-and-effect theories for
> policy making, so that statesmen would know which variables to alter in order
> to effect the desired outcomes. It would bring to the assessment of alternative
> policies a knowledge of relative costs and benefits so that decision-makers
> could select the options with the highest payoff. And once policies were in
> operation, it would provide objective evaluation of their effectiveness so that
> necessary modifications could be made to improve performance.

One manifestation of the scope, pervasiveness, and penetration of these
hopes is the number of evaluation studies actually conducted. While it is
impossible to identify all such studies, as early as 1976 the *Congressional
Sourcebook on Federal Program Evaluations* contained 1,700 citations of
program evaluation reports issued by 18 U.S. executive branch agencies and
the General Accounting Office during fiscal years 1973 through 1975 (Office of Program Analysis, GAO, 1976: 1). The numbers have grown substantially since then. In 1977, federal agencies spent $64 million on program
evaluation and more than $1.1 billion on social research and development
(Abramson, 1978). The third edition of the Compendium of Health and Human Services Evaluation Studies (HHS, 1983) contains 1,435 entries. The
fourth volume of the U.S. Comptroller General's directory of *Federal*

Evaluations (GAO, 1981) identifies 1,429 evaluative studies from various U.S. federal agencies completed between September 1, 1979 and September 30, 1980. *The Policy Analysis Source Book for Social Programs* (1976) is an annotated bibliography containing over 4,000 abstracts of policy analyses and evaluations of federal health, housing, energy, education, and welfare programs.

While the large number of and substantial funding for evaluations suggest great prosperity and acceptance, under the surface and behind the scenes a crisis was building—*a utilization crisis*. Just as by the late 1960s we had discovered that poverty would not go away as easily as we had hoped, so the visions of government based on rational decision making undergirded by scientific truth were beginning to fade. No sooner had the crises of Great Society social programs given rise to calls for greater accountability than scientists responded that their research to serve that purpose was not being used. The utopian hopes for a scientific and rational society, so imminent in the early 1960s, had somehow been postponed. The landing of the first human on the moon had come and gone, but there was still poverty—and research was still not being used as the basis for government decision making.

While the utilization crisis concerned all types of applied social science (see Weiss, 1977), nonutilization seemed to be particularly characteristic of evaluation studies. Ernest House (1972: 412) put it this way: "Producing data is one thing! Getting it used is quite another." Williams and Evans (1969: 453) wrote that "in the final analysis, the test of the effectiveness of outcome data is its impact on implemented policy. By this standard, there is a dearth of successful evaluation studies." Wholey et al. (1970: 46) concluded that "the recent literature is unanimous in announcing the general failure of evaluation to affect decision-making in a significant way." They go on to note that their own study "found the same absence of successful evaluations noted by other authors (Wholey et al., 1970: 48)." Cohen and Garet (1975: 19) found that "there is little evidence to indicate that government planning offices have succeeded in linking social research and decision-making." Seymour Deitchman, in his "Tale of Social Research and Bureaucracy," concluded that "the impact of the research on the most important affairs of state was, with few exceptions, nil" (1976: 390). Weidman et al. (1973: 15) concluded that "on those rare occasions when evaluations studies have been used . . . the little use that has occurred [has been] fortuitous rather than planned." In 1972, Carol Weiss viewed underutilization as one of the foremost problems in evaluation research:

> Evaluation research is meant for immediate and direct use in improving the quality of social programming. Yet a review of evaluation experience suggests that evaluation results have not exerted significant influence on program decisions [Weiss, 1972c: 10-11].

This conclusion was echoed by four prominent commissions and study committees: the U.S. House Committee on Government Operations, Research and Technical Programs Subcommittee (1967); the Young Committee report published by the National Academy of Sciences (1968); the Report of the Special Commission on the Social Sciences for the National Science Foundation (1968); and the Social Science Research Council's prospective on the Behavioral and Social Sciences (1969).

British economist L. J. Sharpe reported that the situation was the same in Europe. He reviewed the European literature and commission reports on utilization of social scientific knowledge and concluded that "we are brought face to face with the fact that it has proved very difficult to uncover many instances where social science research has had a clear and direct effect on policy even when it has been specifically commissioned by government" (1977: 45). Ronald Havelock of the Knowledge Transfer Institute has observed that "there is a gap between the world of research and the world of routine organizational practice, regardless of the field" (1980: 13). Bridging that gap to increase research utilization has proved a difficult challenge, requiring new kinds of communications linkages (Rothman, 1980).

Standards of Excellence for Evaluation

One major step toward increasing evaluators' commitment to evaluation use has been the development of standards for evaluation that make it clear that *evaluations ought to be useful.*

In the past many researchers took the position that their responsibility was merely to design studies, collect data, and publish findings; what decision makers did with those findings was not their problem. This stance removed from the evaluator any responsibility for fostering use and placed all the blame for nonuse or underutilization on decision makers.

This academic aloofness from the messy world in which decisions are made and research findings are translated into action has long been a characteristic of basic scientific research. Before about 1978, the criteria for judging evaluation research could scarcely be differentiated from criteria for judging basic research in the traditional social and behavioral sciences. Technical quality and methodological rigor were the primary concerns of researchers. Use was not an issue. Methods decisions dominated the evaluation decision-making process. Methodological rigor meant experimental designs, quantitative data, and detailed statistical analysis. Whether decision makers understood sophisticated statistical analyses was not the researcher's problem. Validity, reliability, measurability, and generalizability were the dimensions that received the greatest attention in judging evaluation research proposals and reports (see Bernstein and Freeman, 1975). Indeed, evaluators concerned about increasing utilization often called for ever more methodologically rigorous evaluations to increase the validity of findings, thereby supposedly compelling decision makers to take findings seriously.

By the late 1970s, however, it was becoming increasingly clear that greater methodological rigor was not going to solve the utilization problem. Program staff and funders were becoming openly skeptical about spending scarce funds on evaluations they couldn't understand and seldom viewed as really useful. Evaluators were being asked to be "accountable" just as program staff were supposed to be accountable. The questions emerged with uncomfortable directness: Who will evaluate the evaluators? How will evaluation be evaluated? Thus, professional evaluators began discussing standards.

The most comprehensive effort at developing standards was hammered out over five years by a 17-member committee appointed by 12 professional organizations, with input from hundreds of practicing evaluation professionals. The standards published by the Joint Committee on Standards for Educational Evaluation (1981) dramatically reflect the ways in which the practice of evaluation has developed and changed during the last decade. Just prior to publication, Dan Stufflebeam, Chair of the Committee, summarized the committee's work as follows:

> The standards that will be published essentially call for evaluations that have four features. These are *utility, feasibility, propriety* and *accuracy*. And I think it is interesting that the Joint Committee decided on that particular order. Their rationale is that an evaluation should not be done at all if there is no prospect for its being useful to some audience. Second, it should not be done if it is not feasible to conduct it in political terms, or practicality terms, or cost effectiveness terms. Third, they do not think it should be done if we cannot demonstrate that it will be conducted fairly and ethically. Finally, if we can demonstrate that an evaluation will have utility, will be feasible and will be proper in its conduct, then they said we could turn to the difficult matters of the technical adequacy of the evaluation, and they have included an extensive set of standards in this area [Stufflebeam, 1980: 90; emphasis in the original].

It is not an exaggeration, in my opinion, to characterize the shift in perspective represented by the new standards as "a scientific revolution" (Kuhn, 1970). Taking the standards seriously means looking at the world quite differently. Unlike the traditionally aloof stance of basic researchers, evaluators are now called on to take responsibility for use—no more playing the game of blame the decision maker. *Implementation of a utility-focused, feasibility-conscious, propriety-oriented, and accuracy-based approach to evaluation requires situational responsiveness, methodological flexibility, multiple evaluator roles, political sophistication, and substantial doses of creativity* (Patton, 1981). The standards of the Evaluation Research Society (1980) articulate these same themes.

In later chapters some of the specific standards related to increased utilization will be presented. At this point it is sufficient to note the clear mandate for evaluation use that is contained in the standards. "The Utility Standards are intended to ensure that an evaluation will serve the practical information needs of given audiences" (Joint Committee, 1981: 19). Concern about how to actually realize the mandate for increased evaluation use remains a dominant focus among professional evaluators—a concern reflected in the 1985 Toronto joint meeting of the American Evaluation Association and the Canadian Evaluation Society. The theme of that meeting was "The Uses of Evaluation."

We are called back, then, to the early morning scene that opened this chapter. Decision makers lament the disappointing results of evaluation research, complaining that the findings do not tell them what they need to know. And evaluators complain about many things, "but their most common complaint is that their findings are ignored" (Weiss, 1972d: 319). The question remains: What do we have to do to produce useful evaluation studies that are actually used?

Utilization-Focused Evaluation:
A Comprehensive Approach

The question of how to enhance the usefulness and actual use of program evaluation is sufficiently complex that a piecemeal approach based on isolated prescriptions for practice is likely to have only piecemeal impact. The overall problem of underutilization of program evaluation will not be solved by compiling and following some long list of evaluation axioms. Real world circumstances are too complex and unique to be routinely approached through the application of isolated pearls of evaluation wisdom. It is like trying to live your life according to Ben Franklin's *Almanac* or any of the full range of proverbial gems that constitute our cultural heritage. At the moment of decision, you reach into your socialization and remember, "He who hesitates is lost." But then again, "Fools rush in where angels fear to tread." Advice to young evaluators is no less confusing: "Work closely with decision makers to establish trust and rapport," but "maintain distance from program decision makers to guarantee objectivity and neutrality."

What is needed is a comprehensive approach to program assessment that provides an overall framework within which the individuals involved can proceed to develop an evaluation design with built-in utilization appropriate to the unique circumstances they encounter. In program evaluation, as in life, it is one's overall philosophy integrated into pragmatic principles that provides a guide to action. It is to that end that this book is directed: the development of a comprehensive utilization-focused approach to evaluation.

Since original publication in 1978, the ideas Utilization-Focused Evaluation have tested and applied in hundreds of evaluations in the United States and throughout the world. This reservoir of experience provides strong confirmation that evaluation can be useful, and that utility—*and actual use*—can be enhanced through a utilization-focused approach. Evidence to that effect will be presented throughout this book.

The next chapter considers the question of how to define utilization. This problem is approached empirically by asking a sample of federal decision makers and evaluators about the actual impact of studies in which they have been involved. The results of these interviews suggest that what is typically characterized as underutilization or nonutilization of evaluation can be attributed in substantial degree to a definition of utilization that is too narrow and fails to take into consideration the nature of actual decision-making processes in most programs.

Based on a redefinition of utilization in Chapter 2, the third chapter links the processes of utilization to specific decision makers and evaluation information users. Part II considers alternative ways of determining the content or subject of an evaluation. In refining evaluation questions (Chapter 4), a series of options is made available to evaluators as they interact with decision makers and evaluation users to focus key evaluation issues. Those options include utilization-focused goals clarification (Chapter 5), implementation evaluation (Chapter 6), and framing the evaluation question in the context of the program's theory of action (Chapter 7). Part III turns to methods and data analysis, including alternative paradigms of evaluation measurement and design.

Each chapter elaborates the theme that runs throughout the book: namely, that utilization is affected by every aspect of an evaluation, from initial conceptualization to data analysis and interpretation. By paying attention to utilization each step along the way, evaluators can substantially enhance usefulness and *actual use*. Part IV integrates this theme and the separate ideas contained within it to present an overview of the utilization-focused approach to evaluation.

In Search of Impact

A modern version of an ancient Asian story (adapted from Shah, 1964: 64) is helpful in explaining the nature of the search for utilization contained in this book.

It is said that a man once found his neighbor down on his knees under a street lamp looking for something.

"What have you lost, friend?"

"My key," said the man on his knees.

"After a few minutes of searching, the neighbor asked, "Where did you drop it?"

"In that dark pasture," replied his friend.

"Then why, for heaven's sake, are you looking here?"

"Because there is more light here."

The easy and perhaps obvious place to look for utilization is in the concrete decisions made by evaluators and decision makers after a study is completed. What we shall find, however, is that the search for evaluation use takes us into the "dark pasture" of decisions made before any evaluation data are ever collected. The reader will find relatively little in this book about what to do when a study is over. At that point the potential for utilization has been largely determined. Utilization-focused evaluation emphasizes what happens from the very beginning of a study that determines its eventual impact—before a final report is ever produced. The key to utilization will be found on the path the evaluation takes before the findings are exposed to the general light of public scrutiny.

Chapter 2

UTILIZATION IN PRACTICE:

AN EMPIRICAL PERSPECTIVE

Utility is in the eye of the user.

—Halcolm

A Setting

Picture a middle-aged and obviously aging man sitting in his overpadded and obviously aging chair. He is slouched in front of the television set watching a football game. It appears he has been sitting there watching football games for several days—college games, all-star games, play-off games, Monday night football. It is the December-January American football holiday marathon season. He has several days growth of beard on his face; a beer can is held loosely in one hand, with several empties on the floor around his chair. The only movement is from the images on the screen. Even upon close inspection it is hard to tell whether he is awake or asleep.

Stage left, enter his wife and her neighbor friend. As they pass through the room, the wife pauses by his chair and reflects aloud to her neighbor, "The question I ponder is not whether there is life after death but, rather, whether there is life after birth."

Defining Use

The question here is not whether some evaluation heaven exists where the souls of virtuous studies ascend after their physical remains have been laid to rest in an agency library or other cemetery for public documents. The question is whether there is life after birth. From the moment of birth—nay, from the moment of conception—how does the evaluation grow and develop, and as it grows and develops, how does it make its presence felt in the world around it? Does the existence of that evaluation make a difference? Does it have an impact on its environment? Or do evaluators, as a species, have an overly glorified, anthropocentric image of the importance of their work?

One might well construct a metaphysics of evaluation from the preceding questions. But my purpose is more immediate and practical: to define utilization. Tracing the utilization of any particular evaluation necessitates a definition of use so as to be able to recognize its presence or absence in any given case. The evaluation literature reviewed in the last chapter was overwhelming in its agreement that evaluation studies are not used in decision making. But how would we recognize use if it occurred? What would life after birth be like for an evaluation study? What is the opposite of nonuse?

There can be no absolute definition of evaluation utilization because "use" depends in part on the values of user. As Eleanor Chelimsky (1983: 155) has observed, "The concept of usefulness . . . depends upon the perspective and values of the observer. This means that one person's usefulness may be another person's waste."

Most of the literature on program evaluation never explicitly defines utilization. But there is an implicit definition: Utilization occurs when there is an immediate, concrete, and observable effect on specific decisions and program activities resulting directly from evaluation findings. This definition is derived from the usual stated purpose of program evaluation, which is to gather data that can be used to make judgments about program effectiveness. If such data are gathered, then a judgment ought to follow—a judgment that leads directly to concrete action and specific decisions. Carol Weiss (1972c: 10) made this view explicit: "Evaluation research is meant for immediate and direct use in improving the quality of social programming." It is of this immediate and direct use that Weiss was speaking when she concluded that "a review of evaluation experience suggests that evaluation results have generally not exerted significant influence on program decisions" (1972c: 11).

Study of Utilization

If evaluation use is to be increased, it might be helpful to try to find a few positive examples that deviate from this norm of nonuse. We could then study those examples of excellence to learn how to increase utilization. I once participated in a study in which we wanted to talk directly to users of evaluation to find out how *they* defined use. In effect, we used an inductive strategy. We began without a preconceived definition of utilization and let a conceptualization of what use looks like emerge from the responses of federal decision makers. That study and the interview responses of those decision makers marked the beginning of the formulation of the utilization-focused approach to evaluation presented in this book.[1]

We conducted follow-up studies of 20 federal health evaluations. We attempted to assess the degree to which these evaluations had been used and to identify the factors that affected varying degrees of utilization. Given the pessimistic nature of most writings on utilizations, we began our study fully expecting our major problem would be to find even one evaluation that had had a significant impact on program decisions. What we found was considerably more complex and less dismal than our original impressions led us to expect. Program evaluation is used, but not in ways we anticipated. The understanding of utilization that emerged from this study is central to the utilization-focused approach to evaluation presented in this book.

A Sample of "Evaluations"

The 20 case studies that constituted the sample in this study were national health program evaluations. They were selected from among 170 evaluations on file in the Office of Health Evaluation.[2] The process of selecting evaluation studies for inclusion in the sample necessitated developing a very simple operational definition of evaluation. The definition offered in the first chapter was too restrictive for sampling purposes, so we applied only two quite simple criteria in coding HEW studies as "evaluations": (1) There existed some actual operating program (2) about which some kind of systematic data were collected. Fewer than half of the 170 health studies classified by HEW as "evaluations" met these two simple criteria. This was because a large number of those studies were nonempirical think pieces or policy research studies aimed at social indicators in general rather than evaluation of specific programs.

For reasons of confidentiality, neither the actual programs evaluated nor the titles of the evaluation studies can be reported. However, we can present a general description of the final random sample. The 20 cases include 4 mental health evaluations, 4 health training programs, 2 national assessments of laboratory proficiency, 2 evaluations of neighborhood health center programs, studies of 2 health services delivery systems programs, a training program on alcoholism, a health regulatory program, a federal loan forgiveness program, a training workshop evaluation, and 2 evaluations of specialized health facilities.

The types of evaluation studies in the final group of 20 cases ranged from a three-week program review carried out by a single internal evaluator to a four-year evaluation that cost $1.5 million. Six of the cases were internal evaluations and 14 were external.

Data on Utilization:
The Interviewees

Because of very limited resources, it was possible to select only three key informants to be contacted and intensively interviewed about the utilization of each of the 20 cases in the final sample. These key informants were (1) the government's internal project officer (PO) for the study, (2) the person identified by the project officer as being either the decision maker for the program evaluated or the person most knowledgeable about the study's impact, and (3) the evaluator who had major responsibility for the study. Most of the federal decision makers interviewed had been or now are office directors (and deputy directors), division heads, or bureau chiefs. Overall, these decision makers represented over 250 years of experience in the federal government.

The evaluators in our sample were a rather heterogeneous group. Six of the 20 cases were internal evaluations, so the evaluators were federal administrators or researchers. In one case the evaluation was contracted from one unit of the federal government to another, so the evaluators were also federal researchers. The remaining 13 evaluations were conducted by private organizations or nongovernment employees, although several persons in this group either had formerly worked for the federal government or have since come to do so. Evaluators in our sample represented over 225 years of experience in conducting evaluative research.

Interviews ranged in length from one to six hours, with an average length of about two hours. Interviews were taped and transcribed for analysis. In this chapter we will only be concerned with the section of the interview that asked directly about evaluation use. Our question was as follows:

> Now we'd like to focus on the actual impact of this evaluation study. We'd like to get at any ways in which the study may have had an impact—an impact on program operations, on planning, on funding, on policy, on decisions, on thinking about the program, and so forth. From your point of view, what was the impact of this evaluation study on the program we've been discussing?

Following a set of probes and additional questions, depending upon the respondents' initial answers, we asked a question about the nonprogram impacts of the evaluations:

> We've been focusing mainly on the study's impact on the program itself. Sometimes studies have a broader impact on things beyond an immediate program, things like general thinking on issues that arise from a study, or position

papers, or legislation. To what extent and in what ways did this evaluation have an impact on any of these kinds of things?

The analysis of the interviews began with general discussions in which the 17 interviewers shared their perceptions about their own interviews. Three staff members then independently read all interviews looking for patterns and themes. These processes led to the formation of tentative hypotheses about dominant themes. The interview transcripts were then examined again, searching for evidence supporting these tentative hypotheses as well as for contradictory evidence and counterexamples. Quotes extracted from the interviews as examples of particular points were then independently examined by other staff members to check for context and accuracy. Only those findings about which there was a high degree of consensus are reported in the pages that follow.

The Findings on Utilization

In response to the first question on impact, 78% of responding decision makers and 90% of responding evaluators felt that *the evaluation had had an impact on the program*. Moreover, 80% of responding decision makers and 70% of responding evaluators felt these specific evaluation studies had had identifiable nonprogram impacts.

The number of positive responses to the questions on impact is quite striking considering the predominance of the theme of nonutilization in the evaluation literature. The main difference here, however, may be that the actual participants in each specific evaluation process were asked to define

impact in terms that were meaningful to them and their situations. Thus, none of the impacts described was of the type in which new findings from an evaluation led directly and immediately to the making of major, concrete program decisions. The more typical impact was one in which the evaluation findings provided additional pieces of information in the difficult puzzle of program action, permitting some reduction in the uncertainty within which any federal decision maker inevitably operates.

The most dramatic example of utilization reported in our sample was the case of an evaluation of a pilot program. The program administrator had been favorable to the program in principle, was uncertain what the results would be, but was "hoping the results would be positive." The evaluation proved to be negative. The administrator was "surprised, but not alarmingly so. . . . We had expected a more positive finding or we would not have engaged in the pilot studies" (DM367: 13).[3] The program was subsequently ended, with the evaluation carrying "about a third of the weight of the total decision" (DM367: 8).

This relatively dramatic impact stood out as a clear exception to the more typical pattern, in which evaluation findings constitute additional input into an evolutionary process of program action. One decision maker with 29 years' experience in the federal government, much of that time directing research, gave the following report on the impact of the evaluation study about which he was interviewed:

> It served two purposes. One is that it resolved a lot of doubts and confusions and misunderstandings that the advisory committee had. . . . And the second one was that it gave me additional knowledge to support facts that I already knew, and, as I say, broadened the scope more than I realized. In other words, the perceptions of where the organization was going and what it was accomplishing were a lot worse than I had anticipated . . . but I was somewhat startled to find out that they were worse, yet it wasn't very hard because it was partly confirming things that I was observing [DM232: 17].

He goes on to say that, following the evaluation,

> we changed our whole functional approach to looking at the identification of what we should be working on. But again I have a hard time because these things, *none of these things occurred overnight, and in an evolutionary process it's hard to say, you know, at what point it made a significant difference or what point did it merely verify and strengthen the resolve that you already had* [DM232: 17].

This decision maker had become highly involved in applied government research, including his initiation of the study in our sample, because he believed research can help reduce uncertainty in decision making:

As time went on I more clearly recognized that I was not satisfied with having to make program decisions that I was making or that others were making based on "professional judgment." Not that it's bad or anything, it's just that it's pretty shaky at times, and you know, you always sit back and say, "now if I hadn't done that and done something else, what would have been the result?" So it's nice to find that there are better ways of doing it [DM232: 25].

Still, his assessment of the actual impact of the evaluation was quite constrained: "It filled in the gaps and pieces that various ones really had in their orientation to the program" (DM232: 12) and "it verified my suspicions" (DM232: 24).

Respondents frequently had difficulty assessing the degree to which an evaluation study actually affected decisions made after completion of the evaluation. This was true, for example, in the case of a large-scale evaluation effort that had been extremely expensive and had taken place over several years' time. The evaluation found some deficiencies in the program, but the overall findings were quite positive. Changes corresponding to those recommended in the study occurred when the report was published, but those changes could not be directly and simply attributed to the evaluation:

The staff was aware that the activities in the centers were deficient from other studies that we had done, and they were beefing up these budgets and providing technical assistance to some of the projects and improving mental health activities. Now I can't link this finding and that activity. Again that confirms that finding and you say, eureka, I have found [the program] deficient, therefore I will [change] the program. That didn't happen. [The] deficiency was previously noted. A lot of studies like this confirmed what close-by people knew and they were already taking actions before the findings. *So you can't link the finding to the action, that's just confirmation. . . . The direct link between the finding and the program decision is very diffuse.* [Its major impact was] confirming our setting, a credibility, a tone of additional credibility to the program [DM361: 12, 13].

Moreover, this decision maker felt that additional credibility for the program became one part of an overall process of information flow that helped to some degree reduce the uncertainty faced by decision makers responsible for the program: "People in the budget channels at OMB were, I guess, eager for and interested in any data that would help them make decisions, and this was certainly one useful bit of data" (DM361: 13).

The kind of impact we found, then, was that evaluation research provided some additional information that was judged and used in the context of other available information to help reduce the unknowns in the making of difficult decisions. The impact ranged from "it sort of confirmed our impressions . . . confirming some other anecdotal information or impression that we had" (DM209: 7, 1) to providing a new awareness carrying over into other programs:

Some of our subsequent decisions on some of our other programs were probably based on information that came out of this study. . . . The most significant
information from this study that we really had not realized . . . made an impact on future decisions with regard to other programs that we carry on
[DM209: 7].

And why did it have this impact?

Well I guess I'll go back to the points I've already made, that it confirmed
some impressionistic feelings and anecdotal information that we had about
certain kinds of things. At least it gave us some hard data on which to base
some future programming decisions. It may not have been the only data, but it
was confirming data, and I think that's important. . . . And you know at the
time this study was conceived, and even by the time it was reported to us, we
really had very little data, and you know, probably *when you don't have any
data, every little bit helps* [DM209: 15].

This reduction of uncertainty emerged as highly important to decision
makers. In some cases it simply made them more confident and determined.
On the other hand, where the need for change is indicated an evaluation
study can help speed up the process of change or provide an impetus for
finally getting things rolling.

Well I think that all we did was probably speed up the process. I think that they
were getting there anyhow. They knew that their performance was being criti-
cized by various parts of the government and the private sector. As I said earlier, we didn't enter this study thinking that we were going to break any new
ground, and when we got finished, we knew that we hadn't. All we did was
document what the people have been saying for a long time—that _____
are doing a lousy job, so what else is new? But we were able to show just how
poor a job they were doing [EV268: 12].

Reducing uncertainty, speeding things up, and getting things finally
started are real impacts—not revolutionary, organization-shaking impacts—
but real, important impacts in the opinion of the people we interviewed.

The view of evaluation use that emerged in our interviews stands in stark
contrast to the image of utilization that is presented as the ideal in the bulk of
the evaluation literature. The ideal held forth in the literature is one of major
impact on concrete decisions. The image that emerged in our interviews is
that there are few major, direction-changing decisions in most programming, and that evaluation research is used as one piece of information that
feeds into a slow, evolutionary process of program development. Program
development is a process of "muddling through" (Lindblom, 1965; Allison,
1971), and program evaluation is part of that muddling.

Neither did we find much expectation that government decision making could be or should be otherwise. One person with 35 years' experience in the federal government (20 of those years in evaluation) put it like this: "I don't think an evaluation's ever totally used. That was true whether I was using them as an administrator or doing them myself" (EV346: 11). Later in the interview he said,

> I don't think the government should go out and use every evaluation it gets. I think sometimes just the insights of the evaluation feed over to the next administrative reiteration, maybe just the right way to do it. That is, [decisions aren't] clearly the result of evaluation. There's a feedback in some way . . . upgrading or a shifting of direction because of it. [Change] is, you know, small and slow [EV 346: 16].

Another evaluator expressed a similar view:

> I think it's just like everything else in life, if you're at the right place at the right time, it can be useful, but it's obviously only probably one ingredient in the information process. It's rather naive and presumptuous on the part of the evaluation community and also it presumes a rationality that in no way fits [EV264: 18].

Our findings, then, suggest that the predominant image of nonutilization that characterizes much of the commentary on evaluation research can be attributed in substantial degree to a definition of utilization that is too narrow in its emphasis on seeing immediate, direct, and concrete impact on program decisions. Such a narrow definition fails to take into account the nature of most actual program development processes. In effect, social scientists have failed to find evidence of research utilization because their narrow definition of utilization excluded the kinds of more limited impacts described by the decision makers we interviewed. In the past, the search for utilization has often been conducted like the search for contraband in the famous Sufi story about Nasrudin the smuggler.

> Nasrudin used to take his donkey across a frontier every day, with the panniers loaded with straw. Since he admitted to being a smuggler when he trudged home every night, the frontier guards searched him again and again. They searched his person, sifted the straw, steeped it in water, even burned it from time to time. Meanwhile he was becoming visibly more and more prosperous.
>
> Then he retired and went to live in another country. Here one of the customs officers met him, years later.
>
> "You can tell me now, Nasrudin," he said. "Whatever *was* it that you were smuggling, that we could never catch you at?"
>
> "Donkeys," said Nasrudin [Shah, 1964: 59].

Utilization of evaluation is there to see, but not if one is looking only for impacts of great moment. As Weiss (1977: 7) points out, many social scientists have come into applied government research with high hopes of rationalizing the system. They entered the arena of applied research expecting to make great policy waves and are disillusioned to find that they have only provided a few cogs in the great gears of program change and development, helped with a decision here or there, made actions more certain for a few decision makers.

Yet the situation seems little different in basic research. Researchers in any field of specialization can count the studies of major impact on one hand. Most science falls into that great amorphous activity called "normal science." Changes come slowly. Individual researchers contribute a bit here and a bit there, reducing uncertainty gradually, over time. Scientific revolutions are infrequent and slow in coming (Kuhn, 1970).

The situation is the same in applied research. Program evaluation is one part of the normal "science" of program decision making. Research affects in ripples, not in waves. Occasionally a major study emerges with great impact. But most applied research can be expected to make no more than a small and momentary splash in the great lakes of organizations. The use of most studies is likely to sound something like this:

> [We expected that it would be used] but in a way of providing background information around the consequences of certain kinds of federal decision making options. But not necessarily in and of itself determining those decisions. In other words, you might have some idea of what the consequences of the decision are, but there might be a lot of other factors you'd take into account in how you would decide.

> It's part of a total atmosphere, and in the balance of things it's contributing another bit of information about the importance of this particular process, but by no means is it the only thing entering into what's going on in a policy review [DM264: 8, 11].

The Life Cycle of Evaluation Studies: A Review

This chapter began by asking whether there is life after birth for evaluations. It ends with what might be an epitaph for the typical evaluation.

EVALUATION EPITAPH

Didn't change the course of history,
My impact is hard to measure.
Used by some, ignored by others,
Would any call it a pleasure?

I provided some new information,
And I got talked about a lot.

Changed some people's thinking.
Worth it? Maybe yes, maybe not.

Cost both time and money.
The program? Not the same.
But it's hard to sort out causes,
And few will remember my name.

Finally, it is important to understand how the view of evaluation use that emerges in this chapter establishes a context for utilization-focused evaluation. The utilization-focused approach is aimed at increasing the likelihood that an evaluation's impact will be substantial, meaningful, and relevant. In that respect, the degree and type of use found in the federal health evaluations can help us be realistic without accepting such levels of use as the upper limit or the best for which one can hope. It is the premise of this book that use of program evaluation can be increased and more carefully targeted, but evaluation findings will seldom have the enormous kind of influence envisioned by those social scientists who hoped to completely rationalize decision-making processes. The potential for enhancing use lies less in its capability for rationalizing decision making than in its capacity to empower the users of evaluation information. The far-reaching implications of this difference in perspective will become clearer as additional findings from our study of utilization are presented in later chapters.

NOTES

1. At the time of the study, I was Director of the Evaluation Methodology Program in the Humphrey Institute of Public Affairs, University of Minnesota. The study was conducted through the Minnesota Center for Social Research, University of Minnesota. The following students participated in the project: Dale Blyth, Nancy Brennan, James Cleary, Joan Dreyer, James Fitzsimmons, Barbara French, Steve Froman, Kathy Gilder, Patricia Grimes, Kathy Guthrie, David Jones, Leah Harvey, Gary Miller, Gail Nordheim, Julia Nutter, Darla Sandhoffer, Jerome Segal, and John Townsend. A shorter version of this study was published under the title, "In Search of Impact: An Analysis of the Utilization of Federal Health Evaluation Research" (Patton et al., 1977).

2. The Office of Health Evaluation coordinated most evaluation research in the health division of the Department of Health, Education, and Welfare in the federal government. In 1971, this office designed a new recordkeeping system that collected abstracts from all "evaluations" coming through that office; 170 evaluations were collected during the period 1971-1973. This became the universe of evaluations from which we chose our final sample.

3. Citations for quotes taken from the interview transcripts will use the following format: (DM367: 13) refers to the transcript of an interview with a decision maker about evaluation study number 367. The quote is taken from page 13 of the transcript. The study numbers and page numbers have been systematically altered to protect the confidentiality of the interviewees. The study numbers do not correspond to any codes used within DHEW. However, (EV201: 10) and (PO201: 6) refer to interviews about the same study, the former being an interview with the evaluator, the latter an interview with the project officer.

Chapter 3

THE PERSONAL FACTOR:
FOSTERING INTENDED USE
FOR INTENDED USERS

> There are five key variables that are absolutely critical to evaluation use. They are, in order of importance: people, people, people, people, and people.
>
> —Halcolm

A Setting

It is shortly after 8 a.m. on a damp summer morning at Snow Mountain Ranch near Rocky Mountain National Park. Some 40 human service and education professionals from all over the country have gathered in a small, dome-shaped chapel to participate in an evaluation workshop. The session begins like this:

> Okay, let's get started. Instead of beginning by my haranguing you about what you should do in program evaluation, we're going to begin with a short evaluation exercise to immerse us immediately in the process. That is, we're going to take an experiential or simulation approach to learning about the stages of program evaluation.

So what I'm going to do is ask you to engage in an exercise as both participants and evaluators (since that's the situation most of you find yourself in anyway in your own agencies and programs—where you have both program and evaluation responsibilities). We're going to share an experience through this exercise to loosen things up a bit . . . perhaps warm you up, wake you up, and allow you to get more comfortable. The exercise will also allow us to test your participant observer skills and provide us with a common experience as evaluators. We'll generate some personal data about the process of evaluation that we can use for discussion later.

So what I want you to do for about the next five minutes is to move around this space, to get up and move around in any way you want to, to explore this environment. You can explore the environment in any ways you want to—touch things, move things, experience different parts of this setting. And while you're observing the physical environments, watch what others do. Then after about five minutes I'll ask you to find a place where you feel comfortable to write down your observations about the exercise, what you observed, and also to evaluate the exercise. Experience, explore, observe, and evaluate. That's the exercise.

Oh yes, there are two rules. First, I'd prefer that you not talk to anyone, and secondly, I'd prefer that no one leave the room. The exercise works best if people hang around for it! But otherwise, you're free to explore, and remember, while you are participating in this experience, this exercise, you're also evaluating it.

At the end of the exercise the participants were asked to write an evaluation report based on their own observations of what had occurred. Several people were then asked, on a voluntary basis, to share with the group what they had written.

First Observer: People slowly got up. Everybody looked kind of nervous 'cause they weren't sure what to do. People moved out toward the walls, which are made of rough wood. The lighting is kind of dim. People sort of moved counterclockwise. Every so often there would be a nervous smile exchanged between people. The chairs are fastened down in rows so it's hard for people to move in the center of the room. A few people went to the stage area, but most stayed toward the back and outer part. The chairs aren't too comfortable but it's a quiet, mellow room. The exercise showed that people are nervous when they don't know what to do.

Second Observer: The room is hexagonally shaped with a dome-shaped ceiling. Fastened-down chairs are arranged in a semicircle with a stage in front that is about a foot high. A podium is at the left of the small stage. Green drapes hang at the side. Windows are small and triangular. The floor is wood. There's a coffee table in back. Most people went to get coffee. A couple people broke the talking rule for a minute. Everyone returned to about the same place they had been before after walking around. It's not a great room for a workshop, but it's okay.

Third Observer: People were really nervous about what to do because the goals of the exercise weren't clear. You can't evaluate without clear goals so people just wandered around. The exercise shows you can't evaluate without clear goals.

Fourth Observer: I said to myself at the start, this is a human relations thing to get us started. I was kind of mad about doing this because we've been here a half hour already and we haven't done anything that has to do with evaluation. I came to learn about evaluation not to do T-group stuff, or nonverbal communications stuff. So I just went to get coffee and I talked to someone because I didn't like the rule about not talking, but the other person was really nervous about breaking the rule. I didn't like wasting so much time on this.

Fifth Observer: I felt uneasy too, but I think it's natural to feel uneasy when you can't talk and aren't sure what to do. But I liked walking around looking at the chapel and feeling the space. I think some people got into it, but we were stiff and uneasy. People avoided looking at each other. Sometimes there was a nervous smile when people passed each other, but by kind of moving in a circle most people went the same direction and avoided looking at each other. I think I learned something about myself and how I react to a strange, nervous situation.

The five observers had five different perspectives on the same experience. The exercise and reports were followed by a discussion of what it would take to produce a more focused set of observations and evaluations. Suggestions included establishing clear goals; making up criteria for what is being evaluated; figuring out what is supposed to be observed in advance so everyone can observe it; giving clearer directions of what to do; stating the purpose of evaluation; and training the evaluators so that they all know how to observe the same thing.

The problem is that before any of these things can be done, a prior step is necessary. This prior step constitutes the first stage in utilization-focused evaluation. It is this first step that is the concern of this chapter.

The First Step in the Evaluation Process

It is clear from the literature on program evaluation that most evaluations are aimed at assessing the relative degree of program goal attainment—that is, how effective the program is in attaining measurable goals. It is also clear that the purpose of the evaluation should be explicitly stated; that concrete evaluative criteria for program success should be established; and that the measurement procedures and instruments should be appropriate to the goals. All of these are important issues in any evaluation. The question is this: Who will make the decisions about these issues?

Clearly and explicitly identifying people who can benefit from an evaluation is so important that evaluators have created a special term for evaluation users: They are called *stakeholders*. Stakeholders are people who have a stake—a vested interest—in evaluation findings. For any evaluation there are multiple stakeholders: program funders, staff, administrators, clients, and others with a direct, or even indirect, interest in program effectiveness. Stakeholders are decision makers and information users who have questions about a program. The purpose of a utilization-focused evaluation is to answer stakeholders' questions. This necessitates clearly and explicitly identifying primary stakeholders so that their questions can be determined—and answered through evaluation.

The workshop exercise that opened this chapter illustrates the importance of clearly identifying primary evaluation stakeholders. The participants in that exercise observed different things in part because they were interested in different things. They "evaluated" the exercise in different ways, and many had trouble "evaluating" the exercise at all.

The first step in the utilization-focused evaluation is identifying the primary intended users of the evaluation.

Consider again the workshop exercise. The participants observed different things and were unable to evaluate what happened in part because they

did not know for whom they were writing. There were several potential users of evaluation information on the exercise:

(1) As workshop leader, I might want to evaluate the extent to which the exercise accomplished my objectives.
(2) Each individual participant might conduct a personal evaluation in terms of his or her own criteria.
(3) The group could establish consensus goals for the exercise, which would serve as focus for the evaluation.
(4) The bosses, agency directors, and funding boards who paid for participants to attend might want an assessment of the exercise in terms of a return on the resources they have invested for staff training.
(5) The Snow Mountain Ranch director might want an evaluation of the exercise in terms of the appropriateness of the chapel for such workshop activities.
(6) The building architects might want an evaluation of how participants responded to the space they designed.
(7) A group of professional workshop facilitators might want to evaluate the exercise as to its effectiveness for opening a workshop.
(8) Ecological psychologists or human relations trainers might want to assess the effects of the exercise on participants.
(9) Experiential learning educators might want an assessment of the use of such an exercise as an experiential learning tool.
(10) The janitors of the chapel might want an evaluation of the work engendered for them by an exercise that permits moving things around (which sometimes occurs to destructive proportions when the exercise has been used with loose furniture).

This list of people potentially interested in the evaluation (stakeholders) could be expanded. The evaluation question in each case would likely be different. I would have different evaluation information needs as workshop leader than would the camp director; the architects' information needs would differ from the janitors' "evaluation" question; the evaluation criteria of individuals would differ from those reached by the total group through some consensus-formation process.

This long discourse on the nature of differential perception is not aimed at simply making the point that different people see things differently and have varying needs. I take that to be on the order of a truism. The point is that this truism is regularly and consistently ignored in the design of evaluation studies. To target an evaluation at the information needs of a specific person or at a group of identifiable and interacting persons is quite different from what is usually referred to as "identifying the audience" for an evaluation. Audiences are amorphous, anonymous entities. Nor is it sufficient to identify an agency or organization as a recipient of the evaluation report. Organizations are an impersonal collection of hierarchical positions. *People, not organiza-*

tions, use evaluation information. I shall elaborate on these points later in this chapter, when discussing how most evaluations manage to avoid fostering intended use for intended information users. First, I want to present data from our utilization of federal health evaluations study that illustrate and elaborate this first step in utilization-focused evaluation. In the course of presenting these data, I hope it will become clearer how one identifies primary stakeholders and intended users, and why they are the key to the utilization process.

Factors Affecting the Use of Evaluation and the Emergence of the Personal Factor

We asked respondents to comment on how, if at all, each of 11 factors extracted from the literature on utilization had affected utilization of their study. These factors were methodological quality, methodological appropriateness, timeliness, lateness of report, positive or negative findings, surprise of findings, central or peripheral program objectives evaluated, presence or absence of related studies, political factors, decision maker-evaluator interactions, and resources available for the study. Finally, we asked respondents to "pick out the single factor you feel had the greatest effect on how this study was used."

From this long list of questions only two factors emerged as consistently important in explaining utilization: (1) a political considerations factor to be discussed in Chapter 11 and (2) a factor we have called "the personal factor." This latter factor was unexpected, and its clear importance to our respondents has, we believe, substantial implications for the use of program evaluation. *None of the other specific literature factors about which we asked questions emerged as important with any consistency.* Moreover, when these specific factors were important in explaining the use or nonuse of a particular study, it was virtually always in the context of a larger set of circumstances and conditions related to either political considerations or the personal factor.

The personal factor is the presence of an identifiable individual or group of people who personally cared about the evaluation and the information it generated. Where such a person or group was present, evaluations were used; where the personal factor was absent, there was a correspondingly marked absence of evaluation impact. The personal factor represents the leadership, interest, enthusiasm, determination, commitment, assertiveness, and caring of specific, individual people. These are the people who are actively seeking information to reduce decision uncertainties so as to increase their ability to predict the outcomes of programmatic activity and enhance their own discretion as decision makers. These are the primary users of evaluation.

Data on the Importance of the Personal Factor

The personal factor emerged most dramatically in our interviews when, having asked respondents to comment on the importance of each of our 11 utilization factors, we asked them to identify the single factor that was most important in explaining the impact or lack of impact of that particular study. Time after time, the factor they identified was not on our list. Rather, they responded in terms of the importance of individual people:

> *Item:* I would rank as the most important factor this division director's interest, [his] interest in evaluation. Not all managers are that motivated toward evaluation [DM353: 17].

> *Item:* [The single most important factor that had the greatest effect on how the study got used was] the principal investigator. . . . If I have to pick a single factor, I'll pick people any time [DM328: 20].

> *Item:* That it came from the Office of the Director—that's the most important factor. . . . The proposal came from the Office of the Director. It had had his attention and he was interested in it, and he implemented many of the things [DM312: 21].

> *Item:* [The single most important factor was that] the people at the same level of decision making in [the new office] were not interested in making decisions of the kind that the people [in the old office] were, I think that probably had the greatest impact. The fact that there was no one at [the new office] after the transfer who was making programmatic decisions [EV361: 27].

> *Item:* Well, I think the answer there is in the qualities of the people for whom it was made. That's sort of a trite answer, but it's true. That's the single most important factor in any study now that's utilized [EV232: 22].

> *Item:* Probably the single factor that had the greatest effect on how it was used was the insistence of the person responsible for initiating the study that the Director of _____ become familiar with its findings and arrive at judgment on it [DM369: 25].

> *Item:* [The most important factor was] the real involvement of the top decision makers in the conceptualization and design of the study, and their commitment to the study [DM268: 9].

While these comments concern the importance of interested and committed individuals in studies that were actually used, studies that were not used stand out in that there was often a clear absence of the personal factor. One evaluator, who was not sure how his study was used but suspected it had not been, remarked,

> I think that since the client wasn't terribly interested . . . and the whole issue had shifted to other topics, and since we weren't interested in doing it from a research point of view . . . nobody was interested [EV264: 14].

Another highly experienced evaluator was particularly adamant and articulate on the theory that the major factor affecting utilization is the personal energy, interests, abilities, and contacts of specific individuals. When asked to identify the one factor that is most important in whether a study gets used, he summarized his viewpoint as follows:

> The most important factor is desire on the part of the managers, both the central federal managers and the site managers. I don't think there's [any doubt], you know, that evaluation should be responsive to their needs, and if they have a real desire to get on with whatever it is they're supposed to do, they'll apply it. And if the evaluations don't meet their needs, they won't. About as simple as you can get. *I think the whole process is far more dependent on the skills of the people who use it than it is on the sort of peripheral issues of politics, resources.* . . . Institutions are tough as hell to change. You can't change an institution by coming and doing an evaluation with a halo. Institutions are changed by people, in time, with a constant plugging away at the purpose you want to accomplish. And if you don't watch out, it slides back [EV346: 15-16].

His view had emerged early in the interview when he described how evaluations were used in the U.S. Office of Economic Opportunity (OEO):

> In OEO it depended on *who* the program officer was, on the program review officials, on program monitors for each of these grant programs. . . . Where there were aggressive program people, they used these evaluations whether they understood them or not. They used them to affect improvements, direct allocations of funds within the program, explain why the records were kept this way, why the reports weren't complete or whatever. Where they, where the program officials in OEO were unaggressive, passive—*nothing!*
>
> Same thing's true at the project level. Where you had a program director who was aggressive and understood what the hell the structure was internally, and he used it as leverage to change what went on within his program. Those who weren't—nothing [EV346: 5].

At another point he said, "The basic thing is how the administrators of the program view themselves, their responsibilities. That's the controlling factor" (EV346: 8).

The same thing emerged in his comments about each possible factor. Methodological quality, positive or negative findings, the degree to which the findings were expected—he always returned eventually to the themes of managerial interest, competence, and confidence. *The person makes the difference.*

Our sample included another rather adamant articulation of this premise. An evaluation of a pilot program involving four major projects was undertaken at the instigation of the program administrator. He made a special effort to make sure that his question (i.e., Were the pilot projects capable of being extended and generalized?) was answered. He guaranteed this by personally taking an active interest in all parts of the study. The administrator had been favorable to the program in principle, was uncertain what the results would be, but was hoping that the program would prove effective. The evaluation findings were, in fact, negative. The program was subsequently ended, with the evaluation carrying considerable weight in that decision (DM367: 8).

The evaluator interview on this case completely substantiated the administrator's description. The findings were specific and clear. The program was not refunded. Thus, the evaluation had a substantial, direct effect on that decision. The question then becomes why this study had such significant utilization. The answer from the decision maker was brief and to the point:

> Well, [the evaluation had an impact] because we designed the project with an evaluation component in it, so we were expected to use it and we did. . . . Not just the fact that [evaluation] was built in, but the fact that we built it in on purpose. That is, *the agency head and myself had broad responsibilities for this, wanted the evaluation study results and we expected to use them. Therefore, they were used. That's my point.* If someone else had built it in because they thought it was needed, and we didn't care, I'm sure the use of the study results would have been different [DM367: 12].

The evaluator (an external agent selected through an open request-for-proposal process) completely agreed:

> *The principal reason [for utilization] was because the decision maker was the guy who requested the evaluation and used its results. That is, the organizational distance between the policymaker and the evaluator was almost zero in this instance. That's the most important reason it had an impact. . . . It was the fact that the guy who was asking the question was the guy who was going to make use of the answer* [EV367: 12].

What emerges here is a picture of a decision maker who knew what information he wanted, an evaluator committed to answering the decision maker's question, and a decision maker committed to using that information. The result was a high level of utilization in making a decision contrary to the decision maker's initial personal hopes. In the words of the evaluator, the major factor explaining use was

> that the guy who's going to be making the decision is aware of and interested in the findings of the study and has some hand in designing the questions to be answered, that's a very important point [EV367: 20].

The decision maker's conclusion is so similar that it sounds like collusion:

> Evaluation research. Well I guess I would affirm that in many cases it has no impact for many of the reasons that the literature has suggested. But if I were to pick out factors that made a positive contribution to its use, one would be that the decision makers themselves wanted the evaluation study results. I've said that several times. If that is not present, it is not surprising that the results aren't used [DM367: 17].

This point was made often in the interviews. One highly placed and highly experienced administrator offered the following advice at the end of a four-hour interview:

> Win over the program people. Make sure you're hooked into the person who's going to make the decision in six months from the time you're doing the study, and make sure that *he* feels it's *his* study, that these are *his* ideas, and that it's focused on *his* values. . . . I'm sure it enters into personality things [DM283: 40].

The personal factor applies not just to use but to the whole evaluation process. Several of the studies in our sample were initiated completely by a single person because of personal interests and information needs. One study in particular stands out because it was initiated by a new office director with no support internally and considerable opposition from other affected agencies. The director found an interested and committed evaluator. The two worked closely together. The findings were initially ignored because there was no political heat at the time, but over the ensuing four years the director and evaluator personally worked to get the attention of key congressmen. They were finally successful in using personal contacts. The evaluation contributed to the eventual passing of significant legislation in a new area of federal control. From beginning to end, the story was one of personal human effort to get evaluation results used.

The specifics vary from case to case, but the pattern is markedly clear: Where the personal factor emerges, where some individual takes direct, personal responsibility for getting the information to the right people, evaluations have an impact. Where the personal factor is absent, there is a marked absence of impact. Use is not simply determined by some configuration of abstract factors; it is determined in large part by real, live, caring human beings.

This conclusion is supported by other studies on the uses of applied research. Glaser and Taylor (1969: iii) studied utilization by comparing five applied research projects rated as successful by NIMH staff and five rated as unsuccessful. They concluded that successful applied research is characterized by *high communication;* awareness and *involvement* with persons and groups within and outside the immediate environment from its *earliest moments.* . . . . The focus of the research was aimed at a *felt need* which enjoyed a shared interest from other people. Ipso facto, therefore, the product was readily marketable. Potential consumers were involved and informed. They encouraged *early efforts* at *dissemination* of findings, and were ready to consider implications for utilization [italics in original].

Charles Windle of NIMH investigated factors that affected the success of 15 evaluation studies of NIMH's Community Health Centers Program. These were evaluations contracted from the 1% monies of the Community Mental Health Centers Act, funds authorized specifically for program evaluation by the 90th Congress. He reviewed all such evaluations that had products available by the summer of 1972. His investigation revealed that

the factor most closely related to ratings of success was closeness of relationships between the contractor and N.I.M.H. staff. This closeness seemed both to orient the research toward potential utility and to enhance the likelihood that N.I.M.H. staff would utilize the products [Windle, n.d.: 11].

Such findings are sometimes interpreted as meaning simply that the *amount* of contact between decision makers and evaluators should be increased. But our data on the personal factor suggest that increased contact with the wrong persons (i.e., people who are not oriented toward the use of evaluative information) is likely to accomplish little. It is the nature and quality of interactions between evaluators and decision makers that is at issue. My own experience suggests that where the right people are involved (i.e., people who care about the evaluation and its utilization), the amount of direct contact can sometimes be reduced because the interactions that do occur are of such high quality.

In a quite different and more systematic way, Ronald Havelock (1968) has demonstrated the highly personal nature of knowledge utilization. Drawing heavily on the vast diffusion of innovations literature (see Rogers, 1962; Rogers and Shoemaker, 1971), he identifies particular roles that are fulfilled in a utilization or dissemination process. There are "leaders," "defenders," "innovators," "conveyors," "linking agents," and others who provide the personal mechanisms for information transmittal and use. What emerges quite clearly in Havelock's analysis is that the qualities and characteristics of individual people make a difference in the utilization process.

The linkage between evaluation information and decision making can best be made at the level of individual people, because it is individuals who experience uncertainty and seek ways to increase their discretion. The personal factor helps to bridge the gap between knowledge and action. As Lazarsfeld and Reitz (1975: 98) argue, "this gap can only be filled by creative thinking which responds with guesses of varying degrees of risk." This creativity resides in individuals. Attention to the personal factor is the mechanism for identifying both creative decision makers and creative evaluators.

The Focus on People Who Can Use Information

The focus in utilization-focused evaluation is on intended use for intended users. This definition of utilization has five major implications.

First, this means finding and bringing together people who want to know something. It means locating people who are able and willing to use information. Researchers and decision makers who care about seeing evaluation results used must take seriously the importance of identifying who needs what information under what conditions for what purposes. Primary stakeholders, relevant decision makers, and interested information users are the specific individuals who want evaluative information. Relevancy in the context of the personal factor means finding people who have a genuine interest in evaluation data—persons who are willing to take the time and effort to interact with evaluators about their information needs and interests. Thus, the first step in utilization-focused evaluation is to answer seriously and searchingly the question posed by Marvin Alkin (1975a): "Evaluation: Who Needs It? Who Cares?"

Second, formal position and authority are only partial guides in identifying primary stakeholders and information users. Evaluators must find strategically located people who are enthusiastic, committed, competent, interested, and assertive. Our data suggest that more may be accomplished by working with a lower-level person displaying these characteristics than by working with a passive, disinterested person in a higher position.

Third, regardless of what a request-for-proposal (RFP) calls for, the most valuable information with the highest potential for use is that information which directly answers the questions of the individual(s) identified as the primary stakeholders(s). RFPs may be written by individuals other than the decision makers who really need and want the evaluation information. It behooves evaluators to clarify the degree to which an RFP fully reflects the information needs of interested government officials, board members, funders, managers, or others.

Fourth, attention to the personal factor not only can assist evaluators' efforts to increase use, but also can aid decision makers' efforts to find evaluators who will provide them with relevant and useful information. Evaluators who are both interested in and knowledgeable about what they are doing, and who are committed to seeing their findings used in answering decision makers' questions, will provide the most useful information to those decision makers.

Fifth, there are political implications for both evaluators and decision makers in explicitly recognizing and acting on the importance of the personal factor. To do so is also to accept the assumption that decision making in modern organizations is likely to continue to be partly a personal and political process rather than an entirely rationalized and scientific process. Under personal or political conditions, the actions and interests of individual people make a difference. People are more than the positions they occupy.

In the remaining chapters of this book we shall explore the implications of the personal factor for other steps in the utilization-focused approach to evaluation. Prior to that, however, it may be helpful to contrast our first step in conceptualizing evaluation with other beginning strategies. There are several ways of doing evaluation *without* identifying who will use the information obtained, but these approaches reduce evaluation's utilization potential.

Strategies for Reducing Evaluation Use

First, and most common, evaluators can make themselves the major decision makers for the evaluation. This can happen by default (no one else is willing to do it), by intimidation (clearly, the evaluator is the expert), or simply by failing to think about or seek primary stakeholders. This means that the evaluators answer their own questions according to their own interests, needs, and priorities. Others may have occasional input here and there, but it is essentially an evaluation by the evaluator, for the evaluator, and of the evaluator. These conditions are a great boom for conducting basic scientific research under the funding guise of evaluation research, but such studies are seldom of use to program people, whose reaction is likely to be, "It's a great study, really well done. We can see you did a lot of work. But it doesn't tell us anything we want to know, so it's not really useful to us."

A second strategy for reducing use is to use the standard "identification of audience" approach. Audience, however, is not an identifiable group of people organized to have regular and systematic input into the evaluation. Audience refers to groups of largely anonymous faces: the "feds," state officials, the legislature, funders, clients, the program staff, the public, and so forth. But if specific individuals are not identified from these audiences and organized in a manner that permits meaningful involvement in the evaluation process, then utilization may be reduced.

In the absence of identifying specific individuals as information users, the evaluator must speculate on the audience's information needs, thus remaining, in effect, the decision maker for the evaluation. Carol Weiss's popular book, *Evaluation Research*, will serve as an example of the nuance I am emphasizing here. After an excellent discussion on how different groups, audiences, and decision makers need different information and the impossibility of any one evaluation answering everyone's questions, she counsels, "With all the possible uses for evaluation to serve, the evaluator has to make choices" (Weiss, 1972b: 15).

What fundamentally distinguishes utilization-focused evaluation from other approaches is that the evaluator does not alone carry this burden for making choices about the nature, purpose, content, and methods of evaluation. These decisions are shared by an identifiable and organized group of intended users. They are "organized" in that they are brought together, face to face if at all possible, as a group or task force to work with the evaluator and participate in making decisions about the evaluation.

A third way of reducing use is to focus on decisions and information instead of on decision makers and information users. This approach is epitomized by Mark Thompson (1975: 26, 38), who defines evaluation as "marshalling of information for the purposes of improving decisions," and makes the first step in an evaluation "identification of the decision or decisions for which information is required." Thompson simply assumes throughout his model that decision makers and information users are already identified and organized. Thus, the focus is the decision itself.

But again, it is left up to the evaluator to decide what data are actually needed.

The decision-oriented approach stems from the rational social scientific model of how decision making occurs; that is, there is a clear-cut decision to be made; information is needed to make the decision; the social scientist supplies the information; and the decision is then made in accordance with that information. But this model fits neither the real world utilization process (described in Chapter 2) nor the political nature of evaluation (Chapter 11).

It can, indeed, be important, even crucial, to orient evaluations toward future decisions. But identification of such decisions, and the implications of those decisions for the evaluation, are best made in conjunction with specific information users who come together to decide how the evaluation can gather what data for what purposes. Discussion of the future uses of the evaluation is an important part of the process of building commitment on the part of decision makers to actually use the information gathered during the evaluation. But determining what information is needed for what purposes is not left solely to the discretion of the evaluator. The evaluator genuinely *shares* power and expertise with an identifiable and organized group of intended users at every step along the way. The responsibility for making program decisions is theirs. The responsibility for determining what information they need in order to make future decisions is also theirs. If they are unwilling to meet those responsibilities prior to data collection, there is no reason to believe that they will really use the findings after the data are available.

A fourth way that utilization potential is diminished at the outset of an evaluation is simply to decide automatically that the funders of the evaluation, of the program, or both, are the relevant information users. In some cases this is accurate: Funders may be among those interested in using evaluative information. But there are many other reasons why evaluations are funded—to give the appearance of being interested in evaluation; because legislation or licensing requires evaluation; or because someone thought it had to be written into the budget proposal. Just because someone controls evaluation purse strings does not mean that they have an evaluation question. Often, they simply believe that evaluation is a good thing, ought to be done, helps programs, and keeps people on their toes. They do not care about the content of a specific evaluation, they only care that evaluation— any evaluation—takes place. They mandate the process, but not the substance. Under such conditions (which are not unusual) there is considerable opportunity for identifying and working with genuinely interested stakeholders to formulate relevant evaluation questions and a correspondingly appropriate design.

Finally, a fifth way that utilization potential is diminished during the conceptualization of the process is to target evaluations at organizations rather than at individuals. When the organization is the identified consumer of evaluation, specific decision makers and information users do not have to be identified and organized, and usually they are not.

Sociologists have a very precise view of how best to understand and study organizations. It is a view that has had substantial impact on evaluation researchers, management analysts, and administrative sciences. It is also a view largely devoid of individual people. Indeed, the personal factor is anathema to much sociology. Organizations are made up of positions. Skills, powers, rules, roles, and rewards attach to these positions. Since Max Weber's seminal essay on bureaucracy, sociologists have viewed the interchangeability of people in organizations as the hallmark of organizational rationality in modern society. Under their ideal norms of bureaucratic rationality, it does not matter *who* is in a position, only that the position be filled using universalistic criteria. The position, the set of positions, and the organizational social structure mold the individual to function rationally in that position. Weber argued that bureaucracy makes for maximum efficiency precisely because the organization of role-specific positions in an unambiguous hierarchy of authority and status renders action calculable and rational without regard to personal considerations or particularistic criteria.

It is this view of the world that has permeated the minds of evaluators when they say that their evaluation is for "the federal government" or any other organizational entity. But organizations do not consume information; people do—individual, idiosyncratic, caring, uncertain, searching people. *Who* is in a position makes all the difference in the world to information use.

To ignore the personal factor is to diminish utilization potential from the outset. To target evaluations at organizations is to target them at nobody in particular—and, in effect, not to really target them at all.

Supporting Research on the Personal Factor

James Burry (1984) of the UCLA Center for the Study of Evaluation has done a thorough review of the voluminous literature on evaluation utilization. That review was the basis for a synthesis of factors that appear to have a bearing on the degree to which evaluation information may be used (Alkin et al., 1985). The synthesis grew out of empirical research on evaluation utilization (Alkin et al., 1979), and organizes the various factors in three major categories: human factors, context factors, and evaluation factors.

> Human factors reflect evaluator and user characteristics with a strong influence on use. Included here are such factors as people's attitudes toward and interest in the program and its evaluation, their backgrounds and organizational positions, and their professional experience levels.
>
> Context factors consist of the requirements and fiscal constraints facing the evaluation, and relationships between the program being evaluated and other segments of its broader organization and the surrounding community.
>
> Evaluation factors refer to the actual conduct of the evaluation, the procedures used in the conduct of the evaluation, and the quality of the information it provides [Burry, 1984: 1].

The Alkin et al. (1979, 1985) framework and the Burry (1984) review represent the most comprehensive efforts to date to pull together the evaluation literature on utilization. The primary weakness of the synthesis and the framework is that the factors are undifferentiated in terms of importance. The synthesis represents a checklist of factors that can influence evaluation, and the literature that is synthesized suggests the conditions under which certain factors will emerge as important, but no overall hierarchy is suggested by the synthesis; that is, a hierarchy that places more importance on certain factors as necessary and/or sufficient conditions for evaluation use.

At a 1985 conference on evaluation use sponsored by the UCLA Center for the Study of Evaluation, with support from the National Institute of Education, I asked Jim Burry if his review of the literature suggested any factors as particularly important in explaining use. He answered without hesitation:

> There's no question about it. The personal factor is far and away the most important. You're absolutely right in saying that the personal factor is the most important explanatory variable in evaluation use. The research of the last five years confirms the primacy of the personal factor [Burry, 1985].

Another framework that supports the importance of the personal factor is the "Decision-Oriented Educational Research" approach of Cooley and Bickel (1985). Although the label for this approach implies a focus on decisions rather than people, in fact the approach is built on a strong "client orientation." This client orientation means that the primary intended users of decision-oriented educational research are clearly identified and then involved in all stages of the work through ongoing dialogue between the researcher and the client. Cooley and Bickel present case evidence to document the importance of being client-oriented.

Support for the importance of the personal factor also comes from the work of the Stanford Evaluation Consortium, one of the leading places of ferment and reform in evaluation during the late 1970s and early 1980s. Cronbach and associates in the Consortium summarized major reforms needed in evaluation thinking by publishing a provocative set of 95 theses, following the precedent of Martin Luther. Among their theses was this observation on the personal factor:

> Nothing makes a larger difference in the use of evaluations than the personal factor—the interest of officials in learning from the evaluation and the desire of the evaluator to get attention for what he knows [Cronbach et al., 1980: 6].

Beyond Just Beginning

In this chapter the personal factor has been identified as a critical consideration in enhancing evaluation use. The importance of the personal factor is the underlying justification for beginning an evaluation by identifying and organizing primary intended evaluation users. Once identified and organized, evaluators can interact with these primary users throughout the evaluation, not just at the beginning. For there is a sixth approach to evaluation that also diminishes utilization potential: namely, to identify and organize primary decision makers and information users at the outset of the study, and then ignore them until the final report is ready.

Identification and organization of primary intended users is not just an academic exercise performed for its own sake. The purpose of involving specific people who can use information is to enable them to establish direction for and commitment to the evaluation every step along the way. The personal factor is important from initiation of the study through the design and data collection stages as well as in the final report and dissemination parts of the process. If decision makers have shown little interest in the study in its earlier stages, our data suggest that they are not likely to suddenly show an interest in using the findings at the end of the study. They won't be sufficiently *prepared* for use.

Thus, the centrality of the personal factor in contributing to evaluation use has implications for all aspects and stages of program evaluation, not just at the stage at which findings are disseminated. The remainder of this book investigates those implications—implications for how an evaluation is conceptualized (Chapters 4-7), methods decisions (Chapter 8), and analysis approaches (Chapter 9). Prior to considering the next steps in utilization-focused evaluation, the final section of this chapter presents five premises that summarize the perspective developed thus far. Additional premises will be presented in the concluding chapter.

UTILIZATION-FOCUSED EVALUATION PREMISES

The first premise is that concern for utilization should be the driving force in an evaluation. At every point at which a decision about the evaluation is being made—whether the decision concerns the focus of study, design, methods, measurement, analysis, or reporting—the evaluator asks, "How would that affect the uses of this evaluation?"

The second premise is that concern for utilization is ongoing and continuous from the very beginning of the evaluation. Use isn't something one becomes interested in at the end of an evaluation. By the end of the evaluation, the potential for use has been largely determined. From the moment decision makers and evaluators begin conceptualizing the evaluation, decisions are being made which will affect in major ways how the evaluation will be used.

The third premise is that evaluations should be user-oriented. This means that the evaluation is aimed at the interests and information needs of specific, identifiable people—not vague, passive audiences. Therefore, the first step in utilization-focused evaluation is identifying the primary intended users of the evaluation. This first step is the personal factor in action.

The fourth premise is that, once identified, these intended evaluation users should be personally and actively involved in making decisions about the evaluation. Working actively with people who have a stake in the outcomes of an evaluation (the "stakeholders") is aimed at increasing the potential for use by building a genuine commitment to and understanding of the evaluation over the course of the evaluation process.

The fifth premise is that there are multiple and varied interests around any evaluation. Program staff, administrators, clients, public officials, and community leaders all have an interest in evaluation, but the degree and nature of their interests will vary. The process of identifying and organizing stakeholders to participate in an evaluation process should be done in a way that is sensitive to and respectful of these varied and multiple interests. At the same time, it must be recognized that resource, time, and personnel limitations will make it impossible for any single evaluation to answer all possible questions, or to give equal attention to all possible users. The first priority, then, is *intended use for users*.

This notion was put quite succinctly by Baltasar Gracian (1647) in *The Art of Worldly Wisdom*. He observed,

It is a great misfortune to be of use to nobody;
scarcely less to be of use to everybody.

PART II

DIFFICULT CHOICES AND MULTIPLE OPTIONS

Deciding What to Evaluate

Desiderata for the Indecisive

Go placidly amid the noise and haste, and remember what peace there may be in avoiding options. As far as possible, without surrender, be on good terms with the indecisive. Cultivate them. Avoid people who ask you to make up your mind; they are vexations to the spirit. Enjoy your indecisiveness as well as your procrastinations. Exercise caution in your affairs lest you be faced with choices, for the world is full of trickery. But let this not blind you to what virtue there is; many persons strive for the high ideal of mindless tranquility; and everywhere life is full of the joys of avoidance. You are a child of the universe, no less than the trees and the stars; you have a right to do and think and be absolutely nothing. And whether or not it is clear to you, no doubt the universe is unfolding as it should. Therefore be at peace in your oblivion. Therein lies happiness.

Halcolm's
Indesiderata

Chapter 4

FOCUSING EVALUATION QUESTIONS

Human propensities in the face of evaluation: feline curiosity; stultifying fear; beguiling distortion of reality; ingratiatory public acclamation; inscrutable selective perception; profuse rationalization about whys and why nots; and apocalyptic anticipation. In other words, the usual run-of-the-mill human reactions to uncertainty.

Once past these necessary initial indulgences, it's possible to get on to the real evaluation issues: What's worth knowing? How will we get it? How will it be used?

Meaningful evaluation answers begin with meaningful questions.

—Halcolm

A Setting

In 1976, the Northwest Regional Educational Laboratory contracted with the Hawaii State Department of Education to evaluate Hawaii's innovative 3-on-2 Program. The 3-on-2 Program is a team teaching approach in which three teachers work with two regular classrooms of primary-age children. Some classes combined children in multiage groupings. Walls between classrooms were removed so that three teachers and 40 to 60 children shared one large space. The program was aimed at greater individualization, greater cooperation and planning among teachers, and increased diversity of resources available to students in a single classroom.

The Northwest Lab research team proposed an advocacy-adversary evaluation model. Two teams were created; by coin toss one was designated the advocacy, the other the adversary team. The task of the advocacy team was to make the program look as good as possible. The advocates were charged with supporting the proposition that Hawaii's 3-on-2 Program is effective and ought to be continued. The adversaries were to attack the program; they were charged with marshalling all possible evidence demonstrating that the program ought to be terminated. The evaluation project director served as arbiter between the two teams (NWREL, 1977).

The advocacy-adversary model was a combination debate-courtroom approach to evaluation. As concern about the politics and pressures of evaluation grew in the early 1970s, and as critics of evaluation argued with increased vociferation that single evaluators could not maintain neutrality and objectivity throughout the evaluation process, support for the notion of the advocacy-adversary model grew (see Wolf, 1975; Kourilsky, 1974; Owens, 1973). It was an intriguing idea and an alluring prospect.

I became involved as a resource consultant on classroom structure in November of 1976. The two teams were about to begin site visits to observe classrooms, and I was asked by the project director to assist them in developing a framework for systematically observing 3-on-2 classrooms.

When I arrived on the scene, I perceived and personally felt the exhilaration of the competition. I said to myself:

> These are no staid academic scholars. They are athletes training for the contest that will reveal who is best. These are lawyers prepared to use whatever means necessary to fully represent their clients. These are two teams that have become openly secretive about their respective strategies. Each team wants to present the best case it can. These are highly experienced and professional evaluators engaged in a battle not only of data but also of wits. The prospects are interesting indeed.

Just before I left Hawaii, the two teams began to prepare their final reports. As they discussed the content of the reports among themselves and various information users, a concern emerged among some of the evaluators about the narrow focus of the evaluation question. As the evaluators addressed the primary issue of whether the Hawaii 3-on-2 program should be continued or terminated, the question was raised as to whether other information about how to change the program, how to make it better without terminating it, might not be more useful given the political realities of the situation. Was it possible that a great amount of time, effort, and money was directed at answering the wrong question?

Two members of the evaluation teams summarized the problem in their published *post mortem* of Hawaii's 3-on-2 advocacy-adversary evaluation:

As we became more and more conversant with the intricacies, both educational and political, of the Hawaii 3-on-2 Program, we realized that Hawaii's decision-makers should not be forced to deal with a simple save-it-or-scrap-it choice. Middle ground positions were more sensible. Half-way measures, in this instance, probably made more sense. But there we were, obliged to do battle with our adversary colleagues on the unembellished question of whether to maintain or terminate the 3-on-2 Program [Popham and Carlson, 1977: 5].

As planned and hoped for, the results of the Hawaii 3-on-2 evaluation did focus on the right question, and the results were used by the originally identified upper-level decision makers. The results of a survey of Hawaii education officials reported by William Wright and Thomas Sachse at the 1977 Meeting of the American Educational Research Association showed that decision makers got the information they wanted. But the most important evidence that the evaluation focused on the right question comes from actions taken by decision makers following the evaluation. In the summer of 1979, Dean Nafziger, NWREL's Director of Evaluation, Research, and Assessment, wrote me to provide an update on the Hawaii 3-on-2 evaluation. After noting that the decision makers were clearly identified as state legislators, members of the State Board of Education, and the superintendent, he wrote,

Their clear charge was that we should help them make a decision about maintaining the program or dropping it entirely. On the basis of the evaluation, the decision makers decided to eliminate the 3 on 2 program. The final phasing out of the program is scheduled for the upcoming year. As you can see, then, we maintained attention to the information needs of the *true* decision makers, and adhered to those needs in the face of occasional counter positions by other evaluation audiences. . . .

If a lesson is to be learned it is this: an evaluator must determine who is making the decisions and keep the information needed by the decision makers as the highest priority. In the case of the Hawaii 3 on 2 evaluation, the presentation of program improvement information would have served to muddle the decision making process.

The Hawaii 3-on-2 evaluation is exemplary in showing how the right information to the right people can make a difference. But it's seldom easy to know just what the right information is.

An Evaluation Fantasy

As I listened to the conversations in Hawaii, I began to fantasize about how a conversation might go between program officials and evaluators if it had turned out, as Popham and Carlson worried it might, that an advocacy-adversary evaluation would not provide needed information for making program changes. My fantasy, which really deserves the touch of an Art Buchwald, went something like this:

> *Program officials:* We are very much looking forward to the results of your study. As you know, we have been experiencing a high rate of inflation and a declining school-age population. Under these conditions, with reduced federal aid, our program is simply too expensive to maintain as is.
>
> *Evaluators:* Do you mean you've already made the decision to terminate the program before the evaluation is completed?
>
> *Program officials:* Oh, no! Nothing like that. All we've decided is that the program has to be changed. In some schools the program has been very successful and effective. Teachers like it; parents like it; principals like it. How can we terminate such a program? Other schools have only gone along because they were forced to, or because of getting extra money, or to save a teacher position when enrollments declined. In some places the two-classroom space has been subdivided into what is essentially three self-contained classrooms. We know that.
>
> What's more, it's the kind of program that has some strong political opposition and some strong political support. So there's no question of terminating the program, and there's no question of keeping the program the same.
>
> *Evaluators:* I see. But you realize that the evaluation has two teams. One team will present data to show why the program should be continued. The other will present data to show why the program should be ended.
>
> *Program officials:* Ah, yes, we know. And that will be very interesting. We are looking forward to the presentation. But afterwards we trust you will give us answers to our practical questions. We hope you will tell us how to reduce the size of the program, how to make it more cost-effective where possible, and how to increase the overall quality of the program by setting up ways for eliminating ineffective sites and increasing support to successful sites. We don't want to interfere with your evaluation presentation. After all, you are the evaluators. But after the evaluation, maybe you can tell us the answers to these questions, too.
>
> *Evaluators:* Of course we want to be helpful in any way we can, but you realize those aren't the questions we've been studying. We've been studying the question of whether to keep the program or end the program. That's what the final reports will deal with.
>
> *Program officials:* Yes, yes, the final reports should be very interesting. But afterwards you can answer our real questions. There's no question of ending the program or keeping it the same. So afterwards we hope you will tell us how to improve the program, make it better. You can do that, can't you?

Identifying and Focusing Evaluation Questions

The practice of evaluators answering the wrong question, or no question at all, is widespread. The most common complaint I hear about evaluation is that "it didn't tell us what we needed to know. It didn't answer our questions." Such a response is not, however, inevitable.

Once primary evaluation users have been identified and organized, the second step in utilization-focused evaluation is to *identify and focus the relevant evaluation questions*. This is an interactive process between evaluators and the primary intended users of the evaluation. It can be a difficult, even painful process, because deciding what will be evaluated means deciding what will *not* be evaluated. Programs are so complex and have so many levels, goals, and functions that there are always more potential study foci than there are resources to examine them. Moreover, as human beings we have a limited capacity to take in data and juggle complexities. We can deal effectively with only so much at one time. The alternatives have to be narrowed and a choice made about which way to go.

This problem of focus is by no means unique to program evaluation. Management consultants find that a major problem for executives is focusing their energies on priorities. The trick in meditation is learning to focus on a single mantra, koan, or image. Professors have trouble getting graduate students to analyze less than the whole of human experience in their dissertations. And evaluators have trouble getting intended users to focus evaluation issues.

Identifying and focusing relevant evaluation questions means dealing with several basic concerns. What is the purpose of the evaluation? How will the information be used? What will we know after the evaluation that we do not know now? What can we do after the evaluation that we cannot do now for lack of information? These are not simply rote questions. The answers to these and related questions will determine everything else that happens in an evaluation. As evaluators and primary information users interact around these questions, the evaluation begins to take shape.

Formative and Summative Evaluation Questions

First, it is important to clarify at the outset whether the primary purpose of the evaluation is to make an overall judgment about the effectiveness of a program or to collect information that can be used primarily for program development and improvement. The labels for this distinction were introduced by Michael Scriven (1967: 40-43) in discussing evaluation of educational curriculum. He called the former "summative evaluation" and the latter "formative evaluation." The distinction has since become a fundamental evaluation typology and the terms are now applied more broadly than they were by Scriven.

Summative evaluations are aimed at determining the essential effectiveness of programs and are particularly important in making decisions about continuing or terminating an experimental program or demonstration project. As such, summative evaluations are often useful to funders. *Formative evaluations*, in contrast, focus on ways of improving and enhancing programs not only in their initial development, but at any point in the life of a program. Formative information is particularly useful to program administrators and staff.

Summative evaluation questions are these: Has the program been effective? Should it be continued? Is it worthwhile? Did the program bring about (cause) the desired outcomes?

Formative evaluation questions include these: What are the strengths and weaknesses of the program? How can the program be improved? What's working well and what isn't working so well? What are the reactions of clients, staff, and others to the program? What are their perceptions about what should be changed?

These fundamentally different questions have important implications for methods. Summative evaluations typically seek to draw causal inferences about the effects of a program; the preferred design is experimental and outcomes are measured statistically (Mark and Cook, 1984: 66). Formative evaluations rely more heavily on site visits, direct observations of program activities, surveys, and in-depth interviews (Patton, 1980a). Formative evaluations can also be based on information systems that monitor program efforts and outcomes regularly over time to provide feedback for fine-tuning the program. The "decision-oriented educational research" of Cooley and Bickel (1985) builds such an information system aimed at formative evaluation through what they call "monitoring and tailoring."

In terms of the distinction between evaluation research and program evaluation discussed in Chapter 1, summative evaluations tend to be conclusion-oriented whereas formative evaluations tend to be action-oriented.

For any given evaluation, the formative-summative distinction can be critical. Formative and summative evaluations involve significantly different research foci. The same data seldom serve both purposes well. When a program evaluation question is framed in summative terms and summative data are collected, program decision makers may not receive much-needed formative information for program change and improvement. They fail to receive the needed information because the evaluation question is not framed in formative terms. It is thus important to identify the primary purpose of the evaluation at the outset. Other decisions about what to do in the evaluation can then be made in accordance with how well the primary purpose will be served.

There is another important reason for knowing about formative and summative evaluations. These terms have become so commonplace and central to the language (translated: jargon) of evaluation that no self-respecting evaluator would leave home without them. They are the code words that permit entry into the select company and cocktail parties of professional evaluators. Practice saying them glibly to show friends, lovers, and evaluation users that you are in the know.

Alternative Questions from Alternative Definitions of Evaluation

Beyond the distinction between formative and summative evaluations, alternative strategies for focusing evaluations are implied in alternative definitions of evaluation. Different definitions of evaluation reveal important differences in what various evaluators emphasize in their work.

(1) The classic approach of Ralph Tyler (1950) was to emphasize goals and objectives, so, for him (and for the thousands of educators and researchers schooled in his approach), evaluation is the process of determining the extent to which the goals and objectives of a program are being attained. Basing evaluation on delineation and measurement of clear, specific, and measurable goals has been so important that the entire next chapter is devoted to the goals-based strategy for focusing evaluations.

(2) Many social scientists emphasize scientific rigor in their evaluation models, and that emphasis is reflected in their definition of the field. For these social scientists, evaluation involves primarily the application of rigorous social science methods to the study of programs (e.g., Bernstein and Freeman, 1975; Cook et al., 1977; Boruch and Rindskopf, 1984; Mark and Cook, 1984). These evaluators emphasize the importance of experimental designs and quantitative measures. Methodological concerns focus evaluations in this tradition.

(3) Another common emphasis in evaluation definitions is on the comparative nature of the process. Evaluation is the process of *comparing* the relative costs and benefits of two or more programs. The principles and definitions that undergird evaluation models emphasizing the comparative nature of the process have emerged in part as a reaction to the narrowness of evaluation when defined as measuring relative attainment of a single program's goals (Alkin and Ellett, 1984). The focus here is this: How do different programs compare?

(4) Still another emphasis comes from evaluators who highlight the valuation part of evaluation. From this perspective, evaluation is judgment of a program's value. The final judgment, this ultimate determination of relative merit or worth, is the *sine qua non* of evaluation (see Worthen and Sanders, 1973: 22-26, 120-122; Guba and Lincoln, 1981: 35-36).

(5) Some evaluation practitioners focus on the generation of data for decision making and problem solving. This perspective goes beyond making judgments or assigning relative values. The emphasis is on choices, decisions, and problem resolution. It is quite possible to decide that one thing is better than another (e.g., program X versus program Y) without taking any concrete action with regard to program X or program Y. When evaluation is

defined as a problem-solving process (Gephart, 1981), or as a process that provides information for decision making (Thompson, 1975), some action process that goes beyond valuation is given primary emphasis in the definition. Thus, the evaluation is focused on a problem or decision.

(6) Yet another strategy is the systems analysis approach (e.g., Rivlin, 1971; Rossi et al., 1979). This approach looks at the relationship between program inputs and outputs. It uses quantitative data to relate differences in programs or policies to variations in select indicators of program impact. The question is this: What combination of inputs and implementation strategies will most efficiently produce desired outcomes? One of the main antecedents for this approach was systems analysis as developed in the U.S. Department of Defense for military planning (House, 1980: 22).

(7) Finally, there is the definition of evaluation used in this book (see Chapter 1), which emphasizes providing useful and usable information to specific people. The strategy for bringing focus to a utilization-focused evaluation is to find out what the intended users want and need to know. This means that the evaluation may be focused on questions, issues, problems, decisions, goals, system relationships, values, comparisons—*whatever provides the most meaningful framework for working with evaluation users.*

These seven different approaches to evaluation emphasize different parts of the evaluation process. These varying emphases reflect varying values about what is important. There is no single set of evaluation questions, and no single approach, that will always work. There are many, many alternative evaluation questions and approaches. Appendix II lists 30 different types of evaluation. The next section suggests how to work with stakeholders to find out what type of evaluation they are expecting.

Discovering Stakeholders' Definitions and Expectations

A reasonable starting place in working with stakeholders is to find out how *they* think about and define evaluation. Rather than unilaterally defining evaluation, the utilization-focused evaluator will work to discover the perceptions, confusions, expectations, and beliefs about evaluation of those people who will be the primary users of the evaluation. It is then possible to build on that knowledge to develop shared understandings about evaluation options and potential processes. It is often appropriate to simply ask the people with whom one is working to associate freely in a stream-of-consciousness fashion with the word evaluation: "When you hear the word evaluation, what comes to mind?" This can be a verbal exercise or a written one, done in small groups or a large gathering. Notice, however, that I did not ask participants in this process to *define* evaluation. The question, "Who can give me a definition of evaluation?" clearly implies a single right answer, and the wary participant will suspect that the evaluator will eventually pronounce the correct definition, but only after making several participants look stupid. Definitions are thus perceived as academic playthings to be used in a game at which the researcher is sure to win, so why participate? I'm not looking for skill at constructing or repeating definitions. I'm looking for perceptions and synonyms that will provide clues to tacit definitions held by people in the situation in which I'm working. With these perceptions made explicit, it is possible to consider various alternatives and end by defining evaluation in a way that is relevant to the people who are going to use the evaluation.

Some cautions are in order when defining evaluation in any particular setting or for some special purpose. First, no single-sentence definition of evaluation will suffice to fully capture the complex practice of evaluation with its many nuances. Second, different definitions serve different purposes, one especially important function being to serve as a foundation for a particular model or perspective on evaluation. Third, there are fundamental disagreements within the field about the essence and boundaries of evaluation. Fourth, people who propound a particular definition often have some ego investment in their special perspective, whether because they developed it, were trained according to it, or are part of a group in which that definition is esteemed; any critique of a definition, in such cases, can be taken as a personal attack, a good many people finding it difficult to separate criticism of their ideas from criticism of them personally. Fifth, people on the outside looking in (and many within the field) are often confused and uncertain about just what evaluation is. Sixth, there is no reason to expect an early end to either the disagreements or the confusion. As Samuel Butler explained the problem in "Higgledy-Piggledy,"

> Definitions are a kind of scratching and generally leave a sore place more sore than it was before.

The reason for paying attention to how primary users define evaluation is to help establish a basic direction for the evaluation. What do they expect to have happen? What do they expect to get from the evaluation? From this general sense of direction one can move quickly to a much narrower focus.

Criteria for Utilization-Focused Evaluation Questions

A good utilization-focused evaluation question has several characteristics:

(1) It is possible to bring data to bear on the question; i.e., it is truly an *empirical* question.
(2) There is more than one possible answer to the question; i.e., the answer is not predetermined by the phrasing of the question.

(3) The primary users want information to help answer the question.
(4) The intended users feel they *need* information to help them answer the question.
(5) The primary users want to answer the question for themselves, not just for someone else.
(6) They care about the answer to the question.
(7) The intended users can indicate how they would use the answer to the question; i.e., they can specify the relevance of an answer to the question for future action.

A brief elaboration of these major criteria follows.

THE EMPIRICAL CRITERION

Utilization-focused evaluation questions are empirical questions; that is, it is possible to bring data to bear on them and the answer is not predetermined by the phrasing of the question. Evaluation involves systematically collecting and analyzing empirical information for the purpose of making judgments and taking action. The making of judgments and decisions necessarily involves values. But value questions in and of themselves are not answerable empirically. It is critical, therefore, to separate the empirical question from the values question in the phrasing of the evaluation issue.

Let me illustrate this point with an example from teacher centers. Teacher centers have emerged as an alternative to isolated in-service programs on a school-by-school basis. A teacher center is a program aimed at providing resources, ideas, assistance, direction, and encouragement to teachers. Through the Department of Education, the federal government has put a great deal of money into teacher centers. The federal government requires evaluation. For many, the evaluation issue centers on the question of *improvement*. Are the schools improving? Are teachers being helped? Are children doing better? In a review of the program's development, one teacher center planner and advocate has argued that assessment of teacher effectiveness "will have to be in terms of verifying individual teachers' improvement in classroom performance over time" (Devaney, 1977: 7).

Assessing improvement necessarily involves making a judgment about whether an observed impact is desirable or undesirable. It is important to separate the issue of improvement from the related but quite different issue of impact or change. Improvement involves a judgment about whether or not something is better, whereas impact involves the more limited question of whether or not something is different. An observed difference may or may not constitute improvement, depending on who is making the value judgment about whether the change is for better or worse. It is crucial throughout the evaluation process that empirical observations about program impact be kept separate from judgments about whether such impact constitutes improvement.

Suppose a teacher center conducts a series of workshops on the use of resources outside the classroom. As a result, a group of teachers increase field trips by an average of three hours a week. The time spent outside the classroom leads to an average reduction of two hours per week in time spent on reading and arithmetic in class. Clearly, the teacher center has had an impact. Change has occurred. But has teaching improved? The answer depends on how much one values supervised reading and arithmetic compared to other stimulating activities.

Questions of right and wrong, better or worse, are not simple empirical questions. To formulate evaluation questions solely in value terms can sabotage an evaluation from the beginning. The empirical question is not improvement but change. Has the program been effective in changing teachers? Do they think differently? Can they do things now that they could not do before? Do they feel differently? Are different things occurring in classrooms? These are empirical questions. Data to answer such questions can then be used to determine the extent to which such changes constitute improvement according to specific rules.

This is not an esoteric, semantic distinction, but a practical suggestion for distinguishing between that which can be observed (by whatever methods) and that which cannot be observed. Failure to make this distinction can lead to serious misunderstandings throughout the evaluation process. Questions that cannot be answered empirically do not provide a clear focus for utilization-focused evaluation.

QUESTIONS PRIMARY USERS WANT ANSWERED

Utilization-focused evaluation questions focus on issues of interest to identified stakeholders and evaluation users. The questions are something they want answered. This means avoiding questions that decision makers or primary users do not want answered. In almost any program, there are questions of enormous political and personal sensitivity. You can tell when you have stumbled onto such a question because of the uneasy silence it produces, followed by the staff's groping for a way to tactfully change the subject. The most common questions in this category concern opinions about the performance of specific personnel. Personnel evaluation is quite different from program evaluation. Personnel evaluations involve gathering information about the performance of individuals. Program evaluations focus on structural and treatment characteristics of programs. At times there is a narrow line between the two, because personnel performance can, of course, affect program effectiveness. Nevertheless, they represent quite distinct evaluation foci.

I recall one human service program in particular for which we were asked to evaluate the staff development component of the program. In accordance with Peter's Principle, the person in charge of staff development had risen to her own level of incompetence: She was tenured; she had territoriality on that component of the program; she could not be fired and there was no place to which to promote her; she seemed likely to be impervious to change. No one wanted to know what staff, clients, or administrators thought about her—that was data they did not want and could not use. We focused instead on concrete, changeable program activities (e.g., frequency and length of training sessions, content of sessions, participant input, style of training, use of outside resources, and so on).

Research focus is always a difficult issue. Some evaluators seem to have a talent for honing in on personally sensitive questions; their instinct is to go for the kill. Whatever program staff do not want answered, the evaluators do want answered. They are investigators uncovering incompetence and rooting out ineffectiveness. Although I personally take a different approach, I do not deny the right of evaluators to do what they feel they must do—or else resign their commission. But the utilization potential of such evaluators is low. If decision makers and information users do not want a question answered, they will find ways to ignore or discredit the answers proffered. The evaluator can feel righteous about having produced the information, but is not likely to have the satisfaction of seeing it used. There is a Halcolm proverb to express this viewpoint: "You can lead decision makers to information, but you can't make them swallow it." They have to be interested.

QUESTIONS THAT NEED ANSWERING

Utilization-focused questions are those that decision makers feel they need information to answer. This means the answer is not already known. In some cases the reason why program staff do not want a question asked is because they already know with considerable certainty what the answer is. From a utilization point of view, there is no reason to spend a lot of time and money gathering information to tell people things they already know. This is particularly true when a program is relatively chaotic—staff are going in different directions, management is ineffective, clients unhappy. Everyone involved knows things are a mess. The last thing such a program needs is more information to deal with: managerial help, yes; planning assistance, indeed; staff training, without a doubt; but program evaluation, no. Such a program does not suffer from lack of evaluative information, it suffers from a lack of management and direction.

This is a point that must be stressed with decision makers, information users, and program staff. Unless a lack of knowledge and information is part of the problem, program evaluation will not help an organization. All evaluation can do is tell you something you do not already know, or increase your certainty about something of which you were unsure. Evaluations are no panacea for program problems.

An example of this is a daycare program that was losing clients and money. The board knew that the program was poorly located and poorly organized. But instead of relocating and reorganizing, they got a grant to conduct an evaluation. During the evaluation the program folded.

Part of the evaluation interaction process, then, should be aimed at determining what things are already known, what actions can already be taken without further study—and on what aspects of program functioning evaluative information is really needed.

THE PERSONAL INTEREST CRITERION

Utilization-focused questions are of direct personal interest to key stakeholders and primary evaluation users. They want to answer the question for themselves, not just for someone else: they personally care about the answer to the question. The reason for identifying and organizing relevant stakeholders and information users is to be sure that the people who are going to be the primary users of evaluation findings are the same people who decide what the focus of the evaluation will be. This means that the evaluation should focus on *their* information needs—not on their speculations about what someone else wants to know. If the evaluation is for someone else, it behooves the evaluator to make that person part of the identified and organized evaluation task force. A brief example may help illustrate this point.

I sometimes have the opportunity to work at the classroom level with individual teachers. My mandate is to help them improve their teaching, in which case the individual teacher is my primary evaluation information user. The teacher, however, does not necessarily see it that way:

Evaluator: What would you like to have me help you gather information about?

Teacher: Well, I guess we should evaluate student achievement in basic skills.

Evaluator: Do you know how well your students are doing in basic skills?

Teacher: Sure, I know how well they're doing. But the principal and parents don't know.

Evaluator: Well now, as I understand this evaluation, it's purpose is to help you improve your teaching. If there's nothing you need to know and if the evaluation is for the principal, then I should talk to the principal and find out what she wants evaluated. She may already know how well the students are achieving basic skills. Likewise with the parents. If the evaluation is for them, I ought to get them together and find out what they want to know.

At this point we can decide if there is anything the teacher wants to study, or if someone else should become the primary user for the information. My experience is that once people catch onto the idea that it is all right for them to ask their own questions, *questions about which they care,* and that they can conduct evaluations for themselves, not just for someone else, they become quite excited about and committed to the evaluation process.

QUESTIONS AIMED AT FUTURE ACTION

The utilization potential of an evaluation is enhanced if decision makers and information users can indicate during conceptualization how they plan to use information obtained during an evaluation. If they cannot indicate future usefulness at the outset, there is no reason to believe that they will be able to do so after the evaluation.

Providing information for future decisions is one option, keeping in mind that in real programs there are very few decisions of the concrete, single point in time, this-is-the-day-to-make-a-decision variety.

Thus, to say that evaluation questions ought to be framed in a future action context does not mean that they need be aimed at some single future decision, although on occasion that may be possible and appropriate. Rather, more generally, primary evaluation users ought to be able to indicate where their knowledge uncertainties lie, what activities, actions, and options are clouded by those uncertainties, and how evaluative information would increase their potential for doing a better job and making the program more effective. In short, the evaluator attempts to "frame the decision context for the evaluation" (Alkin, 1975b). One way to help guarantee that evaluation studies are geared to collecting information with future action potential is to focus on what Amitai Etzioni calls "moveable" or "malleable" variables. These are factors that are subject to human intervention. Etzioni conceptualizes a continuum from highly immutable conditions (laws of nature) to highly manipulable elements (symbols):

> The first and single most important methodological consideration for a policy researcher is an interest in moveable variables. . . . Within the social realm you can rank order all the variables which characterize the social world as to what is more moveable and what is less moveable. . . . The reason I emphasize this so much is that most of our non-evaluation, non-policy research tends to zero in on the non-moveable variable [Etzioni and Patton, 1976].

In the same vein, Etzioni argues that jobs are usually more malleable than people. He suggests, for example, that rather than trying to make lower socioeconomic persons into punctual, routine-oriented workers, jobs ought to be changed so that employees can carry out their work on a flexible schedule: "Generally I would think that you can demonstrate empirically that jobs can be restructured more readily than people's personalities" (Etzioni and Patton, 1976).

This distinction recalls the point made earlier in this chapter about the difference between personnel evaluation and program evaluation. Program elements are more malleable than personnel. In focusing the evaluation question on future action potential, it is helpful to be sure that the question is aimed at malleable aspects of programmatic activity. From a utilization point of view there is little value in studying a question that would generate information about conditions that are impervious to change.

Duncan MacRae (1976: 283) suggests that the focus on manipulable variables may be too narrow. Nonmanipulable variables are also important because "the consequences of policy choice or of action depend in an *interactive* fashion on manipulated and nonmanipulated variables." The real point is to focus the evaluation on future action potential. Edward Suchman (1972: 55) has emphasized the importance of this orientation:

> Much too often evaluation studies are undertaken when there is very little likelihood that anything will change regardless of how the evaluation comes out. The attitude seems to be "let's do the evaluation and then decide what to do with the results." In such a case, the evaluation is probably unnecessary and certainly inadequately conceived.

Generating Questions

Given these criteria for evaluation questions with high utilization potential, there remains the problem of how to get started. How can an evaluator facilitate the framing of evaluation questions without imposing his or her own questions? I shall suggest one process that I have found particularly helpful. I first used it in an evaluation of the Frontier School Division, Manitoba, Canada.

The Frontier School Division is a geographically immense school district that encompasses much of northern Manitoba. The Deputy Minister of Education in Manitoba thought evaluation might be a way to shake things up, so he asked me to come and meet with them. His own goal was simply to get something started. The actual form and content of the evaluation was to be determined internally, within the Frontier School Division. So I went up to Winnipeg and met with the division administrators, a representative from the parents' group, a representative from the principals' group, and a representative from the teachers' union. I had asked that all constituencies be represented in order to establish a base with all the people who might be involved in using the evaluation. This was to be the initial group of key stakeholders and information users.

Inasmuch as I had been brought in from outside by a superordinate official, it was not surprising that I encountered an atmosphere ranging from defensiveness to outright hostility. They had not asked for the evaluation, and the whole idea sounded unsavory and threatening. In short, the utilization potential for my services seemed minimal.

I began by asking the group to tell me what kinds of things they were interested in evaluating. One administrator responded, "Okay, to begin with we'd like to see the evaluation instruments you've used in assessing other school districts."

I replied that I would be happy to share those instruments with them if they should prove relevant, but it would be helpful to know first what they wanted to evaluate, what kind of information they wanted. They were very appreciative of my concern for their input, so one participant suggested, "We didn't mean that you needed to show us all the instruments. Just show us one so we have an idea of what's going to happen."

I again replied that it was too early to really start talking about instruments. First, we had to identify the evaluation question. Then we would talk about instruments. By then I could tell that I was intensifying their initial suspicions and fears. I was confirming the worst and heightening their resistance by my secretiveness about the content of *my* evaluation scheme. One superintendent decided to try a different tack: "Okay, well, we don't need to see everything at once. How about just showing us one part, say the part that asks about superintendents in the teacher interviews you use."

At that point I was about to throw in the towel, give them some old instruments, and let them use what they wanted out of other evaluations. But I decided to try one other approach first: "Look, maybe your questions will be the same as questions I've used on surveys elsewhere. But I'm not even sure at this point that any kind of survey is appropriate. Maybe you don't need an evaluation. I certainly don't have any questions I need answered about your operations and effectiveness. Maybe you don't either. In which case I'll tell the Deputy Minister that evaluation isn't the way to go. But before we decide to quit, let me ask you to participate with me in a simple little exercise. It's an old complete-the-blank exercise from grade school." I then turned to the blackboard and wrote a sentence in capital letters.

I WOULD LIKE TO KNOW _____ ABOUT FRONTIER SCHOOL DIVISION.

"What I want each of you to do individually is to complete the blank ten times. What are ten things about Frontier School Division that you'd like to know, things you aren't certain about, things that would make a difference in what you do if you had more information? Take a shot at it, without regard to methods, measurement, design, resources, precision—just ten basic questions, real questions about this division."

They did that. Then I divided them into three groups of four people each and asked them to combine their lists together into a single list of ten things that each group wanted to know. They found that there were a lot of items that were similar, that were easily combined. Then we got back together and generated a single list of ten basic things that they would like to know— things that they did not have information on but that they wanted to have information on, information that could make a difference in what they were doing.

The questions generated were somewhat similar to other districtwide educational evaluations because there are only so many things one can ask about a school division. But the questions were phrased in their terms, incorporating important local nuances of meaning and circumstance.

It was important to have a list of questions. The questions needed some additional work to fit all the criteria for high utilization potential, but at least we had some questions they cared about—not my questions but their questions, because during the course of the exercise it had become *their* evaluation. The whole atmosphere had changed. This became most evident as I read aloud the final list of ten items they had generated that morning. One of the items read: "We would like to know what teachers think about the job superintendents are doing and how often superintendents ought to be out in the teachers' classrooms." One of the superintendents who had been most hostile when I first came in said, "That would be dynamite information. We have no idea at all what teachers think about us and what we do. I have no idea if they want me in their classrooms or if they don't want me in the classroom, or how often they think I ought to visit. That could just turn my job around. That would be great to know." We went on down the list and came to a question about the relationship between the classroom and the community. Both the teacher and parent representatives said that nobody had ever thought about that in any real way: "We don't have any policy about that. We don't know what goes on in the different schools. That would be important for us to know."

We spent the rest of the day refining questions, prioritizing, formalizing evaluation procedures, and establishing an agenda for the evaluation process. The hostility had vanished. By the end of the day they were anxious to have me make a commitment to return. They had become excited about doing their evaluation. The evaluation had credibility because the questions were their questions. A month later they found out that budget shifts in the Ministry meant that the central government would not pay for the evaluation. The Deputy Minister told them that they could scrap the evaluation if they wanted to, but they decided to pay for it out of local division funds.

The evaluation was completed in close cooperation with the task force at every step along the way. The results were disseminated to all principals and teachers. The conclusions and recommendations formed the basis for staff development conferences and division policy sessions. The evaluation process itself had an impact on the Division. Over the last several years Frontier School Division has gone through many changes. It is a very different place in terms of direction, morale, and activity than it was on my first visit. Not all those changes were touched on in the evaluation, nor are they simply a consequence of the evaluation. But generating a list of real and meaningful evaluation questions played a critical part in getting things started.

Alternatives to Utilization-Focused Evaluation Questions

There are other ways to solve the problem of focus in the evaluation process. One typical solution to the problem of what to study is for the evaluator to frame questions based largely upon his or her own interests, disciplinary tradition, and theoretical perspective. The evaluator's research agenda is most likely to be paramount where relevant stakeholders and evaluation users have *not* been identified and organized. Under such circumstances who else is there but the evaluator to determine the real focus of the evaluation? The answer to the evaluator's questions may be of some use to the evaluator, but rarely will such an evaluation answer the questions of those who face the day-to-day uncertainties of determining program effectiveness and guiding program improvement.

Decision makers bear considerable responsibility for making sure that their questions are the focus of the evaluation. In our study of the utilization of federal health evaluations, one decision maker described quite cogently the effort involved in making sure that the right question was evaluated.

> The initial design stages went round and round because they [the evaluators] kept trying to answer a different question than the one we wanted answered. . . . If we had dropped it with them right then and said go ahead and do your own thing with it, it would not have been useful. . . . I have a feeling I'm becoming redundant. The greatest single factor [explaining utilization] was that the question *we* wanted answered was the question they did at least try to answer in the study [DM367: 16].

When funds for basic research are scarce, resourceful academicians have found that evaluation funds serve just as well for research support. At a 1975 Theory Symposium sponsored by the University of Minnesota Department of Sociology, Peter Rossi called this the "Robin Hood" approach to evaluation: stealing from the rich (those with evaluation funds) to give to the poor (those in need of basic research funds). A tipoff that scholarly Robin Hoods are on the loose is their long and frequent soliloquies about the importance of using applied research to contribute to basic scientific knowledge. Since the researcher is in a better position than program staff to know what will contribute to basic scientific knowledge, and since one can no more be against contributing to basic scientific knowledge than one can be against progress (sometimes operationalized as increased motherhood, more apple pie, and larger doses of baseball), the evaluation researcher is in the optimal position to determine the research question.

Another closely related way of determining what to study in an evaluation is to let the available methods shape the question. Whatever question can be answered with available evaluator skills, that is the question that will be answered. The usefulness of studying a particular question is thus not at issue.

Economists pose questions in cost-benefit terms; sociologists frame questions that are amenable to study using survey methods; anthropologists think in terms of their own field methods to shape the question; and psychologists look for evaluation questions that will necessitate the use of some test to measure effects on the program's target population.

Another approach to the problem of focus is to try to look at everything at once. This approach can emerge from enthusiastic proponents of evaluation who believe that evaluation is so important it should be applied to everything. At other times the decision to look at multiple issues emerges as a political compromise when consensus about a more limited focus cannot be found. As often as not, evaluations aimed at everything are simply a result of poor conceptualization and failure to think about the issues involved.

There are two dangers in taking on too much. First, as suggested earlier in this chapter, once the evaluation is actually under way, some things end up getting more attention than others. Regardless of intentions, not everything will be studied equally. The second danger is that those participating in the evaluation can become overwhelmed by the complexity and endlessness of it all, particularly if they are new to research. One of the advantages of at least beginning with relatively small-scale, highly focused, and manageable evaluations is that they can provide some immediate reinforcement (through visible results) for demonstrating the utility of evaluation, thereby building staff support for larger scale, longer term, and more complex evaluation efforts.

The opposite case is illustrated by a Manitoba Ministry of Education evaluation system, in which every seven years each school division undertakes a comprehensive study of student achievement, school climate, teacher development, curriculum, administrative effectiveness, community values about education, the school lunch program, the division bus transportation system, extracurricular activities, and basic skills. In short, each division conducts a comprehensive, systematic review of its entire educational mission, using both internal resources and external consultants—thus its name, "the Internal-External Model of Evaluation." At a two-day conference held to introduce the plan to three pilot school divisions, local school officials soon felt overwhelmed by the enormity of the task. They quickly dubbed the system "the internal-external-eternal" model of evaluation. The experiences of that interminable first year bore out the wisdom of the revised label. Without focus, one can generate a great deal of activity with very little useful product.

Utilization Scenarios Based on Evaluation Questions

A good utilization-focused evaluation question is truly empirical; that is, it is possible to bring data to bear on the question; it is not loaded such that the answer is predetermined; it is framed in a clear action context such that intended users can specify how they would use the findings; and intended users want, need, and care about the answer to the question. In Chapters 2 and 3, I defined the primary outcome of utilization-focused evaluation as *intended use by intended users*. Thus, in focusing evaluation questions the intended users should be able to predetermine use without predetermining the actual findings.

Predetermining use can be facilitated by engaging users in utilization scenarios. "If the results came out this way, what would you do? Okay, now suppose the results came out the exact opposite, what would you do then?" Such utilization scenarios should be constructed before data collection to make sure that decision makers have really thought through use implications and options.

Evaluation use can be planned or unplanned. Planned use occurs when the intended use of the evaluation is identified at the beginning; subsequent utilization is then judged by planned or intended use. Unplanned use can occur in any evaluation, but relying totally on the hope that something useful will turn up is a highly risky strategy that results from postponing deliberations on use until the data are collected and analyzed. Eleanor Chelimsky (1983: 160) argues that the most important kind of accountability in evaluation is utilization that comes from "designed tracking and follow-up of a predetermined use to predetermined user." She calls this a "closed-looped feedback process" in which "the policy maker wants information, asks for it, and is interested in and informed by the response" (1983: 160). This perspective solves the problem of defining utilization, addresses the question of who the evaluation is for, and builds in evaluation accountability since the predetermined use becomes the criterion against which the success of the evaluation can be judged.

Focus

This chapter has emphasized the importance of bringing an evaluation into sharp focus. Evaluations can be framed in terms of goals, decisions, issues, problems, values, systems, comparisons—but regardless of approach one must deal with underlying questions. What is the purpose of the evaluation? How will findings be used? What will be known after the evaluation that is not known at the beginning? What's really worth investigating?

The notion here is to focus on those "vital few" facts among the "trivial many" that are high in payoff and information load (MacKenzie, 1972). The "20-80 rule" expresses the importance of focusing on the right information. The 20-80 rule states, as a rule of thumb, that 20% of the facts account for 80% of what is worth knowing (Anderson, 1980: 26).

In working with stakeholders to understand the importance of focus, I typically do an exercise aimed at illustrating and reinforcing the importance of focusing relevant evaluation questions on intended use. It's a very short exercise, and it goes like this:

"We've been talking a lot about focus and its importance. Let's try doing it for a moment.

"Let me ask you to put your right hand out in front of you with your arm fully extended and the palm of your hand turned toward you. Now focus on the center of the palm of your hand. Really look at your hand in a way that you haven't looked at it in a long time. Get to know your hand. Look at the lines—some of them long, some of them short; some of them deep, some of them shallow; some of them relatively straight, some of them nicely curved, and some of them quite jagged and crooked. Look at the colors in your hand—reds, yellows, browns, greens, blues, different shades and hues, and notice the textures, hills and valleys, rougher places and smooth places. Become aware of the feelings in your hand, feelings of warmth or cold, perhaps tingling sensations. (Those of you who, at this point, are having trouble maintaining your attention on the center of your palm may notice you have a problem with focus. . . .)

"Now, keeping your right hand in front of you, I'd like to ask you to extend your left arm and look at your left palm in the same way, not comparatively, but just focus on the center of your left palm in its own terms, looking at it, focusing on it, seeing it, feeling it. . . . Really allow your attention to become concentrated on the center of your left palm . . . getting to know your left hand in a new way. . . .

"Now, with both arms still outstretched I want you to *focus*, with the same intensity that you've been using on each hand, I want you to focus on the center of *both* palms at the same time. [Give participants a little time to try this.] Unless there is something unusual about your eyes you're not able to do that. There are some animals who are able to move their two eyes independently of each other, but human beings do not have that capability. We are only able to look at one thing with intensity at a time. You can go back and forth between the two hands, you can use peripheral vision and get a general look at both hands at the same time, but you can't focus with intensity at the center of both palms at the same time.

"Focusing involves a choice. The decision to look at something is also a decision not to look at something. A decision to see something means that something else will not be seen, at least not with the same acuity. Looking at your left hand or looking at your right hand or looking more generally at both hands provides you with different information and different experiences.

"The same thing is true in the evaluation process. Because of limited time and limited resources, it is never possible to look at everything. It is particularly never possible to look at everything in great depth. Decisions have to be made about what is worth looking at. Choosing to look at one area in-depth is also a decision not to look at something else in-depth. Utilization-focused evaluation suggests that the criteria for making those choices of focus be the usefulness of the resulting information. That information that would be of greatest use for program improvement and programmatic decision making becomes the focus of the evaluation."

Before going on to the next section, I suggest that you take a couple of minutes and experience the exercise for yourself. Focus on your own right hand in the way suggested above, and then your left hand, and then both. Experience the exercise and make your own judgment about the importance, and difficulty, of focus.

A Cautionary Note and Conclusion

The point of paying such close attention to focusing evaluation questions is that utilization potential is thereby enhanced. But a note of temperance may be in order. Increasing utilization potential does not guarantee actual use of findings. There are no guarantees. All one can really do is increase the likelihood of use. Utilization-focused evaluation is time consuming, exhausting, and frequently frustrating. It is a process filled with options, ambiguities, and uncertainties. When things go wrong, as they often do, you may find yourself asking a personal evaluation question: How did I ever get myself into this craziness?

But when things go right; when decision makers care; when the evaluation question is important, focused, and on target; when you begin to see programs changing even in the posing of the questions—then evaluation can be exhilarating, energizing, and fulfilling. It is a creative, challenging process. It involves people in that most splendid of human enterprises—the application of intellect and emotion to the search for answers that will improve human effort and activity. It seems a shame to waste all that intellect and emotion studying the wrong question. Thus, it is worth taking the time to identify and focus relevant evaluation questions.

Chapter 5

BEYOND THE GOALS CLARIFICATION GAME

Mulla Nasrudin was a Sufi guru.[1] A king who enjoyed Nasrudin's company, and also liked to hunt, commanded him to accompany him on a bear hunt. Nasrudin was terrified.

When Nasrudin returned to his village, someone asked him: "How did the Hunt go?"

"Marvelously!"

"How many bears did you see?"

"None."

"How could it have gone marvelously, then?"

"When you are hunting bears, and you are me, seeing no bears at all is a marvelous experience" (Shah, 1964: 61).

Evaluation of the Bear Project

If this tale were updated by means of an evaluation report, it might read something like this:

This is a study undertaken for His Majesty's Ministry of the Interior, under the auspices of the Department of Natural Resources, for the Division of Parks, Section on Hunting, Office of Bears. This is a study of the relationship between the number of bears sighted on a hunt and the number of bears shot

BEAR HUNTING

on a hunt. Our hypothesis is that there is a direct, linear relationship between the sighting of bears and killing of bears. The data were collected on a recent royal hunting expedition. The sample size is therefore somewhat small and generalizations cannot be made with confidence. In effect this is an exploratory case study, Campbell and Stanley (1963) Research Design No. 1.

The data support the hypothesis at the 0.001 level of statistical significance. Indeed, the correlation is perfect. The number of bears sighted was zero, and the number of bears killed was zero. In no case was a bear killed without first being sighted. We therefore recommend that in future projects new Royal regulations be implemented requiring that bears first be sighted before they are killed.

Respectfully submitted,

The Incomparable Mulla Nasrudin
Royal Evaluator

Whose Goals Will Be Evaluated?

Although this evaluation report may be statistically somewhat less rigorous than the average evaluation study, it shares one major characteristic with almost all other reports of this genre: namely, it is impossible to tell whether or not it answers anyone's question. Who decided that the goal evaluated should be the number of bears killed? Perhaps the project staff simply used the hunt as a format for getting royal (federal) money to conduct field trips and the real good is a heightened sensitivity to nature, a closer relationship between Nasrudin and the king, a reduction of Nasrudin's fear of bears, or an increase in the king's power over Nasrudin. It may even be possible (likely!) that different characters in the situation have different objectives and would like different outcome measures. If so, it seems unlikely that all characters will be interested in the same evaluation data. Who will decide what it all means? For Nasrudin, the data indicated a "marvelous" outcome. Other decision makers might read the data differently.

In utilization-focused evaluation, focusing the evaluation on the degree to which goals have been attained is one way of deciding what to evaluate. The problem of whose goals will be evaluated is solved in the first step of utilization-focused evaluation when primary intended users of the evaluation are identified and involved in the evaluation. They decide whose goals and which goals will be the focus of the evaluation. As the Sufi story on hunting bears illustrates, it is impossible to separate the issue of goals clarification from the issue of whose goals will serve as primary evaluation criteria.

The Centrality of Goals in Evaluation

This chapter is a critical review of strategies for identifying and clarifying program goals. Traditionally, evaluation has been synonymous with measuring goal attainment. Goals have played a particularly important part in education evaluations (Morris and Fitz-Gibbon, 1978). Peter Rossi (1972: 18) has stated that "a social welfare program (or for that matter any program) which does not have clearly specified goals cannot be evaluated without specifying some measurable goals. This statement is obvious enough to be a truism." In a major review of the evaluation literature in education, Worthen and Sanders (1973: 231) concluded that

if evaluators agree in anything, it is that program objectives written in unambiguous terms are useful information for any evaluation study. Thus, program objectives and specifications become an extremely important consideration when an evaluation study is constructed.

And Carol Weiss (1972b: 24-26) has noted that "the traditional formulation of the evaluation question is: to what extent is the program succeeding in reaching its goals?" This question assumes that goals can be identified, but goal identification and clarification can be a difficult process. Weiss has explained that "the goal must be clear so that the evaluator knows what to look for." But clarity is itself an elusive goal: "the evaluation question sounds simple enough in the abstract. . . . But what looks elementary in theory turns out in practice to be a demanding enterprise. . . . Thus begins the long, often painful process of getting people to state goals in terms that are *clear*, *specific*, and *measurable*" (italics in original).

Discussions of program and organizational goals are characterized by solemnity. One cannot read much evaluation literature without encountering serious treatises on the centrality and importance of identifying and clarifying program goals, and this solemnity seems to carry over into evaluators' discussions of goals with program staff.

There may be no more deadly way to begin a program staff meeting than by stating that the purpose of the meeting is to identify and clarify program goals and objectives. If evaluators are second only to tax collectors in the hearts of program staff, I suspect that it is not because staff fear evaluators' judgments about program success, but because they hate constant questioning about goals.

The Goals Clarification Game

Goals clarification meetings are frequently conducted like the 20 questions game played at parties. Someone thinks of an object in the room and then the players are allowed 20 questions to guess what it is. In the goals clarification game, the evaluator has an object in mind (a clear, specific, and measurable goal). Program staff are the players. The game begins with the staff writing down some statement they think is a goal. Then the evaluator inspects the statement and tells the staff how close they have come to the goal he or she has in mind. This process is repeated in successive tries until the game ends. The game can end in one of three ways: The staff gives up (so the evaluator wins and writes the program goals for staff); the evaluator gives up (so the staff gets by with vague, fuzzy, and unmeasurable goals); or, in rare cases, the game ends when staff actually stumbles on a statement that reasonably approximates what the evaluator had in mind. There are at least five reasons why program staff have come to hate this game so much:

(1) They have played the game hundreds of times, not just for evaluators, but for funders, advisory boards, in writing proposals, and even among themselves.
(2) They have learned that when playing the game with evaluators, the evaluators almost always win.
(3) They always come out of the game knowing that they appear fuzzyminded and inept to the evaluator.
(4) It is a boring game.
(5) It is an endless game because each new evaluator comes to the game with a different object in mind. (Clarity, specificity, and measurability are not clear, specific, and measurable criteria, so each evaluator can apply a different set of rules in the game!)

In recent years, however, program staff have become more astute at certain aspects of the goals clarification game. They have developed gambits, gambles, and gammons to counter the traditional goals clarification strategies of evaluators. Such strategies as the goals clarification shuffle, the goals conflict approach, and switching from goals clarification to goals war have made the problems of conceptualizing an evaluation research design increasingly more difficult. Evaluators have responded with their own new techniques to counter the strategic moves of program staff.

The Goals Clarification Shuffle

The ploy of the goals clarification shuffle is used most often by program staff who lose the first round of play but later find that they do not like the goal priorities established by the evaluator. This strategy can also be used by funders, administrators, advisory boards, or any other group of people who want to create evaluation havoc. Like many other dance steps (e.g., the Harlem shuffle, the hustle) this technique has the most grace and style when executed simultaneously by a full group of people. The goals clarification shuffle involves a sudden change in goals and priorities after the evaluator is firmly committed to a certain set of measuring instruments and to a research design. The choreography for this technique is quite simple. The top priority program goal is moved two spaces to either the right or left and four spaces backward. Concurrently, all other goals are shuffled randomly but with style and subtlety. Many variations are possible here. The only stipulation is that the first goal must end up somewhere in the middle, with other goals reordered by new criteria.

The goals clarification shuffle first came into national prominence in 1969, when it was employed as a daring counterthrust to the Westinghouse-Ohio State University Head Start Evaluation. That study evaluated cognitive and affective outcomes of the Head Start Program and concluded that Head Start was largely ineffective (Westinghouse Learning Corporation, 1969; Cicarelli, 1971). However, as soon as the final report was published the goals clarification shuffle was executed before enthusiastic congressional audiences, thus establishing the belief that Head Start's health, nutrition, resource redistribution, cultural, and community goals ought to have been in the spotlight (see Williams and Evans, 1969; Evans, 1971: 402). The result was that, despite the negative evaluation findings, Congress expanded the Head Start program and the evaluators were thrown on the defensive. (It was about this same time that serious concerns over nonutilization of evaluation findings started to be heard on a national scale.)

Conflict Over Goals and the Delphi Counter

Conflict over program goals is frequently a major source of irritation for evaluators trying to identify and clarify those goals. In criminal justice programs, there can be conflict over whether the purpose of the program is punitive (punish criminal offenders for wrongdoing), custodial (keep criminal offenders off the streets), or to provide treatment (rehabilitate and return to society). In education and training programs, there is often conflict over whether the goal of the program is attitude change or behavior change. In welfare agencies, there may be disagreement concerning whether the purpose of the program is to provide long-term services to the needy or short-term crisis intervention services. In health settings, staff dissension may emerge over the relative emphasis to be placed on preventive versus curative medical practice. Virtually anytime a group of people assemble to determine program goals there is potential for undermining the goals clarification process if a "conflict configuration" emerges. The emergence of a conflict configuration can be either premeditated or spontaneous; either way, it usually results in lengthy, frustrating, and inconclusive meetings. In the goals clarification game a conflict configuration is usually an easy play to execute. Someone on the staff simply counters the evaluator's attempts to identify and clarify goals by playing on differences in members' personal values and otherwise engendering disagreements, arguments, and dissensus.

For inexperienced evaluators, a conflict configuration can be devastating. The novice evaluator can get caught up in the conflict and lose all credibility by joining one side or the other. More experienced evaluators have learned to remain calm and neutral in hopes that group members will eventually resolve the conflict themselves. But this is a dangerously passive technique. As with other sports, the best offense is a good defense. One option is for the evaluators to call a halt to the game by asserting that they, as neutral observers, are the only participants sufficiently objective and skilled to be able to write and prioritize goals for the group. This counter, however, leaves the evaluators vulnerable to the goals clarification shuffle at some later point in time.

A more elaborate defense against the goals conflict configuration is the Delphi Technique (Helmer, 1966; Dalkey, 1969). This technique is quite popular among evaluators who hate dealing with committees:

> The Delphi technique, a method of developing and improving group consensus, was originally used at the RAND Corporation to arrive at reliable predictions about the future of technology; hence its oracular name. . . . Delphi essentially refers to a series of intensive interrogations of samples of individuals (most frequently, experts) by means of mailed questionnaires concerning some important problem or question; the mailings are interspersed with controlled feedback to the participants. The responses in each round of questioning are gathered by an intermediary, who summarizes and returns the information to each participant, who may then revise his own opinions and ratings. . . . However antagonistic the initial positions and complex the questions under analysis—competing opinions apparently converge and synthesize when this technique is used [Rosenthal, 1976: 121].

The trick in this goals clarification technique is that participants never meet face to face. Thus, disagreements and arguments never get a chance to surface on a personal, interface level. Moreover, the participants in the process remain anonymous. At the end of the process, a master list of prioritized goals is produced to which everyone consents and for which no one has to take responsibility.

> The technique has proved so successful in producing consensus . . . it is now often adopted in many kinds of situations where convergence of opinion is advisable or desirable . . . avoiding as it does the sundry prima donna behaviors that may vitiate round table discussions [Rosenthal, 1976: 121-122].

Of course, for this process to work, choices must be made—and that can be a problem.

> People are very uncomfortable about making choices . . . even people who should be adept and comfortable with the need to decide can find making the required choices—even hypothetically—extremely painful. Moreover, the choices are made very differently by different people . . . and there were some recorded dissensuses that did not seem to be resolved in the number of iterations used [Adelson et al., 1967: 28].

In some programs the evaluators encounter dissensus so intense that the situation constitutes an open war over goals and values. A "goals war" usually occurs when two or more strong coalitions are locked in battle to determine which group will control the future direction of some public policy or program. Such wars over goals are sparked by highly emotional issues that involve deep-seated values. Evaluations of school busing programs to achieve racial balance are a good example. By what criteria ought busing programs be evaluated? Changed racial attitudes, changed interracial behaviors, changed student achievement, changed property values, and changed neighborhood demographics are all candidates for the honor of being primary program goals. Are school busing and other antiracist programs supposed to achieve desegregation (representative proportions of minority students in all schools) or integration (positive interracial attitudes, cooperation, and interaction)? Many communities, school boards, and school staffs are in open warfare over these issues. Included in such arguments are basic disagreements about the appropriate evaluation criteria to apply (see Cohen and Garet, 1975; Cohen and Weiss, 1977).

In the goals clarification game, an evaluator can anticipate a goals war when two or more coalitions emerge; these coalitions represent fundamentally contrasting values and refuse to agree on goal statements and priorities. The goals war is posed as a fight to the finish, elevating conflict to a level at which the participating coalitions are so suspicious of each other that they

would never allow a list of goals to emerge without face-to-face confrontation (which amounts to saying they would never allow a list of consensus goals to emerge). The goals war opponents insist on open meetings at which interpersonal vendettas can be publicly aired. Efforts to establish consensus about the goals of public housing and land use regulation programs are usually of this order. Environmentalists clash with industrial developers over the purposes of these programs. Hearings on environmental impact statements are another excellent opportunity to observe the goals war strategy in full mobilization. In the health and welfare area, program staffs and funding bodies have recently found themselves on various sides of the war over whether or not abortions should be publicly funded.

Focusing on Useful Information Rather than Goals

Goals wars create serious problems for an evaluator, whether the evaluator is internal or external to the program or organization in which the war is being fought. In the 1960s, evaluation was so narrowly tied to measurement of goals that the evaluator who encountered a goals war, or even a goals shuffle, would be incapacitated. It was assumed that "you needed clearly specified objectives in order to do a good evaluation" (Smith, 1980: 39). However, as discussed in the last chapter, evaluators now have a variety of strategies for use in focusing the evaluation.

Goals clarification and measurement of goal attainment is only one of many strategies. The evaluation need not be undermined because different stakeholders pledge allegiance to conflicting goals. Rather, the skillful evaluator can move the discussion away from goals to the issue of what information is needed for future decision making. Proponents and opponents of school busing for desegregation may never agree on educational goals, but they may well agree on what kinds of information are needed to further enlighten their debate—information about who is bused, at what distances, from what neighborhoods, and with what effects.

In working in program war zones on controversial issues, evaluators do well to heed the evaluation standard on political viability:

> The evaluation should be planned and conducted with anticipation of the different positions of various interest groups, so that their cooperation may be obtained, and so that possible attempts by any of these groups to curtail evaluation operations or to bias or misapply the results can be averted or counteracted [Joint Committee on Standards, 1981: 56].

Concern about the overpoliticalization of goals has led Lee J. Cronbach and associates to warn about the distortions that can enter into a program when program staff pay too much attention to what the evaluator decides to measure. This gives the evaluator the power to determine what activities become primary in a program.

> It is unwise for evaluation to focus on whether a project has "attained its goals." Goals are a necessary part of political rhetoric, but all social programs, even supposedly targeted ones, have broad aims. Legislators who have sophisticated reasons for keeping goal statements lofty and nebulous unblushingly ask program administrators to state explicit goals. Unfortunately, whatever the evaluator decides to measure tends to become a primary goal of program operators [Cronbach et al., 1980: 5].

Although I opened this chapter by poking fun at some of follies of the goals clarification process, I have not meant my sarcasm to be interpreted as an attack on goals. Focusing on goals is one important option in utilization-focused evaluation—but only one option. "One can conduct useful evaluations without ever seeing an objective" (Smith, 1980: 39). Nevertheless, for political, organizational, programmatic, and management reasons, goals specification remains the most common way to focus evaluation and planning processes. I have not been attacking the utility of goals. Rather, I have been suggesting that the goals clarification process has become so formalized in the minds of many evaluators as the primary basis for evaluation that they automatically begin every evaluation with specification of clear, specific, and measurable goals. The goals clarification process has become for them an end in itself, rather than a means to the end of focusing program efforts and determining what information is needed for program improvement and decision making. Still, let me go on record as stating that I am not "antigoals."

Nor will evaluation be well served by dividing people into opposing camps: progoals versus antigoals evaluators. I am reminded of an incident at the University of Wisconsin during the student protests over the Vietnam War. In the early days of the antiwar movement those opposed to the war were often labeled as communists. At one demonstration both antiwar and prowar demonstrators got into a scuffle, so police began making arrests indiscriminately. When one of the prowar demonstrators was apprehended by a police officer, he began yelling, "Don't arrest me. You've got the wrong person. *I'm anticommunist!*"

To which the police officer replied, "I don't care what kind of communist you are, you're going to jail."

Well, I don't care what kind of evaluator you are, to be effective you need the flexibility to evaluate with or without goals. The last chapter suggested ways of beginning to focus an evaluation without explicit attention to goals. The remainder of this chapter will deal with the important skills of helping program staff clarify goals and focusing an evaluation on relative goal attainment. Toward this end, let's return to the goals clarification game and consider the problem of vague or fuzzy goals.

Fuzzy Goals

Many programs have such broad aims and are so unclear in their direction that evaluators searching for goals are sure to be frustrated. Classic examples of such programs are the community-action and model-cities programs that were part of the 1960s Great Society thrust in the United States (Weiss and Rein, 1969). Interactions with staff in such broad-aim programs recall Alice's conversation with the Cheshire Cat in Wonderland:

> "Would you tell me, please, which way I ought to go from here?"
>
> "That depends a good deal on where you want to get to," said the Cat.
>
> "I don't much care where," said Alice.
>
> "Then it doesn't matter which way you go," said the Cat.
>
> "So long as I get somewhere," Alice added as an explanation.
>
> "Oh, you're sure to do that," said the Cat, "if you only walk long enough."

It is now conventional wisdom that if you don't know where you want to get to, then you'll have trouble getting there—and you won't know if or when you've arrived. Fuzzy goals imply precisely this kind of lack of clarity.

Fuzzy goals may be so common because ill-defined ideas characterize much human cognition and reasoning (Zadeh et al., 1975: ix). Manfred Kochen of the Mental Health Research Institute, University of Michigan, has used a model called "fuzzy set theory" to explore and explain fuzzy thinking. Based on conclusions drawn from careful laboratory experiments, Kochen (1975: 407) concludes that "on the whole, fuzzy set theory does seem appropriate for conceptualizing certain aspects of the behavior of perhaps half the population." No wonder evaluators have so much trouble getting clear, specific, and measurable goals! No wonder fuzziness is so common in evaluation!

Moreover, evaluators often have difficulty knowing if staff are genuinely unclear about what they're attempting to accomplish, or if they're simply being shrewd in not letting the evaluator (or others) discover their *real* goals. As Carol Weiss (1972b: 27) has pointed out, there is always more than one possible explanation for fuzziness:

> Fuzziness of program goals is a common enough expression to warrant attention. Part of the explanation probably lies in practitioners' concentration on concrete matters of program functioning and their pragmatic mode of operation. They often have an intuitive rather than an analytical approach to program development. But there is also a sense in which ambiguity serves a useful function: it may mask underlying divergences in intent . . . glittering generalities that pass for goal statements are meant to satisfy a variety of interests and perspectives.

Fuzzy goals, then, may be a conscious strategy for avoiding an outbreak of goals wars among competing or conflicting interests. In such instances the evaluation may be focused on important questions, issues, and concerns without resort to clear, specific, and measurable objectives. However, more often than not the problem may be one of communications rather than deviousness.

COMMUNICATING ABOUT GOALS

Part of the difficulty, I am convinced, is the terminology: *goals and objectives*. These words have taken on an awesome quality that strikes fear in the hearts of program staff. *Goals and objectives* become haunting weights that program staff feel they have to carry around their necks, burdening them, slowing their efforts, and impeding rather than advancing their progress. Helping staff clarify their purpose and direction may mean avoiding use of the term "goals and objectives."

I've observed on many occasions that I can have quite animated and interesting discussions with program staff about such things as this: What are you trying to do with your clients? If you are successful, how will your clients be different after the program than they were before? What kinds of changes do you want to see in your clients? When your program works as you want it to, how do clients *behave* differently? What do they say differently? What would I see in them that would tell me they are different? Program staff can often provide quite specific answers to these questions, answers that reveal their caring and involvement with the client change process, yet when the same staff are asked to specify their *goals and objectives*, they freeze. Clearly, the formal terminology of evaluation carries connotations and authority that are intimidating to such staff members.

Under these conditions I find it is more helpful to stay with the questions about client changes, client differences, what the program can accomplish with clients, and other outcome-oriented questions that get at the content of what we mean when we talk about goals and objectives—but avoid actually using those sinister and terrifying words. After having worked with a group of people for a while, and after having obtained a clear picture of what kind of changes they are trying to bring about, I may then tell them that what they have been telling me constitutes their goals and objectives. This revelation often brings considerable surprise and more than just a little sense of satisfaction that they have actually, without knowing it, been able to specify what they were trying to do. Thus, the sensitive and skilled evaluator can recognize statements of goals and objectives, and even measurement criteria, as program staff answer questions about client change, desired client progress, and differences to be brought about by the program.

On more than one occasion when I have reported back to program staff that what we've been talking about for the last half hour seems to me to constitute a statement of their goals and objectives, they react by saying, "But we haven't said anything about what we would count or any of the measures involved." This, as clearly as anything, I take as evidence of how widespread the confusion is between the conceptualization of goals and their measurement. Communicating meaningfully with program staff about what they are trying to do is a process that should not be encumbered by evaluative jargon or concerns about the state of measurement in social science.

Help program staff to be realistic and concrete about goals and objectives, but don't make them hide what they are really trying to do because they're not sure how to write a formally acceptable statement of goals and objectives, or because they don't know what measurement instruments might be available to get at some of the important things they are trying to do.

Separating the Concept from Its Measurement

As noted earlier, evaluation research is traditionally defined as measuring the extent to which program goals and objectives are attained. Such an approach requires specification of goals and objectives that are *clear, specific,* and *measurable*. This approach usually requires that the statement of the goal include specification of how it will be measured, as, for example, in this statement:

> Student achievement test scores in reading will increase one grade level from the beginning of first grade to the beginning of second grade.

This statement is not, however, a goal statement. The goal is that children improve their reading. This is a statement of *how* that goal will be measured and how much improvement is desired (standard of desirability). Confusing the (1) specification of goals with (2) their measurement and (3) the standard of desirability is a major conceptual problem in many program evaluations.

The conceptualization of program direction in a statement of goals and objectives should be clearly separated from the specification of how those goals and objectives will be measured. The two things are quite different— the goal and its measurement. Conceptually, a goal statement should specify a program direction based on values, ideals, political mandates, and program purpose. Thus, conceptually, goals make explicit values and purpose.

Measurement, on the other hand, provides data indicating the relative state of goal attainment. Measurement depends on the state of the art of social science. Some things we know how to measure with considerable precision. In other areas our indicators are less precise, less clear, and less reliable. *Why should the goals and objectives of social programs be limited by the state of the art of measurement in social science?*

To require that goals be clear, specific, *and* measurable is to require programs to attempt only those things that social scientists know how to measure. Such a limitation is clearly unconscionable. It is one thing to establish a purpose and direction for a program. It is quite another thing to say how that purpose and direction is to be measured. By confusing these two steps and making them one, program goals can become quite limited, meaningless, and irrelevant to what program staff and funders actually want to have happen and do have happen.

To make the point, let me overstate the tradeoff in quite stark terms. In many cases program staff are given a choice between clear, specific, quantitatively measurable goals that are meaningless and irrelevant to what is actually going on in the program *or* broad, general, and "fuzzy" goals that express real program ideals but can only be measured or described with "soft" data. For my part, *I prefer to have soft or rough measures of important goals rather than have highly precise and quantitative measures of goals that no one really cares about.* In too many evaluations, program staff are forced to focus on the latter (meaningless but measurable goals) instead of on the former (meaningful goals with soft measures).

Of course, this tradeoff, stated in stark terms, is only relative. It is desirable to have as much precision as possible and, where appropriate, measures should be quite precise and quantitative. However, by separating the process of goals clarification from the process of goals measurement, it is possible for program staff to focus first on what they are really trying to accomplish and to state their goals and objectives as explicitly as possible *without regard to measurement*, and then to worry about how one would measure actual attainment of those goals and objectives. This makes it possible, over time, to keep the same goals and objectives but to change the measures as the state of the art of measurement progresses.

This recommendation comes out of experience with many programs in which staff have been constrained in their writing of goals and objectives by evaluators who told them they could only have goals and objectives whose measurement they could specify *in advance*. Thus, program staff ended up beginning with the measures that were available and working backward to figure out what goals and objectives could be written from those measures. Given that they seldom had much expertise in measurement, they ended up specifying goals and objectives that amounted to nothing more than counting fairly insignificant behaviors and attitudes that they felt they could somehow quantify.

To summarize, rather than beginning with what can be measured and moving to a statement of goals, when I work with groups on goal clarification I have them write their statement of goals and objectives *without regard to measurement*. Once they have stated as carefully and as explicitly as they can what they want to accomplish, then it is time to figure out what indicators and data can be collected to monitor relative attainment of goals. In my experience, program staff understand and appreciate the importance of separating the concept—the goal—from its measurement. They are able to move back and forth between conceptual level statements and operational (measurement) specifications, attempting to get as much precision as possible in both areas without losing sight of the distinction, uniqueness, and importance of *both* the conceptual statements and the separate measurement specifications.

Writing Meaningful and Useful Goals

(1) Distinguish between outcome goals and activity goals. Outcomes describe what participants in a program will be able to do at the end of the program. "Students will read with understanding." "Participants will stop smoking." Outcome goals state the desired impact of the program. "People in the community will respect the police."

Activity goals describe *how* outcome goals will be achieved; they state the desired experiences that will occur in the program. "Students will read two hours a day." "Participants will openly discuss their dependence on cigarettes." "People in the program will be treated with respect." The next chapter will discuss implementation and process goals in greater detail.

(2) Outcome goals should be clearly outcome-oriented. Program staff often write activity goals thinking that they have stated desired outcomes. An agricultural extension agent told me his goal was "to get fifty farmers to participate in a farm tour." But what, I asked, did he want to result from the farm tour? After some dialogue it became clear that the outcome goal was this:

Farmers will adopt improved milking practices in their own farm operations.

A corporation stated one of its goals for the year as "establishing a comprehensive energy conservation program." After I pointed out that it was perfectly possible to establish a comprehensive energy conservation program without ever saving any energy, I asked, "Was the goal establishing the program or saving energy?" They rewrote the goal:

The corporation will significantly reduce energy consumption.

This goal will stand up over time. Each year, then, specific objectives can be established stating how much energy will be saved (e.g., a reduction of 5%). Measuring energy conservation is also dealt with separately.

(3) It should be possible to conceptualize either the absence of the desired state or an alternative to it. Some goal statements are amazingly adept at saying nothing. I worked with a school board whose overall goal was, "Students will learn." There is no way *not* to attain this goal. It is the nature of the species that young people learn. Fortunately, they can learn in spite of the schools. The issues are *what* and *how much* will they learn.

Another favorite is "increasing awareness." It's fairly difficult to put people through two weeks of training on some topic (e.g., chemical dependency) and *not* increase awareness. Under these conditions, the goal of "increasing awareness of chemical dependency issues" is hardly worth aiming at. Further dialogue revealed that the program staff wanted to change knowledge, attitudes, and behavior.

(4) Each goal and each objective should contain only one idea. There is a tendency in writing goal statements to overload the content.

(5) The statement of goals and objectives should be understandable. Goals should communicate to people a strong sense of direction. If readers of a goals statement have to wade through difficult grammatical constructions and complex interdependent clauses to figure out what is supposed to happen in the division or program, then the staff may find that the specification of goals and objectives will cause them considerably more problems than having found some way of avoiding the exercise altogether. Goal statements should also avoid internal program or professional jargon as much as possible. The general public should be able to make sense of goals and objectives.

(6) Formal goals statements should focus on the most important program outcomes and activities. The statement of goals and objectives should contain all major points that are needed for staff focus and communication to others about that focus. Areas of program endeavor and activity that are of minor importance should be excluded, with a brief paragraph explaining what is excluded. The writing of goals and objectives should not be a marathon exercise in trying to see how long a document one can produce. As human beings, our attention span is too short to focus on pages and pages of goals and objectives. Only write them for the things that matter and for outcomes for which you intend to be held accountable.

(7) Keep goal statements separate from statements of how goals are to be attained. An agricultural extension program had this goal statement: "Farmers will increase yields through the educational efforts of extension including farm tours, bulletins, and related activities." Everything after the word "yields" describes how the goal is to be attained and should be stated separately from the actual goal to keep the goal focused, clear, and crisp.

(8) Separate goals statements from measurement criteria. Advocates of "management by objectives" and "behavioral objectives" often place more emphasis on measurement than on establishing a clear sense of direction (Combs, 1972). The two are related, but not equivalent.

Specification of how goals are to be attained, measurement criteria for evaluation, and other amplifications of goals and objectives should be written in separate columns, or in subsequent documents, so as to keep the actual statements of goals and objectives crisp and clear.

(9) Make the writing of goals a positive experience. Goals clarification exercises are so often approached as pure drudgery that staff hate not only the exercise itself, but also the resulting goals. Goals clarification should be an exciting process of establishing direction and priorities. Goals should be statements of what people care about, what they're aiming for, what they hope to accomplish. Goals should not become a club for assaulting program staff. They should be a tool for helping staff realize their ideals.

(10) Thou shalt not covet thy neighbor's goals and objectives. Goals and objectives don't travel very well. They often involve matters of nuance. It is worth taking the time to construct your own goals so that they reflect your assumptions, your own expectations, and your own intentions in your own language.

There are exceptions to all of these guidelines, particularly the last one. One option in working with groups is to have them review the goals of other programs both as a way of helping staff clarify its own goals and to get ideas about format and content. Evaluators who work with behavioral objectives often develop a repertoire of potential objectives that can be adopted by a variety of programs. The evaluator has already worked on the technical quality of the goals so program staff can focus on selecting the content they want. Where there is the time and inclination, however, I prefer to have a group work on its own goals statement so that participants have the experience of developing goals, know whence they came, and understand what they do and do not contain. They feel a sense of ownership about the goals. This can be part of the training function served by evaluators, increasing the likelihood that staff will have success in future goals clarification exercises.

There are three options in this regard: (1) Staff may simply review and adopt another program's goals. (2) Staff may review another program's goals for ideas, but then adapt those goals or write their own. (3) Staff may begin by struggling with their own goals statement, then compare their goals to those of another program, thereby further clarifying their own statement. We used this latter approach in the Caribbean Agricultural Extension Project. First, each national extension service wrote its own goals, then goals statements were exchanged among countries. The exchanges often led to additions or refinements, but each country ended up with its own unique statement of goals and objectives.

Keeping goals and objectives separate from measurement and implementation strategies (items 7 and 8 above) can be achieved through a matrix like the one in Table 5.1. Some different levels of goals statements are discussed in the next section. Implementation issues are discussed in Chapter 7.

Levels of Goal Statements: From Overall Mission to Specific Objectives

To facilitate the framing of evaluation questions in complex programs, it is often helpful to approach goals clarification at three levels: the overall

TABLE 5.1

Goals	*Outcome Data/ Measurement Criteria*	*How Goals Will Be Attained (Implementation Strategies)*	*Data on Implementation Criteria*
1.			
2.			
3.			
4.			

mission of the program, the goals of specific programmatic units (or subsystems), and the specific objectives that specify client outcomes. The mission statement describes the general direction of the overall program or organization in long-range terms. Mission statements function to carve out the territory within which a program will operate. The statement may specify nothing more than a minimal target population and a basic problem to be attacked. For example, the mission of the Minnesota Comprehensive Epilepsy Program is to improve the lives of people with epilepsy through research, education, and treatment. This tells us that the program is concerned with much more than just medical treatment for individual epileptics. There are also research and educational thrusts to the program. Moreover, research is listed before treatment and, in this case, accurately reflects program priorities. But clearly the general mission of "improving the lives of people with epilepsy" is too vague to serve as an indicator for evaluation purposes.

Goals and objectives can be established for the various thrusts of the program. The terms "goals" and "objectives" have been used interchangeably up to this point, but it is useful to distinguish between them as representing different levels of generality. Goals are more general than objectives and encompass the purposes and aims of program subsystems (i.e., research, education, and treatment in the epilepsy example). Objectives are narrow and specific, stating what will be different as a result of program activities. Objectives specify the concrete outcomes of a program. To illustrate these differences a simplified version of the mission statement, goals, and objectives for the Minnesota Comprehensive Epilepsy Program is presented below. This outline was developed after an initial discussion with the program director. The purpose of the outline was to establish a context for later discussions aimed at more clearly framing specific evaluation questions. In other words, this goals clarification and objectives mapping exercise was used as a means of focusing the evaluation question rather than as an end in itself.

MINNESOTA COMPREHENSIVE EPILEPSY PROGRAM: MISSION STATEMENT, GOALS, AND OBJECTIVES

Program Mission: To improve the lives of people with epilepsy through research, education, and treatment.

Research Component

Goal 1: To produce high quality, *scholarly research* on epilepsy.
  Objective 1: To *publish* research findings in high quality, refereed journals.
  Objective 2: To conduct research on . . .
          a. neurological aspects of epilepsy,
          b. pharmacological aspects of epilepsy,
          c. epidemiology of epilepsy, and
          d. social and psychological aspects of epilepsy.

Goal 2: To produce interdisciplinary research.
  Objective 1: To propose, fund, and conduct research projects that *integrate* principal investigators from different disciplines.
  Objective 2: To increase *interaction* among researchers from different disciplines.

Education Component

Goal 3: To educate health professionals about the nature and conditions of epilepsy so as to change knowledge, attitudes, and behaviors.
  Objective 1: To increase the *knowledge* of health professionals who serve people with epilepsy so that they know . . .
    a. what to do if a person has a seizure,
    b. the incidence and prevalence of epilepsy,
    c. etc.
  Objective 2: To change the attitudes of health professionals so that they
    a. are sympathetic to the needs of epileptics, and
    b. believe in the importance of identifying the special needs of epileptics.
  Objective 3: To change the *behaviors* of health professionals so that they
    a. identify whether or not the person they are serving is epileptic, and
    b. match their services to the specific needs of epileptic persons they serve.

Goal 4: To educate persons with epilepsy about their disorder.

Goal 5: To educate the general public about the nature and incidence of epilepsy.

Treatment Component

Goal 6: To diagnose, treat, and rehabilitate persons with severe, chronic, and disabling seizures.
  Objective 1: To increase seizure control in treated patients.
  Objective 2: To increase the functional independence of treated patients.

Administrative Component

Goal 7: To integrate the separate program components into a comprehensive whole that is greater than the sum of its parts.
  Objective 1: To demonstrate that funding many researchers, clinicians, and educators from different disciplines at one site results in spin-offs and breakthroughs that would not occur if components were funded in isolation from each other.
  Objective 2: To facilitate interaction among participants in different program components.

This outline of goals and objectives is illustrative of several points. First, the only dimension that consistently differentiates goals and objectives is the relative degree of specificity of each: Objectives narrow the focus of goals. There is no absolute criterion for distinguishing goals from objectives; the distinction is always a relative one.

Second, the purpose of constructing this outline must be understood. The purpose was not to fully describe the Comprehensive Epilepsy Program. This outline was generated after a single session with the program director. Its purpose was to facilitate discussion as we attempted to focus on evaluation questions of interest to core staff. It was clear at the outset that there were not sufficient resources to fully evaluate all four component parts of the program. Moreover, different component parts faced different contingencies. The treatment and research components have more concrete outcomes than the education and administrative components. The differences in the specificity of the objectives for the four program components reflect real differences in the degree to which the content and functions of those program subsystems were known at the beginning of the evaluation. Thus, with limited resources and variations in goal specificity, it was necessary to decide which aspects of the program could best be served by evaluation research.

Third, this outline of goals and objectives for the Comprehensive Epilepsy Program is not particularly well written. I have extracted the outline directly from rough notes written during the first meeting with the director. The language in several cases could be more concise; some goals and objectives contain two or more ideas that should be separated so that each ideal is singular and unitary; and there are gaps in the logical ordering of goals and objectives where intervening steps need to be specified. But such inadequacies are of little consequence for the purpose at hand. Once the focus of the evaluation is sharpened and the important evaluation questions have been identified, relevant goals and objectives can be more carefully written. Goals and objectives not relevant to the evaluation can be ignored. At this early point in the evaluation process the outline of program mission statement, goals, and objectives is a tool for sharpening the focus on the central issues about which the decision makers most need information. *Which program components and which goals should be evaluated to produce the most useful information for decision makers?* That is the question. To answer it one does not need technically perfect goal statements. Once the evaluation question is focused, relevant goals and objectives can be phrased in technically impeccable language—if such rephrasing improves the evaluation.

The point here is to avoid wasting time in the construction of grandiose, complex models of program goals and objectives just because the folklore of evaluation prescribes that the first step in evaluation is traditionally identification and clarification of program goals in clear, specific, and measurable terms. In complex programs evaluators can spend so much of their time writing goals that they lose sight of whether or not full elaborations of goals and objectives serve a useful purpose. To further develop the distinction between writing goals for the sake of writing goals and writing them to use as tools in sharpening relevant evaluation questions, it is necessary to consider the issue of prioritization. In utilization-focused evaluation goals are prioritized in a manner quite different from that usually prescribed.

Establishing Priorities:
The Importance Criterion and the Usefulness Criterion

The basic solution to the problems of multiple and conflicting goals is establishing priorities. The usual criterion for prioritizing goals is a ranking or rating in terms of *importance*. Multiattribute-utility measurement (Gardiner and Edwards, 1975) and the decision-theoretic approach to evaluation (Edwards et al., 1975) employ both rankings and ratings of importance. The rating approach works as follows:

> Rate dimensions [goals] in importance, preserving ratios. To do this, start by assigning the least important dimension an importance of 10. (We use 10 rather than 1 to permit subsequent judgments to be finely graded and nevertheless made in integers.) Now consider the next-least-important dimension. How much more important (if at all) is it than the least important? Assign it a number that reflects that ratio. Continue on up the list, checking each set of implied ratios as each new judgment is made. Thus, if a dimension is assigned a weight of 20 while another is assigned a weight of 80, it means that the 20 dimension is one-fourth as important as the 80 dimension [Gardiner and Edwards, 1975: 16].

The reason for prioritizing goals is clear: Evaluations ought to focus on important goals. Thus, with limited resources the evaluator would choose to focus the evaluation on the most important program goals (i.e., the goal ranked first on the list). Data might also be gathered on other goals, but the primary focus of the evaluation is measurement of the degree to which the most important goal is being attained. This is the classical model of outcomes evaluation. But from a utilization perspective this model is inadequate.

The fact that a goal is ranked first in importance does not necessarily mean that decision makers and information users need information about attainment of that goal more than they need information about a less important goal. In utilization-focused evaluation program goals are also prioritized by applying the criterion of usefulness of evaluative information. That goal about which evaluation information would be least useful to decision makers and information users is ranked last; that goal about which evaluative information would be most useful is ranked first. The ranking of goals by the importance criterion is often quite different from the ranking of goals by the usefulness of evaluation information criterion. Consider the following example from the Minnesota Comprehensive Epilepsy Program:

Ranking of Goals by Importance	Ranking of Goals by Usefulness of Evaluative Information to Intended Users
(1) To produce high-quality, scholarly research on epilepsy.	(1) To integrate the separate program components into a comprehensive whole that is greater than the sum of its parts.
(2) To produce interdisciplinary research.	(2) To educate health professionals about the nature and conditions of epilepsy.
(3) To integrate the separate program components into a comprehensive whole that is greater than the sum of its parts.	(3) To diagnose, treat, and rehabilitate persons with severe, chronic, and disabling seizures.
(4) To diagnose, treat, and rehabilitate persons with severe, chronic, and disabling seizures.	(4) To produce interdisciplinary research.

Why the discrepancy? The core program staff did not feel they needed a formal evaluation to monitor attainment of the most important program goal. The publishing of scholarly research in refereed journals was so important that the program director intended to personally monitor performance in that area. Moreover, he was relatively certain about how to facilitate achievement of that goal. There was no specific evaluation question related to that goal that he needed answered. By contrast, the issue of "comprehensiveness" was quite difficult to get at. It was not at all clear how comprehensiveness could be facilitated, although it is third on the importance list. The core program staff were anxious to evaluate the development of comprehensiveness. Such data had high utilization potential.

The education goal, second on the usefulness list, does not even appear among the top four goals on the importance list. Yet information about educational impact was ranked high on the usefulness list because it was a goal area about which the program staff had many questions. The education component was expected to be a difficult, long-term effort. Information about how to increase the educational impact of the Comprehensive Epilepsy Program had high utilization potential.

There are several reasons why a ranking of goals according to the usefulness of evaluative information criterion is likely to differ from the ranking by importance. Sometimes goals ranked first in importance have a long-range time frame; program staff may find it more useful to focus on evaluation of goals with a shorter time span. Second, top priority goals (in terms of importance) may be subject to multiple, nonprogram influences to a greater extent than more immediate goals; thus, data about performance on a lower priority goal may be a more useful indicator to staff of their effectiveness than data on a goal the achievement of which could not be attributed solely to program efforts. For example, in programs where the long-range goal of greatest importance is behavioral change, the evaluation may focus on the more immediate but less important goal of attitude change. Behavior is subject to multiple influences, not many of which are amenable to direct or short-run intervention. Attitudes are more subject to short-term intervention and may be one link in the chain to behavioral change. If resources or design problems do not permit measuring both attitude change and behavioral change, the criterion of generating useful information about attitude change may take precedence over the criterion of evaluating the more important goal of behavioral change.

Another reason for the differences in rankings may be the likelihood of getting definitive findings. It is sometimes difficult to obtain measurable differences on important outcomes such as reduced racism and sexism. Thus, decision makers may opt for evaluation of something about which they can expect to find measurable differences. The choice may be between the likelihood of ambiguous findings about attainment of the most important goal, or clearer findings about the attainment of a less important goal. Evaluators can estimate the probabilities in both cases; in a utilization-focused approach the decision makers and information users make the final decision about which way to go.

In my experience, the most frequent reason for differences in importance and usefulness rankings is variation in the degree to which decision makers already have what they consider good information about performance on the most important goal. At the program level, staff members may be so involved in trying to achieve their most important goal that they are relatively well informed about performance on that goal. Performance on less important goals may involve less certainty for staff; information about performance in that goal area is therefore more useful because it tells staff members something they do not already know.

Earlier, I cited the experience of working with individual school teachers whose primary goal was high student achievement on basic skills. They expected any evaluation to measure such achievement. When asked why they needed information on student achievement, they responded that it was important for the school principal and parents: "Of course, we already know how well our students are achieving because we're with them every day. Testing achievement won't tell us anything new." Once it was clarified that the teachers themselves were the decision makers for the evaluation and they could ask questions that they were interested in, the suggested focus of the evaluation changed: "Well, if the information is for us, we wouldn't measure achievement. Those standardized test don't tell us anything anyway. What we really need is help in how to increase students' self-esteem, how to stimulate their affective development. The cognitive domain will probably always be most important in public schools, but we have a handle on that. The problem is how to figure out what's happening in the affective domain. That would be really useful information!"

What I hope is emerging through these examples is an image of the evaluator as an active-reactive-adaptive problem solver. The evaluator actively solicits information about program contingencies, organizational dynamics, environmental uncertainties, and decision-maker goals in order to focus the evaluation on questions of real interest to identified decision makers and information users. The evaluator works with primary intended users to determine what useful information can be generated in the context of decision maker needs and program realities.

Evaluation of Central or Peripheral Goals?

Prioritization of program goals on the basis of usefulness of evaluation information means that an evaluation might focus on goals of apparent peripheral importance rather than more central program goals. The consequences of evaluating central versus peripheral goals is a matter of some controversy. Those who view evaluation as part of a rational decision-making process (the goal model) stress the importance of evaluating central goals. In her early work, Weiss (1972b: 30-31) offered the following advice to evaluators about how to handle the prioritization process:

> The evaluator will have to press to find out priorities—which goals the staff sees as critical to its mission and which are subsidiary. But since the evaluator is not a mere technician for the translation of a program's stated aims into measurement instruments, he has a responsibility to express his own interpretation of the relative importance of goals. *He doesn't want to do an elaborate study on the attainment of minor and innocuous goals*, while vital goals go unexplored.

One primary reason for focusing on central goals is to provide data for major decisions about a program. But, as demonstrated in Chapter 2, major decisions are rare. Incremental, day-to-day, piecemeal decisions are the basis for most program activity. Taken as a whole, over a long period of time, these bit decisions accumulate to establish basic program direction. Thus, from an incrementalist (satisficing) perspective it is appropriate to focus an evaluation on peripheral program goals because they may be more amenable to immediate action. Incremental decisions tend to be small steps, and evaluation of peripheral objectives may focus on the taking of such small steps. As one evaluator in our utilization of federal health evaluations said,

Although I wouldn't necessarily want to choose between major or minor evaluation studies, the point about minor evaluation studies is well taken. If you have an energetic, conscientious program manager, he's always interested in improving his program around the periphery, because that's where he usually can. And an evaluation study of some minor aspect of his program will enable him to significantly improve [EV52: 17].

In our study of the utilization of federal health evaluations we put the issue to decision makers and evaluators as follows:

Another factor sometimes affecting utilization has to do with whether or not the central objectives of a program are evaluated. Some writers argue that evaluations can have the greatest impact if they focus on major program objectives. What happened in your case?

Only one of 38 respondents felt that utilization was likely to be enhanced by evaluating peripheral goals. The overwhelming consensus was that, at the very least, central goals ought to be evaluated and, where possible, both central and peripheral goals should be studied. As they elaborated, 9 decision makers and 8 evaluators said that utilization had probably been helped by the concentration on central issues. This last sentence, however, reflects an important shift in emphasis. As decision makers talked in their own words about the central versus peripheral question in terms of utilization, they switched from talking about goals to talking about "issues." Utilization is increased by focusing on central issues. *And what is a central issue? It is an evaluation question that someone really cares about.* The subtle distinction here is critical. Evaluations are useful to decision makers if they focus on central issues—which may or may not include achievement of central goals.

A Case Example of Utilization-Focused Evaluation

The best example of the subtle shift from goals to issues in our interviews concerns a highly utilized evaluation of the Hill-Burton Hospital Construction Program by their Office of Program Planning and Analysis. This evaluation is worth looking at in detail because it illustrates the key aspects of utilization-focused evaluation. The evaluation was conducted with 1% funds specifically mandated for evaluation in federal legislation. The director of that office established a permanent committee on evaluation projects to make decisions about how to spend 1% monies for evaluation. The evaluation committee was made up of representatives from all the other branches and services in the division: people from the state Hill-Burton agencies, from the Comprehensive Health Planning agencies, from the health care industry, and regional Hill-Burton people. The committee met at regular intervals just [to] kick around ideas for things we thought ought to be looked at in the program. Every member was free to make suggestions. If the committee thought a suggestion was worthwhile we would usually give the person that suggested it an opportunity to work it up in a little more detail [DM159: 3].

During the interview with the project officer, two of the permanent evaluation committee staff were present. One of them noted that the report reads like a rational goal-model evaluation but was actually developed incrementally.

You'll get the idea that somebody had systematically studied the objectives of the program saying these are the objectives we want to find out: whether or not state agency planning and operating accomplishes these objectives. But I don't think that's the kind of thinking we were actually doing at that time, because . . . none of them knew what they were doing.

So we got started: "Well, we can look at one thing and evaluate it, the formula." And we said, "Well, we can also see what state agencies are doing." See? And it was this kind of seat-of-the-pants approach to the whole situation. That's the way you got into it [PO159: 4].

The evaluation committee members were carefully selected on the basis of their knowledge of central program issues. While this was essentially an internal evaluation, the committee also made use of outside consultants: "We tried to get people who had a knowledge of how the Hill-Burton program functioned" (PO159: 9). As another committee member explained,

In our kind of program, with the long history and complexity of Hill-Burton, there was no lack of things to evaluate. But we felt that there was enough expertise in the program, that this should be the way to proceed and not just the scattering of contracts. . . . Even if you do that, to get some real meat and real meaning and be worth the money requires considerable attention . . . We thought it better to do a few things well than anything sloppily. . . . It's not a scientific process by any means . . . The form of it evolved from the process [PO159: 5].

Looking back on the study, the decision maker reported that this committee was the key to the utilization process:

I think that the makeup of the committee and the makeup of the interview teams, and so forth, was such that it helped this study command quite a deal of attention from the state agencies and among the federal people involved in the program . . . Well, I guess I had as much to do with the selection of the members as anybody. I asked a lot of people's advice, of course, and they had to be approved by the division chief, but my attempt was to have some cross-fertilization between the two organizations and also from the health care industry as well, and I don't think maybe we got quite as much variety in there as I'd like in terms of the background of people, but I think we did pretty well [DM159: 18].

There is no better example in our sample of the first step in utilization-focused evaluation: identification and organization of the primary intended users of the evaluation. And how do you keep a group like this working together? The answer emerged when we asked the decision maker about the evaluation of central versus peripheral goals.

> *Decision maker:* Well, I think this was heavily focused toward the major aspects of the program . . .
>
> *Interviewer:* Do you think the fact that you did focus on major aspects—some of the larger, more important aspects of this program—did that make a difference in how the study was used?
>
> *Decision maker:* Well, I think it probably made a difference in the interest with which it was viewed by people. . . . I think if we hadn't done that . . . if the committee hadn't been told to go ahead and proceed in that order, and given the freedom to do that, the committee itself would have lost interest. The fact that they felt that they were going to be allowed to pretty well free-wheel and probe into the most important things *as they saw them* I think had a lot to do with the enthusiasm with which they approached the task [DM159: 22].

The Hill-Burton case allows us to draw together the points made thus far throughout this book. The study began under conditions of considerable uncertainty. Funding was uncertain, the program faced possible termination, and there was no systematic information about what the 50 state Hill-Burton agencies were doing. A group of interested decision makers and information users were assembled to identify and focus the evaluation question. They began using an incrementalist strategy ("seat-of-the-pants approach") but eventually framed the evaluation question in the context of program goals and objectives. The project officer reported, "Of course, what they got into fairly early in the game was they were going to have to think about criteria. What do state agencies do and what should they be doing?" (PO159: 5). There was always this moving back and forth—action, reaction, adaptation—until the evaluation finally focused on central issues of relevance to the identified and organized decision makers and information users.

Central Objectives and the Personal Factor

In the Sufi story about hunting bears that opens this chapter, the point was made that different participants in the hunt had different goals. Goals and objectives embody personal and collective values. *The evaluation question*

of what goals and objectives will be evaluated cannot be answered until a
prior issue is settled: Whose goals and objectives for the program will be
evaluated? Several respondents in our study commented on the subjective
and personal nature of the idea of "central" program goals, particularly
where a program operates at several levels. Consider the response of a decision maker for one of many Neighborhood Health Center Programs.

Interviewer: To what extent did this evaluation study look at the major aspects of the study?

Decision maker: Well, now, you have a controversy because of different audiences with different real or hypothesized objectives in mind. I mean, the central OEO office when it started said the only value to the program is its
antipoverty consequences. I'm sure the OMB people thought the major program objective was impact on health status. The evaluation clearly did not
address either of those and could not have at the time. So you have a great
difference in perception of program objectives. . . . Now if one takes the
narrower legislative objectives and says, well, did you provide services that
were comprehensive and continuous in community-based settings, emphasizing preventive care and all that junk, then this study did focus on those objectives. And, if not the data, then at least the findings suggest that it met those
objectives. I don't think OMB was ever satisfied with those narrow objectives,
with the objectives stated in the legislation. You know, but that was the way the
world is [DM51: 13].

Different people have different perceptions of central program goals. Yet
evaluators often have a hard time accepting the implications of this relativ-
ism, because they have been taught to evaluate central goals or else their
work is not important. But whether it is the evaluator's opinion about centrality, the funder's, the client's, some special interest group's perspective, or
the viewpoint of program staff, the question of what constitutes central program goals and objectives remains an intrinsically subjective one. It cannot
be otherwise. There is no Jungian collective conscience or consciousness
that the evaluator can tap to determine the centrality, appropriateness, or
morality of program goals. At some point the issue of whose goals will be
evaluated must be addressed. Thus, the question of central versus peripheral
goals cannot really be answered in the abstract. The question thus becomes,
"central from whose point of view?" The personal factor interacts with the
goals clarification process to focus the evaluation question in a utilization-
focused approach.

The personal factor, or what Thompson (1967) called "the variable human," is also important because individuals vary both in their aptitude for
handling uncertainty and in their ability to exercise discretion. Information
is power only for people who know how to use it and are open to using it.
There is no one effective strategy of evaluation in the abstract, separate from

the organizational context in which it is introduced or the information-using capabilities of the people using it. The capacities of those involved make a major difference in which strategies of decision making and evaluation are used. Thus, the challenge for utilization is at least partly one of matching: getting information about the right questions, issues, and goals to the right people.

The purpose of the present chapter has been to suggest ways of adapting the goals clarification game to the particular circumstances, needs, and persons in a specific program. The active-reactive-adaptive approach to framing evaluation questions in the context of program goals means that there is no definitive set of rules for playing the goals clarification game—with one notable exception: *The players whose goals serve to help focus the evaluation should also be the primary intended users of the evaluation.*

There is a substantial body of research indicating that different individuals behave quite differently in the 20 questions game (and, by extension, in any decision-making process). Worley (1960), for example, studied subjects' information-seeking endurance in the game under experimental conditions. Initially, each subject was presented with a single clue and given the option of guessing what object the experimenter had in mind or of asking for another clue. This option was available after each new clue, but a wrong guess would end the game. Worley found large and consistent individual differences in the amount of information sought. Donald Taylor (1965) cites the research of Worley and others as evidence that decision-making and problem-solving behavior is dynamic, highly variable, and contingent upon both situational and individual characteristics. This does not make the evaluator's job any easier. It does mean that the personal factor remains the key to the utilization process. As evidenced in the case of the Hill-Burton permanent committee on evaluation, careful selection of knowledgeable, committed, and information-valuing persons can make a significant difference. The selection process for that committee can serve as a model of how to identify and organize decision makers for evaluation purposes. The goals clarification game is most useful when played by people who are searching for information because it helps them focus on central issues without letting the game become an end in itself and without turning the process into a contest between staff and evaluators.

* * *

Thus far this chapter has focused on ways of making sense out of goals and strategies for making goals clarification more than a combative game between evaluators and intended users of evaluation. Before closing the chapter it is worth considering a strategy that circumvents the goals clarification game altogether.

Goal-Free Evaluation

In the goals clarification game one of the most daring moves is to "goal-free evaluation." This method immediately stops play in the goals clarification game. Philosopher-evaluator Michael Scriven first proposed the idea of goal-free evaluation. Goal-free evaluation essentially means gathering data on a broad array of *actual effects* and evaluating the importance of these effects in meeting demonstrated needs. The evaluator makes a deliberate attempt to avoid all rhetoric related to program goals: No discussion about goals are held with staff and no program brochures or proposals are read; only the program's outcomes and measurable effects are studied.

There are four reasons for doing goal-free evaluation:

(1) to avoid the risk of narrowly studying stated program objectives and thereby missing important unanticipated outcomes;

(2) to remove the negative connotations attached to the discovery of unanticipated effects, because "the whole language of 'side-effect' or 'secondary effect' or even 'unanticipated effect' tended to be a put-down of what might well be the crucial achievement, especially in terms of new priorities" (Scriven, 1972b: 1-2);

(3) to eliminate the perceptual biases introduced into an evaluation by knowledge of goals; and

(4) to maintain evaluator objectivity and independence through goal-free conditions.

In Scriven's (1972b: 2) own words:

It seemed to me, in short, that consideration and evaluation of goals was an unnecessary but also a possibly contaminating step. I began work on an alternative approach—simply the evaluation of *actual* effects against a profile of *demonstrated* needs. I call this Goal-Free Evaluation. . . .

The less the external evaluator hears about the goals of the project, the less tunnel-vision will develop, the more attention will be paid to *looking* for *actual* effects (rather than checking on *alleged* effects).

Scriven (1972b: 3) distrusted the grandiose goals of most projects. Such great and grandiose proposals "assume that a gallant try at Everest will be perceived more favorably than successful mounting of molehills. That may or may not be so, but it's an unnecessary noise source for the evaluator." He saw no reason to get caught up in distinguishing alleged goals from real goals: "Why should the evaluator get into the messy job of trying to disentangle that knot?" He would also avoid goals conflict and goals war: "Why try to decide which goal should supervene?" He even countered the goals clarification shuffle. "Since almost all projects either fall short of their goals or over-achieve them, why waste time rating the goals, which usually aren't what is achieved? Goal-free evaluation is unaffected by—and hence does not legislate against—the shifting of goals midway in a project." Finally, he undermined the fuzziness gambit: "Goals are often stated so vaguely as to cover both desirable and undesirable activities, by almost anyone's standards. Why try to find out what was really intended—if anything?"

Essentially, then, goal-free evaluation means gathering data directly on program effects and effectiveness without risking contamination by goals. Sometimes the result of goal-free evaluation is a statement of goals; that is, rather than being the initial focus of the evaluation process, a statement of operating goals becomes its outcome. Scriven, however, considered this inappropriate:

> It often happens in goal-free evaluation that people use this as a way of working out what the goals are, but I discourage them from trying to do that. That's not the point of it. The outcome is an assessment of the merit of the program. A better way to put the trouble with the name goal-free is to say that you might put it better by saying it is needs-based instead of goal-based. It is based on something, namely the needs of the client or recipient, but it isn't based on the goals of the program people and you never need to know those and you shouldn't ever look at them. As far as the idea that you finally come up with them as a conclusion you'd be surprised the extent to which you don't [Scriven and Patton, 1976: 13-14].

By removing goals from the evaluation process, Scriven completely changed the nature of the interactions between evaluators and program staff. In the language of games, this constitutes a stunning gammon. The term gammon here designates a victory in which the winner overwhelms the opponent by getting rid of all pieces before the opponent gets rid of any. Goal-free evaluation rids an evaluation of goals before program staff have a chance to counter them through fuzziness, conflict, war, or shuffling priorities. Nor can staff disguise real goals by promoting public relations ideals to which they have no operating commitment. The evaluator wins the game by establishing rules that exclude even an entry by opponents. This may be the ultimate gammon in the goals clarification game.

There is another sense in which goal-free evaluation can be considered a gammon. Critics of Scriven, however, are more likely to be referring to the colloquial meaning of gammon—"nonsense intended to deceive"—because goal-free evaluation only appears to get rid of goals. The only goals really eliminated are those of local project staff. Scriven replaced staff objectives with more global goals based on societal needs and basic standards of morality. The real cunning in this gammon is that only the evaluator knows for sure what those needs and standards are, although Scriven (1972b: 3-4) considered such standards to be as obvious as the difference between soap and cancer:

Another error is to think that all standards of merit are arbitrary or subjective. There's nothing subjective about the claim that we need a cure for cancer more than a new brand of soap. The fact that some people have the opposite preference (if true) doesn't even weakly undermine the claim about which of these alternatives the *nation* needs most. So the Goal-Free Evaluation may use needs and not goals, or the goals of the consumer or the funding agency. Which of these is appropriate depends on the case. But in no case is it proper to use *anyone's* goals as the standard unless they can be *shown* to be the appropriate ones *and* morally defensible.

As a philosopher, Scriven may feel comfortable specifying what "the nation needs" and designating standards as "morally defensible." But from a utilization perspective, this simply begs the question of who is served by the information collected. The issue is not which goals are better or worse, moral or immoral, appropriate or inappropriate in any objective sense. The issue is whose goals will be evaluated. Scriven's goal-free model eliminates only one group from the game: local project staff. He directs data in only one clear direction—away from the stated concerns of the people who run the program. He addresses a national audience, legislative funders. But as these audiences are ill-defined and lack organization, I am unconvinced that the standards he applies are other than his very own preferences about what program effects are appropriate and morally defensible. Scriven's denial notwithstanding (cf. Scriven, 1972b: 3), goal-free evaluation simply substitutes the evaluator's goals for those of the project. It is a skillful gammon. Marvin Alkin (1972: 11) is kinder, but makes essentially the same point:

> This term, Goal-Free Evaluation, is not to be taken literally. The Goal-Free Evaluation *does* recognize goals (and not just idiosyncratic ones), but they are to be wider-context goals rather than the specific *objectives* of a program. . . . By "goal-free" Scriven simply means that the evaluator is free to choose a wide context of goals. By his description he implies that a goal-free evaluation is always free of the goals of the specific program and *sometimes* free of the goals of the program sponsor. In reality, then, goal-free evaluation is not really goal-free at all, but is simply directed at a different and usually wide decision audience. The typical goal-free evaluator must surely think (especially if he rejects the goals of the sponsoring agency) that his evaluation will extend at least to the level of "national policy formulators." The question is whether this decision audience is of the highest priority.

It should be noted that Scriven's goal-free proposal assumes both internal and external evaluators. Thus, part of the reason the external evaluators can ignore program staff and local project goals is because the internal evaluator takes care of all that. Thus, again, goal-free evaluation is only partially goal-free. Someone has to stay home and mind the goals while the external evaluators muck around in search of any and all effects. As Scriven (1972b: 4) has argued,

> Planning and production require goals, and formulating them in testable terms is absolutely necessary for the manager as well as the internal evaluator who keeps the manager informed. That has nothing to do with the question of whether the external evaluator needs or should be given any account of the project's goals.

It is ironic that in goal-free evaluation Scriven proposed for evaluators precisely that approach which program staff have long advocated for themselves. This is illustrated by a classic reaction from program staff when evaluators announce that it is necessary to begin by clarifying goals: "We're too busy running the program to spend time clarifying goals. We're trying to accomplish a lot of things in this program. Why should we be tied down to a narrow set of specific, clear, and measurable objectives? Goals will only serve to bias the program and hinder what we're trying to do. This is an action program serving lots of individuals in lots of ways. We don't have time to check some master list of goals all the time to see if what this person needs is on the list. What good are goals, anyway? Has a goal ever fed anyone? Can you get clothes with goals if you're naked? Will goals heal you if you're sick, get you a job if you're unemployed, or educate you if you're nonliterate?"

It would be little wonder if program staff responded negatively to Scriven's double standard that program staff must clarify goals but external evaluators do not have to. Scriven (1972b: 5) anticipated a hostile reaction:

> Now it's important to see why goal-free evaluation is *more* of a threat [than goal-based evaluation]. Primarily this is because the goal-free evaluator is less under the control of management; not only are the main variables no longer specified by management, but they may not even *include* those that management has been advertising. . . . The idea of an evaluator who won't even *talk* to you for fear of contamination can hardly be expected to make the producer rest easy.

But Scriven goes on to admonish local staff that they have no right to fear that goal-free evaluators will misrepresent and harm programs by applying irrelevant and inappropriate criteria derived from some global morality. His final word is quite final; program staff are excluded and their criteria are irrelevant. He completes the gammon with a touch of finesse to which there would seem to be no reply: "If a producer really cares about quality control it won't do to insist that the project's definition of quality must be used" (Scriven, 1972b: 5).

There have been several serious critiques of goal-free evaluation (see Stufflebeam, 1972; Alkin, 1972; Popham, 1972; and Kneller, 1972), but as

Popham (1972: 13) has predicted, goal-free evaluation may become very popular: "I can see future evaluators clamoring for specifically designed goal-free evaluation blinders to protect them from the taint of project goals." In the face of such clamoring, the best strategy for program staff may be emulation rather than hostility or criticism. As many parents of teenagers have discovered, double standards teach most effectively those behaviors that the parents practice but have forbidden to the child. If children learn by example, so may program staff. If evaluators need not know where a program was headed to evaluate where it ended up, why should program staff? They can work backwards as easily as evaluators can. Program staff need only wait until Scriven determines what the program has accomplished and then proclaim those accomplishments as their original goals. Ken McIntyre (1976: 39) has eloquently described just such an approach to evaluation. For the final coup de grace on the part of program staff, he suggests that

> One step remains: your program's goals you need a way of knowing;
> You're sure you've just about arrived, but where have you been going?
> So like the guy who fired his rifle at a ten-foot curtain
> And drew a ring around the hole to make a bull's-eye certain.

> It's best to wait until you're through and then see where you are:
> Deciding goals before you start is riskier by far.
> So if you follow my advice in your evaluation,
> You'll start with certainty, and end with self-congratulation.

Taking Goals Seriously

I noted at the beginning of this chapter that I choose to see the humor in the problem of goal specification. But seeing the humorous side of a situation is not the same thing as taking it lightly. The identification and clarification of program goals can be an important part of a comprehensive evaluation. The techniques described in the preceding pages are serious proposals for dealing with the problems encountered by evaluators as they have attempted to identify and clarify program goals. Those problems are well documented from the experiences of evaluators: vague goals, multiple goals, conflicting goals, public relations goals versus real goals, general versus specific goals, central versus peripheral goals, funder goals versus program staff goals, overt versus covert goals, long-term and short-term goals, matching of evaluation goals to program stages, immeasurable goals, changing goals, subsidiary goals, appropriate and inappropriate goals, nominal and operational goals, morally putrescent or quintessential goals—the list is almost endless.

Evaluators have responded to these problems with a variety of proposals. The Delphi technique (Dalkey, 1969), multiattribute-utility measurement

(Gardiner and Edwards, 1975), and the decision-theoretic approach (Edwards et al., 1975) are all strategies for dealing with the problems of multiple and conflicting goals. Behavioral objectives have been advocated as the answer to problems of vagueness and immeasurability (see Popham, 1969). "Differential evaluation" is a model for deriving objectives at three different stages of program development: the initiation stage, the contact stage, and program implementation (Tripodi et al., 1971). Suchman's proposal (1967: 51-56) for constructing "a chain of objectives" addresses the problem of goals that are too global or general as well as the long-range versus short-range issue. And, of course, goal-free evaluation (Scriven, 1972b) attempts to deal with all of these issues by focusing on actual program effects instead of staff intentions.

All of this attention to goals is a clear indication of the importance evaluators attach to goals identification and clarification. Despite all this concern about goals, social scientists who study organizations are still not sure what goals are, or even if they exist. To put this whole discussion of goals in a more philosophical context, this chapter closes with a question: Do program goals exist in any real sense or is the whole notion of program goals a figment of evaluators' imaginations? The answer is far from obvious. Consideration of this question takes us into that seldom penetrated inner chamber, where our basic assumptions about the nature of social reality reside.

Reification of Goals

To reify is to treat an abstraction as if it were real. There is much debate in the social sciences about which concepts are reified. The idea of goals has been a special target of social scientists concerned with concept reification in organizational analysis. This special interest in reification of organizational goals arises from the centrality of goals in the very definition of organizations (see Parsons, 1960: 17; Blau and Scott, 1962: 1-8; Price, 1968: 3). Cyert and March (1963: 28) assert that *individual people have goals, collectivities of people do not*. They likewise assert that only individuals can act; organizations or collectivities, as such, cannot be said to take action. The future state desired by an organization (its goals) is nothing but a function of individual "aspirations." Silverman (1971: 9) agrees, but adds a special condition:

> To say that an organization has a "goal" may be to involve oneself in some of the difficulties associated with reification. . . . It seems doubtful whether it is legitimate to conceive of an organization as having a goal except where there is an ongoing consensus between the members of the organization about the purposes of their interaction.

Etzioni (1968: 6), on the other hand, argues that collectivities do act and that organizations do have goals, defining an organizational goal as "a desired state of affairs which the organization attempts to realize." This is the dominant structural view in sociology, in which the very conception of "structure implies that the component units stand in some relation to one another and that the whole is greater than simply the sum of its parts" (Blau and Scott, 1962: 2). Far from reification of the concept of organizational goals, structuralists argue that one cannot understand organizations simply as a collection of individuals with personal goals. Organizations develop a *Gestalt:* "The concept of *Gestalt* means that the organized arrangement of elements in a larger whole has a significance of its own, not attributable to the specific character of its elements" (Blau, 1967: 346).

To fully understand the issue of goals reification, it is necessary to frame it in the assumption of rationality that dominates social science perspectives on organizations and decision making. The bureaucratic model of organizations in the tradition of Max Weber (1947) represents most completely the rational view of organizations aimed at maximizing efficiency and effectiveness in attaining goals. The "goal-model of organizations" (Etzioni, 1964: 16-18) is a direct manifestation of assumed bureaucratic rationality:

> The basic elements of the goal model are that (1) the organization exists to achieve stated goals; (2) the organization develops a rational procedure for the achievement of the goals; and (3) the organization is assessed in terms of the effectiveness of goal attainment [Champion, 1975: 40-41].

As evaluators might anticipate, the rational-goals model of organizations has encountered serious operational problems. Sociologists have discovered that organizational goals are extremely difficult to determine. The fact that goals may be considered from so many different points of view for so many different analytical purposes has led to a proliferation of attempts at classifying goals (e.g., Etzioni, 1961; Perrow, 1968, 1970; Hage and Aiken, 1969; Gross, 1969). Studies of organizations usually find it convenient to *assume* organizational goals rather than to study them (see Price, 1968: 4). Azumi and Hage (1972: 414) note that

> Organizational sociologists have found it useful to assume that organizations are purposive. . . . However, it has been much more difficult to actually measure the goals of an organization. Researchers find the purposive image helpful but somehow elusive.

Champion (1975: 41-42) reviewed the sociological literature and concluded,

> The consensus seems to be that organizational goals are difficult to define and that the effectiveness of goal attainment is equally difficult to evaluate. A primary implication for the meaningful application of the goal model in organizational analysis is that it is too complex to use on a large scale.

In brief, social scientists who study goals are not quite sure what they are studying. Goals analysis as a field of study is complex, chaotic, controversial, and confusing. There can be no consensus about the goal of goals because there is not even consensus about the existence of goals. As Thompson (1967: 127) put the dilemma,

> There is obvious danger in reifying the abstraction "organization" by asserting that it, the abstraction, has goals or desires. There is little to be gained, however, by swinging to the other extreme of insisting that the goals of an organization are somehow the accumulated goals of its individual members.

In the end, most researchers follow the pragmatic logic of Perrow (1970: 134):

> For our purposes we shall use the concept of an organizational goal as if there were no question concerning its legitimacy, even though we recognize that there are legitimate objections to doing so. Our present state of conceptual development, linguistic practices, and ontology (knowing whether something exists or not) offers us no alternative.

Evaluators, like Perrow, are likely to come down on the side of practicality. The language of goals will continue to dominate evaluation. There is no final answer to the question of reification because the issue is one of perception, situational usage, and personal assumptions about the nature of reality. But different perspectives about the goal of goals in evaluation have real consequences for the entire evaluation process. Thus, my purpose in introducing the issue of goals reification was twofold. First, I hoped by this discussion to induce at least a modicum of caution and humility among evaluators before they impose goals clarification exercises on program staff. Social scientists who study organizations have demonstrated that classical notions of goal-based organizational rationality have severe limitations in practice. *Difficulties in defining program goals are more likely due to problems inherent in the notion of goals than in staff incompetence, intransigence, or opposition to evaluation.* Failure to appreciate these difficulties, however, can quickly create staff resistance, which is likely to be detrimental to the entire evaluation process.

Second, I hope that this chapter on the problem of goals clarification in general and the discussion of goals reification in particular has established a context for understanding why utilization-focused evaluation does not depend on clear, specific, and measurable objectives as the *sine qua non* of evaluation research. Clarifying goals is neither necessary nor appropriate in every evaluation. In utilization-focused evaluation, framing the evaluation question in the context of program goals is only one option in efforts to identify and focus the relevant evaluation questions. The next two chapters consider additional alternatives for focusing evaluation questions.

The Goals Paradox

This chapter began with an evaluation of Nasrudin's hunting trip in search of bears. For Nasrudin that trip ended with the "marvelous" outcome of seeing no bears. Our hunting trip in search of the goal of goals has no conclusive ending, because the goal will vary from evaluation to evaluation, situation to situation. The process of framing an evaluation question in the context of program goals and objectives is clearly not the straightforward, logical exercise depicted by the classical literature on rational decision making. Decision-making processes in the real world are not purely rational, logical, and deductive. Goals may be no more than figments of our imagination, but they can be useful figments. This is the paradox of goals. Goals are rational abstractions in nonrational systems; they are the rational expression of a highly subjective process. Statements of goals emerge at the interface between the ideals of human rationality and the reality of human values. Therein lies their strength and their weakness. Goals provide direction for action and evaluation, but only for those who share in the values expressed by the goals. Evaluators live inside that paradox.

NOTE

1. Sufi stories, particularly those about the adventures and follies of the incomparable Mulla (Master) Nasrudin, are a means of communicating ancient wisdom:

> Nasrudin is the classical figure devised by the dervishes partly for the purpose of halting for a moment situations in which certain states of mind are made clear. . . . Since Sufism is something which is lived as well as something which is perceived, a Nasrudin tale cannot in itself produce complete enlightenment. On the other hand, it bridges the gap between mundane life and a transmutation of consciousness in a manner which no other literary form yet produced has been able to attain [Shah, 1964: 56].

Chapter 6

IMPLEMENTATION EVALUATION:
WHAT HAPPENED IN THE PROGRAM?

"What color is your parachute?"
asked Richard Nelson Bolles (1982),
and he became a rich man.

"What parachute?" asked Halcolm,
still a poor man, but alive.

One Final Backpacking Trip

An old story is told that through a series of serendipitous events much too convoluted and incredible to sort out here, four passengers found themselves together in a small plane—a priest, a young, unemployed college dropout, the world's smartest man, and the president of the United States. At 30,000 feet the pilot suddenly announced that the engines had stalled, the plane was crashing, and he was parachuting out. He added as he jumped, "I advise you to jump too, but I'm afraid there are only 3 parachutes left . . ." With that dire news he was gone.

The world's smartest man did the fastest thinking, grabbed a parachute and jumped. The president of the United States eyed the other two, put on a parachute and said, "You understand, it's not for myself but for the country." And he jumped.

The priest looked immensely uneasy, "Well, my son, you're young, and after all I am a priest, and, well, it seems only the right thing to do, I mean, if you want, um, just, um, go ahead, and um, well . . ."

The college dropout smiled and handed the priest a parachute. "Not to worry, Reverend. There's still a parachute for each of us. The world's smartest man grabbed my backpack instead of a parachute."

Checking the Inventory

Programs, like airplanes, need all their parts to do what they're designed to do and to accomplish what they're supposed to accomplish. Programs, like airplanes, are supposed to be properly equipped to carry out their assigned functions and guarantee passenger (client) safety. Programs, like air-

planes, are not always so equipped. Regular, systematic evaluations of inventory and maintenance checks help avoid disasters in both airplanes and programs.

Implementation evaluation focuses on finding out if the program has all its parts, if the parts are functional, and if the program is operating as it's supposed to be operating. Implementation evaluation can be a major evaluation focus. Evaluating program implementation involves finding out what is actually happening in the program. Of what does the program consist? Who is participating? What do staff do? What do participants experience? What's working and what's not working? What *is* the program?

An Exemplar

Our study of federal health evaluations turned up one quite dramatic case of evaluation use. A program was established by a state legislature to teach welfare recipients the basic rudiments of parenting and household management. The state welfare department was charged with conducting workshops, distributing brochures, showing films, and training caseworkers on how low-income people could better manage their meager resources and become better parents. A single major city was selected for pilot testing the program, and a highly respected independent research institute contracted to evaluate the program. Both the state legislature and the state welfare department were publicly committed to using the evaluation findings for decision making.

The evaluators interviewed a sample of welfare recipients before the program began. They collected considerable data about parenting, household management, and budgetary practices. Eighteen months later, the same welfare recipients were interviewed a second time. The results showed no measurable change in parenting or household management behavior. In brief, the program was found to be ineffective. These results were reported to the state legislators and the newspapers. Following legislative debate and adverse publicity, the legislature terminated funding for the program—a clear case of using evaluation results to inform a major decision.

Now, suppose we wanted to know why the program was ineffective. That question could not be answered by the evaluation as conducted because it focused entirely on measuring the attainment of intended program outcomes; that is, the extent to which the program changed parenting and household management behaviors of welfare recipients. As it turned out, there is a very good reason why the program was ineffective.

When the funds were allocated from the state to the city, the program quickly became embroiled in the politics of urban welfare. Welfare rights organizations questioned the right of government to tell poor people how to spend their money or rear their children: "You have no right to tell us we have to run our houses like the white, middle class. And who's this French-man Piaget who's going to tell us how to raise American kids?"

As a result of these and other political battles, the program was delayed and further delayed. Procrastination being the better part of valor, no parenting brochures were ever printed; no household management films were ever shown; no workshops were held; and no caseworkers were ever trained.

In short, *the program was never implemented. . . . But it was evaluated!* It was found to be ineffective, and was killed.

The Importance of Implementation Analysis

It is important to know the extent to which a program is effective after it is properly implemented, but to answer that question it is first necessary to know the extent to which the program was, indeed, properly implemented. This chapter considers the meaning and purpose of implementation evaluation from a utilization perspective.

In the spring of 1974, the entire issue of the periodical *Evaluation* was devoted to a consideration of "the human services shortfall." Lynn and Salasin (1974: 4) defined this shortfall as "a large and growing gap between what we expect from government-supported human service systems, and what these systems in fact deliver." The human services shortfall is made up of two parts: (1) failure of implemented programs to attain desired outcomes and (2) failure to actually implement policy in the form of operating programs. Evaluators have directed most of their attention to the first problem by conducting outcomes evaluations, but there is growing evidence that the second problem is equally, if not even more, critical. In a recent book on social program implementation, editor Walter Williams concludes, "the underlying theme of this book is that the lack of concern for implementation is currently *the* crucial impediment to improving complex operating programs, policy analysis, and experimentation in social policy areas" (Williams and Elmore, 1976: 267; italics in original). The preface to the book states the problem quite succinctly.

> The fundamental implementation question remains whether or not what has been decided actually can be carried out in a manner consonant with that underlying decision. More and more, we are finding, the answer is no. So it is crucial that we attend to implementation [Williams and Elmore, 1976: xi].

The problem of making policy operative is fundamental in all realms of government intervention. At the international level, studies collected and edited by John C. de Wilde (1967) demonstrate that program implementation and administration are the critical problems in Third World development plans. Organizational sociologists have documented the particular problem of implementing programs that are new and innovative alongside or into existing programs (e.g., Kanter, 1983; Corwin, 1973; Hage and Aiken, 1970). Diffusion of innovation theorists have thoroughly documented the problems of implementing new ideas in new settings (e.g., Brown, 1981; Rogers et al., 1969, 1971; Havelock, 1973). Then there's the marvelous case study of the Oakland Project by Pressman and Wildavsky (1984). Already a classic on the trials and tribulations of implementation, this description of a Great Society urban development effort is entitled:

Implementation

How Great Expectations in Washington
Are Dashed in Oakland;
Or, Why It's Amazing that
Federal Programs Work at All,
This Being a Saga of the
Economic Development Administration
as Told by Two Sympathetic Observers
Who Seek to Build Morals on a
Foundation of Ruined Hopes

Williams and Elmore (1976: xii) studied implementation analysis and found that it has seldom been taken seriously, much to the detriment of research utilization:

The failure to focus on implementation has blighted not only program administration but also policy research and analysis. In the former case, policy ideas that seemed reasonable and compelling when decisions were made often have become badly flawed and ineffective programs as they drifted down the bureaucratic process. It is not just that the programs fall short of the early rhetoric that described them; they often barely work at all. Ignoring implementation has been equally disastrous for research and analysis. *Indeed, it is possible that past analysis and research that ignored implementation issues may have asked the wrong questions, thereby producing information of little or no use to policy-making* [italics in original].

The notion that asking the wrong questions leads to useless information is fundamental to everything we have discussed. To avoid gathering useless information, it is important to frame evaluation questions in the context of program implementation.

Questions of Focus:
Outcomes Evaluation and Implementation Evaluation

It is perhaps easiest to understand implementation evaluation in contrast to outcomes evaluation. While the ideal evaluation includes both, specific

evaluations vary in emphasis on one or the other. Evaluation has been dominated by an emphasis on measuring outcomes. Outcomes evaluation is typically the comparison of actual program outcomes with desired outcomes
(goals). One of the major reasons goals clarification has received so much
attention is that evaluators have been preoccupied with outcomes evaluation.
Provus (1971: 10-11) has cogently described the predominance of outcomes
evaluation in the field of educational assessment:

> Evaluation of program outcomes establishes performance criteria for pro-
> gram recipients. This approach is represented by all that is most current and
> "scientific" in educational evaluation. Starting with the work of Tyler and the
> perfection of standardized instruments with norms for various populations,
> and continuing with the present interest in group criterion-referenced tests,
> individual situational testing, and unobtrusive measures of performance, the
> preoccupation of the present generation of evaluators has been and continues
> to be with microanalysis of a learner's behavior at various times before and
> after exposure to a lesson, program, treatment, or institution.

In educational research, outcomes evaluation is represented by pretest
versus posttest performance on standardized achievement tests; in criminal
justice programs, outcomes evaluation measures comparative recidivism
rates; in health programs, the outcomes are changes in incidence and prevalence rates; in manpower programs, the outcomes are employment rates; in
drug abuse treatment programs, the outcomes are rates of repeated addiction; and so it goes for each area in the human service delivery system. The
problem with pure outcomes evaluation is that the results give decision
makers very little information upon which to act. Simply knowing that outcomes are high, low, or different does not tell decision makers very much
about what to do. What is missing is information about the actual nature of
the program being evaluated. In the example that provided the setting for this
chapter, the decision makers knew only that the welfare parent training program had no measurable effects; they did not even know whether or not a
program actually existed that could be expected to have effects. Based only
on erroneous outcomes information, they terminated a policy approach that
had never actually been tried. Unfortunately, such inappropriate decisions
based only on outcomes evaluations are not uncommon.

> A serious look at the actual substance of the program being evaluated can pre-
> vent some of the obvious but oft repeated evaluation failures of the past.

> For example, although it seems obvious to mention, it is important to know
> whether a program actually exists. Federal agencies are often inclined to as-
> sume that, once a cash transfer has taken place from a government agency to a
> program in the field, a program exists and can be evaluated. Experienced
> evaluation researchers know that the very existence of a program cannot be
> taken for granted, even after large cash transfers have taken place. Early

evaluations of Title I programs in New York City provide an illustration of this problem. . . . Obvious though it may seem, evaluations continue without either raising or answering the primary question: "Does the program exist?" This error could not arise if evaluation researchers looked carefully and seriously at program content before decisions about evaluation research methods were made [Guttentag and Struening, 1975b: 3-4].

While terminating a policy inappropriately is one possible error when only outcomes data are used, enlarging a program inappropriately is also possible when decision makers have no real information about program operations and implementation. In one instance, a number of drug addiction treatment programs in a county were evaluated, collecting nothing but outcomes data on rates of readdiction for treated patients. All programs had relatively mediocre success rates, except one program that had had 100% success for two years. The county board immediately voted to triple the budget of that program. Within a year, the readdiction rates for that program had fallen to the same mediocre level as other programs. By enlarging the program based on outcomes data, the county board had eliminated the key elements in the program's success—its small size and dedicated staff. The highly successful program had been a six-patient halfway house with one primary staff counselor who ate, slept, and lived that program. He established such a close relationship with each addict that he knew exactly how to keep each one straight. When the program was enlarged, he became administrator of three houses and lost personal contact with the clients. The successful program became only mediocre. Thus, a highly effective program was lost because the county board acted without any information about actual program operations and without an assessment of the basis for the program's success.

If one had to choose between implementation information and outcomes information because of limited evaluation resources, there are many instances in which implementation information would be of greater value. A decision maker can use implementation information to make sure that a policy is being put into operation according to design—or to test the very feasibility of the policy.

Leonard Bickman (1985) has described a statewide evaluation of early childhood interventions in Tennessee that began by asking stakeholders in state government what they wanted to know. The evaluators were prepared to undertake impact studies and expected impact data to be the eventual evaluation priority. However, the interviews with state government stakeholders revealed a surprising sophistication about the difficulties and expenses involved in getting good, generalizable outcomes data in a timely fashion. Moreover, it was clear that key policy makers and program managers "were more concerned about the allocation and distribution of resources than about the effectiveness of projects" (p. 190). They wanted to know whether every needy child was being served. What services were being delivered to whom? State agencies could use this kind of implementation and service delivery information to "redistribute their resources to unserved areas and populations or encourage different types of services" (p. 191). They could also use descriptive information about programs to increase communications among service providers about what ideas were being tried and to assess gaps in services.

> Before asking the more sophisticated (and expensive) questions about effectiveness, policy-makers wanted to know simpler descriptive information. . . . If the currently funded programs could not even be described how could they be improved [Bickman, 1985: 190-191]?

Unless one knows that a program is operating according to design, there may be little reason to expect it to produce the desired outcomes. Furthermore, until the program is implemented and a "treatment" is believed to be in operation, there is little reason to evaluate outcomes. The decision maker on the Hill-Burton evaluation from our utilization of federal health studies made this point quite emphatically:

> When we called the committee together and began to discuss the question of evaluating state agency performance there was no decision at that point that there were actually going to be interviews with the state agencies. That's something that grew naturally out of the discussion of the committee members. They concluded fairly early in their discussions that they were groping in the dark to try and evaluate agencies when they weren't really sure what the agencies were doing. And so the idea to interview them and gather all this information relative to what's going on in the state agencies grew out of the committee's feeling that they needed to know what was going on before they could even attempt an evaluation of whether what was going on was good, bad, or indifferent [DM159: 6].

When outcomes are evaluated without knowledge of implementation, the results seldom provide a direction for action because the decision maker lacks information about what produced the observed outcomes (or lack of outcomes). This is the "black box" approach to evaluation: Clients are tested before entering the program and after completing the program, while what happens in between is a black box. Carol Weiss (1972b: 43) described this approach and its dangers:

> Why should the evaluator be concerned with program input? Haven't we noted earlier that his job is to find out whether the program (whatever it is) is achieving its goals? Does it make any difference to his work whether the program is using rote drill, psychoanalysis, or black magic? There are evaluators

who are sympathetic to such an approach. They see the program as a "black box," the contents of which do not concern them; they are charged with discovering effects. But if the evaluator has no idea of what the program really is, he may fail to ask the right questions.

Most black box evaluations that study outcomes alone do so because of tradition and routine; no thoughtful decision has been made about what kind of evaluative information would be most useful. Nowhere is this better illustrated than in the routine use of standardized achievement tests in educational evaluation.

Unlocking the Black Box of Program Implementation

The first step in unlocking the black box of program implementation is finding out whether or not the program actually moved from an idea to initial implementation. The evaluator asks, "Does the program exist?" According to Williams, the number of programs that fail to ever become operational may be quite high because "the major problem for policy analysis is not in developing relatively sound policy alternatives but in failing to consider the feasibility of implementing these alternatives" (Williams and Elmore, 1976: 268). The crucial implementation stage for Williams occurs between the decision and operation stages, when new programs are being tried for the first time. The weaknesses of the planning process suddenly become quite glaring:

> Surely policymakers at the time of choice ought to have reasonable estimates of the organizational capacity to carry out alternative proposals. But however obvious that may be, few people have ever thought in terms of analyzing implementation during the decision-making stages [W. Williams, 1976: 270]!

This makes the evaluator's job all the more difficult, because it means there are seldom clear criteria for even conceptualizing implementation processes, much less evaluating them.

The further one delves into implementation analysis, the more complex the alternatives become. The black box in pure outcomes evaluations quickly becomes a Pandora's box in more comprehensive evaluation designs with an implementation analysis component. Consider, for example, the Pandorian question of how close an actual program has to be in comparison to its initial proposal or plan before it can be said to be implemented. One decision maker interviewed in our utilization of federal health evaluations study felt that policy makers had been misled into thinking that the evaluation report on his program concerned the ideal program as planned, when in fact only partial implementation had occurred. The report was thus discredited in this decision maker's eyes because he felt its use in congressional hearings had done the program a disservice.

> When you start reading your hearings, for instance, and find them using it as a resource in some ways, frankly, it concerns me a little bit, because I felt like portions of this did not have substantive enough data to be making determinations. That is, how can you judge the effect of the cancellation provision when it wasn't fully implemented at the point in time that the study was using? How could you put any reliance upon a study when the repayment provision wasn't fully implemented? Do you see what I mean? So I didn't put credence in the thing [DM145: 25].

But just how close to the ideal must the program be before it can be said to be fully implemented? The next section discusses this and related issues within the black box of program implementation.

Ideal Program Plans and Actual Implementation

Once the evaluator has determined that at least some activity actually exists (i.e., that there is indeed a program to be evaluated), the next question is this: What should the program look like before it can be said to be fully implemented and operational? This question is difficult to answer because programs are not implemented in the classical, rational fashion of single-mindedly adopting a set of means to achieve a predetermined end. From an incrementalist perspective, programs take shape slowly as decision makers react to multiple uncertainties and emerging complexities. Jerome Murphy makes this point quite emphatically in his study of the implementation of Title V of the Elementary and Secondary Education Act. He found great variation in implementation in the various states. He describes evaluations of those programs as exercises in blaming and scapegoating instead of attempts to understand educational change in the context of organizational dynamics, concluding that the widespread assumption that competently led bureaucracies operate like goal-directed, unitary decision makers may well be a major barrier to dealing with problems of bureaucratic change. Both program evaluations and reform efforts must come to grips explicitly with the enduring attributes of organizations (Murphy, 1976: 96).

Sociologists who study formal organizations, social change, and diffusion of innovations have carefully documented the substantial slippage in organizations between plans and actual operations. For Rogers (1962) it is the difference between trial and adoption; for Smelser (1959) it is the difference between specification, implementation, and routinization; for Mann and Neff (1961) it is the slippage between planning change, taking steps to make change, and stabilizing change; and for Hage and Aiken (1970) it is the difference between initiation, implementation, and routinization of change. In each case, regardless of how these sociologists conceptualize the stages of organizational change and innovations adoption, they emphasize two points: (1) *routinization or final acceptance is never certain at the beginning;* and (2) *the implementation process always contains unknowns that change the ideal so that it looks different when and if it actually becomes operational.*

Hage and Aiken (1970: 100) found that organizational conflict and disequilibrium are greatest during the implementation stage of organizational change. No matter how much planning takes place,

> the human element is seldom adequately considered in the implementation of a new product or service. There will be mistakes that will have to be corrected. Alteration of the existing structure will also create conflicts and tensions among members of the organization.

Barriers to Implementation

Odiorne (1984: 190) studied "the anatomy of poor performance" in the "strategic management of human resources." His analysis documents the gargantuan human obstacles that are typically encountered in the implementation and management of programs. Common problems include staff who give up when they encounter trivial obstacles, people who hang onto obsolete ideas and outmoded ways of doing things, emotional outbursts when asked to perform new tasks, muddled communications, and poor anticipation of problems so that once manageable problems become major management crises (pp. 190-194).

Meyers (1981: 37) has argued that much implementation fails because program designs are "counterintuitive"—they just don't make sense. He adds to the litany of implementation hurdles the following: undue haste, compulsion to spend all allotted funds by the end of the fiscal year, personnel turnovers, vague legislation, severe understaffing, racial tensions, conflicts between different levels of government, and the divorce of implementation from policy (pp. 38-39).

Kantor's (1983) best-selling book *The Change Masters* analyzes barriers to be overcome in implementing new ideas. She studied 115 innovations in more than 100 American companies. Her findings include 10 widely applied "Rules for Stifling Innovation," which help explain why implementation cannot be taken for granted.

RULES FOR STIFLING INNOVATION

(1) Regard any new idea from below with suspicion—because it's new, and because it's from below.
(2) Insist that people who need your approval to act first go through several other levels of management to get their signatures.

(3) Ask departments or individuals to challenge and criticize each other's proposals. (That saves you the job of deciding; you just pick the survivor.)

(4) Express your criticisms freely, and withhold your praise. (That keeps people on their toes.) Let them know they can be fired at any time.

(5) Treat identification of problems as signs of failure, to discourage people from letting you know when something in their area isn't working.

(6) Control everything carefully. Make sure people count anything that can be counted, frequently.

(7) Make decisions to reorganize or change policies in secret, and spring them on people unexpectedly. (That also keeps people on their toes.)

(8) Make sure that requests for information are fully justified, and make sure that it is not given out to managers freely. (You don't want data to fall into the wrong hands.)

(9) Assign to lower-level managers, in the name of delegation and participation, responsibility for figuring out how to cut back, lay off, move people around, or otherwise implement threatening decisions you have made. And get them to do it quickly.

(10) And above all, never forget that you, the higher-ups, already know everything important about this business (Kantor, 1983: 101).

Kantor's insights into the difficulties of implementing change are captured quite succinctly in the concluding "moral" of her data-based story (p. 121):

It is hard to get people to look for ways to improve the productivity of plowing if the earth moving trucks are hauling away the soil.

In addition, as programs take shape power struggles develop:

The stage of implementation is thus the stage of conflict, especially over power. It is the time when the new program results in the greatest disequilibrium in the organization because it is the stage when the program becomes a reality and the members of the organization must actually live with it . . . tempers flare, interpersonal animosities develop, and the power structure is shaken [Hage and Aiken, 1970: 104].

The difference between the ideal, rational model of program implementation and the day-to-day, incrementalist, and conflict-laden realities of program implementation is explained with a minimum of jargon in the following notice found by Jerome Murphy (1976: 92) in the office of a state education agency:

Notice

The objective of all dedicated department employees should be to thoroughly analyze all situations, anticipate all problems prior to their occurrence, have answers for these problems, and move swiftly to solve these problems when called upon. . . .

However . . .

When you are up to your ass in alligators, it is difficult to remind yourself that your initial objective was to drain the swamp.

The Case of Project Follow Through

Evaluation disasters can result from failing to recognize that implementation of program ideals is neither automatic nor certain. The national evaluation of Follow Through is a prime example of such a disaster. Follow Through was introduced as an extension of Head Start for primary-age children. It was a planned variation "experiment" in compensatory education featuring 22 different models of education to be tested in 158 school districts on 70,000 children throughout the nation. The evaluation alone employed 3,000 people to collect data on program effectiveness. Yet, as Alkin (1970: 2) has observed, the evaluation lacked focus from the beginning.

It was simply assumed in the evaluation plan that alternative educational models could and would be implemented in some systematic, uniform fashion. Elmore has rightly pointed out the folly of this assumption:

> Each sponsor developed a large organization, in some instances larger than the entire federal program staff, to deal with problems of model implementation. Each local school system developed a program organization consisting of a local director, a team of teachers and specialists, and a parent advisory group. The more the scale and complexity of the program increased, the less plausible it became for Follow Through administrators to control the details of program variations, and the more difficult it became to determine whether the array of districts and sponsors represented "systematic" variations in program content [Williams and Elmore, 1976: 108].

The Follow Through data analysis showed greater variation within groups than between them; i.e., the 22 models did not show systematic treatment effects as such. Most effects were null, some were negative, but "of all our findings, the most pervasive, consistent, and suggestive is probably this: *The effectiveness of each Follow Through model depended more on local circumstances than on the nature of the model*" (Anderson, 1977: 13; italics in original). In reviewing these findings, Eugene Tucker, of the U.S. Office of Education, suggests that, in retrospect, the Follow Through evaluation should have begun as a formative effort with greater focus on implementation strategies:

It is safe to say that evaluators did not know what was implemented in the various sites. Without knowing what was implemented it is virtually impossible to select valid effectiveness measures. . . . Hindsight is a marvelous teacher and in large scale experimentations an expensive one [Tucker, 1977: 11-12].

Yet the importance of framing evaluation questions in the context of program implementation appears to be a hard lesson to learn. Provus (1971: 27-29) clearly warned against precisely the kind of design used in the Follow Through evaluation at a 1966 conference on educational evaluation of national programs, a conference that included U.S. Office of Education officials. By 1971, he had fully developed and published his "discrepancy evaluation" model, which placed heavy emphasis on implementation evaluation:

An evaluation that begins with an experimental design denies to program staff what it needs most: information that can be used to make judgments about the program while it is in its dynamic stages of growth. . . . Evaluation must provide administrators and program staff with the information they need and the freedom to act on that information. . . .

We will not use the antiseptic assumptions of the research laboratory to compare children receiving new program assistance with those not receiving such aid. We recognize that the comparisons have never been productive, nor have they facilitated corrective action. The overwhelming number of evaluations conducted in this way show no significant differences between "experimental" and "control" groups [Provus, 1971: 11-12].

Ideals and Discrepancies

Provus argued that evaluations had to begin by establishing the degree to which programs were actually operating as desired. Discrepancy evaluation is a comparison of the actual program with the ideal program. These ideals "may arise from any source, but under the Discrepancy Evaluation Model they are derived from the values of the program staff and the client population it serves" (Provus, 1971: 12). Evaluation of programs, even national programs, must begin at the local level because

it follows that if there are types of programs with different developmental characteristics, the development standards for these program types will vary also. . . . This local work is usually of the process assessment type in which evaluators systematically collect and weigh data descriptive of on-going program activity [Provus, 1971: 13].

Provus essentially argued that the nature of the evaluation should be adapted to fit the organizational realities of program development and implementation. *The reality is that actual programs look different from ideal program plans. The evaluation challenge is to assist identified decision makers in determining how far from the ideal plan the program can deviate, and in what ways it can deviate, while still meeting fundamental criteria.* How different can an actual program be from its ideal and still be said to have been implemented? The answer must be clarified between decision makers and evaluators as they conceptualize the evaluation and focus the evaluation question in light of information needs and the particular organizational dynamics of the program being evaluated. Williams outlines the issues for negotiation and clarification as follows:

> At some point there should be a determination of the degree to which an innovation has been implemented successfully. What should the implemented activity be expected to look like in terms of the underlying decision? For a complex treatment package put in different local settings, decisionmakers usually will not expect—or more importantly, *not want*—a precise reproduction of every detail of the package. The objective is performance, not conformance. To enhance the probability of achieving the basic program or policy objectives, the implementation should consist of a realistic development of the underlying decision in terms of the local setting. In the ideal situation, those responsible for implementation would take the basic idea and modify it to meet special local conditions. There should be a reasonable resemblance to the basic idea, as measured by inputs and expected outputs, incorporating the best of the decision and the best of the local ideas [Williams and Elmore, 1976: 277-278].

The implementation of the Oregon Community Corrections Act since 1977 is an excellent illustration of how local people will adapt a statewide mandate to fit local needs and initiatives. In studying variations in implementation of this legislation, Palumbo et al. (1984) found a direct relationship between higher levels of implementation and success in attaining goals. Yet "the implementation factors that lead to more successful outcomes are not things that can easily be transferred from one locale to another" (p. 72).

Local Variations in Implementing National Programs

I would not belabor these points if it were not so painfully clear that implementation processes are so frequently ignored in evaluation research. Edwards et al. (1975: 142) note in their introduction to the decision-theoretic approach to evaluation that "we have frequently encountered the idea that a [national] program is a fixed, unchanging object, observable at various times and places." Because this idea seems so firmly lodged in so many minds and continues to spawn so many evaluation disasters, I feel compelled to prolong this section with one more piece of evidence to the contrary.

Rand Corporation, under contract to the U.S. Office of Education, studied 293 federal programs supporting educational change. It is one of the largest and most comprehensive studies of educational change ever conducted. Rand's Change Agent Study concluded that implementation "dominates the innovative process and its outcomes":

> In short, where implementation was successful, and where significant change in participant attitudes, skills, and behavior occurred, implementation was characterized by a process of mutual adaptation in which project goals and methods were modified to suit the needs and interests of the local staff and in which the staff changed to meet the requirements of the project. This finding was true even for highly technological and initially well-specified projects; unless adaptations were made in the original plans or technologies, implementation tended to be superficial or symbolic, and significant change in participants did not occur [McLaughlin, 1976: 169].

The Change Agent Study found that the usual emphasis in federal programs on the *delivery system* is inappropriate. McLaughlin recommended

> a shift in change agent policies from a primary focus on the *delivery system* to an emphasis on the *deliverer*. An important lesson that can be derived from the Change Agent Study is that unless the developmental needs of the users are addressed, and unless projects are modified to suit the needs of the user and the institutional setting, the promise of new technologies is likely to be unfulfilled [McLaughlin, 1976: 180].

In the context of the examples of evaluation absurdities cited in this chapter, and combined with the works of Provus, Williams, Murphy and others, the Rand Change Agent Study has enormous implications for evaluation use. The conclusion of the RAND study means that *implementation evaluation is critical because program implementation is neither automatic nor certain. It means that implementation evaluation must also be adaptive and focused on users if the evaluation is to be relevant, meaningful, and useful. It means that judging program implementation according to some written-in-stone blueprint is inappropriate and dysfunctional. It means that criteria for evaluating implementation must be developed through a process of interaction with identified and organized primary intended information users in order to determine how they view implementation. It means that evaluators will have to be active-reactive-adaptive in framing evaluation questions in the context of program implementation.*

TYPES OF IMPLEMENTATION EVALUATION

In focusing evaluation questions, there are several alternative types of implementation evaluation. These options deal with different kinds of implementation issues. Moreover, these are not mutually exclusive approaches.

Over time, a comprehensive evaluation might include all five types of implementation evaluation reviewed below.

Effort Evaluation

Effort evaluations focus on documenting "the quantity and quality of activity that takes place. This represents an assessment of input or energy regardless of output. It is intended to answer the questions 'What did you do?'
and 'How well did you do it?'" (Suchman, 1967: 61). Effort evaluation
moves up a step from asking if the program exists to asking how active the
program is. If relatively inactive, it is unlikely to be very effective. Tripodi
(1971) has linked effort evaluations to stages of program development. At
the initiation of a program, evaluation questions focus on getting services
under way. Later in time questions concerning the appropriateness and
quality of services become more important.

An effort evaluation establishes the level of program activity by observing
the degree to which inputs are available and operational at desired levels.
Have sufficient staff been hired with the proper qualifications? Are staff-
client ratios at desired levels? How many clients with what characteristics
are being served by the program? Are necessary materials available? An effort evaluation involves making an inventory of program operations.

Monitoring Programs:
Routine Management Information

Monitoring ongoing programs has become an area of specialization
within evaluation (Grant, 1978). An important way of monitoring program
implementation over time is to establish a management information system
(MIS). This provides routine data on client intake, participation levels, program completion rates, case loads, client characteristics, and program
costs. The hardware and software decisions for an MIS have long-term re-
percussions, so the development of such a routine data collection system
must be approached with special attention to questions of use and problems
of "managing management information systems" (Patton, 1982b). Establishing and using an MIS are often primary responsibilities of internal
evaluators. This has been an important growth area in the field of evaluation
as demands for accountability have increased in human services (Attkisson
et al., 1978; Elpers and Chapman, 1978; Broskowski et al., 1978). The
"monitoring and tailoring" approach of Cooley and Bickel (1985) demon-
strates how an MIS can be client-oriented and utilization-focused.

Implementing a management information system to monitor ongoing
program implementation has its own implementation problems—layers of
implementation on top of one another. These problems can lead to a MIS-

match (Dery, 1981). While there is no shortage of documented MIS problems and disasters (Lucas, 1975), computers and data-based management information systems have brought high technology to local governments (Danziger et al., 1982), evaluation (Gray, 1984; Johnson, 1984), and even Congress (Frantzich, 1982).

Process Evaluation

Another option in implementation analysis is process evaluation. This approach focuses on the internal dynamics and actual operations of a program in an attempt to understand its strengths and weaknesses. Process evaluations focus on why certain things are happening, how the parts of the program fit together, and how people perceive the program. This approach takes its name from an emphasis on looking at how a product or outcome is produced rather than looking at the product itself; that is, it is an analysis of the processes whereby a program produces the results it does. Process evaluation is developmental, descriptive, continuous, flexible, and inductive (Patton, 1980a).

Process evaluations search for explanations of the successes, failures, and changes in a program. Under field conditions in the real world, people and unforeseen circumstances shape programs and modify initial plans in ways that are rarely trivial. The process evaluator sets out to understand and document the day-to-day reality of the setting or settings under study. This means unraveling what is actually happening in a program by searching for the major patterns and important nuances that give the program its character. A process evaluation requires sensitivity to both qualitative and quantitative changes in programs throughout their development; it means becoming intimately acquainted with the details of the program. Process evaluations not only look at formal activities and anticipated outcomes, but also investigate informal patterns and unanticipated consequences in the full context of program implementation and development (Fuller and Rapoport, 1984).

Finally, process evaluations usually include perceptions of people close to the program about how things are going. A variety of perspectives may be sought from people inside and outside the program. For example, Hayman and Napier (1975: 84) describe a variety of ways process data can be collected at the classroom level in educational evaluations: "It is now possible to gather reliable process data in numerous ways—from peers, outside resource people, students, and, of course, the teacher's own observations." These differing perspectives can provide unique insights into program processes as experienced by different people.

A process evaluation can provide useful feedback during the developmental phase of a program. It can also be used to collect implementation data for use in diffusion and dissemination processes. One evaluator in our utilization of federal health evaluations reported that process information had been particularly useful to federal officials in expanding a program nationwide.

> We used as our sample those centers which had been in existence for a year. This was to allow for the start-up problems and, you know, gearing up and getting under speed and all that stuff. The reason they wanted it done when it was done was so that it would be able to affect subsequent centers. . . .
>
> I like to think in terms of programmatic issues, in terms of making a difference in the next center that opened, or in the whole series of things that were required in order for a center to get on the way. . . . *The process evaluations that we did for the centers one by one, one at a time, each of those were affected by the results*. And so, the timing was very critical for that, and I think it was the appropriate time [EV51: 22].

Process evaluation is one of the four major components of the CIPP (context, input, process, product) model of evaluation developed by Stufflebeam et al. (1970, 1971). They consider process evaluation to be an integral part of "a total evaluation model." They see process evaluation in a broad sense, as (1) gathering data to detect or predict defects in the procedural design or its implementation during the implementation stages, (2) providing information for program decision, and (3) establishing a record of program development as it occurs.

Component Evaluation

The component approach to implementation involves a formal assessment of distinct parts of a program. Programs can be conceptualized as consisting of separate operational efforts that may be the focus of a self-contained implementation evaluation. For example, the Hazelden Foundation Chemical Dependency Program typically includes the following components: detoxification, intake, group treatment, lectures, individual counseling, release, and outpatient services. While these components make up a comprehensive chemical dependency treatment program that can be and is evaluated in terms of continued sobriety over time (Patton, 1980b; Laundergan, 1983), there are important questions about the operation of any particular component that can be the focus of evaluation. In addition, linkages between one or more components may become the focus of evaluation.

Bickman (1985: 199) argues that one particularly attractive feature of the component approach is the potential for greater generalizability of findings and more appropriate cross-program comparisons:

The component approach's major contribution to generalizability is its shift from the program as the unit of analysis to the component. By reducing the unit of analysis to a component instead of a program, it is more likely that the component as contrasted to entire programs can be generalized to other sites and other providers. The more homogeneous units are, the more likely one can generalize from one unit to another. In principle, the smaller the unit of analysis within a hierarchy, the more homogeneous it will be. By definition, as programs are composed of components, programs are more heterogeneous than components. It should be easier to generalize from one component to another than to generalize from one program to another.

An example of this process might clarify the point. Any two early childhood programs may consist of a variety of components implemented in several different ways. Knowledge of the success of one program would not tell us a great deal about the success of the other unless they were structured similarly. However, given the diversity of programs, it is unlikely that they would have the same type and number of components. In contrast, if both had an intake component, it would be possible to compare them just on that component. A service provider in one part of the state can examine the effectiveness of a particular component in an otherwise different program in a different part of the state and see its relevance to the program he or she was directing.

Treatment Specification

The treatment specification approach to implementation evaluation involves identifying and measuring precisely what it is about a program that is supposed to have an effect. What is going to happen in the program that is expected to make a difference? How are program goals supposed to be attained? What theory do program staff hold about what they have to do in order to accomplish the results they want? In technical terms, this means identifying independent variables that are expected to affect outcomes (the dependent variables). Treatment specification reveals the causal assumptions undergirding program activity. The treatment specification approach to implementation evaluation means measuring the degree to which specified treatments actually occur. This can be a tricky and difficult task laden with methodological and conceptual pitfalls.

> Social programs are complex undertakings. Social program evaluators look with something akin to jealousy at evaluators in agriculture who evaluate a new strain of wheat or evaluators in medicine who evaluate the effects of a new drug. . . . The same stimulus can be produced again, and other researchers can study its consequences—under the same or different conditions, with similar or different subjects, but with some assurance that they are looking at the effects of the same *thing*.
>
> Social programs are not nearly so specific. They incorporate a range of components, styles, people, and procedures . . . the content of the program,

what actually goes on, is much harder to describe. There are often marked internal variations in operation from day to day and from staff member to staff member. When you consider a program as large and amorphous as the poverty program or the model cities program, it takes a major effort to just describe and analyze the program input [Weiss, 1972b: 43].

Yet unless there is basic information about program intervention activities, the evaluator does not know to what to attribute the outcomes observed. This is the classic problem of treatment specification in social science research and, of course, takes us into the arena of trying to establish causality.

Any new program or project may be thought of as representing a theory or hypothesis in that—to use experimental terminology—the decision-maker wants to put in place a treatment expected to *cause* certain predicted effects or outcomes [Williams and Elmore, 1976: 274; italics in original].

From this perspective, one task of implementation evaluation is to identify and operationalize the program treatment.

Many evaluations, especially experimental design evaluations, equate program treatment specification with comparing programs bearing different labels. Because this practice is so prevalent—and so distorting—the next section is a critique of the labeling approach to treatment specifications, followed by a more extensive explanation of how treatments ought to be specified when this approach is used in utilization-focused evaluation.

Program Implementation and Treatment Identification: The Problem of Labeling the Black Box

This section is a simple sermon on the Pandorian folly attendant upon those who would unlock the black box of program implementation through the reification of program labels. There may be no more widespread contravention of basic research principles in evaluation than the practice of using program labels as a substitute for actual data on program implementation. Labels are not treatments.

My own suspicion is that the reification of program labels is a major source of null findings in evaluation research. Labels lead to the aggregation of effective with ineffective programs that have nothing in common except their label. A 1976 evaluation of Residential Community Corrections Programs in Minnesota is a case in point. The report was prepared by the Evaluation Unit of the Governor's Commission on Crime Prevention and Control. The evaluation report compares recidivism rates for three types of programs: (1) halfway houses, (2) PORT (Probationed Offenders Rehabilitation and Training) projects, and (3) juvenile residences.

The term "halfway house" refers to a "residential facility designed to facilitate the transition of paroled adult exoffenders who are returning to society from institutional confinement." The limitation to adults serves to distinguish halfway houses from juvenile residences which serve juveniles. The identification of paroled ex-offenders as the target population of halfway houses distinguishes the *primary* intervention stage of these projects from the PORT projects in which the primary intervention stage is probation [GCCPC, 1976: 8].

The report presents aggregated outcome data for each type of community corrections program. The evaluators take pride in not analyzing differences among individual projects: "Efforts have been made to avoid leading the reader to the conclusion that any given residential community corrections program is 'better' or 'worse' than another" (GCCPC, 1976: 4). The evaluators recognize the design problems of attributing causality to individual project outcomes, but they have no problem aggregating projects about which they have no systematic implementation data. In effect, they are comparing the outcomes of three labels: halfway houses, PORT projects, and juvenile residences. The evaluators' idea of dealing with the implementation issue is contained in one sentence: "the projects included in this study are in various stages of implementation, but all are at least in their second or third year of funding from the Commission" (GCCPC, 1976: 6). Nowhere in the several hundred pages of the report is there any systematic data presented about the actual nature of the treatment experiences provided in these programs. People go in and people come out; what happens in between is a black box of no interest to the evaluators.

The evaluation concludes that "the evidence presented in this report indicates that residential community corrections programs have had little, if any, impact on the recidivism of program clients" (GCCPC, 1976: 289). These preliminary findings resulted in a moratorium on funding of new residential community corrections, and the final report recommended maintaining that moratorium. With no attention to the meaningfulness of their analytical labels and with no treatment specifications, the evaluators passed judgment on the effectiveness of an $11 million program. Just what is it about a halfway house that leads one to expect reduced recidivism? The evaluators never tell us; nor do they document the presence of the supposed treatment.

The problem with the aggregated comparisons was that they were meaningless. In talking with staff in a few of these community corrections projects, it rapidly became clear that the separate efforts vary tremendously in treatment modality, clientele, and stage of implementation. The comparisons were based on averages, but the averages disguise important differences. There was no such thing as the average project among those settings; yet they were combined for comparative purposes. The report obscured both individual sites that are doing excellent work and those of dubious quality. It included no careful descriptions of individual residences and no data from clients, staff, or others about the actual nature of these programs. The evaluation revealed nothing about what these facilities do; it only stated that, in the aggregate, the facilities were not effective.[1]

Unfortunately, this example is not an exceptional case. One has only to read the journals in any of the disciplines to find comparisons based on aggregations of programs with similar labels, but lacking any implementation or treatment specification data. There are comparisons between "open" schools and "traditional" schools that present no data on relative openness. There are comparisons of individual therapy with group therapy where no attention is paid to the homogeneity of either category of treatment. The list could be expanded ad infinitum. Edwards et al. (1975: 142) confirm the widespread nature of the labeling approach to treatment specification:

> A common administrative fiction, especially in Washington, is that because some money associated with an administrative label (e.g., Head Start) has been spent at several places and over a period of time, that the entities spending the money are comparable from time to time and from place to place. Such assumptions can easily lead to evaluation-research disasters.

Treatment Specification: An Alternative to Labeling

A newspaper cartoon showed several federal bureaucrats assembled around a table in a conference room. The chair of the group was saying, "Of course the welfare program has a few obvious flaws . . . but if we can just think of a catchy enough name for it, it just might work!" (Dunagin, 1977).

Treatment specification for implementation evaluation purposes means getting behind labels to state what is going to happen in the program that is expected to make a difference. It is what Provus (1971: 50) called "a program design. The design tells us what we're evaluating, what we can expect to find out in the field. Our first task is to gather information on the design."

Treatment specification reveals the causal assumptions undergirding program activity. For example, one theory ungirding community corrections is that integration of criminal offenders into local communities is the best way to rehabilitate those offenders and thereby reduce recidivism. It is therefore important to gather information about the degree to which each project actually integrates offenders into the community. Halfway houses and juvenile residences can be run like small-scale prisons, completely isolated from the environment. Treatment specification tells us what to look for in each project to find out if the program's causal theory is actually being put to the test. At this point we are not dealing with the question of how to measure the relevant independent variables in a program theory, but only attempting to specify the intended treatment in nominal terms.

In 1976, the Ramsey County Community Corrections Department in Minnesota wanted to evaluate their foster group home program for juvenile offenders. In discussions with the primary information users, it became clear that there was no systematic data about what Ramsey County foster group homes were actually like. The theory undergirding the program was that juvenile offenders would be more likely to be rehabilitated if they were placed in warm, supportive, and nonauthoritarian environments where they were valued by others and could therefore learn to value themselves. The goals of the program were to make juveniles happy and capable of exercising independent judgment, and to reduce recidivism.

The evaluation question was framed in the context of both program goals and program implementation. A major priority of the evaluation effort was to describe and analyze the Ramsey County Group Home "treatment environment." This priority derived from the fact that at the beginning of the study there was no systematic knowledge about what the homes were actually like. What happens in a group home? What does a juvenile experience? What kind of "treatment" is a youth exposed to in a group home? What are the variations in group homes? Are there certain types that seem to be more successful in terms of the outcomes of (1) providing positive experiences for youth and (2) reducing recidivism?

The data analysis showed that group homes in Ramsey County could be placed along a continuum of which one end represented homes that were highly supportive and participatory and the other represented homes that were nonsupportive and authoritarian. Homes were about evenly distributed along the continua of support versus nonsupport and participatory versus authoritarian patterns; i.e., about half the juveniles experienced homes that tended to be more supportive-participatory and about half tended to be more nonsupportive-authoritarian. Juveniles from supportive-participatory group homes showed significantly lower recidivism rates than juveniles from nonsupportive-authoritarian ones ($r = .33$, $p < .01$). Variations in type of group home environment were also found to be significantly related to other outcome variables (Patton, Guthrie, et al., 1977).

In terms of treatment specification, these data demonstrated two things: (1) in about half of the county's 55 group homes, juveniles were not experiencing the kind of treatment that the program design called for; and (2) outcomes varied directly with nature and degree of program implementation. Clearly it would make no sense to conceptualize these 55 group homes as a homogeneous treatment. We found homes that were run like prisons, homes in which juveniles were physically abused. We also found homes at which young offenders were loved and treated as though they were members of the family. Aggregation of recidivism data from all of these homes into a single average rate would produce null findings in most comparisons with other aggregated programs. But when the treatment is specified and degrees of implementation are measured, it is possible to evaluate quite reasonably the program theory in terms of both feasibility and effectiveness.

Evaluating Treatment Environments: A Social Ecological Approach

Rudolf Moos has drawn on a large body of social science research on business organizations, prisons, families, schools, hospitals, factories, and a broad range of bureaucratic settings to conceptualize certain key dimensions of the environment in organizations, families, and treatment programs. The work of Moos is a model of the treatment specification programs. The group home evaluation just discussed drew heavily on it. Moos (1975: 4) explains his approach as follows:

> The social climate perspective assumes that environments have unique "personalities," just like people. Personality tests assess personality traits or needs and provide information about the characteristic ways in which people behave. Social environments can be similarly portrayed with a great deal of accuracy and detail. Some people are more supportive than others. Likewise, some social environments are more supportive than others. Some people feel a strong need to control others. Similarly, some social environments are extremely rigid, autocratic, and controlling. Order, clarity, and structure are important to many people. Correspondingly, many social environments strongly emphasize order, clarity, and control.

Different social scientists use different terms to describe these dimensions of the environment, but there are many similarities in what they are describing (e.g., Hage and Aiken, 1970; Burns and Stalker, 1961; Anderson and Walberg, 1968). Below are some of the dimensions that are used to specify and distinguish different treatment environments:

Formal	Informal
Centralized	Decentralized
Authoritarian	Participatory (Democratic)
Divisive	Cohesive
Standardized	Individualized
Hierarchical	Egalitarian
Controlled	Expressive
Partitioned	Integrated
Independent Parts	Interdependent Parts
Routinized	Individualized

Isolated	Community-Oriented
Low Communications	High Communications

It is important to understand that *these terms are meant to be descriptive* rather than pejorative, prejudicial, or prescriptive. These terms or dimensions are ways of thinking about the differences among organizations, families, and treatment programs. Under certain conditions one type of organization or program environment may be desirable, while under other circumstances a different type may be desirable.

Moos (1974, 1975, 1979) has taken a comprehensive approach in conceptualizing and operationalizing the treatment environment for purposes of program evaluation. Moos calls his work "a social ecological approach" to evaluation research. He has developed concepts and scales to describe and measure variations in treatment environments for mental health institutions, correctional institutions, family environments, military units, and classrooms. He is working toward a taxonomy of social environments and has already developed nine "social climate scales" in his work at the Social Ecology Laboratory and Psychiatry Research Training Program at Stanford University.

Moos has related his treatment environment variables to a variety of program outcome variables in criminal justice, education, and health settings, with statistically significant and meaningful results. His work takes on added significance because deinstitutionalization is currently the dominant theoretical direction in social intervention. He has developed a set of variables in a well-constructed theoretical framework to evaluate the implementation and effects of deinstitutionalization.

Moos's work constitutes an exemplary model of the contribution evaluation research can make to social science theory. However, from a utilization-focused perspective any theoretical model, including the sophisticated and comprehensive social ecological approach, must be adapted to the specific evaluation needs of identified decision makers and information users. Moos's variables ought not be adopted wholesale; careful consideration must be given to their relevance in representing the nascent theoretical notions of primary intended evaluation information users. In the Ramsey County foster group home evaluation described in the previous section, we did just that. Once evaluation task force members identified the relevant treatment dimensions as "warmth, support, involvement, and participatory family decision making," we showed them some of Moos's factors to see if they were representative and descriptive of the program's intervention theory. With additions, deletions, and adaptations, the Moos conceptual and operational scheme proved very helpful. *But the theoretical formulation process began with identified evaluation task force decision makers—not with a scholarly search of the literature.* The theory tested was that held by primary intended information users and stakeholders.

Evaluators may want to test their own particular theories based on what their disciplinary literature specifies as important independent variables. Where resources are adequate and the design can be managed, the evaluators may prevail upon decision makers to include tests of those theories the evaluators hold dear. But first priority goes to providing intended users with information about the degree to which their own implementation ideals and treatment specifications have actually been realized in program operations. Causal models are often forced on program staff when they bear no similarity to the models on which that staff bases its program activities. The evaluators' research interests are secondary to the information needs of primary intended information users in utilization-focused evaluation.

Implementation Overview: Focusing the Evaluation on Questions of Program Implementation

There is considerable evidence that failure at the implementation stage is a major reason for the human services shortfall and ineffective social programs. Evaluations that have ignored implementation issues (and such evaluations are abundant) may have asked the wrong questions. Thus, to avoid gathering useless or erroneous information *it is important to understand the option of focusing the evaluation on questions of program implementation*. This can be a major element in utilization-focused evaluation, particularly in comprehensive evaluations that also include relating relative implementation to degree of program goals attainment. Evaluation design consists in deciding what kinds of information should be collected for what purposes to answer what questions (Brinkerhoff et al., 1983: 77-88). Successful implementation typically involves a process of adapting the ideal to local conditions, organizational dynamics, and programmatic uncertainties. Utilization-focused evaluators will work with primary information users to determine how far from and in what ways the program can deviate from the ideal plan while still meeting fundamental implementation criteria.

Once the evaluator has determined that the program in question actually exists (the first implementation issue in an evaluation), there are several evaluation options with respect to studying implementation: (1) effort evaluation, (2) ongoing program monitoring, (3) process evaluation, (4) components evaluation, and (5) the treatment specification approach.

Depending on the nature of the issues involved and the information needed, any one, two, or all five of the approaches to implementation evaluation might be employed. The point is that without information about actual program operations, decision makers are extremely limited in their ability to interpret performance data or to improve program functioning. Effort evaluations, ongoing program monitoring, component evaluation, the treatment specification approach, and process evaluations answer different questions and focus on different aspects of program implementation. The key is to match the type(s) of evaluation to the information needs of specific stakeholders and intended information users. One of the decision makers we interviewed in our utilization study was emphatic on this point:

> Different types of evaluations are appropriate and useful at different times. . . . HEW tends to talk about evaluation as if it's a single thing. Whereas the important thing is a better understanding within HEW that there are different types of evaluation. That it should not be used as EVALUATION! Using the word generically, as a generic word, is harmful. . . . We ought to stop using evaluation as if it's a single homogenous thing [DM111: 29].

Implementation evaluation is one of the options from which stakeholders and intended evaluation users can choose as the evaluator works with them to focus evaluation questions. Not all final evaluation designs will include implementation data. Variations in implementation may already be known to decision makers, or information other than implementation may be more important, relevant, and useful given the uncertainties they face. Thus, whether implementation evaluation is part of the final design depends on the particular evaluation questions that emerge as the focus of study. What is crucial is that during the process of framing the evaluation questions the issue of implementation analysis is raised. Evaluators have a responsibility in their active-reactive-adaptive interactions with stakeholders to explore evaluation options so that they can decide what information is most useful in the particular circumstances at hand.

NOTE

1. I am indebted to two colleagues for their critiques of this evaluation: Malcolm Bush, Urban Affairs and Education, Northwestern University, and Thomas Dewar, School of Public Affairs, University of Minnesota.

Chapter 7

THE PROGRAM'S THEORY OF ACTION:

CONCEPTUALIZING CAUSAL LINKAGES

That evil is half-cured whose cause we know.

—Shakespeare

Mountaintop Inferences

The difficulty of making causal inferences has been thoroughly documented by philosophers of science (e.g., Bunge, 1959; Nagel, 1961). When reading on the subject as a graduate student, I marveled at the multitude of mathematical and logical proofs necessary to demonstrate that the world is a complex place. I offer instead a simple Sufi story to establish a framework for this chapter's discussion of the relationship between means and ends.

The incomparable Mulla Nasrudin was visited by a would-be disciple. The man, after many vicissitudes, arrived at the hut on the mountain where the Mulla was sitting. Knowing that every single action of the illuminated Sufi was meaningful, the newcomer asked Nasrudin why he was blowing on his hands. "To warm myself in the cold, of course," Nasrudin replied.

Shortly afterward, Nasrudin poured out two bowls of soup, and blew on his own. "Why are you doing that, Master?" asked the disciple. "To cool it, of course," said the teacher.

At that point the disciple left Nasrudin, unable to trust any longer a man who used the same process to cause different effects—heat and cold (adapted from Shah, 1964: 79-80).

Reflections on Causality in Evaluation

In some cases, different programs use divergent processes to arrive at the same outcome; in others, various programs use similar means to achieve different outcomes. Sometimes competing treatments aimed at the same goal operate side by side in a single program. The task of sorting out causal linkages is seldom an easy one.

Stated quite simply, the causal question in evaluation research is this: Does the implemented program lead to the desired outcomes? However, in previous chapters it has become clear that delineating either program implementation or program outcomes is a complex task, and establishing the linkages between implementation and outcomes is even more difficult. To what extent and in what ways do the process, activities, and treatments of the program cause or effect the behaviors, attitudes, skills, knowledge, and feelings of the target population? One need know very little about research to know that it is not possible to establish causality in any final and absolute sense when dealing with the complexities of real programs in which treatments and outcomes are never quite pure, single, and uncontaminated. We cannot provide definitive answers but we can arrive at some reasonable estimation of the likelihood that particular activities have had an effect.

> One admits that causal thinking belongs completely on the theoretical level and that causal laws can never be demonstrated empirically. But this does not mean that it is not helpful to *think* causally and to develop causal models that have implications that are indirectly testable [Blalock, 1964: 6].

Evaluation data are never completely clear-cut and absolute; studies are always flawed in some way, and there are always questions of reliability and validity. Error-free instruments do not and cannot exist in the measurement of complex human, social, behavioral, and psychological phenomena. Then of what good is all this?

Evaluation is only of use if one believes that some systematic information is better than none. Evaluation has meaning only if one believes that a rough idea of the relationship between program activities and outcomes is preferable to relying entirely upon hope and good intentions. Evaluation does not provide final answers, but *it can provide direction*. Thus, evaluation does not lead to final statements about causal linkages, but can reduce uncertainty about such linkages. Therein lies its potential utility.

Elucidating and Testing the Program's Theory of Action

To venture into the arena of causality is to undertake the task of theory construction (Blalock, 1964: 5). This chapter suggests some simple conceptual approaches to theory construction in evaluation aimed at elucidating and testing the program's theory of action. Utilization-focused evaluation involves quite a different approach to theory from that usually taken in either social science or evaluation research.

Evaluation often ignores theoretical issues altogether. Evaluators are accused of being technicians who simply collect data without regard to the theoretical relevance of possible empirical generalizations. Certainly pure outcomes evaluations are nontheoretical. Moreover, in many cases what decision makers need and want is quite specific data relevant to narrow, technical issues that are helpful in monitoring or fine-tuning program operations.

However, evaluation is by no means inherently nontheoretical. It can be theoretical in the usual scientific sense of deductive, logical systems constructed to model causal linkages among general variables (see Hage, 1972). Specific program operations are then modeled after the theory and monitored to test it. The deductive approach usually draws on dominant theoretical traditions in specific scholarly disciplines to construct models of the relationship between program treatments and outcomes. Many illustrations of this approach to evaluation as a theory-testing exercise are chronicled in Rossi and Freeman (1982) and Boruch et al. (1978).

By way of contrast to logical, deductive theory construction, a utilization-focused approach to theory construction is inductive, pragmatic, and highly concrete. *The evaluator's task is to delineate and test the theory or theories held by primary intended evaluation information users. The causal model to be tested is the causal model upon which program activities are based.* First priority goes to providing primary stakeholders with information about the degree to which their own implementation ideals and treatment specifications actually achieve the desired outcomes through program operations. The evaluator's own theories and academic traditions can be helpful in clarifying the program's theory of action, but reality-testing the decision makers' theory of programmatic action is primary; the evaluator's scholarly interests are secondary.

The importance of understanding the program's theory of action as perceived by key stakeholders is explained in part by basic insights from the sociology of knowledge and work on "the social construction of reality" (Berger and Luckmann, 1967; Schutz, 1967; Holzner and Marx, 1979). This work is built on the observation of W. I. Thomas that *situations that are perceived and experienced as real are real in their consequences for what people do.* Elucidating and testing stakeholders' theory of action (i.e., their perceptions about what the program does to produce desired outcomes) will have consequences for what those stakeholders think and do. Utilization-focused evaluation challenges decision makers, program staff, and funders to empirically test their theories of programmatic action.

The inductive approach to user-oriented evaluation theory construction presented here is simple and straightforward. It is neither elegant nor esoteric. Its purposes are twofold: (1) to fill in the conceptual gaps in formulation of program action and aims so as to (2) identify information gaps that can be used to focus relevant evaluation questions.

What Is a Program's Theory of Action?
A Means-Ends Hierarchical Chain of Objectives

Outcomes evaluations generally focus on goal attainment (Chapter 5) whereas implementation evaluations focus on the means of attaining goals (Chapter 6). Another strategy in considering alternative evaluation questions is the linking together of means and ends. The construction of a means-ends hierarchy for a program constitutes a comprehensive description of the program's theory of action. The notion of a programmatic theory of action is derived from James Thompson's (1967: 2) conceptualization of organizational action as "rooted on the one hand in desired outcomes and on the other hand in beliefs about cause/effect relationships." Understanding and delineating the program's theory of action can be an extremely important conceptual technique for assisting primary stakeholders in focusing meaningful evaluation questions.

Suchman recommended beginning the construction of a "chain of objectives" by trichotomizing objectives into immediate, intermediate, and ultimate goals. The linkages between these levels actually comprise a continuous series of actions wherein immediate objectives logically precede intermediate goals and therefore must be accomplished before higher-level objectives. Taken together, the program's goals constitute a chain. Any given objective in the chain is the outcome of the successful attainment of the preceding objective and, in turn, is a precondition to attainment of the next higher objective.

> Immediate goals refer to the results of the specific act with which one is momentarily concerned, such as the formation of an obesity club; the intermediate goals push ahead toward the accomplishment of the specific act, such as the actual reduction in weight of club members; the ultimate goal then examines the effect of achieving the intermediate goal upon the health status of the members, such as reduction in the incidence of heart disease [Suchman, 1967: 51-52].

In practice, the chain of objectives for a program has more than three links. In Chapter 5, the Minnesota Comprehensive Epilepsy Program mission statement, goals, and objectives were described. This three-tier division was useful to get an overview of the program as an initial step in identifying what evaluation information would be most useful. Once that initial focus is selected, a more detailed, multitiered chain of objectives can be constructed. For example, the epilepsy program had educational, research, treatment, and administrative goals. Once the research goal was selected by decision makers as most in need of evaluation, a more thorough chain of objectives was constructed. Table 7.1 illustrates the difference between the initial three-tier conceptualization and the more refined multitier chain of objectives. To have constructed such a detailed, multitier chain of objectives for all seven epilepsy goals would have taken a great deal of time and effort. By using the simple, three-tier approach initially, it was possible to then focus on those goal areas in which a full chain of objectives or hierarchy of means and ends were to be developed.

The full chain of objectives constitutes a program's theory of action. Any particular paired linkage in the theory of action, however, represents an outcome and its means of implementation. As one constructs a hierarchical chain of objectives, it becomes clear that there is only a relative distinction between ends and means: "Any end or goal can be seen as a means to another goal, [and] one is free to enter the 'hierarchy of means and ends' at any point" (Perrow, 1968: 307). *In utilization-focused evaluation, the decision about where to enter the means-ends hierarchy is made on the basis of what information would be most useful to the primary intended evaluation users.*

Identifying Critical Validity Assumptions

The purpose of thoroughly delineating a program's theory of action is to assist stakeholders in making explicit their assumptions about the linkages and activities necessary for the accomplishment of ultimate outcomes. They can then focus the evaluation on those critical linkages where information is most needed at that particular point in the life of the program. This is what Suchman (1967) called making explicit the program's "validity assumptions," i.e., beliefs about cause-effect relationships. The epilepsy decision makers *assume* that publications in scholarly journals get new knowledge to medical practitioners. Validity assumptions are, however, subject to empirical tests. Does the assumed cause-effect relationship hold? For example, many intervention or social change programs are built on the validity assumptions that (1) new information leads to attitude change and (2) attitude change affects behavior. These assumptions are testable. Does new knowledge change attitudes? Do changed attitudes lead to changed behaviors?

It is not possible to test all the validity assumptions or evaluate all the means-ends linkages in a program's theory of action.

TABLE 7.1

Initial and Refined Epilepsy Program Theory of Action

Initial Conceptualization of Epilepsy Program

Program Mission: To improve the lives of people with epilepsy through research.

Program Goal: To publish high quality, scholarly research on epilepsy.

Program Objective: To conduct research on neurological, pharmacological, epidemiological, and social psychological aspects of epilepsy.

Refined Conceptualization of Epilepsy Chain of Objectives

1. Reduce epilepsy incidence and prevalence.
2. Provide better medical treatment for people with epilepsy.
3. Increase physicians' knowledge of better medical treatment for epileptics.
4. Disseminate findings to medical practitioners.
5. Publish findings in scholarly journals.
6. Produce high quality research findings on epilepsy.
7. Establish a program of high quality research on epilepsy.
8. Assemble necessary resources (personnel, finances, facilities) to establish a research program.
9. Identify and generate research designs to close knowledge gaps.
10. Identify major gaps in knowledge concerning causes and treatment of epilepsy.

Immediate → Intermediate → Ultimate

It is impossible to secure proof of the effectiveness of everything one wishes to do. Nor is it desirable. Operating personnel must proceed on the basis of the best available knowledge at the time. The question is one of how freely such validity assumptions are made and how much is at stake [Suchman, 1967: 43].

In a utilization-focused evaluation, the evaluator works with the primary intended information users to identify the critical validity assumptions where reduction of uncertainty about causal linkages could make the most difference.

Delineating a full set of validity assumptions in constructing a program's theory of action can reveal both major information gaps and major conceptual gaps in program planning. Leonard Rutman (1980) has argued that unless the program plan makes conceptual sense and there is substantial reason to believe in its validity assumptions, there is no reason to waste resources on an evaluation; in brief, he considered a reasonably defensible theory of actions, or set of validity assumptions, to be one of the criteria for establishing the "evaluability" of a program. Unless a program meets minimal evaluability criteria, it cannot usefully be evaluated (Wholey, 1979; Rutman, 1984).

The problem with relying on the evaluator's assessment of the reasonableness of programmatic validity assumptions is that what the evaluator believes is less important that what program staff and decision makers believe. The usefulness of evaluation process is in helping program staff and decision makers delineate and test their validity assumptions. Evaluation is a mechanism for *reality-testing* stakeholder assumptions. An evaluator can have greater impact by helping program staff and decision makers empirically test their causal hypotheses than by telling them such causal hypotheses are nonsense. Not only does the wheel have to be recreated from time to time, its efficacy has to be restudied and reevaluated to demonstrate its usefulness. Likewise, the evaluator's *certain belief* that square wheels are less efficacious than round ones may have little impact on those who believe that square wheels are effective. The evaluator's task is to delineate the belief in the square wheel and then to assist the believers in designing an evaluation that will permit them to *test for themselves* their own perceptions and hypotheses. This does not mean that the evaluator ought not to suggest and test alternative hypotheses, but first priority goes to evaluation of validity assumptions in the theory of actions held by primary intended information users.

Filling in the Conceptual Gaps

Helping stakeholders identify conceptual gaps in the theory of action is quite different from telling them that their validity assumptions are unreasonable, though the evaluator will want to sensitively facilitate examination of the reasonableness of linkages in the stated theory of action. The means-ends relationships delineated ought to be reasonable in the sense that actions are ignored.

The difference between passing judgment on the viability or validity of a theory of action and filling in the gaps may be illustrated as follows. Rutman (1977) has argued that programs to use prison guards as counselors to inmates ought never have been evaluated (e.g., Ward et al., 1971) because, on the face of it, the idea is nonsense. Why would anyone ever believe that such a program could work? But clearly, whether they should have or not, many people did believe that the program would work. The evaluator's task is to fill in the conceptual gaps in this theory of action so that critical evaluative information needs can be identified. For example, are there initial selection processes and training programs for guards? Are guards supposed to be changed during such training? The first critical evaluation issue may be whether prison guards can be trained to exhibit desired counselor attitudes and behaviors. The trainability of prison guards in human relations skills can be evaluated without even implementing the full contact program.

Filling in the gaps in the program's theory of action goes to the heart of the implementation question. What series of activities must take place before there is reason to even hope that impact could be demonstrated? If intervening activities and objectives will not be or cannot be implemented, then evaluation of ultimate outcomes is not very useful.

> There are only two ways one can move up the scale of objectives in an evaluation: (a) by proving the intervening assumptions through research, that is, changing an assumption to a fact, or (b) by assuming their validity without full research proof. When the former is possible, we can then interpret our success in meeting a lower-level objective as automatic progress toward a higher one. . . .
>
> When an assumption cannot be proved . . . we go forward at our peril. To a great extent the ultimate worth of evaluation for public service programs will depend upon research proof of the validity of assumptions involved in the establishment of key objectives [Suchman, 1967: 57].

The National Clean Air Act is a good example of legislation in which policy and planning activity have focused only on initial objectives and ultimate goals, with little delineation of crucial intervening objectives. The ultimate goal is cleaner air; the target of the legislation is a handful of engines that each auto manufacturer tests before going to mass production. Authorization for mass production is given if these prototypes operate under carefully controlled conditions for 50,000 miles. Cars that fail pollution tests as they leave the assembly line are not withheld from dealers. Cars on the road are not inspected to make sure that pollution control equipment is still in place and functioning properly. Prototypes are tested for 50,000 miles, but most cars are eventually used for 100,000 miles, with pollution in older cars being much worse than that in new ones. In short, there are many intervening steps between testing prototype automobiles for pollution control compliance and increasing air quality. As Bruce Ackerman (1977: 4) explains,

> Over a period of time the manufacturers will build cleaner and cleaner prototypes. Billions of dollars will be spent on the assembly line to build devices that *look* like these prototypes. But until Congress, the EPA and the states require regular inspections of all cars on the road, very little will come of all this glittering machinery.
>
> Indeed, we could save billions if we contented ourselves with dirtier prototypes, but insisted on cleaner cars. . . . Congressmen themselves woefully exaggerate the importance of their votes for cleaner prototypes. They simply have no idea of the distance between prototype and reality. They somehow imagine that the hard job is technological innovation and that the easy job is human implementation.

Delineating the full theory of action involves identifying both major conceptual gaps and major information gaps. The conceptual gaps are filled by logic, discussion, and policy analysis. The information gaps are filled by evaluation research.

Filling in the Information Gaps: The New School Case

Once the conceptual gaps in the theory of action are delineated, the issue of evaluation focus remains. Determining the evaluation question is not simply a process of mechanically beginning by evaluating lower order validity assumptions and then moving up the hierarchy. Not all linkages in the hierarchy are amenable to testing; different validity assumptions require different resources for evaluation; data-gathering strategies vary for different objectives. All of these considerations are important, but most important is determining what information would be most useful at a particular point in time. This means selecting what Murphy calls "targets of opportunity" in which additional information could make a difference to the direction of incremental, problem-oriented program decision making:

> In selecting problems for analysis, targets of opportunity need to be identified, with political considerations specifically built into final choices. Planning activity in a certain area might be opportune because of expiring legislation, a hot political issue, a breakdown in standard operation procedures, or new research findings. At any time, certain policies are more susceptible to change than others [Murphy, 1976: 98].

Targets of opportunity are simply those evaluation questions about which primary information users care. Having information about and answers to those select questions can make a difference in what is done in the program. Those validity assumptions in a theory of action about which there is already a high degree of certainty are not good targets of opportunity; those program activities to which decision makers are fully committed for political, moral, or other value reasons are likely to be poor targets of opportunity; but those validity assumptions about which there is uncertainty and for which reduction in that uncertainty is a matter of concern to decision makers make excellent targets of opportunity. An example from an evaluation of the New School of Behavioral Studies in Education, University of North Dakota, illustrates this.

The New School of Behavioral Studies in Education was established as a result of a statewide study of education conducted between 1965 and 1967. The New School was to provide leadership in educational innovations with an emphasis on individualized instruction, better teacher-pupil relationships, an interdisciplinary approach, and better use of a wide range of learning resources (Statewide Study, 1967: 11-15). In 1970, the New School gained national recognition when Charles Silberman described the North

Dakota Experiment as a program that was resolving the "crisis in the class-room" in favor of open education.

The New School established a master's degree teaching intern program in which interns replaced teachers without degrees so that the latter could return to the university to complete their baccalaureates. The cooperating school districts released those teachers without degrees who volunteered to return to college and accepted the master's degree interns in their place. Over four years the New School placed 293 interns in 48 school districts and 75 elementary schools, both public and parochial. The school districts that cooperated with the New School in the intern program contained nearly one-third of the state's elementary school children.

A task force of teachers, professors, students, parents, and administrators was formed by the dean of the New School to evaluate its programs. In working with that task force, I constructed the theory of action shown in Table 7.2. The objectives stated in the first column are a far cry from being clear, specific, and measurable, but they were quite adequate for discussions aimed at focusing the evaluation question. The second column lists validity assumptions underlying each linkage in the theory of action. The third column shows that there are measures that can be used to evaluate objectives at any level in the hierarchy. Ultimate objectives are not inherently more difficult to operationalize. Operationalization and measurement are separate issues to be determined after the focus of the evaluation has been decided.

When the Evaluation Task Force discussed Table 7.2, members decided they already had sufficient contact with the summer program to assess the degree to which immediate objectives were being met. They also felt they had sufficient experience to be comfortable with the validity assumption linking objectives six and seven. With regard to the ultimate objectives, the task force members said that they needed no further data at that time in order to document the outcomes of open education (objectives one and two), nor could they do much with information about the growth of the open education movement (objective three). However, a number of critical uncertainties surfaced at the level of intermediate objectives. Once students left the summer program for the one-year internships, program staff were unable to carefully and regularly monitor intern classrooms. It was not certain what variations existed in the openness of the classrooms, nor was it at all certain how local parents and administrators were reacting to intern classrooms. These were issues about which information was wanted and needed. Indeed, for a variety of personal, political, and scholarly reasons, these issues made quite good evaluation targets of opportunity. The evaluation therefore focused on three questions: (1) To what extent are summer trainees conducting open classrooms during the regular year? (2) What factors are related to variations in openness? (3) What is the relationship between variations

TABLE 7.2

The New School Theory of Action: A Hierarchy of Goals, Validity Assumption Linkages, and Evaluation Criteria

Hierarchy of Objectives	Validity Assumption Linkages	Evaluative Criteria
I. Ultimate Objectives		
1. Prepare children to live full, rich, satisfying lives as adults.		1. Longitudinal measures of child and adult satisfaction, happiness, and success.
	Children whose affective and cognitive needs are met will lead fuller, richer, more satisfying lives as adults.	
2. Meet the affective and cognitive needs of individual children in North Dakota and the United States.		2. Measures of student affective and cognitive growth in open and traditional schools.
	More open classrooms will better meet the affective and cognitive needs of individual children.	
3. Facilitate and legitimize the establishment and maintenance of a larger number of more open classrooms in North Dakota and the United States.		3. Measures of increases in the number of open classrooms in North Dakota and the United States over time and measures of the influence of the New School on the number of open classrooms.
	Parents and administrators will favor and expand open education once they have experienced it firsthand.	
II. Intermediate Objectives		
4. Provide parents and administrators in North Dakota with a firsthand demonstra-		4. Measures of parent and administrator attitudes towards New School classrooms

tion of the advantages of open education.

5. Provide teachers and teachers-in-training with a one-year classroom experience in conducting an open classroom.

6. Provide teachers and teachers-in-training with a summer program in how to conduct an open classroom.

III. Immediate Objectives

7. Provide teachers and teachers-in-training with a personalized and individualized learning experience in an open learning environment.

Teachers who have experienced the New School summer program can and will conduct open classrooms during the following intern year that are visible to local parents and administrators.

Teachers who have experienced the summer program can and will conduct open classrooms.

In order to learn about open education it is best to experience it. Teachers teach the way they are taught.

and open education, and measures and analysis of the factors affecting their attitudes.

5. Measures of the degree of openness of New School teaching intern classrooms and the factors affecting the degree of openness of these classrooms.

6. Measures of teacher attitudes, teacher understanding, and teacher competency before and after the New School Program.

7. Measures of the degree in which the New School training program is individualized and personalized, and measures of the cognitive and affective growth of teachers in the New School Program.

in classroom openness and parent/administrator reactions to intern classrooms?

At the onset, nothing precluded evaluation at any of the seven levels in the hierarchy of objectives. There was serious discussion of all levels and alternative foci. In terms of the educational literature, the issue of the outcomes of open education could be considered most important; in terms of university operations, the summer program would have been the appropriate focus; but in terms of the information needs of the primary decision makers and intended information users on the task force, evaluation of the intermediate objectives had the highest potential for generating useful information.

In order to obtain the resources necessary to conduct this evaluation, Vito Perrone, dean of the New School, had to make unusual demands on the U.S. Office of Education (OE). The outcomes of the New School teaching program were supposed to be evaluated as part of a national OE study. Perrone argued that the national study, as designed, would be useless to the New School. He talked the OE people into allowing him to spend the New School's portion of the national evaluation money on a study designed and conducted locally. The subsequent evaluation was entirely the creation of the local task force described above, and produced instruments and data that have become an integral part of the North Dakota program (see Pederson, 1977). The national study produced large volumes of numbers (with blanks entered on the lines for North Dakota) and, as far as I can tell, was of no particular use to anyone.

Developing a Theory of Action as an End in Itself: Program Design Skills

Thus far this discussion of theory of action has been aimed at demonstrating the value of this conceptual strategy as a way of focusing evaluation questions and identifying the information needs of primary stakeholders. On occasion, assisting program staff or decision makers to articulate their programmatic theory of action is an end in itself. Evaluators are called on not only to gather data but also to assist in program design. Knowing how to turn a vague discussion of the presumed linkages between program activities and expected outcomes into a formal written theory of action can be an important service to a program. This is an example of *using the evaluation process to improve a program.*

Evaluation use takes many forms, not only use of findings. The work of Palumbo et al. (1985) on the Community Corrections Act of Oregon nicely illustrates the use of evaluation to (1) conceptualize a major piece of statewide legislation from vague policies into a formal implementation-outcomes hierarchy; (2) design practical, programmatic linkages; and (3) construct a viable, street-wise theory of action.

On many occasions, then, the evaluation data collection effort may include discovering and formalizing a program's theory of action. In such cases, rather than being a means of facilitating the process of focusing evaluation questions, the theory of action can be the primary focus of analysis in the evaluation. This means moving beyond discussing the theory of action to gathering data on it. Such was the case in an evaluation I did of a wilderness program funded by the Fund for the Improvement of Postsecondary Education.

The program involved taking professionals in higher education into wilderness areas in the American Southwest to backpack, climb mountains, kayak, and river raft. The program was aimed at "personal and professional growth that would have an institutional impact." Program staff, through past and personal experiences, knew that wilderness experiences could have a powerful influence on people, but they weren't sure of either the nature or source of the influence. Their evaluation questions were these: What happens to people in this wilderness program? What seems to have the most impact? How do the wilderness experiences carry over to nonwilderness experiences in institutions of higher education? What are we really doing? Through participant observation, follow-up interviews, discussions with staff and participants, and analysis of participant writings, I helped the program staff formally conceptualize and describe their theory of action. This helped them better focus their efforts, helped participants understand their experiences, and helped communications with funders.

There are many such examples. I worked with a multifaceted home nursing program for the elderly to help them sort out which of the many, many things they did were really central to the outcomes they wanted. As a member of an evaluation task force for farming systems research, I worked with colleagues to identify the critical elements of "a farming systems approach" and place those elements in a hierarchy that constituted a developmental theory of action. In these and many other cases my primary contributions were program design and conceptualization skills that combined stakeholder discussions with observations of the program to develop a theory of action. Once developed, the theory of action served to focus future program efforts *and* future evaluation questions.

This leads us to a discussion of how evaluation questions change and develop over time as a program changes and develops. Evaluation can make an ongoing contribution to program improvement as program staff and other primary stakeholders learn to use evaluation concepts to shape and test program ideas. This ongoing, developmental role for evaluation is particularly important for internal evaluators to cultivate.

Unlike most external evaluators, who encounter a program at a particular point in time, make their contribution, and leave, perhaps never to have contact with the program again, internal evaluators are there for the long haul. They need to be particularly sensitive to how evaluation can serve different needs over time, including program design functions and accountability functions. In this way internal evaluators help build an *institutional memory* for a program or organization, a memory made up of lessons learned, ideas cultivated, and skills developed over time. This means internal evaluators especially need to understand, appreciate, and take into consideration the "social learning" (Stone, 1985) that comes from evaluation within organizations over time, a topic elaborated in the next section.

Temporal Sequences and Evaluation Questions: The Timing of Evaluation

The theory of action is at least partially temporal in conceptualization because it progresses from immediate objectives to ultimate goals. Part of the test of a theory of action is the temporal logic of the hierarchy. In causal language, it is impossible for an effect or outcome to precede its cause. It is important, however, that temporal sequence not be exaggerated. Once a program is in operation, the relationships between links in the causal hierarchy are likely to be recursive rather than unidirectional. The implementation and attainment of higher-level objectives interact with the implementation and attainment of lower-order objectives through feedback mechanisms, interactive configurations, and cybernetic systems. Program components may be conceptually distinct in the formal version of a theory of action, but in practice these analytically distinct components, links, and stages are highly interdependent and dynamically interrelated. In short, the cause-effect relationships may be mutual, multidirectional, and multilateral. Open classrooms affect the opinions and actions of parents, but parent reactions also affect the degree of openness of classrooms; classroom climate and school curriculum affect student achievement, but variations in student achievement also affect school climate and curriculum. Once again, the means-ends distinction proves to be somewhat arbitrary and simplified, but there is no avoiding such simplification: "Put simply, the basic dilemma faced in all sciences is that of how much to oversimplify reality" (Blalock, 1964: 8). The challenge is to construct simplifications that pass the dual tests of usefulness and accuracy.

Identifying the temporal sequence represented by a theory of action does not mean that evaluation automatically or necessarily begins by focusing on lower-order objectives and relationships. The focus of the evaluation may depend to some extent on the point in the developmental life of the program at which the evaluation takes place. In our study of the utilization of federal health evaluations, we asked evaluators and decision makers about this issue. For the 20 federal health evaluations in our study, 8 were done early in the life of new programs, 8 were conducted on established programs that had been operating for a number of years, and 2 evaluations occurred as part of the program's swan song (i.e., the program was already in the process of being terminated); in the 2 remaining cases, the evaluator and decision maker gave different information about the timing of the study in question. None of our respondents thought that the timing of the evaluation as an isolated factor had much direct effect on utilization. Timing does, however, become important in the context of other factors, particularly as it affects the information that decision makers need and want.

Just as there are no clear criteria about how close actual program implementation should come to ideal program plans, so there are no fixed criteria about when in the life of a program it is appropriate for an evaluation to occur. In several of our case studies, there were conflicts between evaluators and decision makers over this issue. One decision maker objected to a summative evaluation being done too soon.

What we felt—we being those of us closely associated with the program— what we felt all along was that this was too soon to try to evaluate the program. There just was not enough experience. Now would be a much better time, after the program has been in operation for 6 to 7 years [DM40: 9].

In contrast, an evaluator offered a justification for early summative evaluation.

Interviewer: Would you say that this point in the life of the program when the evaluation was done, did that have any effect on how the study was used?

Evaluator: Yeah, I think so. I think it allowed the government to get off the hook before it had established massive and well developed constituencies out there. I mean, that's a very important point. Typically when you go out to do an experimental or quasi-experimental design on a program that's been operating for a long time, you're dealing with programs that have built up a constituency. It's damn tough for the feds to cancel it. In this case I was out there from the very beginning and so we were able to kind of nip in the bud what could have been otherwise a bummer idea [EV148: 14].

When the program's complete theory of action has been formulated and is taken into consideration, it becomes possible to consider the question of evaluation timing in terms of what information is most relevant at a particular point in time. From this point of view *evaluation is an ongoing process examining different questions at different times.* As one decision maker put it,

I think the whole evaluation process is . . . a dynamic part of the planning and implementation of the program and as long as there is a program it has to continue. Like, you know, you don't do an early evaluation and say, "Fine, this confirms what we're doing. We'll just keep on doing it"—and never take another look at it. Nor do you wait until you say, "Well, we've reached the half life, or whatever radioactivity there is in the program, and now we'll do an evaluation" [DM119: 18].

Another decision maker expressed a firm belief in the importance of matching the focus of the evaluation to the stage of program development.

Now it takes three to five years to build a new, you know, a new multimillion dollar anything, let alone a health delivery institution. . . .

There are different evaluation objectives at different points in the development of a program. There are different levels of evaluation. . . . In the early years you do what I call operational and management analysis/evaluation. You know, are they operating the way they said? They said they're gonna provide services to 10,000 people in two years. . . . Well, that can be monitored in the early years.

Now, if one then wants to hypothesize that there are other impacts, well, that takes much longer. If one wants to even hypothesize health impact, which I am not prepared to do, or antipoverty impact, then that is probably a much longer range kind of thing. It may even be a generational study [DM51: 14]!

This decision maker emphasized the point that different questions emerge at different points in the life of a program, just as different questions are relevant at different levels in a program's theory of action. Tripodi et al. (1971: 40) have formalized this idea in an evaluation they call

differential evaluation which means simply that an evaluation of a social program should be geared primarily to the present stage of program development. In this context, different evaluation questions are suggested for different program stages.

They outline different questions for studying program effort, program effectiveness, and program efficiency at three different program stages— initiation, contact, and implementation.

Edwards et al. (1975: 145) warn against such attempts to routinely match a type of evaluation to a stage of evaluation. They believe the *decision problems are the same at all stages:* "Is this program a good idea? If so, what can we do to make it work as well as possible? If not, how can we devise something better, given our constraints?" They believe that the ideal evaluation technique would be aimed at assessing program merit on a continuous basis:

In short, we cannot see any hard-and-fast lines to distinguish program evaluation at different stages in its life span. We therefore squirm about language or methods that imply such distinctions, or suggest that different techniques are appropriate for different states of program evaluation [Edwards et al., 1975: 146].

This caution is useful in reminding us that *there are no automatic decisions in evaluation*. Knowing the stage of program development does not automatically define the appropriate evaluation question. It can be helpful to be aware that evaluation questions can differ greatly at different points in the life of the program and at different levels in a program's theory of action. Different information is useful to different decision makers at different times. Sensitivity to these issues increases the possibility of timing a particular type of evaluation to mesh with the decision maker's information needs and capabilities. *The right time to conduct a particular type of evaluation is when it will provide relevant and useful information to primary intended evaluation information users.*

Comparing Theories of Action

There is much emphasis in evaluation research on comparing different programs to see which is more effective or efficient. Comparisons are basic to social scientific methods. Etzioni (1964: 17) suggests that comparative frameworks are fundamental to evaluation research so that "rather than comparing existing organizations to ideals of what might be, we may assess their performances relative to one another."

Evaluations can be designed to compare the effectiveness of programs with the same goal, but if those goals do not bear the same importance in the two programs' theories of action, the comparisons may be misleading. Before undertaking a comparative evaluation, it is useful to compare programmatic theories of action in order to understand the extent to which apparently identical or similarly labeled programs are in fact comparable.

Programs with different goals simply cannot be fairly compared to each other on a unidimensional basis. Teacher centers provide an example. The U.S. Office of Education has suggested that teacher centers should be evaluated according to a single set of universal outcomes. But Sharon Feiman (1977) has shown that teacher centers throughout the country vary substantially in both program activities and goals.

Feiman described three types of teacher centers: "behavioral," "humanistic," and "developmental." Table 7.3 summarizes the variations among these types of centers.

It would seem that, at least to some extent, different teacher centers are trying to accomplish different outcomes. The three models cannot be com-

TABLE 7.3
Variations in Types of Teacher Centers

Type of Center	Primary Process of Affecting Teachers	Primary Outcomes of the Process
1. Behavioral Centers	Curriculum specialists directly and formally instruct administrators and teachers.	Adoption of comprehensive curriculum systems, methods, and packages by teachers.
2. Humanistic Centers	Informal, nondirected teacher exploration; "teachers select their own treatment."	Teachers feel supported and important; pick up concrete and practical ideas and materials for immediate use in their classroom.
3. Developmental Centers	Advisors establish warm, interpersonal, and directive relationship with teachers working with them over time.	Teachers' thinking about what they do and why they do it is changed over time; teacher personal development.

pared to determine which one is most effective because they are trying to do different things. Evaluation can help determine the extent to which each of the outcomes have been attained for each specific program, but it cannot determine which outcome is most desirable—that is a values question (see Chapter 4). Because each theory of action is different, evaluation of each program type will be different.

On the other hand, Feiman has conceptually created only three models of operational teacher centers. Each is characterized by a specific process linked to a specific set of desired outcomes. But theoretically there are nine models, one model for each combination of process and outcome. In practice there is a nearly endless variety of mixes, with some teacher centers undoubtedly using all three processes. To make comparisons, general variables that cut across program types must be identified and operationalized. Careful treatment specification (Chapter 6) linked to relevant program outcomes can provide useful evaluation information that permits meaningful comparisons of different programs' theories of action. For example, several variables derived from the work of Hage (1965), Patton (1973), and Moos (1974) might be constructed to describe and compare teacher centers.

(1) Centralization-Decentralization: the degree to which teachers share in center decision making.

(2) Formality-Informality: the degree to which the interaction between the teachers and the center staff is based on their respective status positions and standard role expectations.

(3) Individualization-Standardization: the degree to which different teachers can do different things in different ways at different speeds with different criteria for success.

(4) Diversification-Homogeneity of Learning Resources: the range of forms of learning stimuli and resources incorporated into the activities, curriculum, and experiences of the center.

(5) Peer Interaction: the degree to which the activities, curriculum, physical arrangement, and organization of the classroom contribute to peer interaction as an experiential basis for teachers to learn from.

(6) Integration-Segmentation: the degree to which the activities of the center are blended into a relatively integrated whole.

These treatment specification variables can be linked to changes in teachers' feelings, attitudes, behaviors, and skills to test both program-specific and more general theories of action, depending upon the information needs of identified decision makers and information users. While such cross-sectional analyses of different programs cannot establish firm causal relationships, multivariate techniques can facilitate the creation of quite useful and valid causal inferences for theory testing (Blalock, 1964; Rossi and Freeman, 1982).

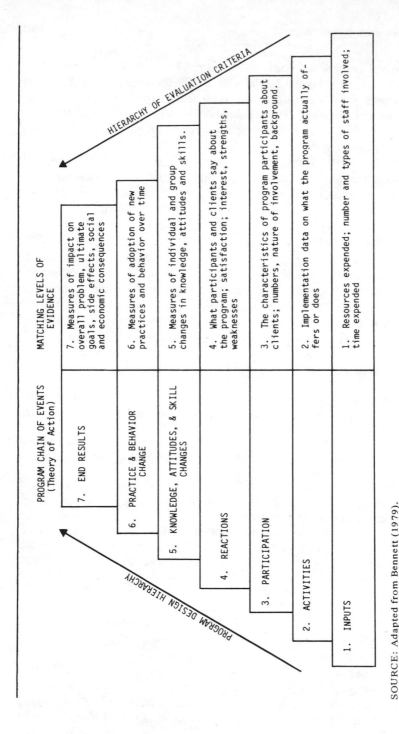

SOURCE: Adapted from Bennett (1979).

Figure 7.1 Hierarchies of Program Design and Evaluation Evidence

Matching a Theory of Action with Levels of Evidence

Claude Bennett (1979, 1982) has conceptualized a relationship between the "chain of events" in a program and the "levels of evidence" needed for evaluation. Although his work was aimed specifically at evaluation of cooperative extension programs (agriculture, home economics, and 4-H/youth), his ideas are generally applicable to any program. Figure 7.1 depicts a general adaptation of Bennett's model.

The model suggests a typical chain of program events: (1) Inputs (resources) must be assembled to get the program started; (2) activities are then undertaken to (3) get people (clients, students, program participants) involved; (4) participants react to what they experience, which leads to (5) changes in knowledge, attitudes, and skills, (6) behavior and practice changes, and, finally, (7) overall impacts, both intended and unintended.

This model explicitly and deliberately places highest value on attaining ultimate social and economic goals (e.g., increased agricultural production, increased health, and a higher quality of community life). Actual adoption of recommended practices and specific changes in client behaviors are necessary to achieve ultimate goals, and are valued over knowledge, attitude, and skill changes. People may learn about some new agricultural technique (knowledge change), believe it's a good idea (attitude change), and know how to apply it (skill change)—but the higher-level criterion is whether they actually begin *using* the new technique (i.e., change their agricultural practices). Participant reactions (satisfaction, likes, and dislikes) are lower still on the hierarchy. All of these are outcomes, but they are not equally valued outcomes. The bottom part of the hierarchy identifies means necessary for accomplishing higher-level ends; namely, in descending order, (3) getting people to participate, (2) providing program activities, and (1) organizing basic resources and inputs to get started.

Utilization-Focused Evaluation Theory of Action

Interestingly, this same hierarchy can be applied to evaluating evaluations. Figure 7.2 shows a hierarchy of evaluation accountability. In utilization-focused evaluation the purpose is to improve programs and increase the quality of decisions made. To accomplish this ultimate end a chain of events must unfold: (1) Resources are devoted to the evaluation, including stakeholder time and inputs; (2) questions are focused, the evaluation is designed, and data are collected; (3) key stakeholders and primary users are involved throughout the process; (4) they react to their involvement (we hope in positive ways); (5) the evaluation process and findings provide knowledge and new understandings, which are the basis for (6) adoption of recommendations and actual use of evaluation information (7) to improve the program and make decisions. Each step in this chain can be evaluated. Figure 7.2 shows the evaluation question that corresponds to each level in the action hierarchy.

Causal Theorizing in Perspective

Our least deed, like the young of the land crab, wends its way to the sea of cause and effect as soon as born, and makes a drop there to eternity.

—Thoreau (1838)

While causal linkages may never be established with certainty, the delineation of assumed causal relationships in a chain of hierarchical objectives can be a useful exercise in the process of focusing the evaluation question. While it may not be appropriate to construct a detailed theory of program action for every evaluation situation, it is important to understand and consider the option. Framing the evaluation question in the context of the program's theory of action is another alternative available in utilization-focused evaluation. This approach includes the construction of a means-ends hierarchy, the specification of validity assumptions linking means and ends, consideration of comparative criteria across different programs, and attention to the temporal sequence in the hierarchy of objectives so as to time a particular type of evaluation with the decision makers' information needs at a particular point in the life of a program.

Attention to theoretical issues can provide useful information to stakeholders when *their* theories are formulated and reality-tested through the evaluation process. Theory construction is also a mechanism by which evaluators can link particular program evaluation questions to larger social scientific issues for the purpose of contributing to scientific knowledge through empirical generalizations. But in a utilization-focused approach to evaluation research, the initial theoretical formulations originate with identified stakeholders and intended information users; scholarly interests are adapted to the evaluation needs of relevant decision makers, not vice versa.

It is important, then, to ask causal questions, even though evaluation data may only provide an approximate picture of what is really happening. It is also important to interpret the results with prudence and care. Consider the wisdom of Buddhism:

One day an old man approached Zen master Hyakujo. The old man said, "I am not a human being. In ancient times I lived on this mountain. A student of

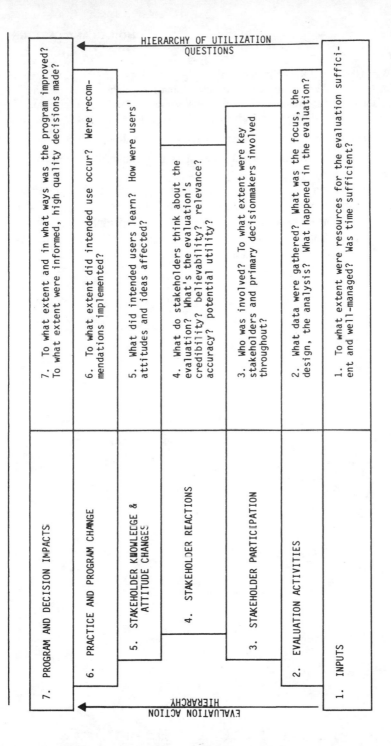

Figure 7.2 Hierarchy of Evaluation Accountability: Evaluating Evaluation

the Way asked me if the enlightened were still affected by causality. I replied saying that they were not affected. Because of that I was degraded to lead the life of a wild fox for five hundred years. I now request you to answer one thing for me. Are the enlightened still affected by causality?"

Master Hyakujo replied, "They are not deluded by causality."

At that the old man was enlightened [adapted from Hoffman, 1975: 138].

Causal evaluation questions can be enlightening; they can also lead to delusions. Unfortunately, there is no clear way of telling the difference. It is nevertheless important to consider causal questions, especially when others are not doing so. But never force the issue—you might be degraded to lead the life of a wild fox for five hundred years!

PART III

APPROPRIATE METHODS

Blow Hard Evaluation

This is the story of three little pigs who built three little houses for protection from the BIG BAD WOLF.

The first pig worked without a plan, building the simplest and easiest structure possible with whatever materials happened to be laying around, mostly straw and sticks.

When the BIG BAD WOLF appeared, he had scarcely to huff and puff to blow the house down, whereupon the first pig ran for shelter and protection to the house of the second pig.

The house of the second pig was prefabricated in a most rigorous fashion with highly reliable materials. Architects and engineers applied the latest techniques and most valid methods to the design and construction of these standardized, prefabricated models. The second pig had a high degree of confidence that his house could withstand any attack.

The BIG BAD WOLF followed the first pig to the house of the second pig and commanded, "Come out! Come out! Or by the hair on my chinny-chin-chin, I'll huff and I'll puff and I'll blow your house down."

The second pig laughed a scornful reply: "Huff and puff all you want. You'll find no weaknesses in this house, for it was designed by experts using the latest and best scientific methods guaranteed not to fall apart under the most strenuous huffing and puffing." So the BIG BAD WOLF huffed and puffed, and he huffed and puffed some more, but the structure was solid, and gave not an inch.

In catching his breath for a final huffing and puffing, the BIG BAD WOLF noticed that the house, although strong and well built, was simply sitting on top of the ground.

There was no foundation at all. The house had been purchased and set down on the local site with no attention to establishing a firm connecting foundation that would anchor the house in its setting. As different settings require very different site preparation with appropriately matched foundations, the prefabricated kit came with no instructions about how to prepare a local foundation. Understanding all this in an instant, the sly wolf ceased his huffing and puffing. Instead, he confidently reached down, got a strong hold on the underside of the house, lifted, and tipped it over. The second pig was shocked to find himself uncovered and vulnerable. He would have been easy prey for the BIG BAD WOLF had not the first pig, being more wary and therefore more alert, dashed out from under the house pulling his flabbergasted brother with him. Together they sprinted to the house of the third pig, crying "wee wee wee" all the way there.

The house of the third pig was the source of some controversy in the local pig community. It was unlike any other house. It was constructed of a hodgepodge of local materials and a few things borrowed from elsewhere. It incorporated some of the ideas seen in the prefabricated houses designed by experts, but those ideas had been altered to fit local conditions and the special interests and needs of the third pig. The house was built on a strong foundation, well anchored in its setting and carefully adapted to the specific conditions of the spot on which the house was built. Although the house was sometimes the object of ridicule because it was unique and different, it was also the object of envy and praise, for it was evident to all that it fit quite beautifully and remarkably in that precise location.

The BIG BAD WOLF approached the house of the third pig confidently. He huffed and puffed his best huffs and puffs. The house gave a little under these strenuous forces, but it did not break. Flexibility was part of its design, so it could sway and give under adverse and changed conditions without breaking and falling apart. Being firmly anchored in a solid foundation, it would not tip over. The BIG BAD WOLF soon knew he would have no pork chops for dinner that night.

Following the defeat of the BIG BAD WOLF, the third pig found his two brother pigs suddenly very interested in how to build big houses uniquely adapted to and firmly grounded in a specific location, structures able to withstand the onslaughts of the most persistent blowhards. They opened a consulting firm to help other pigs. The firm was called "Wee wee wee, all the way home."

—From Halcolm's
Evaluation Fairy Tales

Chapter 8

THE METHODOLOGY DRAGON:
THE PARADIGMS DEBATE IN PERSPECTIVE

It is easier to select a method for madness than a single best method for evaluation, though attempting the latter is an excellent way of achieving the former.

—Halcolm

What Does a Dragon Look Like?

A children's story tells of a boy named Han who was the poor gatesweeper
of an ancient Chinese city. One day a messenger brought word that the wild
horsemen of the north were coming to destroy the city. The Mandarin called
together his councillors: the leader of the merchants, the captain of the army,
the wisest of the wise men, and the chief of the workmen. The council decided that the only hope of saving the city was to pray to the Great Cloud
Dragon for help. The next morning a small fat man arrived at the gate where
the boy Han was sweeping. The old man had a long white beard, a shiny bald
head, and he leaned on a long staff. He told Han that he was the Great Cloud
Dragon come to save the city.

Han was quite surprised. "You don't look like a dragon," he said.

"How do you know?" asked the little old man. "Have you ever seen one?"

"No, I guess not. I will take you to the Mandarin, Honorable Dragon."

The Mandarin was busy meeting with his councillors. He was not happy about being disturbed. When Han humbly introduced the little old man as the Great Cloud Dragon, the Mandarin became very angry. "Don't be ridiculous. He's a fat man who is tracking dirt on my fine carpets. Away with him."

"I have come to help you," said the little fat man. "But if you want a dragon to help you, you must treat him with courtesy. I have come a long way. Give me something to eat and something to drink and speak to me politely, and I will save the city."

The Mandarin was unimpressed. "Everybody knows what dragons look like. They are proud lords of the sky. They wear gold and purple silk. They look like Mandarins."

"This is no dragon," said the captain of the army. "Everyone knows that dragons are fierce and brave, like warriors. The sight of them is like the sound of trumpets. They look like captains of the army."

"Nonsense!" interrupted the leader of the merchants. "Dragons are rich and splendid. They are as comfortable as a pocketful of money. They look like merchants. Everyone knows that."

"You are all wrong," said the chief of the workmen. "Everyone knows that dragons are strong and tough. Nothing is too hard for them to do. They look like workmen."

It remained only for the wisest of the wise men to speak. "The one thing that is known—and indeed I can show it to you in 47 books—is that dragons are the wisest of all creatures. Therefore they must look like wise men."

At that moment screams and yells were heard outside. On the horizon the dark mass of wild horsemen could be seen. The councillors pushed the little old man aside and ran away to hide.

"Well," said Han. "I don't think we have much time. The enemy will be here soon. I don't know whether you are a dragon or not, but if you are hungry and thirsty, please do me the honor of coming into my humble house."

The old man ate and drank, then he said to Han, "For your sake I will save the city." The wild horsemen were nearly to the gate. The little man blew a great breath. A huge storm arose which caught the horsemen and drove them away. As the storm subsided the little fat man said to Han, "Now I will show you what a dragon looks like." As he sprang up into the air his changed form filled the sky. According to the story, "He grew taller than the tallest tree, greater than the greatest tower. He was the color of sunset shining through rain. Scales covered him, scattering light. His claws and teeth glittered like diamonds. His eyes were noble like those of a proud horse. He was more beautiful and more frightening than anything Han had ever seen. He flew high, roaring, and vanished into the deep sky."

Han went through the city telling the hiding people that the dragon had saved them. The Mandarin rewarded Han and named him the Honorable Defender of the city. "We are saved," said the Mandarin. "But best of all we know what a dragon looks like. He looks like a small, fat, bald old man" (adapted from Williams, 1976).

Everyone Knows What a Dragon Looks Like

Science begins with definitions and classification systems. The awesome complexity of reality is simplified and ordered by defining and classifying selected elements within that reality. What we sometimes lose sight of is that *all scientific systems of definition and classification are perceptual, artificial, and arbitrary. Whose definitions prevail at any given time and place is a matter of politics, persuasion, and preference.* It is in the nature of things that there can never be an absolute definition of what a dragon looks like.

Every stage in evaluation research involves the processes of definition and classification. One first has to decide what a decision maker looks like. Then we classify goals according to whether they are vague or clear, general or specific, measurable or immune to measurement. Program implementation is defined and programs are classified by type, size, mission, evaluability, and effectiveness. Variables are defined to describe treatment environments and program interventions. We even classify types of evaluations: formative and summative; goal-free and goal-based outcomes evaluation and implementation evaluation; effort, process, and treatment specification approaches. In *Creative Evaluation* (Patton, 1981), I identified 132 different types of evaluation. Finally, we come to the methodological issues. For program people, methodology is the not-so-friendly dragon of measurement and design, breathing fire and numbers, questionnaires and equations.

Occasionally I am successful in convincing students or colleagues that evaluation questions ought to stem from the information needs of primary stakeholders and intended evaluation users. They will agree that, to be useful, evaluations ought to assess decision makers' goals, examine their ideals of program implementation, and test their theories of program action. During the conceptual phase of the evaluation, these students and colleagues are sympathetic to the importance of a consultative role for evaluators working with stakeholders and intended users to arrive at crucial definitions of the problem. Where we part company is in the role to be played by stakeholders in making measurement and design decisions. "The evaluator is nothing," they argue, "if not an expert in methods and statistics. Clearly social scientists ought to be left with full responsibility for operationalizing program goals and determining data collection procedures." Edwards and Guttentag (1975: 456) are prime examples of this perspective: "The decisionmakers' values determine on what variables data should be gathered. The researcher then decides how to collect the data." But utilization-focused evaluation takes a different approach.

Making Data Collection Decisions

There can be no acting or doing of any kind, till it be recognized that there is a thing to be done; the thing once recognized, doing in a thousand shapes becomes possible.

—Thomas Carlyle

Once primary intended users are identified and the focus of the evaluation is determined, methods decisions must be made. This is the third step in utilization-focused evaluation. However, the criteria applied and the processes used for making methods decisions in utilization-focused evaluation are significantly different from traditional evaluation approaches. This chapter and the next will explore the consequences for evaluation methods of being utilization-focused.

There are a variety of methodological options to consider. I have never attempted to list a thousand such options for any evaluation a la Thomas Carlyle, but I've no doubt it could be done. I would certainly never try the patience of primary stakeholders with a thousand options, but I do expect to work with them to consider the strengths and weaknesses of a more delimited set of methodological possibilities.

In utilization-focused evaluation, the researcher has no intrinsic rights to unilaterally make critical design and data collection decisions. Quite the contrary; it is crucial that intended users participate in the making of measurement and methods decisions so that they understand the strengths and weaknesses of the data—and so that they believe in the data. Utilization potential can be severely diminished if stakeholders are excluded at the critical operationalization stage when making data choices.

The primary focus in making evaluation methods decisions should be on getting the best possible data to adequately answer primary stakeholders' evaluation questions given available resources and time. The emphasis is on *appropriateness and credibility*—measures, samples, and comparisons that are appropriate and credible to address key evaluation issues. The Joint Committee's (1981) evaluation standards are quite clear on this point:

Utility Standard on Information Scope and Selection: Information collected should be of such scope and selected in such ways as to address pertinent questions about the object of the evaluation and be responsive to the needs and interests of specified audiences.

A consensus has gradually emerged in the professional practice of evaluation that evaluators need to know a variety of methodological approaches in order to be flexible and responsive in matching research methods to the nuances of particular evaluation questions and the idiosyncracies of specific stakeholder needs (Young and Comtois, 1979). Evaluators are encouraged to use multiple methods to overcome the weaknesses of any one particular approach (Reichardt and Cook, 1979).

The problem is that this ideal of evaluators being situationally responsive, methodologically flexible, and sophisticated in using a variety of methods runs headlong into the realities of the evaluation world. Those realities include limited resources, political considerations of expediency, and the narrowness of disciplinary training available to most evaluators—training that imbues them with varying degrees of methodological prejudice.

The problem of methodological prejudice has been a major concern in evaluation. Much of that concern has centered on a debate about the relative merits of qualitative and quantitative methods. This debate had its origins in competing traditions within the social sciences, so as evaluation research emerged as a special application of social science methods, the debate carried over into evaluation. The first edition of this book entered full force into the debate as it raged at that time. Since then, the opposing positions have been considerably moderated as a consensus has emerged that the real issues are methodological flexibility and appropriateness—not one approach as absolutely right or wrong, better or worse across the board. This chapter reviews that debate by way of elucidating some of the methodological choices available to evaluators.

The concerns that sparked the debate remain relevant because much social science training is still quite narrow. Most social scientists are most comfortable with those methods that are central to their primary discipline. They have been trained to study the world in a particular way. That particular way of viewing the world becomes so second nature that it takes on the characteristics of a world view or a paradigm. The paradigms debate has been a prominent and persistent topic in the evaluation literature (Rust, 1977; Cronbach, 1975, 1982; Reichardt and Cook, 1979; Heilman, 1980; Guba and Lincoln, 1981; Lincoln and Guba, 1985) and a regular feature at meetings of professional evaluators.

THE PARADIGMS DEBATE

A paradigm is a world view, a general perspective, a way of breaking down the complexity of the real world. As such, paradigms are deeply embedded in the socialization of adherents and practitioners: Paradigms tell them what is important, legitimate, and reasonable. Paradigms are also normative, telling the practitioner what to do without the necessity of long existential or epistemological consideration. But it is this aspect of paradigms that constitutes both their strength and their weakness—their strength in that it makes action possible, their weakness in that the very reason for action is hidden in the unquestioned assumptions of the paradigm.

> Scientists work from models acquired through education and through subsequent exposure to the literature often without quite knowing or needing to know what characteristics have given these models the status of community paradigms. . . . That scientists do not usually ask or debate what makes a particular problem or solution legitimate tempts us to suppose that, at least intuitively, they know the answer. But it may only indicate that neither the question nor the answer is felt to be relevant to their research. Paradigms may be prior to, more binding, and more complete than any set of rules for research that could be unequivocally abstracted from them [Kuhn, 1970: 46].

Evaluation research was initially dominated by the natural science paradigm of hypothetico-deductive methodology. This dominant paradigm emphasized quantitative measurement, experimental design, and multivariate, parametric statistical analysis as the epitome of "good" science. This basic model for conducting evaluation research came from the tradition of experimentation in agriculture, which gave us many of the basic statistical and experimental techniques most widely used in evaluation research.

> The most common form of agricultural-botany type evaluation is presented as an assessment of the effectiveness of an innovation by examining whether or not it has reached required standards on prespecified criteria. Students—rather like plant crops— are given pretests (the seedlings are weighed or measured) and then submitted to different experiences (treatment conditions). Subsequently, after a period of time, their attainment (growth or yield) is measured to indicate the relative efficiency of the methods (fertilizer) used. Studies of this kind are designed to yield data of one particular type, i.e., "objective" numerical data that permit statistical analyses [Parlett and Hamilton, 1976: 142].

By way of contrast, the alternative to the dominant quantitative/experimental paradigm was derived from the tradition of anthropological field studies. Using the techniques of in-depth, open-ended interviewing and personal observation, the alternative paradigm relies on qualitative data, naturalistic inquiry, and detailed description derived from close contact with the targets of study.

In utilization-focused evaluation, neither of these paradigms is intrinsically better than the other. They represent alternatives from which the utilization-focused evaluator can choose; both contain options for primary stakeholders and information users. *Issues of methodology are issues of strategy, not of morals* (see Homans, 1949). Yet it is not easy to approach the selection of evaluation methods in this adaptive fashion. The paradigmatic biases in each approach are quite fundamental. Great passions have been aroused by advocates on each side. Kuhn (1970: 109-110) has pointed out that this is the nature of paradigm debate:

> To the extent that two scientific schools disagree about what is a problem and what is a solution, they will inevitably talk through each other when debating the relative merits of their respective paradigms. In the partially circular arguments that regularly result, each paradigm will be shown to satisfy more or less the criteria that it dictates for itself and to fall short of a few of those dictated by its opponent. . . . Since no paradigm ever solves all problems it defines and since no two paradigms leave all the same problems unanswered, paradigm questions always involve the question: Which problem is it more significant to have solved?

In utilization-focused evaluation, the answer to that question is personal and situational rather than absolute.

The Dominant Paradigm in Its Days of Ascendance

The most explicit affirmation of the dominance of the hypothetico-deductive paradigm as *the* scientific method in evaluation research is in the meta-evaluation work of Bernstein and Freeman (1975). The purpose of the Bernstein-Freeman study was to assess the quality of evaluative research. What is of interest to us here is the way Bernstein and Freeman operationalized or measured "quality." The quality variables they identified and measured represented a fully explicit description of the dominant evaluation research paradigm—experimental and quantitative scientific methods. Table 8.1 shows how they coded their major indicators of quality; a higher number represents higher-quality research. What emerges is a picture of high-quality evaluation as completely quantitative data obtained through an experimental design and analyzed with sophisticated statistical techniques. But their definition of quality ignored whether the information collected was relevant, understandable, or useful from the point of view of stakeholders, or even whether the methods and measurements used were appropriate to the problem under study. For Bernstein and Freeman, the quality of evaluation research was judged entirely by its conformance with the dominant, hypothetico-deductive paradigm.

There was a broad consensus that this was the most desirable approach to evaluation research. Bernstein and Freeman cited Suchman (1967), Caro (1971), and Rossi and Williams (1972) in support of their quality coding scheme. Wholey et al. (1970: 93) considered evaluations conducted according to the dominant paradigm to be the only kind worthy of federal support: "Federal money generally should not be spent on evaluation of individual local projects unless they have been developed as field experiments, with

TABLE 8.1
Bernstein and Freeman (1975) Codings of
Evaluation Quality Variables

Variable Measuring Some Aspect of Evaluation Quality	Coding Scheme (where higher coding number represents higher quality)
Process Procedures	
Sampling	1 = Systematic random
	0 = Nonrandom, cluster, or nonsystematic
Data analysis	2 = Quantitative
	1 = Qualitative and quantitative
	0 = Qualitative
Statistical procedures	4 = Multivariate
	3 = Descriptive
	2 = Ratings from qualitative data
	1 = Narrative date only
	0 = No systematic material
Impact Procedures	
Design	3 = Experimental or quasi-experimental randomization and control groups
	2 = Experimental or quasi-experimental without both randomization and control groups
	1 = Longitudinal or cross-sectional without control or comparison groups
	0 = Descriptive, narrative

equivalent treatment and control groups." The Social Science Research Council (Reicken and Boruch, 1974) aimed quite explicitly at reinforcing the dominance of the hypothetico-deductive paradigm in evaluation and policy research. Peter Rossi (1972) reported general consensus about the most desired evaluation research methods at a conference on evaluation and policy research sponsored by the American Academy of Arts and Sciences in 1969; this concern was identical to the model found most desirable by Bernstein and Freeman.

A cursory skimming of major educational and social science research journals would confirm the dominance of the hypothetico-deductive paradigm. In their widely used methodological primer, Campbell and Stanley (1963: 3) called this paradigm "the only available route to cumulative progress." It was this belief in and commitment to the natural science model on the part of the most prominent academic researchers that made the hypothetico-deductive paradigm dominant. As Kuhn (1970: 80) explains, "a paradigm governs, in the first instance, not a subject matter but rather a group of practitioners." Those practitioners most committed to the dominant paradigm were found in universities, where they employed the scientific method in their own evaluation research and nurtured students in a commitment to that same methodology (see Bernstein and Freeman, 1975).

The problem from a utilization-focused evaluation perspective is that the very dominance of the hypothetico-deductive paradigm, with its quantitative, experimental emphasis, appeared to have cut off the great majority of its practitioners from serious consideration of any alternative evaluation research paradigm or methods. The label "research" had come to mean the equivalent of employing the "scientific method," of working within the dominant paradigm. There was, however, an alternative.

The Emergence of the Alternative Paradigm

The alternative methodological paradigm was derived most directly from anthropological field methods. More generally, this naturalistic inquiry paradigm draws on work in qualitative methodology, phenomenology, symbolic interactionism, ethnomethodology, and the general notion or doctrine of *Verstehen* ("understanding"). Kenneth Strike (1972: 28) described this tradition as follows:

> The basic dispute clustering around the notion of *verstehen* has typically sounded something like the following: the advocates of some version of the *verstehen* doctrine will claim that human beings can be understood in a manner that other objects of study cannot. Men have purposes and emotions, they make plans, construct cultures, and hold certain values, and their behavior is influenced by such values, plans, and purposes. In short, a human being lives in a world which has "meaning" to him, and, because his behavior has meaning, human actions are intelligible in ways that the behavior of nonhuman objects is not.

In short, the Verstehen approach assumes that the social sciences need methods different from those used in agricultural experimentation and natural science because human beings are different from plants. The alternative paradigm stresses understanding that focuses on the meaning of human behavior, the context of social interaction, and the connections between subjective states and behavior. The tradition of Verstehen places emphasis on the human capacity to know and understand others through sympathetic introspection and reflection based on detailed description gathered through direct observation, in-depth, open-ended interviewing, and case studies.

Evaluation came to have advocates for and practitioners of alternative methodological approaches. Robert Stake's "responsive approach to evaluation" was an early alternative to the dominant paradigm.

> Responsive evaluation is an alternative, an old alternative, based on what people do naturally to evaluate things; they observe and react. The approach is not new. But this alternative has been avoided in district, state, and federal plan-

ning documents and regulations because it is subjective and poorly suited to formal contracts. It is also capable of raising embarrassing questions [Stake, 1975: 14].

Stake recommended responsive evaluation because "it is an approach that trades off some measurement precision in order to increase the usefulness of the findings to persons in and around the program" (ibid). Also clearly embodying the alternative paradigm was the "illuminative evaluation" approach of Parlett and Hamilton (1976: 144):

> Illuminative evaluation takes account of the wider contexts in which educational programs function. Its primary concern is with description and interpretation rather than measurement and prediction. It stands unambiguously within the alternative anthropological paradigm. The aims of illuminative evaluation are to study the innovatory program: how it operates; how it is influenced by the various school situations in which it is applied; what those directly concerned regard as its advantages and disadvantages; and how students' intellectual tasks and academic experiences are most affected. It aims to discover and document what it is like to be participating in the scheme, whether as teacher or pupil, and, in addition, to discern and discuss the innovation's most significant features, recurring concomitants, and critical processes. In short, it seeks to address and illuminate a complex array of questions.

Competing Paradigms

We now have before us the broad outlines of two contrasting evaluative research paradigms. In a very real sense these were opposing and competing paradigms. In our utilization of federal health evaluation studies, every respondent answered methodological questions with reference to these competing paradigms. Respondents would typically begin by explaining any reasons for departure of the particular study in question from the dominant paradigm ideal of quantitative measures obtained through an experimental design. Studies were described as "hard" or "soft" along a continuum in which "harder" was clearly better. There were frequent stories of conflicts over methods.

The paradigms debate highlighted a series of methodological dimensions along which there are variations in emphasis. These dimensions focus attention on some of the options available in making methods decisions. The next sections describe these options as they emerged in the paradigms debate.

Quantitative and Qualitative Data: Different Perspectives on the World

Quantitative measurement relies on the use of instruments that provide a standardized framework in order to limit data collection to certain predetermined response or analysis categories. The experiences of people in programs and the important variables that describe program outcomes are fit into these standardized categories to which numerical values are then attached. By contrast, the evaluator using a qualitative approach seeks to capture what people's lives, experiences, and interactions mean to them in their own terms and in their natural settings. Qualitative data provide depth and detail. Depth and detail emerge through direct quotation and careful description. The extent of depth and detail will vary depending on the nature and purpose of a particular study.

Considering trade-offs between breadth and depth leads to consideration of the relative strengths and weaknesses of qualitative and quantitative data. Qualitative methods permit the evaluator to study selected issues in depth and detail; the fact that data collection is not constrained by predetermined categories of analysis contributes to the depth and detail of qualitative data. Quantitative methods, on the other hand, require the use of a standardized stimulus so that all experiences of people are limited to certain response categories. The advantage of the quantitative approach is that it is possible to measure the reactions of many subjects to a limited set of questions, thus facilitating comparison and statistical aggregation of the data. By contrast, qualitative methods typically produce a wealth of detailed data about a much smaller number of people and cases.

Quantitative data permit the complexities of the world to be broken into parts and assigned numerical values. Quantitative data come from questionnaires, tests, standardized observation instruments, and program records. To obtain quantitative data, it is necessary to be able to categorize the object of interest in ways that permit counting. Quantitative data are parsimonious, easily computerized, and amenable to statistical analysis. Statistical techniques make it possible to analyze a great deal of data systematically according to accepted operational procedures.

Qualitative data consist of detailed descriptions of situations, events, people, interactions, and observed behaviors; direct quotations from people about their experiences, attitudes, beliefs, and thoughts; and excerpts or entire passages from documents, correspondence, records, and case histories. The detailed descriptions, direct quotations, and case documentation of qualitative methods are raw data from the empirical world. The data are collected as open-ended narrative without attempting to fit institutional activities or peoples' experiences into predetermined, standardized categories such as the response choices that comprise typical questionnaires or tests.

Sociologist John Lofland suggested that there are four elements in collecting qualitative data. First, the qualitative evaluator must get close enough to the people and situation being studied to be able to understand the depth and details of what goes on. Second, the qualitative evaluator must aim at capturing what actually takes place and what people actually say: the perceived facts. Third, qualitative data consist of a great deal of pure description of people, activities, and interactions. Fourth, qualitative data consist of direct quotations from people, both what they speak and what they write down.

> The commitment to get close, to be factual, descriptive and quotive, constitutes a significant commitment to represent the participants in their own terms. This does not mean that one becomes an apologist for them, but rather that one faithfully depicts what goes on in their lives and what life is like for them, in such a way that one's audience is at least partially able to project themselves into the point of view of the people depicted. They can "take the role of the other" because the reporter has given them a living sense of day-to-day talk, day-to-day activities, day-to-day concerns and problems. . . .
>
> A major methodological consequence of these commitments is that the qualitative study of people in situ is a process of discovery. It is of necessity a process of learning what is happening. Since a major part of what is happening is provided by people in their own terms, one must find out about those terms rather than impose upon them a preconceived or outsider's scheme of what they are about. It is the observer's task to find out what is fundamental or central to the people or world under observation [Lofland, 1971: 4].

Quantitative information tends to be viewed as "hard" data, whereas qualitative data tend to be viewed as "soft." Statistical presentations tend to have more credibility, to seem more like "science," whereas qualitative narratives tend to be associated with journalism.

Kuhn (1970: 184-185), in his discussion of science paradigms, observed that the values scientists hold help them choose between alternative ways of practicing their discipline: "The most deeply held values concern predictions: they should be accurate; quantitative predictions are preferable to qualitative ones." Kuhn was writing mainly about natural scientists, but it is clear that the same values were enthusiastically embraced by social scientists and early evaluation researchers. Not only were quantitative predictions preferable to qualitative ones, but qualitative analyses in general had little legitimacy beyond certain limited exploratory situations.

The danger of this methodological status hierarchy was that it denigrated those who employed qualitative methodology. Bernstein and Freeman (1975) even ranked evaluations that gathered *both* quantitative and qualitative data as lower in methodological quality than those which gathered only quantitative data. The problem was the advocacy of statistics to the virtual exclusion of other types of data. C. Wright Mills (1961: 50) observed in this regard that the dominance of statistical methodology led to a "methodological inhibition" that he called "abstracted empiricism." The problem with abstracted empiricism was that "it seizes upon one juncture in the process of work and allows it to dominate the mind."

The earlier dominance of quantitative methods severely limited the kinds of questions asked and the types of problems studied. Although most phenomena are not intrinsically impossible to measure quantitatively, certain types are clearly easier to measure numerically. It is easier to measure the number of words a child spells correctly than to measure that same child's ability to use those words in a meaningful way. It is easier to count the number of minutes a student spends reading books in class than it is to measure what reading means to that student.

Quantitative advocates assumed the necessity, desirability, and even the possibility of applying some underlying empirical standard to social phenomena. By way of contrast, qualitative researchers assume that some phenomena are not amenable to numerical mediation. *The point here is that different kinds of problems require different types of data.* If we only want to know the number of words a child can spell or the frequency of interaction between children of different races in desegregated schools, then statistical procedures are appropriate. However, if we want to understand the relevance of the words a child uses to that child's life situation, or the meaning of interracial interactions, then some form of qualitative methodology (such as participant observation, in-depth interviewing, or systematic fieldwork) that allows the researcher to obtain firsthand knowledge about the empirical social world in question may well be more appropriate.

> If the problems upon which one is at work are readily amenable to statistical procedures, one should always try them first. . . . No one, however, need accept such procedures, when generalized, as the only procedures available. Certainly no one need accept this model as a total canon. It is not the only empirical manner.
>
> It is a choice made according to the requirements of our problems, not a "necessity" that follows from an epistemological dogma [Mills, 1961: 73-74].

One evaluator in our federal utilization study had personally struggled with this choice between qualitative and quantitative data. He was evaluating community mental health programs, and reported that quantitative measures frequently failed to capture real differences among programs. For example, he found a case in which community mental health staff cooperated closely with the state hospital. On one occasion, he observed a therapist from the community mental health center accompany a seriously disturbed client on the "traumatic, fearful, anxiety-ridden trip to the state hospital." The therapist had been working with the client on an out-patient basis. After commitment to the state facility, the therapist continued to see the client weekly and assisted that person in planning toward and getting out of the state institution and back into the normal community as soon as possible. The evaluator found it very difficult to measure this aspect of the program quantitatively.

> This actually becomes a *qualitative* aspect of how they were carrying out the mental health program, but there's a problem of measuring the impact of that

qualitative change from when the sheriff used to transport the patients from that county in a locked car with a stranger in charge and the paraphernalia of the sheriff's personality and office. The qualitative difference is obvious in the possible effect on a disturbed patient, but the problem of measurement is very, very difficult. So what we get here in the report is a portrayal of some of the qualitative differences and a very limited capacity of the field at that time to measure those qualitative differences. *We can describe some of them better than we can measure them* [EV5: 3].

A more extended example may help to illustrate the importance of seeking congruence between the phenomenon studied and the research methodology employed for the study. The example concerns the key issue of the extent to which educational innovation makes a difference in children's achievement. After examining some four decades of educational research, John Stephens (1967) concluded that educational innovation makes little difference. "But," asked Edna Shapiro (1973: 542), "can such a judgment be made when the researcher has sampled only an extremely narrow band of measurement within a constant and equally restrictive situation?"

Shapiro asked this question after finding no achievement test differences between (1) children in an enriched Follow Through program modeled along the lines of open education and (2) children in comparison schools not involved in Follow Through or other enrichment programs. *When the children's responses in the test situation were compared, no differences of any consequence were found. However, when observations of the children in their classrooms were made, there were striking differences between the Follow Through and comparison classes.* Based on systematic observations, the Follow Through (FT) classrooms

> were characterized as lively, vibrant, with a diversity of curricular projects and children's products, and an atmosphere of friendly, cooperative endeavor. The non-FT classrooms were characterized as relatively uneventful, with a narrow range of curriculum, uniform activity, a great deal of seat work, and less equipment; teachers as well as children were quieter and more concerned with maintaining or submitting to discipline [Shapiro, 1973: 529].

Observations also revealed that the children behaved differently in these two types of environments. Yet standardized achievement tests failed to detect these differences. Shapiro suggests that there were factors operating against the demonstration of differences that call into question traditional ways of gauging the impact and effectiveness of different kinds of school experience. *The testing methodology, in fact, narrowed the nature of the questions that were being asked and predetermined nonsignificant statistical results.*

> I assumed that the internalized effects of different kinds of school experience could be observed and inferred only from responses in test situations, and that

the observation of teaching and learning in the classroom should be considered auxiliary information, useful chiefly to document the differences in the children's group learning experiences.

The rationale of the test, on the contrary, is that each child is removed from the classroom and treated equivalently, and differences in response are presumed to indicate differences in what has been taken in, made one's own, that survives the shift to a different situation.

The findings of this study, with the marked disparity between classroom responses and test responses, have led me to reevaluate this rationale. This requires reconsideration of the role of classroom data, individual test situation data, and the relation between them. *If we minimize the importance of the child's behavior in the classroom because it is influenced by situational variables, do we not have to apply the same logic to the child's responses in the test situation, which is also influenced by situational variables* [Shapiro, 1973: 532-534; emphasis added]?

Shapiro elaborated and illustrated these points at considerable length. Her conclusion went to the heart of the problem posed by the previous dominance of a single methodological paradigm in evaluation research: *"Research methodology must be suited to the particular characteristics of the situations under study. . . . An omnibus strategy will not work"* (Shapiro, 1973: 543; emphasis added).

At first, some evaluators were willing to recognize that qualitative data might be useful at an exploratory stage of research prefatory to quantitative research. What they denied was that qualitative data can be a legitimate basis for systematic evaluation, or theory construction.

Gathering qualitative data is an alternative that not only employs different methods but also asks different questions. As Kuhn (1970: 106) has explained, one of the functions of scientific paradigms is to provide criteria for choosing problems that can be assumed to have solutions: "Changes in the standards governing permissible problems, concepts, and explanations can transform a science." It was the failure of the dominant natural science paradigm to answer important questions like those raised by Shapiro that gradually made serious consideration of the alternative paradigm so crucial for evaluation research.

The emergent consensus in evaluation now seems to be that *both* qualitative and quantitative data are valued and recognized as legitimate. There is widespread recognition that evaluators must be able to use a variety of methods in evaluating programs. Evaluators are encouraged to be sophisticated and flexible in matching research methods to the nuances of particular evaluation questions and the idiosyncracies of specific decision maker needs (Patton, 1982a). There are no logical reasons why qualitative and quantitative methods cannot be used together. *Qualitative Evaluation Methods* (Patton, 1980a) describes conditions under which qualitative methods are particularly appropriate in evaluation research. Sometimes quantitative methods alone are most appropriate. But in many cases both qualitative and quantitative methods should be used together.

Wherever appropriate, multiple methods should be used. Where multiple methods are used, the contributions of each kind of data should be fairly assessed. In many cases this means that evaluators working in teams will need to work hard to overcome their tendency to dismiss certain kinds of data without first considering seriously and fairly the merits of those data.

Naturalistic and Experimental Inquiry Options

The paradigms debate was in part a debate about the relative importance of causal questions in evaluation. Those evaluators who believe that the most important and central function of evaluation is to measure the effects of programs on participants in order to make valid causal inferences are strong advocates of randomized experiments as "the standard against which other designs for impact evaluation are judged" (Boruch and Rindskopf, 1984: 121). In advocating experimental designs, evaluators such as Campbell and Boruch (1975) have demonstrated the power and feasibility of randomized experiments for a variety of programs (Boruch et al., 1978). The concerns that permeate these writings are concerns about increasing "rigor," "well-controlled settings," reducing threats to internal validity, and precise estimates of program effects.

Naturalistic inquiry is distinguished from experimental inquiry by the extent to which the investigator or evaluator attempts to avoid controlling or manipulating the situation, people, or data under study. The extent to which any particular investigator engages in naturalistic inquiry varies along a continuum (Guba, 1978). It is certainly possible for an investigator to enter a field situation and try to control what happens just as it is possible for the experimentalist to control only the initial assignment to groups, then to watch what happens "naturally." The important distinction is between relative degrees of calculated manipulation. A naturalistic inquiry strategy is selected when the investigator wants to minimize research manipulation by studying natural field settings; experimental conditions and designs are selected when the evaluator wants to introduce a considerable amount of control and reduce variation in extraneous variables.

Willens and Raush (1969: 3) define naturalistic inquiry as "the investigation of phenomena within and in relation to their naturally occurring context." In their extensive review of naturalistic inquiry in educational evaluation, Guba and Lincoln (1981) identify two dimensions along which types of scientific inquiry can be described: the extent to which the scientist manipulates some phenomenon in advance in order to study it, and the extent to which constraints are placed on output measures; that is, the extent to which predetermined categories or variables are used to describe the phenomenon under study. They then define "naturalistic inquiry" as a "discovery-oriented" approach that minimizes investigator manipulation of the study setting and places no prior constraints on what the outcomes of the research will be. Naturalistic inquiry is thus contrasted to experimental research, in which, ideally, the investigator attempts to control conditions of the study completely by manipulating, changing, or holding constant external influences and in which a very limited set of outcome variables is measured.

Wolf and Tymitz (1976-1977: 6) describe naturalistic inquiry as an approach aimed at understanding

> actualities, social realities, and human perceptions that exist untainted by the obtrusiveness of formal measurement or preconceived questions. It is a process geared to the uncovering of many idiosyncratic but nonetheless important stories told by real people, about real events, in real and natural ways. The more general the provocation, the more these stories will reflect what respondents view as salient issues, meaningful evidence, and appropriate inferences. . . . Naturalistic inquiry attempts to present "slice-of-life" episodes documented through natural language and representing as closely as possible how people feel, what they know, and what their concerns, beliefs, perceptions, and understandings are.

Under real field conditions, where the evaluator wants to know about life and work in program settings, naturalistic inquiry replaces the static snapshots of traditional survey research with a dynamic, process orientation. In seeking to understand dynamic processes, the naturalistic inquiry evaluator eschews the fixed comparisons of pre-post experimental designs. Instead, the evaluator sets out to understand and document the day-to-day reality of the program(s) under study. The evaluator makes no attempt to manipulate, control, or eliminate situational variables or program developments, but accepts the complexity of a dynamic and evolving program reality.

Qualitative data can be collected in experimental designs in which participants have been randomly divided into treatment and control groups. Likewise, some quantitative data may be collected in naturalistic inquiry approaches. Such combinations and flexibility are still rather rare, however. Experimental designs predominantly aim for statistical analyses, whereas qualitative data are the primary focus in naturalistic inquiry.

Deductive and Inductive Approaches

Another important issue in the paradigms debate has been the relative value and feasibility of deductive and inductive research strategies. An evaluation approach is inductive to the extent that the evaluator attempts to make sense of the situation without imposing preexisting expectations on the program setting. Inductive designs begin with specific observations and build toward general patterns. Categories or dimensions of analysis emerge from open-ended observations as the evaluator comes to understand program patterns that exist in the empirical world under study.

This contrasts with the hypothetico-deductive approach of experimental designs, which requires the specification of main variables and the statement of specific research hypotheses *before* data collection begins. A specification of research hypotheses based on an explicit theoretical framework means that general principles provide the framework for understanding specific observations or cases. The evaluator must then decide in advance what variables are important and what relationships among those variables can be expected.

The strategy of inductive designs is to allow the important analysis dimensions to emerge from patterns found in the cases under study without presupposing what the important dimensions will be. The qualitative methodologist attempts to understand the multiple interrelationships among dimensions that emerge from the data without making prior assumptions or specifying hypotheses about the linear or correlative relationships among narrowly defined, operationalized variables. In short, the inductive approach to evaluation means that an understanding of program activities and outcomes emerges from experience with the setting. Theories about what is happening in a setting are grounded in direct program experience rather than imposed on the setting a priori by hypothetico-deductive constructions.

Evaluation research can be inductive in two ways. Within programs, an inductive approach begins with the individual experiences of participants, without pigeonholing or delimiting what those experiences will be in advance of fieldwork. Between programs, the inductive approach looks for unique institutional characteristics that make each setting a case unto itself. At either level, generalizations may emerge when case materials are content analyzed, but the initial focus is on full understanding of individual cases, before those unique cases are combined or aggregated. This means that evaluation findings are grounded in specific contexts; theories that result from the findings will be grounded in real-world patterns (Glaser and Strauss, 1967).

In evaluation the classic deductive approach is measuring relative attainment of predetermined clear goals in a randomized experiment that permits precise attribution of goal attainment to identifiable program treatments. In contrast, the classic inductive approach is goal-free evaluation, in which the evaluator gathers qualitative data on actual program impacts through direct observations of program activities and in-depth interviews with participants, all without regard to stated, predetermined goals. A more straightforward contrast is between closed-ended questionnaires and open-ended interviews. A structured, multiple-choice questionnaire requires a deductive approach because items must be predetermined based on some theory or preordinate criteria about what is important to measure. An open-ended interview, on the other hand, permits the respondent to describe what is meaningful and salient without being pigeonholed into standardized categories.

In practice, these approaches are often combined. Some evaluation questions are determined deductively while others are left sufficiently open to permit inductive analyses based on direct observations. Our study of federal health program evaluation use was partly deductive in that we tested propositions derived from the theoretical literature, but the study was also inductive in that we left undefined the major dependent variable (i.e., utilization) and asked interviewees to define utilization in a way meaningful to them.

Thus, the paradigms debate has sharpened our understanding of the strengths and weaknesses of each strategy. While the quantitative/experimental paradigm is largely hypothetico-deductive and the qualitative/naturalistic paradigm is largely inductive, an evaluation can include elements of both strategies. Indeed, there is often a flow from inductive approaches (to find out what the important questions and variables are; i.e., exploratory work) to deductive hypothesis testing aimed at confirming exploratory findings, then back again to inductive analysis to look for rival hypotheses and unanticipated or unmeasured factors. In the actual practice of utilization-focused evaluation, both inductive and deductive strategies should be part of the evaluator's repertoire.

From Objectivity Versus Subjectivity to Fairness and Balance

In the paradigms debate, a qualitative/naturalistic approach to evaluation research frequently stimulated charges of subjectivity—a label regarded as the very antithesis of scientific inquiry. Objectivity was considered the *sine qua non* of the scientific method. To be subjective meant to be biased, unreliable, and nonrational. Subjective data implied opinion rather than fact, intuition rather than logic, impression rather than confirmation. Evaluators were advised to avoid subjectivity and make their work "objective and value-free."

In the paradigms debate, the means advocated by scientists for controlling subjectivity through the scientific method were the techniques of the dominant experimental/quantitative paradigm. Yet the previous section observed that quantitative methods can work in practice to limit and even bias the kinds of questions that are asked and the nature of admissible solutions.

Michael Scriven (1972a: 94) has insisted that quantitative methods are no more synonymous with objectivity than qualitative methods are synonymous with subjectivity:

Errors like this are too simple to be explicit. They are inferred confusions in the ideological foundations of research, its interpretations, its application. . . . It is increasingly clear that the influence of ideology on methodology and of the latter on the training and behavior of researchers and on the identification and disbursement of support is staggeringly powerful. Ideology is to research what Marx suggested the economic factor was to politics and what Freud took sex to be for psychology.

The possibility that "ideological" preconceptions can lead to dual perspectives about a single phenomenon goes to the very heart of the contrasts between paradigms. Two scientists may look at the same thing, but because of different theoretical perspectives, assumptions, or ideology-based methodologies, *they may literally not see the same thing* (Petrie, 1972: 48). Indeed, Kuhn (1970: 113) argued that

something like a paradigm is prerequisite to perception itself. What a man sees depends both upon what he looks at and also upon what his previous visual-conceptual experience has taught him to see. In the absence of such training there can only be, in William James' phrase, "a bloomin' buggin' confusion."

As the parable of Han and the Dragon that opened this chapter illustrates, perceptions of the world (and of dragons) vary depending on how one has been trained. The Mandarin thought a dragon must look like a proud lord—a Mandarin. The captain of the army was convinced that a dragon would look like a warrior. The merchant, the chief workman, and the wise man each defined and perceived the dragon in a different way. They could each look at the same thing, but because of different ideology-based definitions, assumptions, and perspectives, they literally would not see the same thing. There may even be people whose preconceived definitions of the world tell them that no such things as dragons exist!

It is in this context that the dominant paradigm's claim of achieving objectivity can be called ideology. It is not possible for us to view the complexities of the real world without somehow filtering and simplifying those complexities. In the final analysis, this means that we are always dealing with perceptions, not "facts" in some absolute sense. "The very categories of things which comprise the 'facts' are theory dependent" (Petrie, 1972: 49) or, in this case, paradigm dependent. It is this recognition that led Howard Becker (1970: 15) to argue that "the question is not whether we should take sides, since we inevitably will, but rather whose side we are on."

A major difference between the paradigms was, and is, their respective views on the nature of reality and thus the role of research in predicting reality. The quantitative/experimental paradigm conceives of science as the search for truth about a singular reality, thus the importance of objectivity. The qualitative/naturalistic paradigm searches for perspective and understanding in a world of multiple "realities," thus the inevitability of subjectivity. Although the possibility of attaining objectivity and truth in any absolute sense has become an untenable position in evaluation, the negative connotations associated with the term "subjectivity" make it an unacceptable alternative. There is a solution.

Utilization-focused evaluation, being practical in orientation, replaces the traditional search for truth with a search for useful and balanced information, and replaces the mandate to be objective with a mandate to be fair and conscientious in taking account of multiple perspectives, multiple interests, and multiple realities. In this regard, Egon Guba (1981: 76-77) suggests that evaluators could learn a great deal by adopting the stand of investigative journalists.

> Journalism in general and investigative journalism in particular are moving away from the criterion of objectivity to an emergent criterion usually labeled "fairness." . . . Objectivity assumes a single reality to which the story or evaluation must be isomorphic; it is in this sense a one-perspective criterion. It assumes that an agent can deal with an object (or another person) in a nonreactive and noninteractive way. It is an absolute criterion.
>
> Journalists are coming to feel that objectivity in that sense is unattainable. . . .
>
> Enter "fairness" as a substitute criterion. In contrast to objectivity, fairness has these features:
>
> * It assumes multiple realities or truths—hence a test of fairness is whether or not "both" sides of the case are presented, and there may even be multiple sides.
>
> * It is adversarial rather than one-perspective in nature. Rather than trying to hew the line with *the* truth, as the objective reporter does, the fair reporter seeks to present each side of the case in the manner of an advocate—as, for example, attorneys do in making a case in court. The presumption is that the public, like a jury, is more likely to reach an equitable decision after having heard each side presented with as much vigor and commitment as possible.
>
> * It is assumed that the subject's reaction to the reporter and interaction between them heavily determines what the reporter perceives. Hence one test of fairness is the length to which the reporter will go to test his own biases and rule them out.
>
> * It is a relative criterion that is measured by *balance* rather than by isomorphism to enduring truth.
>
> Clearly, evaluators have a great deal to learn from this development.

The Joint Committee's (1981) standards on evaluation reflect this change in emphasis:

Priority Standard on Balanced Reporting: The evaluation should be complete and fair in its presentation of strengths and weaknesses of the object under investigation, so that strengths can be built upon and problem areas addressed.

Accuracy Standard on Defensible Information Sources: The sources of information should be described in enough detail so that the adequacy of the information can be assessed.

The next section discusses an issue closely related to concerns about objectivity—namely, the problem of how close to get to the program and people being evaluated. Too much closeness may compromise "objectivity." Too much distance may diminish insight and understanding.

The Continuum of Distance from Versus Closeness to the Program

The quantitative/experimental paradigm prescribes distance in order to guarantee neutrality and objectivity. This component has become increasingly important with the professionalization of the social science and educational research establishment. Professional comportment connotes cool, calm, and detached analysis without personal involvement or bias.

The qualitative/naturalistic paradigm questions the necessity of distance and detachment, assuming that without empathy and sympathetic introspection derived from personal encounters the observer cannot fully understand human behavior. Understanding comes from trying to put oneself in the other person's shoes, from trying to discern how others think, act, and feel. John Lofland (1971) explains that methodologically this means getting close to the people being studied through attention to the minutiae of daily life, through physical proximity over a period of time, and through development of closeness in the social sense of intimacy and confidentiality. "The commitment to get close, to be factual, descriptive, and quotive, constitutes a significant commitment to represent the participants *in their own terms*" (Lofland, 1971: 4).

The commitment to closeness is based on the assumption that the inner states of people are important and can be known. From this assumption flows a concern with meaning, mental states, and world view. It is at this point that the alternative paradigm intersects with the phenomenological tradition (see Bussis et al., 1973). Attention to inner perspectives does not mean administering attitude surveys. "The inner perspective assumes that understanding can only be achieved by actively participating in the life of the observed and gaining insight by means of introspection" (Bruyn, 1966: 226). Actively participating in the life of the observed means, at a minimum, being willing to get close to the program being evaluated.

A commitment to get close to the program and a willingness to view participants in their own terms implies an openness to the phenomenon under study that is relatively uncontaminated by preconceived notions and categories (i.e., is inductive).

> In order to capture the participants "in their own terms" one must learn *their* analytic ordering of the world, *their* categories for rendering explicable and coherent the flux of raw reality. That, indeed, is the first principle of qualitative analysis [Lofland, 1971: 7; italics in original].

In the Shapiro study of Follow Through open classrooms, it was her closeness to the children in those classrooms that allowed her to see that something was happening that was not captured by standardized tests. She could see differences in children, and could understand differences in the meaning of their different situations. She could feel their tension in the testing situation and their spontaneity in the more natural classroom setting. Had she worked solely with data collected by others or only at a distance, she would never have discovered the crucial differences in the classroom settings she studied—differences that actually allowed her to evaluate the innovative program in a meaningful and relevant way.

Again, it is important to note that the admonition to get close to the data is in no way meant to deny the usefulness of quantitative methodology. Rather, it means that statistical portrayals must always be interpreted and given human meaning. One evaluator in our utilization of federal health evaluations expressed frustration at trying to make sense out of data from over 80 projects when site visit funds were cut out of the evaluation: "There's no way to evaluate something that's just data. You know, you have to go look" (EV111: 3).

That many quantitative methodologists fail to ground their findings in qualitative understanding poses what Lofland calls a major contradiction between their public insistence on the adequacy of statistical portrayals of other humans and their personal everyday dealings with and judgments about other human beings:

> In everyday life, statistical sociologists, like everyone else, assume that they do not know or understand very well people they do not see or associate with very much. They assume that knowing and understanding other people require that one see them reasonably often and in a variety of situations relative to a variety of issues. Moreover, statistical sociologists, like other people, assume that in order to know or understand others one is well advised to give some conscious attention to that effort in face-to-face contacts. They assume, too, that the internal world of sociology—or any other social world—is not understandable unless one has been part of it in a face-to-face fashion for quite a period of time. How utterly paradoxical, then, for these same persons to turn around and make, by implication, precisely the opposite claim about people they have never encountered face-to-face—those people appearing as numbers in their tables and as correlations in their matrices [Lofland, 1971: 3]!

Closeness to the data is not the only legitimate way to understand human behavior. For certain questions and for situations involving large groups, distance is inevitable, but for others face-to-face interaction is both necessary and desirable. This returns us to the recurrent theme of matching the evaluation methods to the problem.

In thinking about the issue of closeness to the phenomenon under study, it is useful to remember that many major contributions to our understanding of the world have come from scientists' personal experiences. One finds many instances in which closeness to the data made key insights possible— Piaget's closeness to his children, Freud's proximity to and empathy with his patients, Darwin's closeness to nature, and even Newton's intimate encounter with an apple.

In short, closeness does not make bias and loss of perspective inevitable; and distance is no guarantee of objectivity.

Of Variables and Wholes

The quantitative/experimental paradigm requires operationalization of independent and dependent variables that can be analyzed statistically. Outcomes must be identified and measured as specific variables. Treatments and programs must also be conceptualized as discrete, independent variables. The characteristics of program participants are also described by standardized, quantified dimensions. Sometimes the variables measured are of direct interest and relevance, as when primary program goals are measured directly (e.g., student achievement test scores, recidivism statistics for a group of juvenile delinquents, or sobriety rates for participants in chemical dependency treatment programs). At other times, the variables measured are indicators of a larger construct. For example, community well-being is a general construct that may be measured by such specific indicators as crime rates, fetal deaths, divorce, unemployment, suicide, and poverty (Brock et al., 1985). These variables are statistically manipulated or added together in some linear fashion to test hypotheses and draw inferences about the relationships among separate indicators, or the statistical significance of differences between measured levels of the variables for different groups. The essential logic of this approach is as follows: (1) Key program outcomes and treatments can be represented by separate independent variables; (2) these variables can be quantified; and (3) relationships among these variables are best portrayed statistically.

The primary critique of this logic by qualitative/naturalistic paradigm adherents is that such an approach (1) oversimplifies the complexities of real-world experiences, (2) misses major factors of importance that are not easily quantified, and (3) fails to portray a sense of the program and its impacts as a "whole." The qualitative/naturalistic paradigm is *holistic* in orientation. The holistic approach assumes that the whole is greater than the sum of its parts; it also assumes that a description and understanding of a program's context is essential to an understanding of the program. Thus, it is insufficient simply to study and measure the parts of a situation by gathering data about isolated variables, scales, or dimensions. In contrast to experimental designs that manipulate and measure the relationships among a few carefully selected and narrowly defined variables, the holistic approach to research design gathers data on any number of aspects of the setting under study in order to assemble a complete picture of the social dynamic of the particular situation or program. This means that at the time of data collection each case, event, or setting under study is treated as a unique entity, with its own particular meaning and its own constellation of relationships emerging from and related to the context within which it exists.

The advantages of using variables and indicators are parsimony, precision, and ease of analysis. Where key program elements can be quantified with validity, reliability, and credibility, and where necessary statistical assumptions can be met (e.g., linearity, normality, and independence of measurement), statistical portrayals can be quite powerful and succinct.

The advantage of qualitative portrayals of holistic settings and impacts is that greater attention can be given to nuance, setting, interdependencies, complexities, idiosyncracies, and context.

John Dewey (1956a: 5-6) advocated a holistic approach to both teaching and research if one was to reach into and understand the world of the child.

> The child's life is an integral, a total one. He passes quickly and readily from one topic to another, as from one spot to another, but is not conscious of transition or break. There is no conscious isolation, hardly conscious distinction. The things that occupy him are held together by the unity of the personal and social interests which his life carries along. . . . [His] universe is fluid and fluent; its contents dissolve and re-form with amazing rapidity. But after all, it is the child's own world. It has the unity and completeness of his own life.

Deutscher (1970: 33) adds that despite the totality of our personal experiences as living, working human beings, we have focused in our research on parts to the virtual exclusion of wholes:

> We knew that human behavior was rarely if ever directly influenced or explained by an isolated variable; we knew that it was impossible to assume that any set of such variables was additive (with or without weighting); we knew that the complex mathematics of the interaction among any set of variables was incomprehensible to us. In effect, although we knew they did not exist, we defined them into being.

Although most scientists would view this radical critique of variable analysis as too extreme, I find that teachers and practitioners often voice the same criticisms. Narrow experimental results may lack relevance for innovative teachers because they have to deal with the whole in their classrooms. The reaction of many program staff to scientific research is like the reaction of Copernicus to the astronomers of his day: "With them," he observed, "it is as though an artist were to gather the hands, feet, head, and other members for his images from diverse models, each part excellently drawn, but not related to a single body, and since they in no way match each other, the result would be monster rather than man" (Kuhn, 1970: 83). How many program staff have complained of the evaluation research monster?

It is no simple task to undertake holistic evaluation, to search for the Gestalt in programs. The challenge for the participant observer is "to seek the essence of the life of the observed, to sum up, to find a central unifying principle" (Bruyn, 1966: 316). Again, Shapiro's work (1973) in evaluating innovative Follow Through classrooms is instructive. She found that test results could not be interpreted without understanding the larger cultural and institutional context in which the individual child is situated.

In utilization-focused evaluation, neither the holistic approach nor variable analysis represents an omnibus strategy appropriate to all situations and problems. It is in reaction to the previous dominance of statistical analysis as *the* scientific approach in evaluation research that the potential of more holistic evaluation strategies has more recently emerged. As one of the most famous of all Sufi stories illustrates, touching only one part of an elephant, as each of the nine blind men did, can give quite a distorted picture of what the whole elephant looks like.

Two Views of Change

The paradigms debate is in part a debate about how best to understand and study change. The two paradigms conceptualize and measure change in quite different ways for quite different purposes.

The quantitative/experimental paradigm typically involves gathering data at two points in time, pretest and posttest, and compares the treatment group to the control group on standardized measures. Ideally participants are assigned to treatment and control groups randomly, or, less ideally, are matched on critical background variables. Such designs assume an identifiable, coherent, and consistent treatment. Moreover, they assume that, once introduced, the treatment remains relatively constant and unchanging. In some designs, time series data are gathered at several predetermined points rather than just at pretest and posttest. The purpose of these designs is to determine the extent to which the program (treatment) accounts for measurable changes in participants in order to make a summative decision about the value and effectiveness of the program in producing desired change (Mark and Cook, 1984; Boruch and Rindskopf, 1984).

In contrast, the qualitative/naturalistic paradigm conceives of programs as dynamic and developing, with "treatments" changing in subtle but important ways as staff learn, as clients move in and out, and as conditions of delivery are altered. The primary interest of qualitative/naturalistic evaluators is describing and understanding these dynamic program processes and their holistic effects on participants so as to provide information for program improvement (formative evaluation). Thus, part of the paradigms debate has been about the relative utility, desirability, and possibility of understanding programs from these quite different perspectives for different purposes.

The quantitative/experimental/summative approach is most relevant for fairly established programs with stable, consistent, and identifiable treatments and clearly quantifiable outcomes, in which a major decision is to be made about the effectiveness of one treatment in comparison to another (or no) treatment.

The qualitative/naturalistic/formative approach is especially appropriate for developing, innovating, or changing programs in which the focus is on program improvement, facilitating more effective implementation, and exploring a variety of effects on participants. This can be particularly important early in the life of a program or at major points of transition. As an innovation or program change is implemented, it frequently unfolds in a manner quite different from what was planned or conceptualized in a proposal. Once in operation, innovative programs are often changed as practitioners learn what works and what does not, and as they experiment, grow, and change their priorities. This, of course, creates frustration and hostility among evaluators who expect specifiable, unchanging treatments to relate to specifiable, predetermined outcomes. Evaluators have been known to do everything in their power to stop program adaptation and improvement so as not to interfere with their research design (see Parlett and Hamilton, 1976). The deleterious effect this may have on the program itself, discouraging as it does new developments and redefinitions in midstream, is considered to be a small sacrifice made in pursuit of higher-level scientific knowledge. But there is a distinct possibility that such artificial evaluation constraints will contaminate the program treatment by affecting staff morale and participant response.

Were some science of planning and policy or program development so highly evolved that initial proposals were perfect, one might be able to sympathize with these evaluators' desire to keep the initial program implementation intact. In the real world, however, people and unforeseen circumstances shape programs, and initial implementations are modified in ways that are rarely trivial.

Under conditions in which programs are subject to change and redirection, the naturalistic evaluation paradigm replaces the fixed treatment or outcomes emphasis of the experimental paradigm with a dynamic orientation. A dynamic evaluation is not tied to a single treatment or to predetermined goals or outcomes but, rather, focuses on the actual operations of a program over a period of time. The evaluator sets out to understand and document the day-to-day reality of the setting or settings under study. He or she makes no attempt to manipulate, control, or eliminate situation variables or program developments, but takes as a given the complexity of a changing reality. The data of the evaluation are not just outcomes but changes in treatments and patterns of action, reaction, and interaction.

A dynamic perspective requires sensitivity to both qualitative and quantitative changes in programs throughout their development, not just at some endpoint in time. The evaluation is process-oriented. Process evaluation is built on subjective inferences in the sense that the investigator attempts to develop empathy with program participants and understand the changing meaning of the program in the participant's own terms; process evaluation requires getting close to the data, becoming intimately acquainted with the details of the program. Thus, process evaluation includes a holistic orientation to evaluation research, observing not only anticipated outcomes but also unanticipated consequences, treatment changes, and the larger context of program implementation and development.

Again, the issue is one of matching the evaluation design to the program, of meshing evaluation methods with decision maker information needs. The point of contrasting fixed experimental designs with dynamic process designs in the paradigms debate was to release evaluators "from unwitting captivity to a format of inquiry that is taken for granted as the naturally proper way in which to conduct scientific inquiry" (Blumer, 1969: 47). Nowhere is this unwitting captivity better illustrated than in those agencies that insist— in the name of science—that all evaluations must employ experimental designs. Two examples will illustrate this problem. In Minnesota, the Governor's Commission of Crime Prevention and Control required experimental evaluation designs of all funded projects. A small Native American alternative school was granted funds to run an innovative crime prevention project with parents and students. The program was highly flexible; participation was irregular and based on self-selection. The program was designed to be sensitive to Native American culture and values. It would be a perfect situation for formative, responsive evaluation. Instead, program staff were forced to create the illusion of an experimental, pretest and posttest design. The evaluation design interfered with the program, wasted staff time and resources, and became an example par excellence of forcing the collection of worthless information under the guise of maintaining scientific standards.

The second example is quite similar, but concerns the Minnesota Department of Education. The state monitor for an innovative arts program in a free school insisted on quantitative, standardized test measures collected in pretest and posttest situations; a control group was also required. The arts program was being tried out in a free school as an attempt to integrate art and basic skills. Students were self-selected and participation was irregular; the program had multiple goals, all of them vague; even the target population was fuzzy; and the treatment depended on who was in attendance on a given day. The free school was a highly fluid environment for which nothing close to a reasonable control or comparison group existed. The teaching approach was highly individualized, with students designing much of their program of study. Both staff and students resented the imposition of rigid, standardized criteria that gave the appearance of a structure that was not there. Yet the Department of Education insisted on a static, hypothetico-deductive evaluation approach.

On the other hand, the direction of the design error is not always the imposition of overly rigid experimental formats. Campbell and Boruch (1975) have shown that many evaluations suffer from an underutilization of more rigid designs. They make a strong case for randomized assignment to treatments by demonstrating six ways in which quasi-experimental evaluations in compensatory education tend to underestimate effects.

Matching methods to programs and decision maker needs is a creative process that emerges from a thorough knowledge of the organizational dynamics and information uncertainties of a particular context. Regulations to the effect that all evaluations must be of a certain type serve neither the cause of increased scientific knowledge nor that of greater program effectiveness—thus the active-reactive-adaptive role of the utilization-focused evaluator.

Alternative Sampling Logics

The quantitative/experimental/summative paradigm emphasizes randomization and probabilistic sampling sufficient in size to permit valid generalizations and appropriate tests of statistical significance. The qualitative/naturalistic/formative paradigm is built on "purposeful sampling" of information-rich cases (Patton, 1980: 100-107). The depth and detail of qualitative methods typically focus on a small number of case studies, too small for confident generalizations. Cases are selected because they serve a particular purpose—thus the term "purposeful sampling."

When the evaluation or policy question is aimed at generalizations, some form of random, probabilistic sampling is the design of choice. A needs assessment, for example, aimed at determining how many residents in a county have some particular problem would suggest the need for a random sample of county residents.

Case studies, on the other hand, become particularly useful when one needs to understand some particular problem or situation in great depth, and when one can identify cases rich in information—rich in the sense that a great deal can be learned from a few exemplars of the phenomenon in question. For example, a great deal can often be learned about how to improve a program by studying select drop-outs, failures, or successes. Stake (1978:

32) has argued that good case studies can "provide different and better knowledge" about a program than statistical generalizations "by providing more valid portrayals, better bases for personal understanding of what is going on, and solid grounds for considering action."

The best-selling management book *In Search of Excellence* (Peters and Waterman, 1982) studied 50 corporations with outstanding reputations for excellence to learn lessons about what these exemplars were doing right. The problem with this approach is yielding to the temptation to inappropriately generalize case study findings to the entire population, as when Tom Peters generalized the lessons from *In Search of Excellence* to all of corporate America—indeed, to all organizations of all kinds in the world! It is precisely such overgeneralizations that have led advocates of randomized, probabilistic sampling to be suspicious of case studies and purposeful sampling.

On the other hand, qualitative methodologists are suspicious of generalizations based on statistical inference at a single point in time. Findings based on samples, however large, are often stripped of their context when generalizations are made—particularly generalizations across time and space. Cronbach (1975) has observed that generalizations decay over time; that is, they have a half-life much like radioactive materials. Guba and Lincoln (1981: 62) are particularly critical of the emphasis on generalizations in the quantitative/experimental ("scientific") paradigm because, they ask, "What can a generalization be except an assertion that is context free? . . . [Yet] *It is virtually impossible to imagine any human behavior that is not heavily mediated by the context in which it occurs*."

Cronbach et al. (1980) have offered a middle ground in the paradigms debate with regard to the problem of generalizability and the relevance of evaluations. They argue against experimental designs that are so focused on carefully controlling cause and effect that the findings are largely irrelevant beyond that highly controlled experimental situation. On the other hand, they are equally concerned that entirely idiosyncratic case studies will yield little of use beyond the case study setting. They suggest instead that designs balance depth and breadth, realism and control, so as to permit reasonable "extrapolation" (1980: 231-235). Unlike the usual meaning of the term "generalization," an extrapolation clearly connotes that one has gone beyond the narrow confines of the data to think about other applications of the findings. Extrapolations are modest speculations on the likely applicability of findings to other situations under similar, but not identical, conditions. Extrapolations are logical, thoughtful, and problem-oriented rather than purely empirical, statistical, and probabilistic. Extrapolations are particularly helpful when based on information-rich samples and designs (i.e., evaluations that produce useful information carefully targeted and highly relevant to stakeholder concerns). Users of evaluation will usually expect evaluators to thoughtfully extrapolate from their findings in the sense of pointing out lessons learned and potential applications to future efforts. Sampling strategies in utilization-focused evaluation should be planned with the stakeholders' desire for extrapolation in mind.

The exchange of views in the paradigms debate has done much to publicize the strengths and weaknesses of both randomized, probabilistic sampling aimed at highly valid conclusions and purposefully sampled case studies aimed at information-rich and highly meaningful conclusions. Understanding these strengths and weaknesses has increased evaluator options to use both approaches in a single evaluation. For these alternative approaches are by no means incompatible. Indeed, they make for a powerful combination. Larger samples of statistically meaningful data can address questions of incidence and prevalence (generalizations) while case studies add depth and detail to make interpretations more meaningful and grounded. Such designs can also introduce a balance between concerns about individualization and standardization, the topic of the next section.

Uniformity or Diversity: Different Foci

The quantitative/experimental paradigm requires the variety of human experience to be captured along standardized scales. Individuals and groups can be described as exhibiting more or less of some trait (self-esteem, satisfaction, competence, knowledge), but everyone is rated or ranked on a limited set of predetermined dimensions. Statistical analyses of these dimensions emphasize central tendencies (averages and deviations from those averages). Critics of standardized instrumentation and measurement are concerned that such an approach only captures quantitative differences, thereby missing significant qualitative differences and important idiosyncrasies. Critics of statistics are fond of telling about the person who drowned in a creek with an average depth of six inches; what was needed was some *in-depth* information about the 6-foot pool in the middle of one part of the creek.

The qualitative/naturalistic paradigm is especially sensitive and pays particular attention to uniqueness, whether this be individual uniqueness or the uniqueness of program, community, home, or other unit of analysis. The inductive strategy of qualitative methods permits the evaluator to enter a program without first pigeonholing participants and staff. When comparing programs, the qualitative evaluator begins by trying to capture the unique, holistic character of each program with special attention to context and setting. Patterns across individuals or programs are sought only after the uniqueness of each case has been described.

Quantitative evaluation researchers sometimes recognize individuality when they discuss "disordinal interactions"; that is, treatments interacting with individual variables in program experiments. This simply means that there may be some innovations that work better for certain types of clients rather than showing across-the-board effects. Both Cronbach (1964b) and Kagan (1966) have expressed the belief that the discovery method works better for some students than for others; some students will perform better with inductive teaching, and some will respond better to didactic teaching. Stolurow (1965) has also suggested that learning strategies interact with individual variables.

Although such suggestions are hardly news to teachers (they know that children learn in different ways, though they do not always know how to take those differences into account in their teaching), disordinal interactions have rarely been uncovered in experimental research. Bracht and Glass (1968: 449) report that, while there are convincing arguments as to why one should expect disordinal interactions, "the empirical evidence for disordinal interactions is far less convincing than the arguments." In point of fact, the actual search for disordinal interactions is rare—most researchers do not bother with the difficult statistical analyses necessary or fail to measure relevant variables:

> the *molarity* (as opposed to the *molecularity*) of both personological variables and the treatments incorporated into many experiments *may* tend to obscure disordinal interactions which *might* be observable when both the variables and the treatments are more narrowly defined. . . . Searching for such interactions with treatments as necessarily complex as instructional curricula may be fruitless [Bracht and Glass, 1968: 451-452].

In effect, Bracht and Glass tend to dismiss the question rather than call into question the methodology that fails to find and predict individual differences. But for program staff, particularly staff in innovative programs aimed at individualizing treatment, the question cannot be dismissed. Indeed, for these staff, the central issue in the treatment process is how to identify and deal with individual differences in clients. Any serious and prudent observer knows that such differences exist, but experimental designs consistently fail to uncover them (e.g., Shapiro, 1973).

Where the emphasis is on individualization of teaching or on meeting the needs of individual clients in social action programs, an evaluation strategy is needed that can take the individual into account. A methodology that takes the individual into account must be sensitive both to unique characteristics in people and programs and to similarities among people and generalizations about treatments.

When the evaluation is aimed at improvement of a specific program, when the information collected is for participants and not just scientists, when the concern is for individuals rather than broad generalizations, an inductive case study approach that identifies unique characteristics and idiosyncracies can be invaluable. Case studies can and do accumulate. Anthropologists have built up an invaluable wealth of case study data that includes both idiosyncratic information and patterns of culture.

Using both quantitative and qualitative approaches can permit the evaluator to address questions about quantitative differences on standardized variables and qualitative differences reflecting individual and program uniquenesses. *The more a program aims at individualized outcomes, the greater the appropriateness of qualitative methods. The more a program emphasizes common outcomes for all participants, the greater the appropriateness of standardized measures of performance and change.*

WHITHER THE EVALUATION METHODS PARADIGMS DEBATE? THE DEBATE HAS WITHERED

Evaluation is much too important to be left to the methodologists.

—Halcolm

The history of the paradigms debate parallels the history of evaluation. The earliest evaluations focused largely on quantitative measurement of clear, specific goals and objectives. With the widespread social and educational experimentation of the 1960s and early 1970s, evaluation designs were aimed at comparing the effectiveness of different programs and treatments through rigorous controls and experiments. This was the period when the quantitative/experimental paradigm dominated, as represented by the Bernstein and Freeman (1975) critique of evaluation quality and such popular texts as Campbell and Stanley (1963), Weiss (1972b), Suchman (1972), Rutman (1977), and the first edition of *Evaluation* (Rossi et al., 1979).

By the middle 1970s, the paradigms debate was becoming a major focus of evaluation discussions and writings (Parlett and Hamilton, 1972; Cronbach, 1975; Patton, 1975a). By the late 1970s, the alternative qualitative/ naturalistic paradigm had been fully articulated (Guba, 1978; Patton, 1978; Stake, 1978). During this period, concern about finding ways to increase utilization became predominant in evaluation (see Chapter 1) and evaluators began discussing standards. A period of pragmatism and dialogue followed, during which calls for and experiences with multiple methods and a synthesis of paradigms became more common (Rist, 1977; Reichardt and Cook, 1979; House, 1980).

One of the clearest signals that the debate was withering came with the publication of the Joint Committee Standards (1981), which gave equal attention, weight, and credence to qualitative and quantitative analyses. Indeed, the Joint Committee was absolutely diligent and precise about this equality of treatment by stating two accuracy standards of identical wording except for the words "quantitative" and "qualitative."

Standard on Analysis of Quantitative Information
> Quantitative information in an evaluation should be appropriately and systematically analyzed to ensure supportable interpretations.

Standard on Analysis of Qualitative Information
> Qualitative information in an evaluation should be appropriately and systematically analyzed to ensure supportable interpretations [Joint Committee on Standards, 1981: 98].

The advice of Cronbach et al. (1980: 7), in their important book on reform of program evaluation, was widely taken to heart:

> The evaluator will be wise not declare allegiance to either a quantitative-scientific-summative methodology or a qualitative-naturalistic-descriptive methodology.

Signs of detente and pragmatism now abound. The second editions of *Evaluation* (Rossi and Freeman, 1982) and *Evaluation Research* (Rutman, 1984) are more balanced and cognizant of methodological diversity. Carol Weiss is revising her important primer on *Evaluation Research* and tells me that a major focus of revision will be greater attention to qualitative methods. Pragmatism, methodological tolerance, flexibility, and concern for appropriateness rather than orthodoxy now characterize the practice, literature, and discussions of evaluation.

The withering of the paradigms debate was made most impressive to me at the 1982 annual meeting of the "May 12" evaluation group at UCLA. The May 12 group is an informal gathering of distinguished evaluators who annually assemble to discuss the issues of the day. During two days in California that distinguished group could find nothing of import about which to argue. In contrast to past sessions, and despite the varying methodological backgrounds and preferences of participants, there was general agreement on the values of methodological flexibility, pragmatism, and eclecticism.

There are ten developments that seem to me to explain the withering of the paradigms debate:

(1) Evaluation has emerged as a genuinely interdisciplinary field of professional practice. Evaluation first emerged as a specialization within separate social science and educational disciplines. The methods expertise of evaluators was closely tied to the methodological focus of their discipline of origin. In recent years, however, courses and programs have emerged for training evaluators that focus attention on evaluation as an interdisciplinary, practical, professional, and problem-solving effort. This has permitted more balanced training and a more balanced approach to methods that emphasizes methodological appropriateness rather than disciplinary orthodoxy.

(2) *The utilization crisis focused attention on the need for methodological flexibility.* When the utilization crisis emerged in the 1960s, there were two major recommendations for increasing evaluation use. One recommendation focused on increased methodological rigor as a way of increasing the accuracy, reliability, and validity of evaluation data, and thereby increasing use. The second set of recommendations focused on increasing attention to stakeholder needs, giving greater attention to evaluation processes as political and problem solving, and matching methods to questions. Methodological rigor alone has not proven an effective strategy for increasing utilization. Direct attention to issues of use, as in utilization-focused evaluation, has proven effective.

(3) *The articulation of professional standards by evaluation associations has emphasized methodological appropriateness rather than paradigm orthodoxy.* The Joint Committee Standards (1981) and the standards of the Evaluation Research Society (1980) both emphasized accuracy within a clear utilization context. The standards provided a basis other than methodological rigor for judging evaluations, and therefore introduced the possibility of using a variety of methods, including qualitative ones, and still doing evaluations that were judged of high quality.

(4) *The accumulation of practical evaluation experience during the last fifteen years has reduced paradigms polarization.* The practical experience of evaluators in attempting to work with programs to improve their effectiveness has led evaluators to become pragmatic in their approaches to methods issues, and in that pragmatism has emerged a commitment to do what works rather than a commitment to methodological rigor for the sake of rigor.

(5) *The strengths and weaknesses of both quantitative/experimental methods and qualitative/naturalistic methods are now better understood.* In the original debate quantitative/experimental methodologists tended to attack some of the worst examples of qualitative/naturalistic evaluations while the qualitative/naturalistic evaluators tended to hold up for critique the worst examples of quantitative/experimental approaches. With the accumulation of experience and confidence, exemplars of both qualitative and quantitative approaches have emerged with corresponding analyses of the strengths and weaknesses of each. This has permitted more balance and a better understanding of the situations for which various methods are most appropriate.

(6) *A broader conceptualization of evaluation, and of evaluator training, has reduced the centrality of methods in evaluation, and has therefore reduced the centrality of the methods debate.* Early definitions of evaluation were fairly narrow in emphasizing goal attainment and the application of scientific methods to the study of programs. More recent definitions of evaluation, including the one in this book (Chapter 1), emphasize providing information for program improvement and decision making. This broader conceptualization has directed attention to the political nature of evaluation,

the need to integrate evaluation into program processes, working with stake-holders throughout the evaluation process, and laying a solid foundation for the use of evaluation. This broader view of evaluation has made methods less central and thereby reduced the centrality of the methods paradigms debate.

(7) *Advances in methods approaches have strengthened diverse applications to evaluation problems.* This is especially true of qualitative/ naturalistic methods in which a great deal of work has gone on in the last ten years addressing questions of the validity and reliability of evaluation data that is qualitative in nature. The paradigms debate, in part, increased the amount of qualitative work being done, created additional opportunities for training in qualitative methods, and brought attention by methodologists to problems of increasing the quality of qualitative data. As the quality of qualitative methods has increased, as training in qualitative methods has improved (e.g., Levine et al., 1980), and as claims about qualitative methods have become more balanced, the attacks on qualitative methods have become less strident. Likewise, quantitative-experimental methodologists have become more flexible and modest, reducing the extent to which those techniques were the subject of attack.

(8) *Support for methodological eclecticism from major figures in evaluation has increased methodological tolerance.* When eminent scientists such as Donald Campbell and Lee J. Cronbach began publicly recognizing the contributions that qualitative methods could make to social science research and evaluation, the acceptability of qualitative-naturalistic approaches was greatly enhanced. Ernest House (1977: 18), in describing the role of "qualitative argument" in evaluation research, notes that "when two of the leading scholars of measurement and experimental design, Cronbach and Campbell, strongly support qualitative studies, that is strong endorsement indeed." In my own work I have found increased interest in and acceptance of qualitative methods in particular and multiple methods in general.

(9) *Evaluation professional societies have supported exchanges of views and high-quality professional practice in an environment of tolerance and eclecticism.* The evaluation professional societies and journals serve a variety of people from different disciplines who operate in different kinds of organizations at different levels, in and out of the public sector, and in and out of universities. This diversity and opportunities to exchange views and perspectives have contributed to the emergent pragmatism, eclecticism, and tolerance in the field.

(10) *There is increased experience in combining qualitative and quantitative approaches.* As evaluators worked to focus evaluation questions and gather useful information, they began using multiple methods and a variety of data sources to elucidate evaluation questions. Initial efforts at merging quantitative and qualitative perspectives often proved difficult. Qualitative and quantitative data were often difficult to integrate, and when doubts were

raised or conflicts emerged it was often the qualitative data that bore the larger burden of proof. An excellent article by M.G. Trend (1978) described the difficulties of getting fair consideration of qualitative data in a major ABT Associates study. The Trend article is an excellent description of qualitative data being rejected when they do not support quantitative findings.

The 1980 meetings of the Society of Applied Anthropology in Denver included a symposium on the problems encountered by anthropologists participating in teams in which both quantitative and qualitative data were being collected. The problems they shared were stark evidence that qualitative methods were typically perceived as exploratory and secondary when used in conjunction with quantitative/experimental approaches. When qualitative data supported quantitative findings, that was icing on the cake. When qualitative data conflicted with quantitative data, the qualitative data have often been dismissed or ignored.

Despite these difficulties, there have now emerged positive examples in which qualitative and quantitative data have worked together. Fetterman (1980, 1984) has had considerable success in reporting and integrating both kinds of data. He used qualitative data to understand quantitative findings, and quantitative data to broaden qualitative interpretations. Maxwell et al. (1985) demonstrated how an ethnographic approach can be combined with an experimental design within a single study framework. Another area of integration has emerged in evaluations that include a large number of case sites in a large-scale study; Firestone and Herriott (1984) have demonstrated how quantitative logic can contribute to the interpretation of qualitative data as the number of sites in a study grows. The theoretical basis for combining qualitative and quantitative methods has been well articulated (Reichardt and Cook, 1979; Patton, 1982a).

Thus, there are positive signs that evaluators have become much more sophisticated about the complexities of methodological choices and combinations. The evaluations cited above provide concrete examples of methods integration. This evidence also suggests that integrating qualitative and quantitative methods will continue to be a difficult task requiring great sensitivity and respect for the strengths of each approach and recognition of the weaknesses of each data set.

* * *

All in all, these trends and factors suggest that the paradigms debate has significantly withered. The focus is now on methodological appropriateness rather than orthodoxy, methodological creativity rather than rigid adherence to a paradigm, and methodological flexibility rather than following a narrow set of rules.

The methodological dragon has been tamed.

BEYOND PARADIGMS

The paradigms debate helped elucidate the complexity of choices available in evaluation. It also demonstrated the difficulty of moving beyond narrow disciplinary training to make decisions based upon what information is most useful rather than what information is collected traditionally in one's discipline. It is premature to say that the practice of evaluation is now completely characterized by flexibility and attention to methodological appropriateness rather than disciplinary orthodoxy, but it is fair to say that the goals have shifted dramatically in this direction.

Accompanying this shift in emphasis has been a recognition that there are no rigid rules for making methods decisions. Corollaries to this lack of rules are as follow: (1) There is no single best plan for an evaluation, (2) there is no perfect design, and (3) there are always errors and ambiguities. These observations will be explored further in the next chapter. These observations lead from orthodoxy to trade-offs and negotiations. With the paradigms debate in perspective, the methodology dragon can cease to be a drag on methodological flexibility and creativity. The debate over which paradigm was the right path to *truth* has been replaced in evaluation by a paradigm of choices.

The Paradigm of Choices

With its roots in the social sciences and educational research, evaluation originally emerged as a methodological solution to real world decision-

making problems. Evaluation was methods driven. The primary concerns in any evaluation centered on design, measurement, and analysis decisions.

Evaluation has grown and matured beyond that original, narrow methodological focus. Table 8.2 summarizes the contrasting themes of the paradigms debate and describes the synthesis that is emerging with the shift in emphasis from methodological orthodoxy to methodological appropriateness and utility. *Utilization-focused evaluation is utility driven rather than methods driven.* Methods are employed in the service of relevance and use, not as their master. This has opened up the paradigm of choices. Methods decisions *follow* identification of primary stakeholders and focusing relevant evaluation questions. Like a child losing its innocence, evaluation research has grown beyond the simple days when the answer to every evaluation problem was the administration of a standardized test to experimental and control groups.

Today's evaluator must be sophisticated about matching research methods to the nuances of particular evaluation questions and the idiosyncracies of specific decision maker needs. The evaluator must have a large repertoire of research methods and techniques available to use on a variety of problems. Thus, today's evaluator may be called on to use any and all social science research methods, including analyses of quantitative data, questionnaire results, secondary data analysis, cost-benefit and cost-effectiveness analyses, standardized tests, experimental designs, unobtrusive measures, participant observation, and in-depth interviewing.

The utilization-focused evaluator works with stakeholders to design an evaluation that includes any and all data that will help shed light on evaluation questions, given constraints of resources and time. Such an evaluator is committed to research designs that are relevant, rigorous, understandable, and able to produce useful results that are valid, reliable, and believable. On many occasions—indeed, for most evaluation problems—a variety of data collection techniques and design approaches will be used. Multiple methods and triangulation of observations contribute to methodological rigor.

Selecting methods is no longer a matter of the dominant paradigm versus the alternative paradigm, of experimental designs with quantitative measurement versus holistic-inductive designs collecting qualitative data. The debate and competition between paradigms is being replaced by a new paradigm—a paradigm of choices. The paradigm of choices recognizes that different methods are appropriate for different situations.

The next chapter discusses how methods decisions are different when an evaluation is utility driven rather than methods driven.

TABLE 8.2

The Evaluation Methods Paradigms Debate Summary of Emphases: Theses, Antitheses, Syntheses

	Theses: Originally Dominant "Scientific" Paradigm	Antitheses: Originally Competing Alternative Paradigm	Syntheses: Utilization-Focused Evaluation, a Paradigm of Choices
Purpose	Summative	Formative	Intended use for intended users
Measurement	Quantitative data	Qualitative data	Appropriate, credible, useful data
Design	Experimental designs	Naturalistic inquiry	Creative, practical, situationally responsive designs
Researcher stance	Objectivity	Subjectivity	Fairness and balance
Inquiry mode	Deduction	Induction	Either or both
Conceptualization	Independent and dependent variables	Holistic interdependent system	Stakeholder questions and issues
Relationships	Distance, detachment	Closeness, involvement	Collaboration, consultative
Approach to study of change	Pre-post measures, time series, static portrayals at discrete points in time	Process-oriented, evolving, capturing ongoing dynamism	Developmental, action-oriented: What needs to be known to get program from where it is to where it wants to be?

Relationship to prior knowledge	Confirmatory, hypothesis testing	Exploratory, hypothesis generating	Either or both
Sampling	Random, probabilistic	Purposeful, key informants	Combinations, depending on what information is needed
Primary approach to variations	Quantitative differences on uniform, standardized variables	Qualitative differences, uniquenesses	Flexible: Focus on comparisons most relevant to intended users and evaluation questions
Analysis	Descriptive and inferential statistics	Case studies, content and pattern analysis	Answers to stakeholders' questions
Types of statements	Generalizations	Context-bound	Extrapolations
Contribution to theory	Validating theoretical propositions from scientific literature	Grounded theory	Describing, exploring, and testing stakeholders' and program's theory of action
Goals	Truth, scientific acceptance	Understanding, perspective	Utility, relevance: Acceptance by intended users

Chapter 9

EVALUATIONS WORTH USING:

UTILIZATION-FOCUSED METHODS DECISIONS

I am easily satisfied
with the very best.

—Winston Churchill

The Very Best Evaluation

It would all be so much easier if everyone agreed on what constitutes the very best. Even in the glory days of the dominant paradigm, when there was considerable agreement that the very best was randomized true experiments, different methodologists still rated actual studies quite differently. McTavish et al. (1975) used eminent social scientists to judge and rate the research quality of 126 federal studies. They found that "there appear to be important and meaningful differences between raters in their professional judgments about a project's methodology" (p. 63). One has only to read the debates over studies of student achievement and educational inequality (e.g., between Coleman and Cain in Rossi, 1972) or the "White Flight Debate" (Pettigrew and Green, 1977; Coleman, 1977) to know that methodologists disagree about the proper way to conduct research and interpret findings.

Eva Baker is Director of the UCLA Center for the Study of Evaluation and the editor of *Educational Evaluation and Policy Analysis (EEPA)*. As editor, she established a strong system of peer review for *EEPA*, requiring three independent reviewers for every article. Eva recently told me that in several years as editor *she has never published an article on which all three reviewers agreed the article was good!*

That's an extraordinary statement to people who think that there are clear scientific standards for what constitutes good work. Editor Baker's experience is less surprising to those inside science who understand that a major thrust of methodological training in graduate school is learning how to pick apart and attack any study. There are no perfect studies. And there cannot be, for there is no agreement on what constitutes perfection.

This has important implications for methods decisions in evaluation. There are no universal and absolute standards for judging methods. The paradigms debate highlighted the different criteria that could be applied in judging methods. The consensus that has emerged from the paradigms debate is that evaluation methods are to be judged on the basis of appropriateness, utility, practicality, credibility, and relevance. These criteria are necessarily situational and context-bound. One cannot judge the adequacy of methods used in a specific evaluation without knowing the purpose of the evaluation, the intended uses of the findings, the resources available, and the trade-offs negotiated.

Judgments about validity and reliability, for example, are necessarily and appropriately relative rather than absolute in that the rigor and quality of an evaluation's design and measurement depend on the purpose and *intended use* of the evaluation. The accuracy standards of the Joint Committee on Standards (1981) make it clear that validity and reliability of an evaluation depend on the intended use(s) of the evaluation.

Valid Measurement: The information-gathering instruments and procedures should be chosen or developed and then implemented in ways that will assure that the interpretation arrived at is valid *for the given use*.

Reliable Measurement: The information-gathering instruments and procedures should be chosen or developed and then implemented in ways that will assure that the information obtained is sufficiently reliable *for the intended use* [Joint Committee, 1981: 98; emphasis added].

Involving Primary Intended Users in Methods Decisions

The third step in utilization-focused evaluation involves working with primary intended users to make methods decisions. Since methods decisions always involve trade-offs and choices, and since scientists and methodologists disagree about what criteria to apply in negotiating trade-offs, stakeholders' criteria take on added importance. Stakeholders can understand methods options. Stakeholders need to be involved in making choices so that they clearly understand the strengths and weaknesses of various approaches. Since intended users have the most at stake in an evaluation, their criteria for what constitutes a good evaluation become the primary focus for methods decisions. This chapter is about how to involve stakeholders in methods decisions.

Cronbach et al. (1980: 7) have observed that "merit lies not in form of inquiry but in relevance of information." My experience with stakeholders suggests that they would rather have "soft data" about an important question than "hard data" about an issue of minor relevance. Obviously the ideal is hard data about important questions, whatever "hard data" may mean in a particular context. But in the real world of trade-offs and negotiations, too often what can be measured determines what is evaluated, rather than deciding first what is worth evaluating and then doing the best one can with methods. Relevance and utility are the driving forces in utilization-focused evaluation; methods are employed in the service of relevance and use, not as their master.

There are no rigid rules that can be provided for making data collection methods decisions in evaluation. Cronbach (1982: 239) observed that designing an evaluation is as much art as science: "Developing an evaluation is an exercise of the dramatic imagination." The art of evaluation involves creating a design and gathering information that is appropriate for a specific situation and particular policymaking context. In art there is no single, ideal standard. Beauty is in the eye of the beholder, and the evaluation beholders include decision makers, policymakers, program managers, and the general public. Thus, for Cronbach, there are no preferred measures or ideal measures, not even in a particular situation. Any given design is necessarily an interplay of resources, possibilities, creativity, and personal judgments by the people involved.

> There is no single best plan for an evaluation, not even for an inquiry into a particular program, at a particular time, with a particular budget [Cronbach, 1982: 231].

This chapter explores the implications of this observation for working with stakeholders to design useful and appropriate evaluations rather than attempting to design studies that are immune from methodological criticism. There simply is no such immunity. Thus, instead of engaging in the futile effort to please the scientific community, utilization-focused evaluation strives to attain the more modest and attainable goal of pleasing primary intended users. This does not mean that utilization-focused evaluations are less rigorous. It means the criteria for rigor may be different from the traditional canons of science.

CREDIBILITY AND USE

Use is related directly to credibility. Credibility is a complex notion that includes the perceived accuracy, fairness, and believability of the evaluation. It also depends on the extent to which the evaluation is understandable. Concern about credibility is a major theme in the Joint Committee's standards (1981). Evaluators are admonished to be "both trustworthy and competent" so that findings will achieve "maximum credibility and acceptance" (p. 24). Report clarity, full and frank disclosure of data strengths and weaknesses, balanced reporting, defensible information sources, valid and reliable measurement, and justified conclusions are all specific standards aimed at credibility as a foundation for use.

For information to be useful and to merit use, it should be as accurate and believable as possible. Limitations on the degree of accuracy should be stated clearly. Research by Weiss and Bucuvalas (1980) found that decision makers apply "truth tests" (whether data are believable and accurate) and "utility tests" (whether data are relevant) in deciding how seriously to pay attention to research and evaluation findings. Decision makers want highly accurate and trustworthy data. This means they want data that are valid and reliable. But in the politically charged environment of evaluation, these traditional scientific concepts have taken on some new and broader meanings.

Evaluation Validity

House (1980: 249) has suggested that validity means "worthiness of being recognized." For the typical evaluation this means being "true, credible, and right" (p. 250). Different approaches to evaluation establish validity in different ways. The important part of House's contribution from the point of view of utilization-focused evaluation is that he applies the notion of validity to *the entire evaluation*, not just data from an evaluation. An *evaluation* is perceived as valid in a global sense that includes the overall approach used, the stance of the evaluator, the nature of the process, the design, and the way in which results are reported. Both the evaluation *and* the evaluator must be perceived as trustworthy for the evaluation to have high validity.

Alkin et al. (1979: 245) found in their studies of evaluation use that "for evaluations to have impact, users must believe what evaluators have to say." The believability of an evaluation depends on much more than the perceived scientific validity of the data and findings. Believability depends on the users' perceptions of and experiences with the program being evaluated, users' prior knowledge and prejudices, the perceived adequacy of evaluation procedures, and the users' trust in the evaluator (Alkin et al., 1979: 245-247). Trust, believability, and credibility are the underpinnings of overall evaluation validity.

It is important to understand how overall evaluation validity differs from the usual, more narrow conception of validity in scientific research. Validity is usually focused entirely on data collection procedures, design, and technical analysis.

A measure is scientifically valid to the extent that it captures or measures the concept (or thing) it is intended to measure. Validity is often difficult to establish, particularly for new instruments. Over time scientists develop a consensus about the relative validity of often-used instruments, such as major norm-referenced standardized educational tests. Rossi et al. (1979) discuss three common criteria for validity of quantitative instruments.

> *(1) Consistency with usage:* A valid measurement of a concept must be consistent with past work that used that concept. Hence, a measure of adoption must not be in contradiction to the usual ways in which that term has been used in previous evaluations of interventions.
>
> *(2) Consistency with alternative measures:* A valid measure must be consistent with alternative measures that have been used effectively by other evaluators. Thus, a measure must produce roughly the same results as other measures that have been proposed, or, if different, have sound conceptual reasons for being different.
>
> *(3) Internal consistency:* A valid measure must be internally consistent. That is, if several questions are used to measure adoption, the answers to those questions should be related to each other as if they were alternative measures of the same thing [Rossi et al., 1979: 170-171].

Qualitative data collection (e.g., such techniques as participant observation and in-depth, open-ended interviewing) poses different validity problems. In qualitative methods, validity hinges to a greater extent on the skill, competence, and rigor of the researcher because the observer or interviewer *is* the instrument. Guba and Lincoln (1981: 113) comment on this validity problem as follows:

> Since as often as not the naturalistic inquirer is himself the instrument, changes resulting from fatigue, shifts in knowledge, and cooptation, as well as variations, resulting from differences in training, skill, experience among different "instruments," easily occur. But this loss in rigor is more than offset by the flexibility, insight, and ability to build on tacit knowledge that is the peculiar province of the human instrument.

Validity is also a concern in using official statistics. Evaluators frequently use government statistics as social indicators to measure changes in phenomena of interest, such as health or crime statistics. Hudson (1977: 88-89) discussed at length the validity problems of crime statistics:

> First, officially collected information used as measures of program outcomes are, by their very nature, indirect measures of behavior. For example, we have no practical or direct way of measuring the actual extent to which graduates of correctional programs commit new crimes. Second, the measurements pro-

vided are commonly open to serious problems. For example, the number of crimes known to authorities in most situations is only a fraction of the number of crimes committed, although that fraction varies from crime to crime. . . . The growing willingness of victims of sexual assault to report their crimes to the police and actively cooperate in prosecution is an example of the manner in which public attitudes can affect officially recorded rates of crime.

Of the various criteria used to measure recidivism, that of arrest appears to be especially problematic. Recidivism rates based on arrest do not tell us whether those arrested have, in fact, returned to criminal behavior but only that they are presumed to have done so. . . .

The widespread discretion exercised by the police to arrest is a further source of invalidity. For example, it is probably reasonable to expect that the number of individuals arrested for a particular type of crime within a jurisdiction is to some extent a direct reflection of changing police policies and not totally the function of changing patterns of law-violating behavior. In addition to the power of deciding when to arrest, police also have discretionary authority to determine which of a number of crimes an individual will be arrested for in a particular situation. Thus, if policy emphasis is placed upon combating burglary, this may affect decisions as to whether an arrestee is to be arrested for burglary, simple larceny, or criminal damage to property. In short, the discretion of the police to control both the number and types of arrests raises serious validity problems in evaluations which attempt to use this measure of program outcome.

In summary, then, validity problems are of concern for the overall credibility of the evaluation as well as the trustworthiness of the evaluator and for all kinds of data collection—quantitative measures, questionnaires, qualitative observations, government statistics, and social indicators. The precise nature of the validity problem varies from situation to situation, but the evaluator must always be concerned about the extent to which the data collected are credible and actually measure what is supposed to be measured. The next section examines a validity issue of special, though not unique, concern to evaluators: the issue of face validity.

The Believability of Data:
Face Validity in Utilization-Focused Measurement

Involving identified stakeholders and intended information users in measurement and design decisions is based on the finding that use is enhanced if users believe in and have a stake in the data (Alkin et al., 1979). Belief in the data is increased by understanding it; understanding is enhanced by involvement in the painstaking process of making decisions about what data to collect, how to collect it, and how to analyze it. Stakeholders who acquiesce to the expertise of the evaluator may later find that they neither understand nor believe in the evaluation data. By the same token, evaluators can expect low utilization if they rely on the mysticism of their scientific priesthood to establish the credibility of data rather than relying on the understanding of decision makers directly involved with it.

One of the best ways to facilitate stakeholder understanding of and belief in evaluation data is to place a high value on *face validity* of evaluation instruments. Face validity concerns "the extent to which an instrument looks as if it measures what it is intended to measure" (Nunnally, 1970: 149). An instrument has face validity if stakeholders can look at the items and understand what is being measured. Face validity, however, is generally held in low regard by measurement experts. Predictive validity, concurrent validity, construct validity—these technical approaches are much preferred by psychometricians. Nunnally (1970: 149) considers face validity to have occasional public relations value when data are gathered for the general public: "Less logical is the reluctance of some administrators in applied settings, e.g., industry, to permit the use of predictor instruments which lack face validity." Yet from a utilization perspective, it is perfectly logical for decision makers to want to understand and believe in data they are expected to use. Nunnally (1970: 150) disagrees: "Although one could make a case for the involvement of face validity in the measurement of constructs, to do so would probably serve only to confuse the issues." It is little wonder that evaluators, many of whom cut their measurement teeth on Nunnally's textbooks, have little sympathy for the face validity needs of stakeholders. Nor is it surprising that such evaluators complain that their findings are not used. Consider the following case.

The board of directors of a major industrial firm decided to decentralize organizational decision making in hopes of raising worker morale. The president of the company hired an organizational consultant to monitor and evaluate the decentralization program and its effects. From the literature on the sociology of organizations, the evaluator selected a set of research instruments designed to measure decentralization, worker autonomy, communication rates and patterns, worker satisfaction, and related organizational dimensions. The scales had been generated empirically and used by sociologists to measure organizational change in a number of different settings. The factorial composition of the scales had been established. The instruments had high predictive validity and construct validity, but they had low face validity.

The evaluator selected a simple pretest and posttest design with nine months separating pre- and postadministration of the instruments. Data analysis showed no statistically significant changes between pretest and posttest. The evaluator reported that the decentralization program had not been implemented successfully and that worker morale remained low.

These negative findings were reported for the first time at a meeting of the board. The president of the company had a considerable stake in the success of the program; he did not have a stake in the evaluation data. He did what decision makers frequently do in such cases—he began to attack the data.

President: How can you be so sure that the program has not been implemented? How did you determine that the program is inefficient?

Evaluator: We collected data using the best instruments available. I won't go into all the technical and statistical details of factor analysis and Cronbach's alpha. Let me just say that these scales have been shown to be highly valid and reliable.

Take this scale on "individual autonomy." It's made up of ten items. Each item is an indicator of "autonomy." For example, the best predictor item in this particular scale asks respondents: (a) "Do you take coffee breaks on a fixed schedule?" or (b) "Do you go to get coffee whenever you want to?"

President: [visibly reddening and speaking in an angry tone] Am I to understand that your entire evaluation is based on some kind of questionnaire that asks people how often they get coffee, that you never personally talked to any workers or managers, that you never even visited our operations?

Am I to understand that we paid you $20,000 to find out how people get their coffee?

Evaluator: Well there's a lot more to it than that, you see . . .

President: That's it! We don't have any more time for this nonsense. Our lawyers will be in touch with you about whether we want to press fraud and malpractice charges!"

Clearly the president was predisposed to dismiss any negative findings. But suppose the evaluator had gone over the measurement and design decisions with the president before gathering data. Suppose the evaluator had shown him the items, explained what they were supposed to indicate, and then asked, "Now, if we administer these questionnaires with these items measuring these factors, will they tell you what you want to know? Does this kind of evaluation make sense to you? Are you prepared to act on this kind of data? Would you believe the results if they came out negative?"

Such an exchange might not have made a difference. It is not easy to get decision makers to look carefully at instrumentation in advance, nor do evaluators want to waste time explaining their trade. Decision makers are just as happy not being bothered with technical decisions—after all, that is why they hired an evaluator in the first place, to design and conduct the evaluation! But the costs of such attitudes to use can be high. Utilization-focused evaluation makes the face validity of instrumentation—determined before data are collected—a major criterion in evaluation measurement. Data analysis, data interpretation, and data use are all facilitated by attention to face validity criteria.

The Credibility of Evaluation Designs

Face validity criteria can also be applied to design questions. Does the design make sense? Is the decision maker interested in a comparison of group A against group B? Is the sample size sufficiently large to be believable? The evaluator can be sure that decision makers will have opinions about these issues after the data are collected, particularly if findings are negative. By engaging the information users in consideration of these issues before data are collected, the data are likely to be more credible and more useful. Consider the following case.

At an evaluation workshop for human service agencies, the marketing director for a major retail merchandising company had come to find out how to get more mileage out of his marketing research department. He told the following story.

Two years earlier (1975) he had spent a considerable sum researching the potential for new products for his company's local retail distribution chain. A carefully selected sample of 285 respondents had been interviewed in the Minneapolis-Saint Paul greater metropolitan area. The results indicated one promising new line of products for which there appeared to be growing demand. He took this finding to the board of directors with a recommendation that the company make a major capital investment in the new product line. The board, controlled by the views of its aging chairman, vetoed the recommendation. The reason: "If you had presented us with opinions from at least a thousand people we might be able to move on this item. But we can't make a major capital commitment on the basis of a couple of hundred interviews."

The marketing director tactfully tried to explain that increased sample size would have made only a marginal reduction in possible sampling error. The chairman remained unconvinced, the findings of an expensive research project were ignored, and the company missed out on a major opportunity: The item they rejected was citizens-band radios, the hottest selling new retail item in the country less than a year after the survey results were rejected by the board!

It is easy to laugh at the board's mistake, but the marketing director was not laughing. He wanted to know what to do. I suggested that next time he check out the research design with the board before collecting data, going to them and saying, "Our statisticians estimate that a sample of 285 respondents in the Twin Cities area will give us an accurate picture of market potential. Here are the reasons they recommend this sample size. . . . Does that make sense to you? If we come in with the recommendations based on 285 respondents, will you believe the data? Can you confidently act on the basis of this research design?"

If the board responds positively, then utilization potential is enhanced. Of course, there are no guarantees. But at least the evaluator has done all that can be done. If the board says the sample is too small, then the survey might as well include more respondents—or be cancelled. There is little point in implementing a design that is known in advance to lack credibility.

Reliability

Validity focuses on the meaning and meaningfulness of data; reliability focuses on consistency of results. A measure is reliable to the extent that essentially the same results are produced in the same situation, and that these results can be reproduced repeatedly as long as the situation does not change. For example, in measuring the height of an adult person, one should get essentially the same results over time. Measuring attitudes, however, is more difficult because one can never be sure if a measured change means the attitude has changed or if the data collection is unreliable.

In essence, reliability concerns the problem of error in data collection. Evaluation measures can be seductive in their apparent precision. To say, for example, that a student has scored in the seventieth percentile on a standardized achievement test sounds terribly precise and scientific. It is easy to forget that the numbers are merely probabilistic indicators of real things; the numbers are not the thing. Eminent psychologist Ann Anastasi (1973: XI) commented on this kind of confusion with regard to IQ scores: "One still hears the term 'IQ' used as though it referred, not to a test score, but to a property of the organism." In other words, the numbers that come out of standardized tests or other evaluation instruments are not embedded in the genes or on the foreheads of students or clients. They are only rough approximations of some characteristic at a specific point in time under particular conditions. Test results or questionnaire responses are only one piece of information about a person or a group—a piece of information that must be interpreted in connection with other information we have about that person or group. Test scores and other evaluation data, then, are neither good nor bad. They are pieces of information that are subject to considerable error— and that are more or less useful depending on how they are gathered, interpreted, applied, and used or abused.

All kinds of statistical information are subject to error and unreliability. I have chosen to focus on standardized tests as an example in this section on errors because nonscientists seem particularly subject to a belief in the absolute accuracy of such evaluation instruments. The importance of looking for potential sources of error in any measurement is, however, a principle that applies generally. For many reasons, all tests and other evaluation instruments are subject to some measurement error. Henry Dyer, a president of the highly respected Educational Testing Service (ETS), tells of trying to explain to a government official that test scores, even on the most reliable tests, have enough measurement error that they must be used with extreme caution. The government official, who happened to be an enthusiastic proponent of performance contracting, responded that test makers should "get on the ball" and start producing tests that "are 100% reliable under all conditions."

Dyer's comments on this conversation are particularly relevant to an understanding of error in evaluation instruments. He asks,

> How does one get across the shocking truth that 100% reliability in a test is a fiction that, in the nature of the case, is unrealizable? How does one convey the notion that the test reliability problem is not one of reducing measurement error to absolute zero, but of minimizing it as far as practicable and doing one's best to estimate whatever amount of error remains, so that one may act cautiously and wisely in a world where all knowledge is approximate and not even death and taxes are any longer certain [Dyer, 1973: 87]?

Sources of error are many. For example, continuing with the problems of errors in test scores, there are myriad reasons why a particular student's score may be subject to error. The health of the child on the day the test is given can affect the score. Whether or not the pupil had breakfast can make a difference. Noise in the classroom, a sudden fire drill, whether or not the teacher or a stranger gives the test, a broken pencil, and any number of similar disturbances can change a test score. The mental state of the child—depression, boredom, elation, a conflict at home, a fight with another student, anxiety about the test, a low self-concept—can affect how well the student performs. Simple mechanical errors such as marking the wrong box on the test sheet by accident, accidentally skipping a question, or missing a word while reading are common problems for all of us. Students who have trouble reading will perform poorly on reading tests; but they are also likely to perform poorly on social studies, science, and arithmetic tests because all of these tests require reading. Thus, the test may considerably underestimate the real knowledge of the child.

Some children perform better on tests because they have been taught how to take written tests. Some children are simply better test takers than other children because of their background or personality or how seriously they treat the idea of the test. Some schools make children sit all day long taking test after test, sometimes for an entire week. Other schools give the test for only a half-day or two hours a day to minimize fatigue and boredom. Some children like to take tests; some do not. Some teachers help children with difficult words, or even read the tests along with the children; others do not. Some schools devote their curriculum, or at least some school time, to teaching students what is on the tests. Other schools, notably alternative schools (open classrooms, free schools, street academies), place little emphasis on test taking and paper-and-pencil skills, thus giving students less experience in the rigor and tricks of taking tests.

All these sources of error—and I have scarcely scratched the surface of such possibilities—can seriously affect an individual child's score. Moreover, they have virtually nothing to do with how good the test is, how carefully it was prepared, and how valid its content is for a given child or group. Intrinsic to the nature of standardized testing, these errors are always present to some extent and are largely uncontrollable. They are the reason that statisticians can never develop a test that is 100% reliable.

The errors are more or less serious depending on how a test is used. When looking at test scores for large groups, we can expect that because of such errors some students will perform above their true level and other students will perform below their true score. For most groups, statisticians believe that these errors cancel each other. The overly high scores of some students compensate for the overly low scores of others, so that the group result is relatively accurate. The larger the group tested, the more likely this is to be true.

However, for a specific individual, no other scores are available to make up for the error in his or her score. The only hope is that the questions the student answered wrong because of error will be compensated for by the questions he or she got right either accidentally or by guessing. This type of error compensation is much less reliable in correcting for error than the situation described for large groups. The least reliable result is one individual's answer on a single question. Nothing can compensate for error in this case. Thus, one must be extremely cautious about making too much of results for individuals, particularly on single, specific test questions and short tests.

Different evaluation instruments are subject to different kinds of errors. Measurement errors can also result from the sampling procedures employed, the way instruments are administered, and other design problems. Whether the evaluation includes data from tests, questionnaires, management information systems, government statistics, or whatever—the analysis should include attention to potential sources of error. Statistical procedures are available for computing the relative size of various kinds of error.

The point is that evaluators do their clients a disservice when they treat lightly the problem of errors in evaluation data. Evaluators need not be defensive about errors. Decision makers and information users can be helpful in identifying potential sources of error. In my experience, their overall confidence in their ability to correctly and appropriately use evaluation data is increased when there has been a frank and full discussion of *both* the data's strengths and weaknesses. In this way, evaluators are helping to make evaluation clients more knowledgeable so they will understand what Dyer's government official did not:

> The problem is not one of reducing measurement error to absolute zero, but of minimizing it as far as practicable and doing one's best to estimate whatever amount of error remains, so that one may act cautiously and wisely in a world where all knowledge is approximate and not even death and taxes are any longer certain.

TRADE-OFFS

Different evaluation questions permit different degrees of error. An evaluation that focuses on a major decision that will affect the future continuation of a program, perhaps touching the lives of thousands of people and involving allocations of millions of dollars, will necessarily involve considerable attention to ways of minimizing error. On the other hand, a small-scale, fairly informal, formative evaluation aimed at stimulating staff to think about what they're doing will raise fewer concerns about error. There is a lot of space between these extremes. The amount of precision needed and the degree of error that can reasonably be tolerated will vary from evaluation to evaluation. These are matters to be discussed and negotiated. The next two sections look at additional concerns that commonly involve negotiation and trade-offs. These are decisions about (1) breadth versus depth and (2) the relative generalizability of findings.

The Problem of Focus: Breadth Versus Depth

Deciding what information and how much data to gather in an evaluation involves difficult decisions and trade-offs. Getting more data usually takes longer and costs more, but getting fewer data usually reduces confidence in the findings. Studying a narrow question or very specific problem in great depth may produce clear results but leave other important issues and problems unexamined. On the other hand, gathering information on a large variety of issues and problems may leave the evaluation unfocused and result in knowing a little about a lot of things but not knowing a lot about anything.

Thus, in the methods deliberations some boundaries must be set on data collection. Should all parts of the program be studied, or only certain parts? Should all clients be studied, or only some subset of clients? Should the evaluator aim at describing all program processes, or is there reason to examine only certain selected processes in depth? Should all outcomes be examined, or should the evaluation focus on the attainment of only certain outcomes of particular interest at this time?

In my own experience the problem of establishing focus and priorities is more difficult than the problem of generating potential questions at the beginning of the evaluation. Once a group of decision makers and information users begins to take seriously the notion that they can learn from the collection and analysis of evaluative information, they soon discover that there are lots of things they would like to find out. The evaluator's role is to help decision makers and information users move from a rather extensive list of potential questions to a much shorter list of realistic questions and finally to a focused list of essential and necessary questions. This is a process that goes from divergence to convergence. One begins by generating many possibilities (divergence) and then focuses on a few worthwhile priorities (convergence).

An example of variations in measurement focus may help illustrate the kinds of trade-offs involved. Suppose that a group of educators is interested in studying how a school program affects the social development of children of school age. They want to know if the interaction of children with others in the school setting contributes to the development of social skills. They believe that those social skills will be different for different children, and they are not sure of the range of social interactions that may occur, so they are interested in a descriptive evaluation that will capture variations in experience and individualized outcomes. Still, there are trade-offs in determining the final focus. It is clear that any given child has social interactions with a great many people. The problem in focusing our evaluation research endeavor is to determine how much of the social reality experienced by children we should attempt to describe. In a narrowly focused evaluation we might select one particular set of interactions between teacher and children. Broadening the scope somewhat, we might decide to look at only those interactions that occur in the classroom, thereby increasing the scope of the study to include interactions not only between teacher and child but also among peers in the classroom and between any volunteers and visitors to the classroom and the children. Broadening the scope of the study still more, we might decide to look at all of the social relationships that children experience in schools; in this case we would move beyond the classroom to look at interactions with other teaching personnel in the school—for example, the librarian, school counselors, special subject teachers, the custodian, and/or school administration staff. Broadening the scope of the study still further, the educators might decide that it is important to look at the social relationships children experience in home and in school in order to understand how children experience those settings differently, and therefore to understand better the unique effects of the school. In this case we would include in our design interactions with parents, siblings, and other people in the home. Finally, one might look at the social relationships experienced throughout the full range of societal contacts that children have, including church, clubs, and even mass media contacts.

All of these are potentially important evaluation research questions. Suppose now that we have a set amount of resources—for example, $25,000—to conduct the study. At some level, any of these research endeavors could be undertaken for $25,000. It is immediately clear, however, that there is a trade-off between breadth and depth. A highly focused question like the interactions between teacher and child could consume the entire amount of our resources and allow us to investigate the problem in great depth. On the other hand, we might attempt to look at all social relationships that children experience, but to look at each of them in a relatively cursory way in order, perhaps, to explore which of those relationships is primary. (If school relationships have very little impact on social development in comparison to relationships outside the school, decision makers could use that information to decide whether or not the school program ought to be redesigned to have greater impact on social development or if the school should forget about trying to affect social development directly at all.) The trade-offs involved are the classic trade-offs between breadth and depth.

Considering trade-offs between breadth and depth often leads to consideration of the relative strengths and weaknesses of qualitative and quantitative data. Qualitative methods permit the evaluator to study selected issues in depth and detail; the fact that data collection is not constrained by predetermined categories of analysis contributes to the depth and detail of qualitative data. Quantitative methods, on the other hand, require the use of a standardized stimulus so that all experiences of people are limited to certain response categories. The advantage of the quantitative approach is that it is possible to measure the reactions of many subjects to a limited set of questions, thus facilitating comparison and statistical aggregation of the data. By contrast, qualitative methods typically produce a wealth of detailed data about a much smaller number of people and cases.

There are no rules that tell evaluators what data mix is best. The breadth versus depth trade-off is applicable not just in comparing quantitative and qualitative methods; the same trade-off applies within either quantitative or qualitative methods. The human relations specialists tell us that we can never fully understand the experience of another person. The methods issue is how much time and effort we are willing to invest in trying to increase our understanding about any single person's experience. Again, under conditions of limited resources, we can look at a narrow range of experiences for a smaller number of people.

Take the case of interviews. Interviewing with an instrument that provides a respondent with a largely open-ended stimulus typically takes a great deal of time. In North Dakota when I was studying various aspects of open education, we developed an open-ended interview consisting of 20 questions that were asked of children in grades one to eight in various open classrooms. Those questions consisted of items such as, "What do you like most about school?" and "What don't you like about school?" These interviews took between half an hour and two hours, depending on how articulate students were and how old they were. It would certainly have been possible to have longer interviews. Indeed, I have conducted in-depth interviews with people that ran six to eight hours over a period of a couple of days. On the other hand, it would have been possible to ask fewer questions, to make the interviews shorter, and to obtain less depth.

To illustrate this trade-off between breadth and depth in sampling human behavior, let us consider the full range of possibilities. It is possible (and indeed it has been done) to study a single individual over an extended period—for example, the in-depth study of one day in the life of one child. This necessitates gathering detailed information about every occurrence in that child's life and every interaction involving that child during some period. With a more limited research question we might study several children during a more limited period. With a still more limited research question, or an interview of a half-hour, we could interview yet a larger number of children on a smaller number of issues. The extreme case would be to spend all of our resources and time asking a single question of as many children as we could interview given the resource constraints.

There is no rule of thumb that tells an evaluator precisely how to focus an evaluation question. The extent to which a research question is broad or narrow depends on the resources available, the time available, and the needs of decision makers. In brief, these are choices not between good and bad but among alternatives, all of which have merit.

It's relatively easy to generate a great deal of information with sophisticated evaluations made possible by fairly ample resources. It's also relatively easy to design an extremely simple evaluation with limited resources, one that generates a certain minimum amount of acceptable information. What is more difficult is to generate a great deal of really useful information with extremely scarce resources. The latter challenge seems also to be the most typical.

Internal and External Validity in Design

Trade-offs between internal and external validity have become a major concern in evaluation since Campbell and Stanley (1963: 175) asserted that "internal validity is the sine qua non." Internal validity in its narrowest sense refers to certainty about cause and effect. Did X cause Y? In a broader sense it refers to the "trustworthiness of an inference" (Cronbach, 1982: 106), in the sense that one is reasonably confident about an interpretation. External validity, on the other hand, refers to the degree of confidence one has in generalizing findings beyond the situation that was studied.

Internal validity is increased by exercising rigorous control over a limited set of carefully defined variables. However, such rigorous controls create artificialities that limit generalizability. The highly controlled situation is less likely to be relevant to a greater variety of more naturally occurring, less controlled situations. In the narrowest sense, this is the problem of going from the laboratory into the real world. By contrast, increasing variability and sampling a greater range of experiences or situations typically reduces control and precision, thereby reducing internal validity. The ideal is high internal validity and high external validity. In reality, there are typically trade-offs involved in the relative emphasis placed on one or the other.

Cronbach's discussion of these issues for evaluation is quite comprehensive and insightful. He emphasizes that "both external validity and internal validity are matters of degree and external validity does not depend directly on internal validity" (1982: 170). It is in this context that Cronbach introduces the idea of "extrapolation" rather than generalization. Extrapolation refers to the logical, creative process of thinking about what specific findings mean for other situations rather than the statistical process of generalizing from a sample to a larger population. Findings are typically interpreted in light of stakeholders' and evaluators' experiences, knowledge, and understanding, and applied/extrapolated using all available knowledge including information about quite different situations. This moves the process of interpretation from a focus on what is true or false in some absolute sense to a concern with conclusions that are reasonable, justifiable, plausible, and warranted. In brief, the issue is credibility.

In working with stakeholders to design evaluations that are credible, the evaluator will need to consider the degree to which internal and external validity are of concern, and to emphasize each in accordance with stakeholder priorities.

TRUTH AND UTILITY TRADE-OFFS

Stakeholders want accurate information; they apply "truth tests" (Weiss and Bucuvalas, 1980) in deciding how seriously to pay attention to an evaluation. They also want useful and relevant information. The ideal, then, is both truth and utility. In the real world, however, there are often choices to be made between the extent to which one maximizes truth and the degree to which data are relevant.

The simplest example of such a choice is time. The timelines for evaluation are often ridiculously short. A decision maker may need whatever information can be obtained in three months, even though the researcher insists that a year is necessary to get data of reasonable quality and accuracy. This involves a trade-off between truth and utility. Highly accurate data in a year are less useful to this decision maker than data of less accuracy obtained in three months.

Decision makers regularly face the need to take action with limited and imperfect information. They prefer more accurate information to less accurate information, but they also prefer some information to no information. This is why research quality and rigor are "much less important to utilization than the literature might suggest" (Alkin et al., 1979: 24).

How much weight do stakeholders give to research quality when interpreting evaluation findings? In our own study of utilization, respondents placed little emphasis on methodological quality as a factor explaining use. Of the 15 decision makers who rated the methodological quality of the study about which they were interviewed, one-third rated it as "high," 53% said it was "medium," and only 13% gave the study a "low" rating. Of 17 responding evaluators, there were 41% high, 35% medium, and 24% low ratings. No decision maker and only one evaluator felt that the methodology used was inappropriate for researching the question at issue.

More to the point, only 4 decision makers felt that methodological quality was "very important" in explaining the study's use. *In no case was methodological quality identified as the most important factor explaining either utilization or nonutilization.*

The effects of methodological quality on use must be understood in the full context of a study, its political environment, the degree of uncertainty with which the decision maker is faced, and thus his or her relative need for any and all clarifying information. If information is scarce, then new information, even of dubious quality, may be somewhat helpful. For example, one administrator admitted that the evaluation's methodological rigor could be seriously questioned, but said the study was highly useful in policy discussions:

> The quality and methodology were not even considered. All that was considered was that management didn't know what was going on, the terms, the procedures, the program was foreign to their background. And they did not have expertise in it, so they were relying on somebody else who had the expertise to translate to them what was going on in terms that they would understand [DM312: 17].

Social scientists may lament this situation and feel that the methodology of evaluation research ought to be of high quality for value reasons; that is, because poor-quality studies ought not be used (see Rutman, 1977). *But there is little in our data to suggest that improving methodological quality in and of itself will have much effect on increasing the use of evaluations.* No matter how rigorous the methodology and no matter how sophisticated the statistical manipulations, an evaluation will only be useful in proportion to its relevance to decision makers' questions.

The relative unimportance of methodological quality as a factor explaining use is tempered by the kind of use we found. Were evaluations being used as the major piece of information in making critical one-time decisions, methodological rigor might be paramount. But when evaluation is one part in a larger whole, decision makers displayed less than burning interest in methodological quality. Rather, decision makers were more concerned that findings be at least sufficiently relevant that the data could be used to give some direction to pending action. One evaluator tied the research quality issue to the nature of uncertainty in organizational decision making. This evaluator fully recognized the inadequacies in the data he had collected, but he had still worked with the decision maker to apply the findings, fully recognizing their problematic nature:

> You have to make the leap here from very limited data. I mean, that's what a decision's like. You make it from a limited data base; and, damn it, when

you're trying to use quantitative data and it's inadequate, you supposedly can't make a decision. Only you're not troubled by that. You can use impressionistic stuff. Yeah, your intuition is a lot better. I get a gestalt out of this thing on every program.

This may come as a great shock to you, but that is what you use to make decisions. In Chester Barnard's definition, for example, the function of the executive is to make a decision in the absence of adequate information [EV148: 11].

It is in this context that research substance and relevance become more important to decision makers than research quality. Thus, the evaluator quoted above felt that the payoff from his evaluation was quite exemplary—despite admitted methods inadequacies.

Well it was a pretty small investment on the part of the government—$47,000 bucks. In the evaluation business that's not a pile of money. The questions I had to ask were pretty narrow and the answers were equally narrow and relatively decisive, and the findings were put to use immediately and in the long term. So can you beat that [EV148: 8]?

Another evaluator expressed similar sentiments. In this case the evaluation had to be completed in only three months.

There are a million things I'd do differently. We should have probably spent more time. . . . I personally could not be satisfied with it. At the time, that was probably the best study we could do, but now it isn't, and that's why I couldn't be satisfied with it. . . . I'm satisfied in the sense that some people found it useful. It really was not just kept on a shelf. There were people who paid attention to that study and it had an impact. Now, I've done other studies that I thought were methodologically really much more elegant that were kind of ignored. Sitting on somebody's shelf.

My opinion is that this really modest kind of study probably has had impact all out of proportion to the quality of the research, and that's my feeling. It happened to be at a certain place at a certain time, where it at least talked about some of the things that people were interested in talking about, so it got some attention. And many other studies that I know of that have been done, not just for ASPE, but in HEW, that I would consider of higher quality, haven't really gotten used [EV145: 34].

To fully understand why issues of research quality are not more critical in affecting use, it is helpful to keep in mind that many stakeholders are not highly sophisticated about methodological questions. But what they have learned and what they do know (almost intuitively) is that *the methods and measurements used in any study are open to question and attack*, the point with which this chapter began. As a result, experienced decision makers know that methods are always vulnerable. Knowing this, most program people are more interested in discussing the substance of findings than in the methods used to get the findings. One decision maker interviewed explained his experience with research quality on a community mental health evaluation as follows:

> Well, let me put it in another context. If it were negative findings programmatically we would have hit very hard on the methodology and tried to discredit it. You know, from the program standpoint. But since it was kind of positive findings, we said, "Okay, here it is." If anybody asked us about the methodological deficiencies, we were never reluctant to tell them what we thought they were. *Not many people asked* [DM51: 10].

In addition to feeling that research methods are always open to debate, many decision makers may simply be skeptical about large-scale, elaborately designed, carefully controlled studies. The experience to date is not promising. Cohen and Weiss (1977) reviewed 20 years of policy research on race and schools, and found progressive improvement in research methods (i.e., with use of increasingly rigorous designs and ever more sophisticated analytical techniques). Sample sizes increased, computer technology was introduced, multiple regression and path analytic techniques were employed, and more data-gathering instruments were developed. After reviewing the findings of studies produced with these more rigorous methods as well as the uses made of findings from these studies, Cohen and Weiss (1977: 78) concluded that "these changes have led to more studies that disagree, to more qualified conclusions, more arguments, and more arcane reports and unintelligible results." This comes close to positing a clear negative relationship between methodological sophistication and utilization of research for policy formulation: The greater the improvement of research on a policy question, the greater the confusion will be about what the findings mean.

High-quality research methods and sophisticated analytical techniques are not the ends of evaluation research, they are means to an end. In utilization-focused evaluation, the question of research quality is tied to questions of methodological appropriateness and research relevance. The concern with relevance does not mean that research quality is unimportant. It simply means that quality is not the major factor in determining use. Decision makers cannot wait forever for the perfect study. As one put it,

> You can get so busy protecting yourself against criticism that you develop such an elaborate methodology that by the time your findings come out, who cares? So, I mean, you get a balance—the validity of the data against its relevance. And that's pretty tough stuff. I mean, that's hard business [DM111: 26].

Utilization-focused evaluation combines concern for research quality with concern for relevance by involving stakeholders in the making of critical methods and measurement decisions. As no study is ever methodologically perfect, it is important for stakeholders to know firsthand what imperfections exist—and to be included in deciding which imperfections they will have to live with in making the inevitable leaps from limited data to incremental action.

The Dynamics of Measurement and Design Decisions

Research quality and relevance are not set in stone once an evaluation proposal has been accepted. A variety of factors emerge throughout the life of an evaluation that require new decisions about methods. Actively involving stakeholders in making methods decisions about these issues means more than a one-point-in-time acquiescence to a research design. It is important that stakeholders understand and approve initial evaluation proposals. It is also important that intended information users be involved in methods decisions that affect what the final design will look like. In every one of the 20 federal health studies investigated, there were significant methods differences between the original proposal and the project as executed. While little attention has been devoted in the evaluation literature to the phenomenon of slippage between methods as originally proposed and methods as actually implemented, the problem is similar to that of program implementation (see Chapter 6).

McTavish et al. (1975) studied the research implementation problem in 126 solicited research projects funded across 7 HEW agencies. All 126 projects were rated by independent judges along seven descriptive methodological scales. Both original proposals and final reports were rated; the results showed substantial instability between the two. The researchers concluded,

> Our primary conclusion from the Predictability Study is that the quality of final report methodology is essentially not predictable from proposal or interim report documentation. This appears to be due to a number of factors. First, research is characterized by significant change as it develops over time. Second, unanticipated events force shifts in direction. Third, the character and quality of information available early in a piece of research makes assessment of some features of methodology difficult or impossible. Finally, there appear to be important and meaningful differences between raters in their professional judgments about the project's methodology [McTavish et al., 1975: 62-63].

Earlier in the report, they had pointed out that

> among the more salient reasons for the low predictability from early to late documentation is the basic change which occurs during the course of most research. It is, after all, a risky pursuit rather than a pre-programmed product. Initial plans usually have to be altered once the realities of data or opportunities and limitations become known. Typically, detailed plans for analysis

and reporting are postponed and revised. External events also seem to have taken an expected toll in the studies we examined. . . . Both the context of research and the phenomena being researched are typically subject to great change [McTavish et al., 1975: 56].

If stakeholders are involved only at the stage of approving research proposals, they are likely to be surprised when they see a final report. Even interim reports bear only moderate resemblance to final reports. Thus, the making of decisions about research methods is a continuous process that involves checking out changes as they are made. Changes in the details of research design and measurement can have important consequences when the data are analyzed and interpreted. While it is impractical to have evaluator-stakeholder discussions about every minor change in methods, utilization-focused evaluators prefer to err in the direction of consultative rather than unilateral decision making, when there is a choice. Stakeholders also carry a responsibility to make sure they remain committed to the evaluation. One internal evaluator interviewed in our federal utilization study, still smarting from critiques of his evaluation as methodologically weak, offered the following advice to decision makers:

> I'm not going to throw too many rocks at myself, but let me say something on that point. Very, very often those of us who are doing evaluation studies are criticized for poor methodology, and the people who levy the criticism sometimes are the people that pay for the study. You know, they'll do this more often when the study is either late or it doesn't come up with the answers that they were looking for. But I think that a large share of the blame or responsibility goes on the project monitor from the sponsor for not maintaining enough control, direct hands-on contact with the evaluation as it's ongoing.
>
> I don't think that it's fair to blame a contractor, even those of us within the government who are contractors in a sense to the other government agencies, you can't blame a contractor for developing a poor study approach, a poor methodology, and absolve yourself, if you're the sponsor, of any, you know, association with that. Because it's your role as a project monitor, project officer, whatever you call yourself, to be aware of what those people that you're paying, you know, what they're doing all the time, and to guide them.
>
> We let contracts out and we keep our hands on these contractors all the time. And when we see them going down a road that we don't think is right, we pull them back and we say, "Hey, you know, we disagree." We don't let them go down the road all the way and then say, "Hey fella, you went down the wrong road" [EV32: 15].

Threats to Data Quality

Evaluation methodologists typically focus their attention on threats to internal validity a la the classic text of Campbell and Stanley (1963). These threats to validity are rival hypotheses to consider in positing that a program produced an observed outcome. The observed effect could be due to larger societal changes (history), as when generally increased societal awareness of the need for exercise and proper nutrition contaminates the effects of specific programs aimed at encouraging exercise and proper nutrition. Maturation is a threat to validity when it is difficult to separate the effects of a program from the effects of growing older; this is a common problem in juvenile delinquency programs, as delinquency has been shown to decline naturally with age. Instrumentation used for pre and post measurements can have effects independent of program effects, as when different people administer a test before and after a program, or when raters or observers are different at two points in time. Reactions to measurement and evaluation can affect outcomes independent of program effects, as when students perform better on a posttest simply because they are more familiar with the test the second time; or there can be interactions between the pretest and the program when the experience of having taken a pretest increases participants' sensitivity to key aspects of a program. Problems in sampling and comparisons between nonequivalent groups can reduce the validity of findings based on comparisons. Losing people from a program ("experimental mortality") can affect findings when the pretest and posttest samples are different, as people who drop out of a program, and therefore fail to take a posttest, are likely to be different in important ways from those who stay to the end.

Threats to validity are of concern in both quantitative/experimental designs and qualitative/naturalistic designs, although these threats are manifested in different ways in different designs. For example, reactivity in qualitative methods is primarily a matter of how respondents react to interviewers and observers, whereas reactivity in quantitative measurement focuses on reactions to tests and questionnaires. All evaluation designs, however, must be concerned with reactivity in some form. Guba and Lincoln (1981: 114) concluded that *with regard to threats to validity, naturalistic approaches come off at least as well as experimental approaches*.

The key point is that it is impossible to identify in the abstract and in advance all of the trade-offs involved in balancing concerns for validity, reliability, utility, feasibility, propriety, and accuracy that will need to be considered in any particular situation. Even when faced with the reality of particular circumstances and specific evaluation problems, it often is not possible to determine in advance precisely how a creative design or measurement approach will affect the quality of the data collected. For example, having program staff do client interviews in an outcomes evaluation could (1) seriously reduce the validity and reliability of the data, (2) substantially increase the validity and reliability of the data, or (3) have no measurable effect on data quality. The nature and degree of effect would depend on staff relationships with clients, how staff were assigned to clients for interviewing, the kinds of questions being asked, the training of the interviewers, atti-

tudes of clients toward the program, and so on. Program staff might make
better or worse interviewers than external evaluation researchers, depending on these and other factors.

An evaluator must grapple with these kinds of data quality questions for
all designs. There are no automatic rules one can apply. There is no substitute for thought and analysis based on the specific circumstances and information needs of a particular evaluation.

Threats to Utility

Whereas traditional evaluation methods texts focus primarily on threats
to validity, this chapter has focused primarily on threats to utility. Threats to
utility include the following:

- failure to focus on intended use by intended users;
- inadequate involvement of primary intended users in making methods
  decisions;
- focusing on unimportant issues—low relevance;
- inappropriate methods and measures given stakeholder questions and information needs;
- poor stakeholder understanding of the evaluation generally and findings
  specifically;
- low stakeholder belief and trust in the evaluation process and findings;
- failure to design the evaluation to fit the context and situation;
- low face validity;
- unbalanced data collection and reporting;
- perceptions that the evaluation is unfair;
- low evaluator credibility;
- political naivety; and
- failure to keep stakeholders adequately informed and involved along the way as
  design alterations are necessary.

There is now substantial evidence that paying attention to and working to
counter these threats to utility will increase use. Working collaboratively
with stakeholders to focus on relevant issues, make sure the design is appropriate, increase understanding, build credibility, and establish a commitment to use does increase the usefulness—and actual use—of evaluations.

Designing Evaluations Worth Using:
Reflections on the State of the Art

The first edition of this book was highly critical of traditional evaluation
practices, particularly overattention to threats to validity and underattention
to threats to utility. Although much of the tone of this revised edition may still

come across as critical of standard evaluation practice, I know from direct observation that there is a great deal of creative work being done by evaluators in all kinds of difficult and challenging situations. In the last several years my evaluation work and consulting have brought me into contact with hundreds of evaluators. My observations suggest that what these evaluators have in common is a commitment to do the most and best they can with the resources available, the short deadlines they face, and the intense political pressures they feel—all of which constitute the context for their work. They share a belief that doing something is better than doing nothing, so long as one is realistic and honest in assessing and presenting the limitations of what is done.

This last caveat is important. I have not attempted to delineate all the possible threats to validity, reliability, and utility that may be posed by various designs. This is not a methods, measurement, and design text. My purpose has been to stimulate thinking about how attention to intended use for intended users will affect all aspects of evaluation practice, including methods decisions.

Practical but creative evaluation consists of using whatever resources are available to do the best job possible. There are many constraints. Our ability to think of alternatives is limited. Resources are always limited. This means that data collection will be imperfect, so dissenters from evaluation findings who want to attack a study's methods can always find some grounds for doing so. A major reason for actively involving primary intended information users in making methods decisions is to deal with weaknesses in the design, and consider trade-off threats to data quality, *before* data are generated. By strategically calculating threats to utility, as well as threats to validity and reliability, it is possible to make practical decisions about the appropriateness of traditional approaches as well as the strengths of creative and nonconventional data collection procedures. It is also necessary, at the design stage, to consider threats to feasibility: Can the proposed evaluation design actually be implemented?

Both "truth tests" (whether data are believable and accurate) and "utility tests" (whether data are useful) are important to decision makers, information users, and stakeholders. One is obliged to think about and deal with threats to validity that may reduce the utility of data, just as one is obliged to consider threats to utility that may result from overly elaborate and too-sophisticated designs aimed at reducing threats to validity. One is obliged to take validity and reliability constraints into consideration in data analysis, as those constraints become known in the process of data collection and analysis. One is obliged to be forthright in reporting on the quality of data in an evaluation. But evaluators are not obliged to return the technical, validity-reliability-accuracy criteria to a position of predominance and ascendancy as the primary standards against which an evaluation is judged. As the standards of evaluation make clear, technical concerns for data accuracy should be made in conjunction with concerns for utility, feasibility, and propriety. There is a lot of room for and a substantial need for creative approaches to evaluation to meet the spirit and challenge of these standards, to produce evaluations that are used—and that are worth using.

There are strong themes of both pragmatism and utilitarianism in these observations. In designing evaluations it is worth keeping in mind Patton's Law (General George S.):

> A good plan today is better
> than a perfect plan tomorrow.

Then there is Halcolm's evaluation corollary to Patton's Law:

> Perfect designs aren't.

Chapter 10

THE MEANINGS OF EVALUATION DATA:

ANALYSIS, INTERPRETATION,

AND REPORTING

What is the sound
of one hand clapping?

—Hakuin

This question was first posed by the Japanese Zen Master Hakuin (1686-1769) as a means of facilitating enlightenment. "The disciple, given a Koan [riddle] to see through, was encouraged to put his whole strength into the singleminded search for its solution, to be 'like a thirsty rat seeking for water . . . ,' to carry the problem with him everywhere, until suddenly, if he were successful, the solution came" (Hoffman, 1975: 22). The Koan is a technique originated by the Zen masters to shake their students out of routine ways of thinking and acting, open up new possibilities, and help individual students realize their full potential. The evaluator is engaged in some of these same processes. Utilization-focused evaluation helps decision makers stand outside the program and look at what is happening; evaluations can help shake staff out of routine ways of doing things, open up new possibilities, and help programs realize their full potential.

This comparison of the evaluation process to the Zen search for enlightenment is not frivolous. Religion and philosophy are ultimately personal, perceptual, and interpretive mechanisms for establishing the meaning of life; evaluation is ultimately a personal, perceptual, and interpretive approach to establishing the meaning—and meaningfulness—of program activities. Leaps of faith are often involved in making sense out of research data. The Zen search through Koans consists of three basic parts: a question, an answer, and interpretation/assimilation of the answer in terms of the student's own life; evaluation involves a question, an empirical answer, and interpretation/utilization of the answer in the context of the program's own dynamics. A fundamental tenet of the Koan educational method is that *the question is as important as the answer*; the same principle applies to utilization-focused evaluation. The Zen Master carefully matches the Koan to the student; the responsive evaluator focuses on questions that are relevant to specific stakeholders. In Zen there are many pathways to enlightenment; in paradigm-flexible evaluation there are multiple methods available for use in the search for information. Finally, the Zen student must struggle to make sense out of the answer to the Koanic riddle; in evaluation the meaning of empirical data is always a matter of interpretation, elucidation, and situational application. Consider the following Koanic exchange entitled "A Flower in Bloom."

A monk asked Master Ummon, "What is the pure body of truth?"

Master Ummon said, "A flower in bloom."

Monk: "'A flower in bloom'—what's it mean?"

Master: "Maggot in the shit hole, pus of leprosy, scab over a boil" [Hoffman, 1975: 119].

"What's it mean?" may be a philosophical, religious, or epistemological question. It can also be the very concrete, practical question of researchers or program staff poring over pages of statistical tables and reams of computer printout generated by an evaluation study. In evaluation, the answer one hopes for is that "it means something; it tells us something about what to do." For any given set of data, the answer depends on who is interpreting the data.

The truism that where some people see flowers, others see maggots is regularly and consistently ignored in the design and interpretation of evaluation studies. Too often evaluators and decision makers behave as if there is some body of data out there that has only to be collected in order to reveal what it all means, whether or not it works, and whether or not the program is effective. But such data simply do not exist outside the context of a specific group of people with a particular perspective. It is for this reason that utilization-focused evaluation begins with identification and organization of intended information users. This is also why data analysis and interpretation processes depend on the active participation of these primary information users, because in the end they are the ones who must translate data into decisions and action.

Setting the Stage for Analysis: Utilization Scenarios

The stage can be set for analysis before data are ever collected. Once instruments have been designed—*but before data collection*—it is helpful to have a session with key stakeholders (e.g., evaluation task force members) to conduct a mock or simulated analysis or interpretation session. This session focuses on the action implications of the data.

The evaluator prepares for this session by organizing fabricated results, some positive and some negative, on the most important issues. For example, suppose the major outcome variable for a vocational training program is the job placement rate. The evaluator might present data showing a placement rate of 40% for black participants and 75% for white participants. The stakeholders are asked, "What do these results mean? What actions would you take based on these results? How would you use these data?" This kind of discussion accomplishes four things:

(1) The simulated analysis is a *check on the design* to make sure that all the relevant data for interpretation and use are going to be collected. All too often at the analysis stage evaluators and stakeholders realize that they forgot to ask an important question.

(2) The mock utilization session is a *training exercise* that helps prepare stakeholders for the real analysis later. They learn how to interpret data. Strengths and weaknesses of the design emerge with greater clarity.

(3) Working through a utilization scenario prior to data collection helps *set realistic expectations* about what the results will look like. This is a chance to prepare stakeholders for the necessity of thinking about and interpreting findings in relation to possible actions and ambiguities.

(4) Utilization scenarios can help *build a commitment to use* of the findings— or reveal the lack of such commitment. When stakeholders are unable to deal with how they would use evaluation findings prior to data collection, they are less likely to be able to use findings after data collection. The commitment to use can be cultivated by helping stakeholders think realistically and concretely about how findings might be applied before making a final commitment to actual data collection. The relatively safer atmosphere of a mock analysis can help engender a commitment to use before stakeholders are confronted with real findings.

Quantitative data are fairly easy to fabricate once instruments have been developed. When the evaluation involves primarily qualitative data, it is still possible to construct imaginary findings (e.g., quotations, case studies).

This extra work can pay off with large dividends as stakeholders develop a utilization-focused mindset based on an actual experience of struggling with data. Athletes, performing artists, astronauts, and entertainers spend hundreds of hours preparing for events that take only a few hours. It is not too much to ask stakeholders to spend two hours in a utilization preparation session getting mentally and analytically ready for the climax of an evaluation—the interpretation and application of findings.

Establishing Standards of Desirability

A simulated analysis session is also a prime time to think about and formalize interpretation guidelines or parameters before data collection. With quantitative data this can be done quite precisely by establishing stands of desirability. I like to aim for at least three levels of interpretation:

(1) level at which the program is considered highly effective;
(2) level at which the program is considered adequate;
(3) level at which the program is considered inadequate.

These interpretation standards can be established for all kinds of evaluation data. Suppose one is collecting satisfaction data on a workshop. At what level of satisfaction is the workshop a success? At what level is it merely adequate? At what level of participant satisfaction is the workshop to be judged ineffective? This exercise not only can lead to concrete interpretation standards but may also reveal that satisfaction data alone are an inadequate indicator of effectiveness.

The process of specifying objectives sometimes involves setting standards of desirability. However, objectives are often unidimensional: "75% of the workshop participants will be satisfied." This doesn't tell us what constitutes an outstanding accomplishment, and it doesn't distinguish adequacy from excellence. Nor does it really make it clear if 65% satisfaction is inadequate or merely "lower than we hoped for but acceptable." Moreover, objectives are often set a long time before the program is under way or well before an actual evaluation has been designed. Reviewing objectives and establishing precise standards of desirability just before data collection increases the likelihood that standards for interpretation will be up to date, realistic, and meaningful.

The point is to get stakeholders to think about interpretation and use before they are confronted with actual findings. During the early conceptualization stages of an evaluation, questions of use are fairly general and responses may be vague. The evaluator asks, "What would you do if you had an answer to your evaluation question? How would you use evaluation findings?" These general questions help focus the evaluation. But once the context has been delineated, the evaluation questions focused, and methods selected, the evaluator can pose quite specific data analysis questions— before any data are collected. Stakeholders look at the possible variations in evaluation findings and discuss their implications for action and decision. For example, if recidivism in a community corrections program is 55%, is that high or low? Does it mean the program was effective or ineffective? The program had some impact, but what level of impact is desirable? What level is acceptable? What level spells trouble? These issues can be resolved, to some extent, before the data are collected, thus permitting discussions about interpretation and action in an atmosphere that is not charged with defensiveness, rationalization, and justification.

Suppose, for example, that you are evaluating a local teacher center. One of the evaluation questions concerns the extent to which teachers use the center intensively (three or more times) versus more superficial use (once or twice). Data from one such study (Feiman, 1977: 19-21) is shown in Table 10.1.

Now suppose the staff are given the actual results for the first time with no prior preparation. The staff assemble to discuss the final evaluation.

First staff speaker: Oh, yes, that's about what we'd anticipated.

Second staff speaker: Plus, of course, the data don't include people who come to regular workshops and special classes.

Third staff speaker: Then, too, since only 23 teachers noted on the background forms that they first visited the center during the period of observation, it is not likely that most of the people who came once were first-time visitors. The observation time was really too short.

Fourth staff speaker: Then, too, January and February are bad months, you know, everyone is depressed with winter, and. . . .

Soon it becomes apparent either that the data do not tell the staff much, at least not without other data, or that staff are not prepared to deal with what the data do suggest. This is not at all unusual as a *postevaluation* scenario.

TABLE 10.1
Intensity of Teachers' Use of a Teacher Center

Number of Visits Made by a Teacher to the Center	Number of Visits	Percentage of Total Visitors
1 or 2	185	80.4
3 or more	45	19.6

NOTE: Data are for visits between January 10 and February 28.

Now let us try another scenario. At the outset of the evaluation study, the program staff discuss their notions of what their task is and how teacher change occurs. They decide that the kind of impact they want to have cannot occur in one or two visits to the teaching center: "If teachers don't return after one or two visits, we must be doing something wrong." The period of time in question is a full twelve-month period. Before the data are collected the staff complete the table shown in Table 10.2.

A recordkeeping system must then be established that staff agree to and believe in so that the data have credibility. The teacher center staff have committed themselves to actively engaging teachers on a multiple-contact basis. The data will provide clear feedback about the effectiveness of the program. The key point is that if staff are unwilling or unable to interpret data and set expectancy levels before the evaluation, there is no reason to believe they can do so after the evaluation. In addition, going through this process ahead of time alerts participants to additional data they need in order to make sense of the evaluation; clearly, one table on frequency of visits is only a starting place. Involving staff or other decision makers in such a process helps to clarify the evaluation criteria that are being used. Finally, when stakeholders are involved in establishing these criteria themselves, the involvement helps increase their commitment to use the data for program improvement. Once the evaluation question is formulated in accordance with the basic interests of stakeholders, the same stakeholders ought to be involved in establishing explicit criteria for interpreting the data. Stakeholders thereby commit themselves to taking the process seriously.

Many of the most serious conflicts in evaluation are rooted in the failure to clearly specify standards of desirability in advance of data collection. This can lead both to collection of the wrong data and to intense disagreement about the standards for interpreting data that have already been collected. Without explicit criteria, data can be interpreted to mean almost anything about the program—or to mean nothing at all.

Making Findings Interesting:
Speculating on Results

Another option in setting the stage for analysis and interpretation is having stakeholders speculate about actual results prior to seeing the real data. This can be done prior to data collection or after data collection but prior to actual presentation of findings. The stakeholders are given an analysis table with all the appropriate categories but no actual data (a dummy table). They then fill in the missing data with their guesses of what the results will be.

This kind of speculation helps increase interest in seeing the actual results. (I've even had stakeholders establish a betting pool on the results. Each person puts in a dollar or more, and the person closest to the actual

TABLE 10.2
Teacher Center Standards of Desirability

Interpretation of Data	Percentage and Number of Teachers Who Have Contact with the Center 3 or More Times
We're doing an *outstanding job* of engaging teachers at this level	
We're doing an *adequate job* of engaging teachers at this level	
We're doing a *poor job* of engaging teachers at this level	

results wins the pot. That creates interest! And the winner must be present at the unveiling of the findings to win. Strange how attendance at the presentation of findings is increased under these conditions!)

A second function of having stakeholders write down their guesses is to provide a concrete basis for determining the extent to which actual results come close to expectations. Program staff, for example, sometimes argue that they don't need formal evaluations because they know their clients, students, or program participants so well that evaluation findings would just confirm what they already know. I've found that when staff commit their guesses to paper in advance of seeing actual results, the subsequent comparison often calls into question just how well some staff do know what is happening in the program. At least then program staff and other stakeholders can't just say, "That's just what I expected." There is a data base to determine how much has been learned and confirmed. This can be useful in documenting the extent to which evaluation does provide new insights and understandings.

It is also possible to combine these processes of establishing standards of desirability and speculating on results. Consider, for example, giving stakeholders in a data analysis session a table that presents simple descriptive statistics on participant reactions to a training program. The questions concern satisfaction level, how much was learned, and other typical questions aimed at getting participant feedback. In the data analysis session stakeholders are given the questionnaire items with two columns. The first column asks them to specify what percentage response they would consider desirable, and the second column asks them to consider and specify what percentage response they believe was actually obtained in the evaluation.

Having specified a standard of desirability, and having taken a guess at actual results, stakeholders now have a greater stake in and a framework for looking at the actual findings. The discussion can then focus on the implications of the data falling below, at, or above the desired response, and why the actual findings were different from or the same as what any given participant guessed the results would be. In my experience, such discussions are highly animated and allow stakeholders to become actively involved in the data analysis and interpretation process.

The major limitation of such an approach is that the amount of data presented must be highly focused and limited so that participants are able to deal with the entire process. Carefully constructed tables and highly focused analysis can make such presentations lively, interesting, and quite valuable.

I find that, given the time and encouragement, stakeholders with virtually no methods or statistics training can readily identify the strengths, weaknesses, and implications of the findings. The trick is to move people from passive reception—from audience status—to active involvement and participation.

*   *   *

Constructing utilization scenarios, doing simulated analysis and interpretation sessions with stakeholders, and formalizing speculations on the results are all techniques for setting the stage for use. The next sections discuss how to actually present findings.

CONSIDERING FINDINGS: AN EVALUATION QUARTET

There are four quite separate parts to the process of making sense out of evaluation findings.

(1) Description and Analysis: This involves organizing raw data into a form that reveals the basic results. Description and analysis present the facts of the case and the actual data.

(2) Interpretation: This goes beyond the data to meaning and significance. What do the results mean? What's the significance of the findings? Why did the findings turn out this way? What are possible explanations of the results?

(3) Judgment: This involves explicitly bringing values to bear on the analysis and interpretations. To what extent and in what ways are the results positive or negative? What is good or bad, desirable or undesirable in the program, based on value judgments of merit and worth?

(4) Recommendations: What should be done? What are the action implications of the findings, based on our analysis, interpretation, and judgments? Recommendations should follow from the data analysis, interpretations, and explanations of what the data mean, and judgments about the desirability of what was found.

Stakeholders should be actively involved in all four of these processes so that they fully understand the findings and their implications. Involving stakeholders in these processes requires skills that go well beyond what is taught in statistics courses. Working with stakeholders to analyze and interpret findings is quite different from doing it on one's own as a researcher.

ISSUES IN ANALYSIS

Arranging Data for Ease of Interpretation: Focusing the Analysis

Providing descriptive statistics in a report does not mean simply reproducing the results in relatively raw form. Data need to be arranged, ordered, and presented in some reasonable format that permits decision makers to quickly detect patterns in the data. Consider the three presentations of data shown in Table 10.3. Each of these presents the same data, but the ordering and presentation of the data are different in each case.

The first presentation shows the data in the order in which they appeared on the questionnaire with the percentage responses for each category of response. It is difficult to look at that table and detect patterns in the data. There are a great many numbers and a considerable amount of information to absorb. Working with a group of decision makers in an evaluation task force, they would need several minutes to study this table in order to reasonably discuss the patterns in the data.

The second presentation shows a common way of simplifying the data, by simply dividing the scale at the midpoint and reducing the four categories to two categories. There are times when such an analysis would be very revealing. In this case, such an analysis disguises the real patterns in the data. Decision makers would look at the second presentation in Table 10.3 and conclude that there was no way of using the survey data to establish priorities for programs.

The third presentation arranges the descriptive data in such a way that decision makers can immediately see the pattern in the results. It is important for decision makers to know that when the two highest categories of response are combined, they fail to distinguish among expressed needs. The data in the third table, however, make it clear that there is much more support for employment programs, for example, than for social programs to entertain the disabled and keep them socially busy. Failure to arrange the data as it is shown in the third table is a failure to focus the data analysis for decision makers.

Simplicity in Data Presentations

Unless one is a genius, it is best to aim at being intelligible.

—Anthony Hope

TABLE 10.3
Three Presentations of the Same Data

Expressed Needs of 478 Physically Disabled People	Great Need for This	Much Need	Some Need	Little Need
Presentation 1: Raw results presented in the same order as items appeared in the questionnaire.				
Transportation	35%	36%	13%	16%
Housing	33	38	19	10
Educational opportunities	42	28	9	21
Medical care	26	45	25	4
Employment opportunities	58	13	6	23
Public understanding	47	22	15	16
Architectural changes in buildings	33	38	10	19
Direct financial assistance	40	31	12	17
Changes in insurance regulations	29	39	16	16
Social opportunities	11	58	17	14
Presentation 2: Results divided at the midpoint of the scale.				
Transportation		71%		29%
Housing		71		29
Educational opportunities		70		30
Medical care		71		29
Employment opportunities		71		29
Public understanding		69		31
Architectural changes in buildings		71		29
Direct financial assistance		71		29
Changes in insurance regulations		68		32
Social opportunities		69		31
Presentation 3: Results computed and arranged to highlight patterns in the data.				
Employment opportunities	58%			
Public understanding	47			
Educational opportunities	42			
Direct financial assistance	40			
Transportation	35			
Housing	33			
Architectural changes in buildings	33			
Changes in insurance regulations	29			
Medical care	26			
Social opportunities	11			

William of Occam with his razor would have made an excellent analyst of evaluation data. Look first for the simplest presentation that will handle the facts. Evaluators may need and use sophisticated and complex statistical techniques to uncover the nuances of evaluation data, but simple and straightforward statistical presentations are needed to give decision makers access to evaluation findings.

The social sciences go through fads in which certain kinds of data analysis are particularly favored when one wants to have an article published in a major journal. For awhile multiple regression techniques are all the rage; some journals are particularly enamored of path analysis; still others seem to have a fascination with factor analysis, or log-linear techniques, or a propensity for examining different interactions under varying assumptions and building mathematical models of social processes. These complex and sophisticated techniques have allowed major advances in the analysis of social and behavioral science data. The problem is that very few decision makers understand such techniques; these sophisticated procedures are easily abused and misrepresented when the assumptions on which they rest are violated; and sophisticated statistical presentations are intimidating to nonstatisticians.

When I first joined the evaluation training program at Minnesota, the primary emphasis was on increasing the sophistication of evaluation measurement and data analysis techniques. In attending professional meetings in sociology, psychology, political science, and evaluation during my postdoctoral years of study, there were regular and predictable calls for the implementation of ever more elaborate research designs and the use of increasingly sophisticated analysis techniques in evaluation research. At the same time, I began working on evaluations with decision makers at the federal, state, and local levels. Almost universally I encountered people who were fairly intimidated by percentages, unsure of correlation coefficients, and wary of what they considered to be statistical gobbledygook.

I am not implying that sophisticated techniques, where appropriate and helpful, should not be used. I am suggesting that it is the height of folly to center one's public presentations and decision-making discussions around complex statistical findings. I have been told by some of my colleagues that they make such presentations because they consider it part of their responsibility to educate public officials about statistics. From my observations I would suggest that what they are educating them about is not how to use such statistics but, rather, about the overall uselessness of social science research findings for decision making, and convincing them of the inability of social scientists to communicate in a simple and straightforward manner to those responsible for public policy.

Evaluation, if it is to be accessible to and understandable by key stakeholders, must depart from the trends of the various social science disciplines and return to simplicity as a virtue of data analysis and presentation. This does not mean that one cannot use sophisticated techniques. Rather, it means that having used those techniques to tease out the nuances in the data and to confirm the strength and meaningfulness of discovered relationships, the next step is to creatively think about how to translate those findings into simple, straightforward, and understandable statistics. This means, for example, that the results of a regression analysis might be reduced to nothing more complex than a chi-square table or a set of descriptive statistics (percentages and means). This need not distort the presentation. Quite the opposite, it will usually focus and highlight the most meaningful findings while allowing the investigators to explain in a footnote and/or an appendix that more sophisticated techniques have been used to confirm the simple statistics here presented.

Simplicity as a virtue means that we must reward evaluators for clarity, not complexity. Like the skilled acrobat who makes the most dazzling moves look easy, the audience being unaware of the long hours of practice and the sophisticated calculations involved in what appear to be quite simple movements, evaluators must find ways of so perfecting their public performances that those involved in working with them to make sense out of the data will believe that *even they* can understand and participate in the analysis, all the while being perhaps unaware of the long hours of arduous work involved in sifting through the data, organizing it, arranging it, testing out relationships, taking the data apart, and creatively putting it back together to arrive at that moment of public unveiling.

Simplicity as a virtue means that we are rewarded not for how much we confuse people, but for how much we enlighten them; it means that we emphasize building up others' feelings that they can master what is before them, rather than intimidating them with our own expertise, knowledge, and sophistication. Simplicity as a virtue means separating the complexity of analysis from the clarity of presentation and using the former to inform and guide the latter. Simplicity as a virtue is not simple. In the end it often involves considerably more work and creativity to simplify than simply to rest content with a presentation of the complex statistics as they originally emerged in the analysis. Simplicity as a virtue is not simple, but it can be effective.

Strive for Balance

The counterpoint to my preceding sermon on simplicity is that evaluation findings are seldom really simple. In striving for simplicity, one must be careful to avoid simplemindedness. It is simpleminded to present only one point of view. This happens most often in evaluation when results are boiled down, in the name of simplicity, to some single number—a single percentage, a single cost/benefit ratio, or a single proportion of the variance explained. Striving for simplicity means making the data understandable, but balance and fairness need not be sacrificed in the name of simplicity. Balance means that the complexity and multiple perspectives of a situation can be represented through several different numbers, all of them presented in an understandable fashion. Advertising is based upon the deception of single representations of facts. Evaluation, to maintain credibility and integrity, requires multiple statistical representations for a full and balanced picture of the situation. Some examples may help clarify what I mean.

In his 1972 presidential campaign, Nixon made the claim that "under his administration black incomes had risen faster than white incomes." In the same campaign McGovern made the claim that "after four years of Nixon, blacks were worse off than whites in terms of income." Both statements were true. The distortion comes in that both statements represent only part of the picture. To understand what was happening in the relationship between black and white income one needed more than any single statistic.

Consider the data given in Table 10.4 to illustrate this point. These data illustrate how it is possible for both political statements to be true: Black incomes rose faster than white incomes, but blacks were worse off than whites at the end of the four-year period under study. At a minimum, a balanced view would require *both* the absolute changes and the percentage changes. When a report gives only one figure or the other (i.e., only absolute changes or only percentage changes), the reader has cause to suspect that the full picture has not been presented. A balanced viewpoint requires both kinds of numbers.

A more relevant example for evaluation purposes comes from a study of Internal Revenue Service audits conducted by the U.S. General Accounting Office (GAO). The cover page of the report carried the sensational headline that the study had found that IRS audit procedures in five selected districts missed $1 million in errors in four months:

> These districts assessed incorrect tax estimated to total $1.0 million over a 4-month period because of technical errors, computation errors, or failure to make automatic adjustments.

The IRS response to the GAO report points out that the same audit cases containing the $1 million in errors had revealed over $26 million in errors that led to adjustments in tax. Thus, the $1 million represented only about

TABLE 10.4
Illustrative Data (Constructed)

	Beginning Level	Level Four Years Later	Absolute Amount of Change	Percentage Change
Median White Income	$10,100	$10,706	$606	6
Median Black Income	$ 5,500	$ 6,050	$550	10

4% of the total amount of money involved. Moreover, when one reads the details behind the headline, it turns out that the $1 million resulted from different methods of calculation used by the IRS and the GAO because the GAO included all differences whereas the IRS ignored differences of $100 or less. In the data presented by the GAO it is impossible to tell what proportion of the $1 million involves errors of under $100, which are routinely ignored by the IRS. Finally, a detailed reading of the report also shows that the $1 million error involves cases of two types: instances in which additional tax would be due to the IRS *and* instances in which a refund would be due the taxpayer from the IRS. In point of fact, the $1 million error would result in virtually no additional revenue to the government had all the errors been detected and followed up.

The gross simplification of the evaluation findings and the headlining of the $1 million error represent considerable distortion of the full picture. Simplicity at the expense of accuracy is no virtue; complexity in the service of accuracy is no vice. The point is to make those complex matters accessible to and understandable by the relevant decision makers. The omitted information from the GAO report could not be justified on the basis of simplification. The omission represented distortions of the situation rather than simplification.

Striving for balance means thinking about all the information decision makers need to have for a full picture of the situation under study. It means generally including both numbers representing absolute changes and percentage changes; it means watching for situations in which it is appropriate to report a mean, median, and/or mode in order to fully represent the distribution of data; it means providing different estimates or indicators of an attitude or behavior under study; it means categorizing data in more than one way to see what differences those categorical distributions make; it means providing information about mean, range, and standard deviations (represented as straightforward and understandable confidence limits); and it means finding ways to say the same thing in more than one way to minimize misinterpretation and misunderstanding.

Be Clear About Definitions

A frequent source of misunderstanding in evaluation is confusion about what was actually measured or studied. In workshops on data analysis I give the participants statistics on farmers, on families, and on recidivism. In small groups the participants are asked to discuss the meaning of the different sets of data. Almost invariably they jump right into making interpretations without asking how farmer was defined in the data collection, how family was defined, or what recidivism actually represents in the data at hand. A simple term like "farmer" turns out to be enormously variant in its use and definition. When does the weekend gardener become a farmer, and when does the large commercial farmer become an "agribusinessperson?" There is a whole division of the Census Bureau that wrestles with this problem.

Defining "family" is no less complex. There was a time, not so long ago, when our society may have shared a common definition of family. Now there is a real question about who has to be doing what to whom under what conditions before we call it a family. Before interpreting any statistics on families it would be critical to know how family was defined.

Recidivism is by no means unusual as a concept in evaluation research. But the term offers a variety of different definitions and measures. Recidivism may mean (1) a new arrest, (2) a new appearance in court, (3) a new conviction, (4) a new sentence, (5) or actually committing a new crime regardless of whether the offender is apprehended. The statistics will vary considerably depending on which definition of recidivism is being used.

A "study" was published by the National Federation of Decency concerning the decadent content of Phil Donahue television shows. One of the categories of analysis in the study included Donahue programs that encouraged "abnormal sex." The author of the report later acknowledged that it was probably a bit excessive of the federation to have included breast feeding in this category (Boulder Daily Camera, September 30, 1981: 2). But, then, definitions of abnormal sex do seem to vary somewhat. Any reader of a research report on the subject would be well advised to look with care at the definition used by the researcher. Of course, any savvy evaluator involved in such a study would certainly be careful to make sure that his or her own sexual practices, whatever they might be, were categorized as normal.

In the 1972 presidential campaign, Nixon gained considerable press attention for making a major budget shift from defense spending to spending for social services. One had to listen quite attentively and read quite carefully to learn that all that had happened was moving the Veterans Administration expenditures from the defense side of the ledger to the social services side of the ledger. The statistical changes in proportion of expenditures for different purposes were entirely an artifact of the change in definition of those services.

Such examples are not meant to make people cynical about statistics. Many distortions of this kind are inadvertent, due to sloppiness of thinking, unexamined assumptions, hurrying to complete a final report, or basic incompetence. But those are reasons, not excuses. A Sufi story illustrates the importance of being clear about definitions before drawing conclusions.

Mulla Nasrudin and a friend went to the circus together. Many of the performances were outstanding, but the most dazzling of all was the tightrope walker. All the way home from the performance Mulla's friend kept raving about the performance of the tightrope walker. After awhile the Mulla tired of this conversation, but the companion resisted all attempts to change the subject. Finally, in frustration, Nasrudin said, "It was really not such a great feat as all that to walk a tightrope. I myself can do it."

The companion was angry at Nasrudin's brazen statement, so he challenged him to a substantial wager. He was determined to put an end to Mulla Nasrudin's vain boasting. They set a time for the attempt in the center of the marketplace so that all the village could be witness to who won the wager.

At the appointed hour Mulla Nasrudin appeared with the rope, laid the rope out on the ground, walked along it, and demanded his money.

The friend was incredulous. "But the tightrope must be in the air for you to win the wager!" exclaimed the companion.

"I wagered that I could walk a tightrope," replied Nasrudin. "As everyone can see I have, indeed, walked the tightrope."

The village judicial officer ruled in Nasrudin's favor. "Definitions," he explained to the assembled villagers, "are the things of which laws are made."

They are also the things of which evaluation research are made.

Make Comparisons Carefully and Appropriately

Virtually all data analysis in evaluation ends up in some way being comparative. Numbers in isolation, standing alone without a frame of reference or basis of comparison, seldom make much sense. A recidivism rate of 40% is a meaningless statistic. Is that high or low? Does that represent improvement or deterioration? An error of $1 million in IRS audits is a meaningless number. Some basis of comparison or standard of judgment is needed in order to interpret such statistics. The problem comes in selecting the appropriate basis of comparison. In the example of the IRS audit, the U.S. General Accounting Office believed that the appropriate comparison was an error of zero dollars, absolute perfection in auditing. The IRS considered such a basis of comparison completely unrealistic in either practice or theory, and they suggested a basis of comparison against the total amount of corrections made in all audits.

Skepticism can occur in evaluation analyses when the basis for the comparisons appears to be arbitrary and contrived. It is important to think carefully about what kind of comparisons are appropriate, preferably before data analysis, so that the evaluation question is carefully focused on information that will illuminate the situation and provide a clear basis for action and decision. This is no easy task, for the available choices are quite varied.

The outcomes of a program can be compared to

(1) the outcomes of "similar" programs;
(2) the outcomes of the same program the previous year;

(3) the outcomes of model programs in the field;
(4) the outcomes of programs known to be having difficulty;
(5) the stated goals of the program;
(6) external standards of desirability as developed by the profession;
(7) standards of minimum acceptability, e.g., basic licensing standards;
(8) ideals of program performance; or
(9) guesses made by staff or other decision makers about what the outcomes would be.

Consider the new jogger or running enthusiast. At the beginning, runners are likely to use as a basis for comparison their previous sedentary lifestyle. By that standard, the initial half-mile or one-mile run appears to be pretty good. Then the runner discovers that there are a lot of other people running, many of them running three miles, four miles, five or ten miles a week. By that standard, they haven't done so well, and so they push on. On days when they want to feel particularly good, they compare themselves to all the people who don't run at all. On days when they need some incentive to push harder, they compare themselves to people they know who run twice as much as they do. Some adopt the standards from medical people about the minimum amount of running needed for basic conditioning, something on the order of thirty minutes of sustained and intense exercise a least three times a week. Some measure their progress in miles, others in minutes and hours. Some compare themselves to friends; others get involved in official competitions and races.

In politics it is said that the conservatives compare the present to the past and see all the things that have been lost, while the liberals compare the present to what could be in the future and see all the things yet to be attained. None of these comparisons is right or wrong; they are simply different. Each basis of comparison provides a different perspective, a different way of looking at things, and different information. Evaluators can work carefully with stakeholders to decide which comparisons are appropriate and relevant to give a full and balanced view of what is happening in the program.

INTERPRETATIONS AND JUDGMENTS

The data analysis and interpretation phases in utilization-focused evaluation are where evaluators and stakeholders look at the data together and try to make sense out of it. As noted earlier, it is important to separate analysis and interpretation. Analysis involves organizing the data, constructing appropriate statistical tables, and arranging for the data to be displayed in an orderly, usable format. Interpretation involves deciding what the data mean, providing explanations for the results, and attaching significance to the findings.

In resisting the temptation to bear alone the burden of analysis and interpretation, the evaluator is again viewing the evaluation process as a training opportunity through which decision makers and information users can become more sophisticated about the potential of data-based decision-making approaches over the long term. H.G. Wells anticipated the importance of making statistical thinking accessible to nonstatisticians when he observed,

> Statistical thinking will one day be as necessary for efficient citizenship as the ability to read and write.

For evaluation task force members, that day is now. But incorporating a training perspective in the evaluation process will mean being prepared to deal with statistical reasoning. The logic of qualitative analysis also needs to be made accessible to stakeholders.

As stakeholders come to understand the difference between analysis and interpretation, it is helpful to focus on three aspects of empirical reasoning.

(1) Numbers and qualitative data must be interpreted to have meaning. Numbers are not bad or good, they're just numbers. Judgments have to be made about the accuracy and meaningfulness of numbers. Interpretation means thinking about what the data mean and how they ought to be applied. There are no magic formulas for making interpretations. Statisticians have no corner on the ability to think and reason. Interpretation is a human process, not a computer process. The best guideline may be Einstein's dictum that "the important thing is to keep on questioning."

(2) Data are usually indicators or representations of what the world is like. Just as a map is not the territory it describes, the statistical tables on a program are not the program. They are indicators of what the program is like, but they are not the program. Thus, statistics are a means of increasing understanding about a program; generating statistics is not an end in itself.

(3) As indicators and estimates subject to interpretation, statistics and qualitative data contain varying degrees of error. Thinking within the framework of the culture of science involves probabilities, not absolutes. The switch from absolute judgment (things are or are not) to probabilistic thinking (things are more or less likely) is fundamental to entry into empirical reasoning and careful interpretations.

In utilization-focused evaluations, stakeholders are given an opportunity to make their own interpretations with the guidance, assistance, and facilitation of the evaluator. The utilization-focused evaluator strives to be unobtrusive and supportive so that stakeholders are forced to think about and own their interpretations while at the same time keeping the discussion grounded in the data so that speculation doesn't become wild and unfounded.

Scriven (1967) has strongly advocated the evaluator's responsibility to draw conclusions from data and make judgments about the evaluation results. Others have argued that the evaluator's job is only to supply the data, that the decision makers alone must make the judgments (e.g. Rosen, 1973).

Utilization-focused evaluation incorporates both of these views. The evaluator's job includes making judgments and recommendations, but decision makers and information users are first given an opportunity to arrive at their own conclusions unencumbered by the evaluator's interpretations, judgments, and recommendations. As the evaluator facilitates consideration of findings by stakeholders, there will be opportunities to sensitively and diplomatically make distinctions among analysis, interpretation, judgment, and recommendations as well as for the evaluator to share his or her own perspectives on these issues. An example will help illustrate how such a process can work.

An Example of Utilization-Focused
Data Deliberations by Stakeholders

In the Minnesota Center for Social Research evaluation of Ramsey County foster group homes for juvenile offenders, we collected data from natural parents, foster parents, juveniles, and community corrections staff. The intended information users were the Community Corrections Advisory Board. We worked closely with members of this board in problem identification, research design, and instrumentation. Once the data were collected, we employed a variety of statistical techniques, including alpha factor analysis and stepwise forward regression analysis. We then reduced these findings to some ten pages of data and presented them in simple form in a very readable format. The items with the highest loadings on the factor analysis were presented with frequency distributions; descriptive statistics for major dependent and independent variables were included; a series of simple two-by-two tables showing the relationships among major variables was constructed; and, finally, a correlation matrix and regression equation predicting recidivism were shown. These materials, with no accompanying narrative, were sent to the decision makers. A week later we met with them and discussed their interpretations of the data. At that time they decided to seek broad involvement in the data interpretation, so a half-day meeting was arranged for community corrections staff, welfare department staff, court services staff, and members of the county board. That meeting brought together some 40 of the most powerful elected and appointed officials in the county to interpret the evaluation data.

A major purpose of the evaluation was to describe and conceptualize the group home treatment environment. Variations in recidivism, runaway rates, and juvenile attitudes would then be related to variations in environments. The factor analysis of 56 items designed to measure variations in the group home environment did uncover a single major factor. This factor explained 54% of the variance, with 19 items loading above .45 on that factor. *The first task in data interpretation was to label that factor in such a way that its relationship to dependent variables would represent something meaningful to identified information users.* For this purpose we used the group of 40 county officials.

The meeting began with a brief description of the methods and data, which were then distributed. Participants were divided randomly into groups of four people. Each group was asked to look at the items in Table 10.5 and to label the factor or theme represented by those items in their own words. After 15 minutes, each of the ten groups reported a label; discussion followed. Consensus emerged around the terms "participation and support" as representing one end of the continuum and "authoritarian and nonsupportive" for the other end. We also asked the groups to describe the salient elements in the factor. These descriptions were combined with the labels chosen by the group; the resulting conceptualization—as it appeared in the final evaluation report—is shown in Table 10.6.

The groups then studied accompanying tables showing the relationships between this treatment environment factor and program outcome variables (see Table 10.7). The relationships were statistically significant and quite transparent. Juveniles who reported experiencing more supportive-participatory corrections environments had lower recidivism rates, lower runaway rates, and more positive attitudes. Having established the direction of the data, we discussed the limitations of the findings, methodological weaknesses, and the impossibility of making causal interpretations. Key decision makers were already well aware of these problems. Then, given those constraints, the group was asked for recommendations. The basic thrust of the discussion concerned ways to increase the supportive-participatory experiences of juvenile offenders. *The people carrying on that discussion were the people who fund, operate, and control juvenile offender programs.* The final written evaluation report included the recommendations that emerged from that meeting as well as the evaluators' own conclusions and recommendations. But the final written report took another four weeks to prepare and print; *the utilization process was already well under way before the final report was disseminated.*

Three main points are illustrated here about a utilization-focused presentation of findings. First, nonscientist information users can understand and interpret data when presented with clear, readable, and simplified statistical tables; sophisticated analyses can be reworked and presented in more simplified, tabular form. Second, as experienced data analysts know, the only way to really understand a data set is to live with it, to spend some time getting inside it; busy decision makers are unwilling or unable to spend days at such a task, but a couple of hours of structured time spent in directed data analysis can pay off in greater understanding of and commitment to using the evaluation data. Third, evaluators can learn a great deal from stakeholder interpretations of data if they are open and listen to what people knowledge-

TABLE 10.5

Composition of the Group Home Treatment Environment Scale

The items that follow are juvenile interview items that are highly interrelated statistically in such a way that they can be assumed to measure the same environmental factor. The items are listed in rank order by factor loading (from .76 to .56 for a six-factor alpha solution). This means that when the scores were combined to create a single numerical scale the items higher on the list received more weight in the scale (based on factor score coefficients). What underlying factor or theme is represented by the combination of these questions?

(1) The [group home parent name]s went out of their way to help us.

almost always	30.9%	
a lot of times	10.9%	
just sometimes	34.5%	
almost never	23.6%	Factor loading = .76

(2) At . . . . . .'s personal problems were openly talked about.

almost always	20.0%	
a lot of times	9.1%	
just sometimes	32.7%	
almost never	38.2%	Factor loading = .76

(3) Did you feel like the group home parents tried to help you understand yourself?

almost always	23.6%	
a lot of times	29.1%	
just sometimes	23.6%	
almost never	23.6%	Factor loading = .74

(4) How often did . . . . . .s take time to encourage you in what you did?

almost always	27.3%	
a lot of times	20.0%	
just sometimes	30.9%	
almost never	21.8%	Factor loading = .73

(5) At . . . . . .'s house, how much were you each encouraged to make your own decisions about things? Would you say that you were . . .

almost always	18.9%	
a lot of times	30.2%	
just sometimes	30.2%	
almost never	20.8%	Factor loading = .68

(6) How often did the . . . . . .s let you take responsibility for making your own decisions?

almost always	23.6%	
a lot of times	20.0%	
just sometimes	25.5%	
almost never	30.9%	Factor loading = .67

(continued)

TABLE 10.5 (Continued)

---

(7) We really got along well with each other at . . . . . . 's.

almost always	23.6%
a lot of times	29.1%
just sometimes	32.7%
almost never	14.5% Factor loading = .66

(8) Would the group home parents tell you when you were doing well?

almost always	30.9%
a lot of times	30.9%
just sometimes	29.1%
almost never	9.1% Factor loading = .64

(9) How often were you allowed to openly criticize the group home parents?

almost always	14.8%
a lot of times	7.4%
just sometimes	24.1%
almost never	53.7% Factor loading = .59

(10) How much of the time would you say there was a feeling of "togetherness" at . . . . . . 's?

almost always	27.3%
a lot of times	23.6%
just sometimes	32.7%
almost never	16.4% Factor loading = .59

(11) How much did the . . . . . . s help you make plans for leaving the group home and returning to your real home?

almost always	9.1%
a lot of times	21.8%
just sometimes	21.8%
almost never	47.3% Factor loading = .58

(12) How often would the . . . . . . s talk with you about what you'd be doing after you left the group home?

almost always	7.3%
a lot of times	18.2%
just sometimes	36.4%
almost never	38.2% Factor loading = .58

(13) How much of the time did the kids have a say about what went on at . . . . . . 's?

almost always	13.0%
a lot of times	29.6%
just sometimes	27.8%
almost never	29.6% Factor loading = .56

(continued)

TABLE 10.5 (Continued)

(14) How much were decisions about what you all had to do at the group home made only by the . . . . . . s without involving the rest of you?

almost always	30.9%
a lot of times	18.2%
just sometimes	32.7%
almost never	18.2% Factor loading = .56

(15) How much of the time were discussions at . . . . . . 's aimed at helping you understand your personal problems?

almost always	23.6%
a lot of times	23.6%
just sometimes	18.2%
almost never	34.5% Factor loading = .56

TABLE 10.6
Group Home Treatment Environment Continuum

Description of Group Home Ideal Types

Supportive-Participatory	*Nonsupportive-Authoritarian*
In group homes nearer this end of the continuum juveniles perceive group home parents as helpful, caring, and interested in them. Juveniles are encouraged and receive positive reinforcement. Juveniles are involved in decisions about what goes on in the home. Kids are encouraged to make their own decisions about the things they do personally. There is a feeling of togetherness, of being interested in each other, of caring about what happens now and in the future. Group home parents discuss the future with the kids and help them plan. There is a feeling of mutual support and kids feel that they can openly express their feelings, thoughts, problems, and concerns.	In group homes nearer this end of the continuum juveniles report that group home parents are less helpful, less open with them and less interested in them personally. Juveniles are seldom encouraged to make their own decisions and the parents tend to make decisions without asking their opinions about things. There isn't much planning things together or talking about the future. Kids are careful about what they say, are guarded about expressing their thoughts and feelings. Kids get little positive reinforcement. There is not much feeling of togetherness, support, and mutual caring; group home parents kept things well under control.

NOTE: The descriptions presented here are based on stakeholders' interpretations of the factor analysis in Table 10.5.

able about the program have to say. Just as decision makers do not spend as much time in data analysis as do evaluators, so evaluators do not spend as much time in program analysis, operations, and planning as do decision makers. Each can learn from the other in the overall effort to make sense out of the data and the situation.

TABLE 10.7
Relationship Between Different Home Environments and Recidivism

	No Recidivism	Recidivism	Total
Supportive-Participatory	76%	24%	100%
Homes	(N = 19)	(N = 6)	(N = 25)
Nonsupportive-Authoritarian	44%	56%	100%
Homes	(N = 11)	(N = 14)	(N = 25)

NOTE: Correlation r = .33; Significant at .009 level.

RECOMMENDATIONS

Before looking specifically at the process of generating recommendations, it may be helpful to position recommendations within the overall evaluation process. Evaluations are useful in ways that go beyond a narrow focus on implementing recommendations or making concrete, specific decisions about immediate courses of action. Participation in an evaluation process affects ways of thinking about a program; it can clarify goals, increase (or decrease) particular commitments, and reduce uncertainties; and the process can stimulate insights, the consequences of which may not be evident until some time in the distant future. Recommendations, then, do not bear the full brunt of the hopes for evaluation use.

Nevertheless, recommendations are often the most visible part of an evaluation report. Well-written, carefully derived recommendations and conclusions can be the catalyst that brings all the other elements in an evaluation process together into a meaningful whole. When done poorly, recommendations can become the center of attack, discrediting what was otherwise a professional job because of hurried and sloppy work on a last-minute recommendations section. I suspect that one of the most common reasons evaluators get into trouble when writing recommendations is that they haven't allowed enough time to really think through the possibilities and discuss them with people who have a stake in the evaluation. After months of work on an evaluation, I've known many cases in which the recommendations were generated hours before a final reporting session, under enormous time pressure. In our study of the utilization of federal health evaluations we asked 20 decision makers about the usefulness of the recommendations in the specific evaluation reports they had received. The following reactions were typical:

I don't remember the specific recommendations.

The recommendations weren't very useful or anything we could do much with. It was the overall process that was useful, not the recommendations.

I remember reading them, that's about all.

The recommendations were the least useful part of the report. They looked like they'd been added as an afterthought.

This section includes suggestions for writing practical and useful recommendations. For a more complete and elaborate discussion of these points, see Patton (1982a: 270-295).

Useful and Practical Recommendations

(1) Early in the evaluation the nature and content of the final report should be negotiated with stakeholders and evaluation funders. Not all evaluation reports include recommendations. The kinds of recommendations, if any, to be included in a report are a matter of negotiation.

(2) Recommendations should clearly follow from and be based on the evaluation findings. The processes of analysis, interpretation, and judgment should lead logically to recommendations.

(3) Distinguish different kinds of recommendations. Recommendations that deal directly with central questions or issues should be highlighted and separated from recommendations about secondary or minor issues. Distinctions should be made between summative and formative recommendations. It may be helpful and important to distinguish between recommendations that can be implemented immediately, recommendations that can be implemented in the short term (within six months to a year), and recommendations aimed at the long-term development of the program. In still other cases, it may be appropriate to orient recommendations toward certain groups of people: recommendations for funders, recommendations for program administrators, recommendations for program staff, and recommendations for clients or program participants.

Another way of differentiating between types of recommendations is to clearly specify which recommendations are strongly supported by the data and have the solid support of the evaluator and/or the evaluation task force versus those recommendations that are less directly supported by the data or about which there is dissension among members of the task force. In similar fashion, it is important to distinguish between recommendations that involve a firm belief that some action should be taken and recommendations that are meant merely to stimulate discussion or suggestions that might become part of an agenda for future consideration and action.

The basic point here is that long, indiscriminate lists of recommendations at the end of an evaluation report diffuse the focus and diminish the power of central recommendations. By making explicit the different amounts of emphasis that the evaluator intends to place on different recommendations, and by organizing recommendations so as to differentiate among different kinds of recommendations, the evaluator increases the usefulness of the recommendations as well as the likelihood of the implementation of at least some of them.

(4) Some decision makers prefer to receive multiple options rather than recommendations that advocate only one course of action. This approach begins with a full slate of possible recommendations: terminate the program; reduce funding for the program; maintain program funding at its current level; increase program funding slightly; and increase program funding substantially. The evaluator then builds a case for each of these recommendations, showing which findings, assumptions, interpretations, and judgments combine to support each of the designated options.

(5) Insofar as possible, when making recommendations, particularly major ones involving substantial changes in program operations or policies, evaluators should study, specify, and include in their reports some consideration of the benefits and costs of making the suggested changes, including the costs and risks of not making them.

(6) Focus on actions within the control of intended users. A major source of frustration for many decision makers is that the recommendations in evaluation reports relate mainly to things over which they have no control. For example, a school desegregation study that focuses virtually all its recommendations on needed changes in housing patterns is not very useful to school officials, even though they may agree that housing changes are needed. Is the implication of such a recommendation that the schools can do nothing? Is the implication that anything the school does will be limited to the extent that housing patterns remain unchanged? Or, again, are there major changes a school could make to further the aims of desegregation, but the evaluator got sidetracked on the issue of housing patterns and never got back to concrete recommendations for the school? Of course, the best way to end up with recommendations that focus on manipulable variables is to make sure that in the conceptualization of the evaluation the focus is on manipulable variables, and that focus is maintained right on through to the writing of recommendations.

(7) Exercise political sensitivity in writing recommendations. Ask yourself the questions, "If I were in their place with their responsibilities, their political liabilities, their personal perspectives, how would I react to this recommendation stated in this way? What arguments would I raise to counter the recommendations?" Work with stakeholders to analyze the political implications of recommendations. This doesn't mean recommendations should be weak but, rather, that evaluators should be astute. Controversy may or may not serve the cause of getting findings used. But, at the very least, controversies should be anticipated.

(8) Be careful and deliberate in wording evaluations. Important recommendations can be lost in vague and obtuse language. Powerful recommendations can be diluted by an overly meek style, while particularly sensitive

recommendations may be dismissed by an overly assertive style. Avoid words that confuse or distract from the central message.

(9) Allow time to do a good job on recommendations, time to develop recommendations collaboratively with stakeholders, and time to pilot test recommendations for clarity, understandability, practicality, utility, and accuracy.

(10) Develop strategies for getting recommendations taken seriously. Simply listing recommendations at the end of a report is a minimum. Think about how to facilitate serious consideration of recommendations. Help decision makers make decisions on recommendations, including clear assignment of responsibility for follow-up action and timelines for implementation.

REPORTING

In utilization-focused evaluation, use does not center on the final report. Evaluators have traditionally focused on the final written report as the evaluation climax and the key mechanism for use. From the academic perspective use is achieved through dissemination of a published report (e.g., Fairweather, 1967: 199-210). Traditionally, use is not even an issue until there is something concrete (a report) to use. By contrast, utilization-focused evaluation is concerned with use from the beginning, and the final written report is only one of many mechanisms for facilitating use. The Minnesota Group Home Evaluation reviewed in the last section illustrates this point. Major use was under way well before the report was written. The final report was an anticlimax, and appropriately so.

The data from our study of Federal Health Evaluations indicate that much important reporting is interpersonal and informal. In hallway conversations, in restrooms, over coffee, before and after meetings, over the telephone, and through informal networks the word gets passed along when something useful and important is found. The final sections of this chapter include some suggestions for how to think about reporting findings to increase use. Following these suggestions a summary of utilization-focused evaluation principles for reporting will be presented.

Multiple Strategies for Reporting

The evaluator can work with stakeholders to develop a variety of strategies for reporting evaluation findings. Stakeholders then share not only in developing these strategies but also in carrying them out. Below is a list of possible reporting strategies. This list is by no means exhaustive.

(1) Write and disseminate a complete evaluation report, including an executive summary and appropriate technical appendices.

(2) Write separate executive summaries targeted at specific audiences or stake-holder groups.
(3) Write a carefully worded press release put out to the media by a prestigious office or public figure.
(4) Hold a press conference in conjunction with the press release.
(5) Make verbal presentations to select groups that may include analysis exercises that actively involve participants in analysis and interpretations.
(6) Begin a calculated whispering campaign to spread results through informal channels.
(7) Construct professionally designed graphics, charts, and displays for use in reporting sessions.
(8) Designate and train a findings champion or information broker to carry evaluation findings to practitioners and special stakeholder groups.
(9) Make a short videotape, or audiotape, which professionally presents the results and can be used in analysis sessions and discussions without the presence of the evaluator.
(10) Stage a debate or advocacy-adversary analysis of the findings in which opposing points of view can be fully aired (Patton, 1982a: 250-251).

The combination and scope of strategies used will depend on the nature and importance of the evaluation. The point is to be creative and strategic in facilitating use. In employing these strategies some additional principles can be helpful in planning reporting approaches.

Avoid Surprising Stakeholders

Actively working on data analysis and interpretation with stakeholders means that evaluators cannot wait until they have a highly polished final report prepared to show the results to stakeholders. Use does not center around the final report. Evaluators who prefer to work diligently in the solitude of their offices until they can spring a final report on a waiting world may find that the world has passed them by. The reason is that evaluation feedback is most useful as part of a process of thinking about a program, rather than as a one-shot information input. Thus, evaluation surprises born of the sudden release of final reports are not likely to be particularly well received. Such surprises are more likely to increase than to reduce uncertainty.

In our study of the use of federal health evaluations, we asked about the relationship between surprise findings and use. The question was asked as follows:

Some writers suggest that the degree to which the findings of a study were expected can affect the study's impact. Arguments on this go both ways. Some of them say that surprise findings have the greatest impact because they bring to light new information. Others say that surprises will usually be rejected because they don't fit in with general expectations. What was your reaction to the findings of this study? Were you surprised by the findings, or were they about what you expected?

What we found was that evaluation seldom produces major surprises. There are often minor surprises on peripheral questions, but major surprises on central questions are rare. This relates to the nature of the use we found. Inasmuch as utilization is a gradual process, key decision makers who want information are not sitting back waiting on a single set of evaluation findings. Instead, they are collecting information from multiple sources all the time. Evaluation is one piece of information that feeds into the whole picture. Evaluation findings clarify, illuminate, and provide direction, but they do not determine the whole picture. Active decision makers of the information-using variety thus work to stay in touch with program developments and to avoid the uncertainty of sudden surprises. One decision maker we interviewed made the point that a "good" evaluation process should build in feedback mechanisms that guarantee the relative predictability of the content of the final report.

> If you're a good evaluator you don't want surprises. The last thing in the world you want to do is surprise people, because the chances are surprises are not going to be well received. . . . It isn't a birthday party, and people aren't really looking for surprises. So that if you're coming up with data that is different than the conventional wisdom, you ought, a good evaluation effort I would suggest, would get those ideas floated during the evaluation process so that when the final report comes out, they aren't a surprise.

> So my reaction is that if you were dealing in the world of surprises, you aren't doing a very good evaluation. Now you could come up with findings contrary to the conventional wisdom, but you ought to be sharing those ideas, if you will, with the people being evaluated during the evaluation process to be sure that those surprises don't have any relationship to reality and again working during that process on the acceptance that maybe . . . but if you present a surprise, it will tend to get rejected. See, we don't want surprises. We don't like surprises around here [DM346: 30-31].

The evaluator for this project expressed the same opinion: "Good managers are rarely surprised by the findings. If there's a surprising finding it should be rare. I mean, *everybody's missed this insight except this great evaluator? Nonsense!*" (EV364: 13). Surprise attacks may make for good war strategy, but in evaluation the surprise attack does little to add credence to a study.

Writing Final Reports for Intended Users

The theme running throughout this book is that what happens *before* the final report is written will usually determine use. For that reason relatively little space will be devoted to the actual writing of the final evaluation report. Certainly evaluation reports should be understandable and intelligible. Brief executive summaries are more likely to be read than are full reports. But most important, as with all other aspects of utilization-focused evaluation, the actual format, purpose, and organization of the final report should be discussed and negotiated with stakeholders.

There are many ways to write a final report. (For an excellent review of alternatives, see Datta, 1977.) Recommendations may come at the beginning of the report or at the end; methods sections may be put in the body of the report or in an appendix; and the style of the report can be written as more or less an academic treatise. What matters is that the style and organization of the report make sense to intended users of the evaluation findings.

One evaluator in our federal utilization study described quite lucidly the difference between writing a report according to what he thought had been specified in a project officer's request-for-proposal (RFP) and writing the same report based on personal conversations with the decision maker for whom the study was actually conducted. As the evaluator recalled the situation, the RFP was highly misleading:

> If I had done exactly what the RFP asked for and turned in a report that was responsive to the RFP but not to what I was very clear were the kinds of questions they wanted answered, they would have gotten a different report. As a matter of fact, let me just tell you the essence of the thing. I had almost no direction from the government, as I've said, except that the guy kept saying, well here on point 8, you've got to do 8 on the contract.

> So when I turned in the draft of the report, I did points 1 through 9 and put that in the final report. Then I essentially wrote another report after that and made that the last half of the report. It was a detailed description of the activities of the program, it came to very specific kinds of conclusions. It wasn't what was asked for in the RFP, but it was what they needed to answer their questions. [The decision maker] read it and the comment back was, "It's a good report, except for all that crap in the front."

> Okay, so I turned it around then in the final draft, and put all that crap in the front into an appendix. And if you look at the report it has a big, several appendices. All of that, if you compare that carefully to the contract, all that crap in the appendix is what I was asked to get. All the stuff that constitutes the body of the report was above and beyond the call [EV367: 12].

What emerges here is a picture of a decision maker who knew what information he wanted, an evaluator committed to answering the decision maker's question, and a decision maker committed to using that information. The result was a high level of use in making a decision contrary to the decision maker's initial personal hopes. And in the words of the evaluator, the major factor explaining use was that the guy who's going to be making the decision is aware of and interested in the findings of the study and has some hand in designing the questions to be answered, that's a very important point [EV367: 20].

The decision maker concurred:

Evaluation research. Well I guess I would affirm that in many cases it has no impact for many of the reasons that the literature has suggested. But if I were to pick out factors that made a positive contribution to its use, one would be that the decision makers themselves wanted the evaluation study results. I've said that several times. If that is not present, it is not surprising that the results aren't used [DM367: 17].

THE POWER OF POSITIVE VERSUS NEGATIVE THINKING

There is a general cynicism that permeates much of the writing on evaluation research, a cynicism based on the belief that most evaluations have negative findings. Freeman (1977: 30), in his review, "Present Status of Evaluation Research," expressed the opinion that the preponderance of negative impact findings has diminished evaluation research utilization potential. He recommended that "in view of the experience of the failure of most evaluations to come up with positive impact findings, evaluation researchers probably would do well to encourage the 'biasing' of evaluations in the direction of obtaining positive results." He went on to explain that evaluators ought to play a more active role in helping to design programs that have some hope of demonstrating positive impact, based on treatments that are highly specific and carefully targeted.

The problem with Freeman's perspective is that he reflects the tendency among many evaluators and decision makers to think of evaluation findings in monolithic, absolute, and purely summative terms. In reality, evaluation findings are seldom either completely positive or completely negative. Moreover, as our federal health utilization interviews pointed out, whether findings are interpreted as "positive" or "negative" depends on who is using and interpreting the findings. In our 20 federal health evaluation case studies, respondents described findings as follows:

Basically positive findings	5
Basically negative findings	2
Mixed positive-negative findings	7
Evaluator-decision maker disagreement on nature of findings	6
	—
Total	20

In only one case did any respondents feel that the positive or negative nature of findings explained very much about utilization. Evaluation data, given that they were seldom surprising, were used to help decision makers reduce uncertainty about programmatic activity. Because we encountered few summative decisions, the overall positive or negative nature of the evaluation was not an important factor in explaining use. The positive or negative findings of a particular study constitute only one piece of information that feeds into a larger process; they are thus interpreted in the larger context of other available information. Absolute statements about positive or negative findings are less useful than specific, detailed statements about levels of impact, the nature of relationships, and variations in implementation and effectiveness. The issue is not whether findings are negative or positive, but whether evaluation results contain useful information that can reduce uncertainty and thereby provide direction for programmatic action.

Finally, there is a real sense in which the positive or negative nature of evaluation findings can never be established with any absolute certainty. As Mulla Nasrudin advises, a heavy dose of humility is helpful when making interpretations about the meaning of something. This advice emerged from a teahouse discussion. A monk entered and said,

> "My Master taught me to spread the word that mankind will never be fulfilled until the man who has *not* been wronged is as indignant about a wrong as the man who actually *has* been wronged."

> The assembly is momentarily impressed. Then Nasrudin spoke: "My Master taught *me* that nobody at all should become indignant about anything until he is sure that what he thinks is a wrong is in fact a wrong—and not a blessing in disguise" [Shah, 1964: 58-59].

Dissemination of Findings to Multiple Audiences

Dissemination of findings to audiences beyond intended users is a quite different issue from the kind of use that has been the focus of this book. Studies can have impact on all kinds of audiences in all kinds of ways. As a social scientist, I value and want to encourage the full and free dissemination of evaluation findings. Each of us ought to be permitted to indulge in the fantasy that our evaluation reports will have impact across the land and through the years. But only a handful of studies will ever enjoy (or suffer) such widespread dissemination!

Dissemination efforts will vary greatly from study to study. The nature of dissemination is a matter for negotiation between evaluators and decision makers. However, there are a few principles relevant to dissemination that can be extracted from utilization-focused evaluation.

Different individuals and audiences are interested in a given evaluation for different reasons. The questions addressed in an evaluation will have different meanings for people who were not directly involved in the painstaking

process of focusing the evaluation. Those who become engaged in dissemination efforts must be highly skilled at adapting the evaluation specifics of a
particular study to the program specifics of information users in a different
setting. One highly experienced federal decision maker in our federal utilization study commented at length on the complex nature of disseminating
evaluation at the federal level:

> I think all too frequently evaluation studies come in through a channel of the
> program or evaluation official responsible for the evaluation study, and the
> report gets passed up through the hierarchy to the upper echelon and people
> are too busy to read—particularly to read undigested material. I think the
> character of the presentation is critical. . . . Presentations can sometimes be
> overly superficial, sometimes may suffer from glibness, sometimes may be
> characterized as snow jobs, but, if they're really good they'll come out as
> solid, straightforward presentations. This means that the people making the
> presentations have to be able to translate their idioms into the language that's
> most understandable to different audiences [DM152: 25-26].

Translating evaluation findings into the idioms of particular audiences
may be more of a task than the evaluator alone can easily undertake. Several
writers have commented on the need for training professionals in the specialized role of translating research results for practitioners (e.g., Guba, 1968;
Havelock, 1968; Kirk, 1977). "An effective research utilization system requires linkers to act as an intermediary between researchers and practitioners. Linkers are the bridges that make research results available to
practitioners" (Agarwala-Rogers, 1977: 331).

On a more limited basis, I prefer to make evaluation presentations to
larger audiences a joint venture with one or more of the key stakeholders
with whom I have worked. Such presentations can provide fresh insights to
both evaluator and decision makers, while permitting a balanced view of the
project to the newly targeted audience. Joint efforts can also increase the
relevance of any given presentation by combining evaluator-decision maker
experiences. Achieving relevance is no easy task when multiple agencies are
targeted for dissemination.

> A presentation, for example, to a small group at NIH can address itself essen-
> tially and solely to NIH concerns. A presentation to the heads of the various
> health agencies will have to be above the level of individual concerns to cross-
> agency concerns. The presentation that's made up at the secretary's level, or
> the assistant secretary for planning and evaluation, has got to take into account
> the perspectives of the department, the responsibilities of the department, the
> extent to which the department identifies itself with administration positions,
> the extent to which the department has expressed options, expressed alterna-
> tives to administration positions.

The point is you're talking to people who perceive their roles differently. A person at the HEW level who looks at an activity that has been evaluated at an NIH institute level has a very difficult time relating to the issues involved, generally. The closest he comes to NIH is thinking of NIH in the aggregate. It is hard [DM152: 26].

The difficulty of making evaluations relevant to multiple audiences, each conceptualized in vague and general terms, is what led us to identification and organization of relevant decision makers and information users as the first and most critical step in utilization-focused evaluation. This is also the reason we have focused on utilization as a personal, specific, and interactive process rather than as a general dissemination problem. Dissemination can broaden and enlarge the impact of a study in important ways, but the nature of those long-term impacts are largely beyond the control of the evaluator. What the evaluator can control is the degree to which the information gathered addresses the identifiable concerns of intended information users. That is, indeed, my definition of utilization: intended use by intended users. That is the use for which I take responsibility. Thus, evaluators must cease to think of dissemination as the separate and only utilization component of a project. Utilization considerations enter into the evaluation at the very beginning and at every step along the way. In utilization-focused evaluation, dissemination efforts, far from being the whole cake of utilization, are little more than frosting on the cake. Dissemination is not use.

SUMMARY

Principles for Reporting Findings

This chapter began by comparing efforts to establish the meaning of evaluation data to the Zen search for enlightenment. Evaluation use is ultimately personal, perceptual, and interpretive. What follows is a summary of the suggestions for and principles of reporting presented in this chapter.

(1) Actively involve intended users and key stakeholders in the processes of analysis and interpretation.

(2) Set the stage for active involvement through stimulated analyses and mock interpretation sessions prior to data collection. Such sessions can provide (a) a check on the utility of data to be collected, (b) a training experience for stakeholders in how to deal with data, (c) a process for setting concrete and realistic expectations about what findings will look like, and (d) increased commitment to use.

(3) Standards of desirability can be established before data are collected to guide later data interpretation.

(4) Be creative in finding ways to make the analysis process interesting, for example, by having stakeholders speculate in writing (i.e., guess) before seeing actual results.

(5) Work with stakeholders to separate the four parts of the reporting process: description and analysis, interpretation, judgments, and recommendations.

(6) Organize and focus the findings for easy and practical analysis and interpretation. Stakeholders can only deal with a limited amount of well-organized data.

(7) Simplicity is a virtue in data analysis. Straightforward reporting is a valuable skill; some would say a gift.

(8) Findings should be balanced. This means considering multiple possible interpretations and analyzing various kinds of indicators. Single indicators are seldom adequate in the search for balance. Multiple indicators, multiple analytical approaches, and multiple perspectives are needed for balance. Balance "positive" and "negative" findings as appropriate.

(9) Be clear about definitions.

(10) Make comparisons carefully and appropriately.

(11) Use multiple strategies in reporting findings.

(12) Adapt the content of reports and techniques of reporting to the needs, interests, and capabilities of specific stakeholders and audiences.

(13) Negotiate and plan reporting and dissemination strategies with stakeholders.

(14) Keep in mind the differences between the processes of utilization and dissemination. Utilization is intended use by intended users. Dissemination is making findings available to a variety of audiences.

(15) Help stakeholders assess the findings on a variety of dimensions: relevance, believability, understandability, accuracy, practicality, and, of course, utility.

(16) Develop recommendations carefully, based on findings, and work to get recommendations taken seriously.

* * *

The analysis and interpretation of evaluation data are exciting processes. Many nights have turned into morning before evaluators have finished trying new computer runs to tease out the nuances in some data set. The work of months, sometimes years, finally comes to fruition as data are analyzed and interpreted, conclusions drawn, and alternative courses of action and recommendations considered. The excitement of data analysis and interpretation need not be the sole prerogative of evaluators. Stakeholders can become involved in struggling with data too, increasing both their commitment to and understanding of the findings.

In the spring of 1977, two evaluators from the Minnesota Center for Social Research were on the phone with program staff two or three times a day during data analysis of an educational project that was being evaluated to determine whether it was a valid model for dissemination funding. Program staff shared with evaluators the anxiety and excitement of watching the findings take final shape. Preliminary analyses on initial data appeared to have quite negative implications; as the sample became more complete, the findings began to look quite positive; finally, a mixed picture of positive and negative conclusions was drawn. Because the primary information users were intimately involved in the conceptualization and analysis of the evaluation, there were no last minute attacks on methods to explain away negative findings. The program staff understood the data, whence it came, where it went, and what could be used for program development and improvement. A utilization-focused approach to data analysis engenders commitments to use evaluation findings.

Data analysis is not simply a routine application of technical procedures. It is a creative and demanding process that is too often squeezed into the last few days before a report is due. The purpose of data analysis is to inform decision making. Too much analysis is done for its own sake, the evaluator getting caught up in the fascinating nuances of data dredging and losing sight of the real focus of evaluation. When the evaluator loses sight of the real purpose of data analysis, a fine harvest of numbers and statistics may be accumulated, but without any use ever being made of those numbers and no real consumption of those statistics taking place. A Sufi story illustrates what can happen when data collection and analysis proceed without clear purpose.

Mulla Nasrudin was visiting the village of a relative when he noticed a man in the village going about counting things. Throughout the day the man could be seen going about the village with paper and pen in hand counting all sorts of things—houses, trees, birds, children, stones, etc. When Nasrudin inquired of people in the village he was told that the man was believed to have powerful connections in the capital city and that he was counting things for the ruler. This was an impressive explanation and the Mulla decided to talk further with this distinguished statistician.

"I have noticed your work and, being a little interested in understanding the world myself, I would appreciate an opportunity to learn about the things you have discovered."

The man looked about him on all sides and then asked Nasrudin, "I note that you are a stranger here. Can you be trusted with private information?"

Nasrudin assured the man that he could count on Nasrudin's discretion and that he would treat whatever was told him with complete confidentiality.

"What I have to tell you then is that I have nothing to tell you. All of my business in counting is merely for appearances. I have no other work to do and because the unemployed are quickly conscripted for military service I have adopted this subterfuge to give an impression of being greatly occupied with important dealings. You are the first person who has asked me what my counting means and I cannot tell you for I myself have discovered no purpose in it."

Utilization-focused data collection and analysis has a purpose. That purpose is use—improved programs and better decisions.

PART IV

UTILIZATION:

Theory and Practice

The Universal Evaluation

A long time ago there was a young evaluator who was determined to discover the perfect evaluation instrument, one that would be completely valid, always reliable, and universally applicable. To help him in his quest he set out in search of Halcolm, known far and wide as the wisest evaluator. At the time Halcolm was meditating in distant mountains. Being too impatient to await Halcolm's return from the mountains, the young evaluator journeyed by air, by train, by bus, and finally miles on foot through rough mountain terrain until he found Halcolm's place of retreat.

Young Evaluator: Great Master Halcolm, forgive this intrusion, but I am on a quest for the perfect evaluation instrument.

Halcolm: Tell me about this perfect instrument.

Young Evaluator: I am looking for an instrument that is valid and reliable in all evaluation situations, that can be used to evaluate all projects, all programs, all impacts, all benefits, all people. . . . I am seeking an evaluation tool that *anyone* can use to evaluate *anything*.

Halcolm: What would be the value of such an instrument?

Young Evaluator: It would get rid of all errors in measurement, get rid of politics in evaluation, and make evaluation truly scientific. It would save money, time, and frustration. We'd finally be able to get at the truth about programs.

Halcolm: Where would you use such an instrument?

Young Evaluator: Everywhere!

Halcolm: With whom would you use it?

Young Evaluator: Everyone!

Halcolm: And what brought you to me in this quest?

Young Evaluator: A friend, Amy Block, told me you know more about evaluation than anyone. You have more experience and have thought about evaluation more than anyone. Surely, then, you must know the secret of how all evaluations are ultimately the same. Once I know that secret, I can construct the perfect instrument.

Halcolm: But if I tell you the secret, it will no longer be secret. There will be no quest for the young to undertake. What would become of the process?

Young Evaluator: Who needs it?

Halcolm: (*Silence*)

Young Evaluator: What's the use?

Halcolm: (*Silence*)

Young Evaluator: Just help me focus, please. Am I asking the most important question?

Halcolm: (*Silence*)

Young Evaluator: What do I need to do to get an answer?

Halcolm: (*Silence*)

Young Evaluator: At least tell me something. What methods can I use to find out what I want to know?

Halcolm: I could tell you what little I know about what is universal in evaluation. It is not an instrument. And it is not a secret. But I don't need to tell you. Your last five questions indicate that you already know.

Chapter 11

SITUATIONAL RESPONSIVENESS

AND THE POWER OF EVALUATION

An empirical observation will always hold less sway than an untested belief, except when it doesn't. Every situation is unique, except when it isn't. Power is, except when it is not.

—Halcolm

Politics and Evaluation:
A Case Example

During the 1975-1976 school year, the Kalamazoo Education Association (KEA), Kalamazoo, Michigan, was locked in battle with the local school administration over the Kalamazoo Schools Accountability System. The accountability system consisted of 13 components, including teacher and principal performance objectives, fall and spring standardized testing, teacher-constructed criterion-referenced tests in high school, teacher peer evaluations, and parent, student, and principal evaluations of teachers. The system had received considerable national attention. For example, *The American School Board Journal* editorialized in April (1974: 40) that by the summer of 1974, "Kalamazoo schools probably will have one of the most

comprehensive computerized systems of personnel evaluation and accountability yet devised."

Yet conflict over the school system's accountability program had been
high for several years; charges and countercharges had been exchanged
regularly between the Kalamazoo Education Association and the Office of
the Superintendent of Schools. The KEA, for example, charged that teachers were being demoralized; the superintendent argued that teachers didn't
want to be accountable. Political statements flowed with increasing frequency, making constructive dialogue difficult.

A central issue concerned the degree to which teachers throughout the
system were supportive of or hostile to the accountability system. The KEA
claimed widespread teacher dissatisfaction. The superintendent countered
that the hostility to the system came largely from a vocal minority of mal-
content unionists. The newspapers hinted that the administration might be
so alienating teachers that the system could not operate effectively. School
board members were nervous; an election was approaching and uncertainty
about the administration's ability to manage the schools in the face of what
appeared to be growing teacher hostility was potentially a major political
issue.

Ordinarily, a situation of this kind would continue to be one of charge and
countercharge based entirely on selective perception, with no underlying
data to clarify and test the reality of the opposing positions. But early in
1976, the KEA sought outside assistance from Vito Perrone, dean of the
Center for Teaching and Learning, University of North Dakota. The KEA
proposed that Dean Perrone conduct public hearings at which interested
parties could testify on and be questioned about the operations and consequences of the Kalamazoo Accountability System. Perrone suggested that
such a public forum might become a political circus; moreover, he was concerned that a fair and representative picture of the system could not be developed in such an openly polemical and adversarial forum. He suggested
instead that a survey of teachers be conducted to describe their experiences
with the accountability system and to collect a representative overview of
teacher opinions about their experiences.

Perrone attempted to negotiate the nature of the accountability review
with the superintendent of schools. However, the superintendent indicated
that he and the administration of the schools "could not cooperate" during
the spring of 1976. The administration wanted to postpone the survey until
after the election, when everyone could reflect more calmly on the situation
and when administrators would have more time to cooperate in a review.

After several unsuccessful attempts to involve the school administration
in the review, Perrone, with the concurrence of KEA-MEA-NEA, made a
decision to go forward. The review would include, as the major data source,
teacher responses to a mail survey conducted independently by the Minne-

sota Center for Social Research. The evaluation, then, was limited to providing as concisely as possible a review of the accountability program *from the perspective of teachers*. The evaluation of the accountability system was based on teacher responses to a mail questionnaire sent to all members of the Kalamazoo Education Association the first week of June 1976. The evaluation and research staff of the school system, which is responsible for the accountability system, previewed the survey instrument and made wording suggestions that were incorporated into the final revision of the questionnaire. Of the teachers 61 % anonymously responded to the survey conducted during the last week of the school year.

The results revealed intense teacher hostility toward and fear of the accountability system. It was clear from the survey results that teachers felt the Kalamazoo Accountability System was largely ineffective and inadequate. Of the respondents, 93 % believed that "accountability as practiced in Kalamazoo creates an undesirable atmosphere of anxiety among teachers," 90 % asserted that "the accountability system is mostly a public relations effort," and 83 % rated the "overall accountability system in Kalamazoo" either "poor" or "totally inadequate."

The full analysis of the data, including teachers' open-ended comments, suggested that the underlying problem was a hostile teacher-administration relationship created by the way in which the accountability system was developed (without teacher input) and implemented (forced on teachers from above). The data also documented serious misuse of standardized tests in Kalamazoo.

The school board election eroded the school administration's support, and during the summer of 1976, the superintendent resigned. The new superintendent and school board in 1976-1977 used the Perrone/MCSR report as a basis for starting fresh with teachers. The KEA officials reported a new environment of teacher-administration cooperation in developing a mutually acceptable accountability system.

The evaluation report did not directly cause the changes. Many other factors came to play in Kalamazoo at that time. But the evaluation report was information that reduced uncertainty about the scope and nature of teachers' feelings. A full meeting of the school board was devoted to discussion of the report. Candidates for the job of Kalamazoo superintendent called Dean Perrone to discuss the report and increase their understanding of the system. The evaluation report became part of the political context within which administration-teacher relations developed throughout the 1976-1977 school year. It became information that had to be taken into consideration, and information that had an observable impact on the Kalamazoo school system. The evaluation data were used by teacher union officials to enhance their political position and to increase their input into the accountability system.

The Political Context of Evaluation

Chapter 2 reported that social scientists often fail to find evidence of evaluation utilization because their definition of use is overly grandiose and rational. In particular, the rational social scientific model assumes an objective truth that is above and beyond political perception or persuasion. Scientists become uneasy when one group adopts a set of findings to further its own political purposes, as happened in Kalamazoo. They much prefer that the data serve all parties equally in a civilized search for the best answer. Research and experience suggest, however, that the Kalamazoo case, in which use was conditioned by political considerations, is the norm rather than the exception.

Political considerations are an important part of the situational context for any evaluation. This chapter will focus on how evaluators can adapt evaluation processes to differing situations to enhance use. Situational responsiveness means assessing those factors and conditions that may affect evaluation use so that those factors and conditions can be taken into account in working with stakeholders to design a useful, practical, ethical, and accurate evaluation. The situational factors highlighted in this chapter are politics, organizational conditions, and the relationship of the evaluator to the program being evaluated. The chapter closes with a more general discussion of how evaluators can be active, reactive, and adaptive in order to make evaluations situationally responsive.

In discussing situational responsiveness, this chapter will draw on theories of power and organizational development that provide a scholarly basis for choosing which situational variables to monitor in undertaking a utilization-focused evaluation. By understanding the nature of power in organizations and the relationships of information to power and organizational change, the evaluator will have not only a set of skills to contribute in undertaking an evaluation but also a theoretical perspective in which to ground the application of skills and methods. Let's begin, then, with a look at the political nature of evaluation as a basis for looking at power and information more generally in organizations and programs.

An Empirical Look
at the Political Nature of Evaluation

In studying the utilization of federal health evaluations, we asked evaluators and decision makers about the political factors that affected the impact of the specific studies we were investigating. Early in the interview, after questions on the role of the respondent in the study, the purpose of the study, and its origins, we asked the following question:

Thinking about the study as a whole, it would be helpful for us to have some understanding of the political context within which this particular study took place. Were there any political considerations that you feel directly affected this study?

Near the end of the interview, a question about political considerations was asked again. This time the question came as one of a number asked about factors that influenced the degree of utilization of the findings:

Many writers discuss the importance that political factors can have on the utilization of evaluation research. Evaluations sometimes get caught up in the external politics of programs—or the internal politics of the program. Evaluations can be either used for political purposes—or ignored for political reasons. Were there any political considerations that seem to have affected how this study was used, that affected its impact?

Nine decision makers and ten evaluators said that political considerations had affected how the study was used. In combination, at least one person interviewed in 15 of the 20 cases felt that politics had entered into the utilization process. Nine decision makers and seven evaluators felt that political considerations had been "very important" as a factor explaining use.

The types of politics involved included intra- and interagency rivalries; budgetary fights with the Office of Management and Budget, the administration, and Congress; power struggles between Washington administrators and local program personnel; and internal debates about the purposes or accomplishments of pet programs. Budgetary battles seemed to be the most political. One evaluator was particularly adamant about the political nature of his evaluation from the initiation of the study to the final report: "This was a really hot political issue, and I think that was the really important factor [explaining utilization]" (EV264: 17). The decision maker concurred.

While many evaluators responded affirmatively to the questions on political influences in the evaluation process, their full answers reveal a hesitancy and uneasiness that reflect the tensions between political and scholarly functions. The data from the interviews suggest that many evaluators resolve this tension by disassociating themselves from the political side of evaluation, despite evidence throughout their interviews that they are necessarily a part of the politics of evaluation. Because the utilization-focused approach to evaluation is based on the assumption that evaluation is a highly political process, and that the evaluator shares responsibility for the nature of that process, it is important to understand the implications of evaluators' attempts to disassociate themselves from the political process. The federal health evaluation utilization interviews provide rich source material for this purpose.

Political Innocence and Ignorance

In one of our interviews with an evaluator of mental health programs, the research scientist was particularly forthright about his lack of political sophistication. When asked about the political context of the study, he at first attempted to help the interviewer by suggesting that maybe there were pressures from Congress for evaluation, but then he stopped and said, "We had no knowledge or feeling about political relationships. We are quite innocent on such matters. We may not have recognized it" (EV5: 7). This was from a research scientist with 12 years' experience, "primarily evaluations and then I have done community studies and surveys as incidental to a program operating job" (EV5: 20).

Of the ten evaluators who felt that political considerations had affected utilization, only a few could clearly specify the nature of the political factors involved. For others, there was a vague expectation that politics was involved, but they were not sure just how: "Internally I expect there was. . . . I merely speculate. I expect the director could use it in any number of ways; he may not have done it at all" (EV119: 18). On another study, the decision maker stated that the study had not been used because program funding had already been terminated before the evaluation was completed. When asked about this in a later interview the evaluator replied:

> No, I wasn't aware of all that. Nor was I aware that it was under any serious threat. . . . I'd say the communication on political matters related to the evaluation was not something that came up with us. It was not discussed to my recollection before or after, no, not before, during, or after the conduct of the study [EV97: 12-13].

Part of evaluators' innocence or ignorance about the political processes of utilization stems from a definition of politics that includes only happenings of momentous consequences. Evaluators frequently answered our questions about political considerations only in terms of the overall climate brought on by President Nixon's attacks on welfare programs. They did not define the day-to-day negotiations out of which programs and studies evolve as "politics." One evaluator explained that no political considerations affected the study because "this was not a global kind of issue. There were vested interests all right, but it was not what would be considered a hot issue. Nobody was going to resign over whether there was this program or not" (EV145: 12).

Nine decision makers and five evaluators reported that political considerations played *no* part in the utilization process. It is instructive to look at these cases of "apolitical" evaluations, because on close inspection many were quite political. Consider, for example, the case of an academic researcher who became involved in the study of citizen boards for community mental health programs. At points in the interview, the researcher respondent objected to the term "evaluation" and explained that his was a basic research study, not an evaluation—thus its apolitical nature. When asked early in the interview whether political considerations or political factors of any kind affected the study in any way, he replied, "No. No. I would say no" (EV4: 6). The researcher went on to explain that he required absolute autonomy in the study and no external political pressures were brought to bear. Near the end of the interview, when asked if political considerations in any way affected the utilization of findings, the researcher again responded with a firm "no." In this researcher's mind, the study was clearly an example of academic research—nonpolitical in conception, implementation, and utilization. Consider, then, his responses to other questions in the interview.

Data on the Political Nature of Evaluation

Item: When asked how the study began, the evaluator described a set of personal contacts that he and colleagues made to find NIMH funding for the project:

> We got in touch with some people . . . and they were rather intrigued by this. . . . It came at year's end, as usual, and they had some funds left over from year-end type of things, and they were wondering, you know, who would be willing to take a small amount, and our project was really small in terms of dollars, $26,000-$27,000, somewhere around in there. . . . I'm pretty certain we were not competing with other groups; they felt a sole bid kind of thing wasn't going to get other people angry at all this [EV4: 1, 5-6].

Item: When asked about the purpose of the study, the evaluator replied,

> Well, a couple of things. We were wondering about conflict patterns in different programs' citizen boards. NIMH at that time was somewhat concerned because many of their centers were in high-density ghetto areas, not only cutting across the black population, but Mexican Americans or a mix of the two, or a mix of the three, that is, Puerto Ricans thrown in there. . . .

> The other thing that we were interested in, and to some extent NIMH was also interested in, is that up until the time of the study many of the agencies had boards which were pretty middle-class type boards and what they were wondering, what we were wondering, is that now you put in "poor people," people of other kinds of mixes and all of this, how is that going to work? Is that going to enhance the thing, or is that really going to disturb the system as far as the middle-class people were concerned [EV4: 4]?

Item: The interviewer followed the above response by probing, "Were there any other issues articulated by people at NIMH?" The evaluator responded,

Oh, yeah. They had a young guy who was very much concerned. He, you could say in some ways, was an advocate for, not so much for citizen participation, but just for loosening up the system so to speak . . . and he was very much into this thing, as many of them were, in fact, so he tried to push some of the people to look at things this way. Some of them I felt were pretty conservative and they were afraid that we were rocking the boat by looking at some of this [EV4: 4].

He then described some of the personalities and interactions involved.

Item: The research study included a set of recommendations about how citizen boards should be organized and better integrated into program activities.

Item: The researcher described considerable long-range impact of this study on local centers, on NIMH policy, on later studies, and even on legislation.

The influence is certainly not a direct outcome as far as the study was concerned, but it's a very important by-product of the study in which at that time we kept people talking about citizen evaluation; what does citizen participation truly mean, and so forth. You see, that generated a lot of thinking [EV4: 14].

Item: On release of results, the evaluator said,

We only released the results in a report and we wrote one paper out of it. Now, the fascinating thing, like reverberation, like throwing a pebble in a pond, and then what happens [was that] *Psychology Today* picked up this report and wrote a glowing little review. . . . They looked at seven or eight different NIMH reports and ours seemed to come through for the cheapest amount of money; then they made some nasty comments about the cost of government research [EV4: 10-11].

Item: The researcher recounted a lengthy story about how a member of Ralph Nader's consumer protection staff got hold of the study and then figured out the sample and wrote their own report. He and his colleagues talked with their lawyers but were unable to stop Nader's staff from using and abusing their data and sources, some of whom were identified incorrectly. They were unable to fight Nader's group.

We just don't have that kind of money, so we were furious. Various of us have friends who are lawyers that, you know, we thought that we would go to our lawyer friends and see if they couldn't do something. And they all came back with pretty much the same kind of response. Again, what finally happened was that when their big report came out, using our stuff, parts of our stuff, they gave it to the *New York Times* and various newspapers [EV4: 11-12].

Item: Since the study, the researchers have been involved in a number of regional and national meetings at which they have reported their findings.

> We go to enormous numbers of meetings. We see all kinds of people in all kinds of different settings, and it's not that we want to trumpet this particular study, but you know how it is at meetings, "What are you doing now?" kind of thing, "What have you been doing?" And so we talk about some of these sorts of things . . . and through this study we've sort of become known in a limited circle as "the experts in this sort of thing" [EV4: 20].

He described one such meeting, at which he became involved in an argument with local medical staff.

> The doctors and the more middle-class type of people in mental health work said we were just making too much of a fuss, that things were really, by and large, pretty nice, pretty quiet, going along pretty well. And I remember distinctly in that room, which must have had 200 people that day, the blacks and some of the, well, you might call them militant liberals, whatever labels one would put on them, were whispering to each other . . . and I began to get the tension, feel the tension and the kind of bickerings that were going on [EV4: 19].

Politics by Any Other Name

It is difficult to understand on what basis this researcher can report that the study was above political considerations. By his own testimony, the study must be considered highly politicized from conception to utilization. Personal influence was used to get funding. The research question was conceived in highly value-laden terms: "middle-class boards" versus "poor people boards." Internally there were concerns about "rocking the boat by looking at some of this." The study made controversial recommendations, was cited in national publications, and was used indirectly in legislative processes. The researchers became expert advocates for a certain view of citizen participation, a view about which there was less than complete consensus. *Personal contacts, value-laden definitions, controversial recommendations, subtle pressures to please, advocacy—of such things are politics made.*

The traditional academic values of many social scientists lead them to want to be nonpolitical in their research. Yet they also want to affect government decisions. The evidence is that they cannot have it both ways. To be innocent of the political nature of evaluation is to become a pawn in someone else's game, wittingly or unwittingly—or perhaps more commonly, to miss the game all together. Yet there has been a "rejection of systematic valuative discourse by the contemporary social sciences" (MacRae, 1976: 55).

Gideon Sjoberg (1975: 30), in his comprehensive review of the relationships between politics, ethics, and evaluation research, suggests that most
social scientists fail to understand the political nature of evaluations because
they continue to have

> an unrealistic view of the research process. . . . The conceptualization of the
> scientific process as expressed in most treatises on social research makes it
> impossible to grapple with the political and ethical issues that arise (Sjoberg
> and Nett, 1968), especially in the area of evaluation research.

Social scientists find it difficult to see beyond their own notions of logical
and rational judgments about truth, despite the fact that there is now a large
body of evaluation case studies and experience documenting the political
nature of evaluation (e.g., Cohen, 1970; House, 1973, 1974; Weiss, 1970,
1972, 1975, 1977; Levine and Levine, 1977). The problem is integrating
that experience into evaluation practice and "understanding social research
as a social enterprise" (Sjoberg, 1975: 30).

The Sources of Evaluation's Political Inherency

The political nature of the evaluation process stems from several factors:
(1) The fact that people are involved in evaluation makes it a political
process. Social research as a social enterprise means that the values, perceptions, and politics of everyone involved (scientists, decision makers, funders, program staff) impinge on the evaluation process from start to finish.
(2) The fact that classification systems and categories are involved in
evaluation makes it a political process. People perceive things through fil-
ters called classification systems and categories. The concepts, methods,
theories, and propositions of scientific research are normative and value-
laden. The way in which an evaluation problem is stated necessarily includes
value orientations, specialized cognitive interests, and subjective perceptions about both the nature of social "reality" and what is important to know
about that social reality (see Mayntz, 1977; Gouldner, 1970). The categories and classification systems used directly affect the nature of the data
collected. One of the evaluators interviewed in our utilization study was particularly conscious of the political nature of research categories. When
asked how political considerations affected the study, he responded,

> Well, certainly our decision to look at urban and rural reflected the political
> considerations at the time . . . it reflected the consideration that there are
> problems in the city that are different from problems in rural areas, and that
> this was a national program, so we didn't want to concentrate solely on prob-
> lems in the city and not pay any attention to problems in rural areas. . . . And
> then our decision to use the percent nonwhite, to look at the black and white

issue as one of the dimensions on which we stratified, that certainly reflects, you know, the attention to poor, minority areas and to the whole, well the political and socioeconomic distribution of the population and the projected interpretation of the proportion of mental illness that exists. . . . So to the extent that we used factors that were important at the moment of the study in the politics and the socioeconomic condition of the nation, to that extent we were very much influenced by political considerations. . . . What we tried to do in our sample was to reflect the political and social and economic problems we thought were important at the time [EV12: 7-8].

(3) The fact that empirical data are involved in evaluation makes it a political process. Data always require interpretation. Social science is a probabilistic enterprise. Social scientific data present probabilities and patterns, not final conclusions and facts. Interpretation is only partially a logical, deductive process; it is also a value-laden, political process. Actions taken and decisions based on such data are necessarily best guesses.

(4) The fact that actions and decisions are the desired result of evaluation makes it a political process. Any given programmatic action or decision is a result of multiple factors and influences, a process of doing the best one can with limited information. Evaluation findings are just one input into the complex system of programmatic and organizational functioning. Weighting those inputs is a political activity.

(5) The fact that programs and organizations are involved makes evaluation a political process. Organizations are decision-making systems and, as such, there are tensions between rational and political forces.

[Organizations] may have substantial elements of rationality in the sense of possessing an ordered set of preferences, the procedures for revealing available alternative courses of action and the ability to choose between them in terms of the preference. Rationality is limited, however, by the existence of many preference orders within an organization [Silverman, 1971: 204-205].

There is conflict both within organizations and between organizations, conflicts over the distribution of resources, status, and power. One of the weapons employed in these organizational conflicts is information.

(6) The fact that information is involved in evaluation makes it a political process. Information leads to knowledge; knowledge reduces uncertainty; reduction of uncertainty facilitates action; and action is necessary to the accumulation of power. While the actual role of information in decision making is not always obvious or direct, there is evidence that information can make a difference. Cohen (1970: 214) states the linkage between information and decision making quite succinctly:

Decision-making, of course, is a euphemism for the allocation of resources—money, position, authority, etc. Thus, to the extent that information is an instrument, basis, or excuse for changing power relationships within or among institutions, evaluation is a political activity.

The "Is" and the "Ought" of Evaluation Politics

In effect, then, evaluation is inherently a political process. We have not been discussing whether or not it should be political. The evidence indicates that regardless of what ought to be—and social scientists have largely argued that use of scientific findings ought to be apolitical—the uses of evaluation will be partially political in nature. The degree of politicalization varies, but it is never entirely absent.

In our study of the utilization of federal health evaluations, we found that political factors consistently affected the utilization process, whether or not the decision makers and evaluators were fully aware of the political implications of the study from the outset. Moreover, many decision makers seemed to feel that political awareness is part of the responsibility of being an evaluator. Social scientists, they explained, will not change the political nature of the world, and while several respondents were quite cynical on this point, the more predominant view seemed to be that government would not be government without politics. One highly experienced and particularly articulate decision maker expressed this view quite explicitly:

> A substantial number of people have an improper concept of how politics works and what its mission is. And its mission is not to make logical decisions, unfortunately for those of us who think program considerations are important. Its mission is to detect the will of the governed group and express that will in some type of legislation or government action. And that will is very rarely, when it's pooled nationally, a rational will. It will have moral and ethical overtones, or have all kinds of emotional loads [DM328: 18].

This decision maker clearly believed that politics is in the nature of things. But he also believed that, in terms of a democratic system of government, government decision making ought to be political.

> [Government decision making] is not rational in the sense that a good scientific study would allow you to sit down and plan everybody's life. And I'm glad it's not, by the way. Because I would be very tired, very early, of something that ran only by the numbers. Somebody'd forget part of the numbers. So I'm not fighting the system, but I am saying that you have to be careful of what you expect from a rational study when you insert it into the system. It has a tremendous impact. . . . It is a political, not a rational process. . . . Life is not a very simple thing [DM328: 18-19].

The key word here is process—political process. Evaluation information feeds into and is also part of the process. During our interviews, evaluators in particular tended to separate politics from evaluation, so that evaluation information was perceived as rational and objective while other inputs into the decision-making process were considered subjective and political. One evaluator expressed this view as follows:

> Well, as I said earlier, it didn't have very much impact, in our opinion. The why is very simply that the politics of situations usually outweigh the results of evaluations. . . . It takes a lot of time to satisfy oneself that the grounds for the evaluation were legitimate . . . and that it wasn't colored. And I think if you work in this business long enough, you recognize that evaluations are an input to decision makers . . . politics have an input to a decision maker, and politics probably carry more weight than evaluation [EV131: 8].

Such a dichotomy between evaluation and politics contributes to social scientists' ineffectiveness in attempts to enhance use of their findings because they fail to recognize the fundamentally political and power-laden nature of the information they have collected. In the next section, a theoretical basis for this perspective is explored.

Reducing Uncertainty and Enhancing Power Through Evaluation Information

The utilization-focused approach assumes that evaluation is and necessarily will be political in conceptualization, design, implementation, and utilization. Indeed, this approach assumes that use of evaluation findings will occur in direct proportion to the evaluation's power-enhancing capability. Power-enhancing capability is determined as follows: *The power of evaluation varies directly with the degree to which the findings reduce the uncertainty of action for specific stakeholders.*

This view of the relationship between evaluation information and power is adapted from the organizational theories of Michael Crozier (1964) and James Thompson (1967). Crozier developed his theory from the study of organizational structure and dynamics in a French clerical agency and a tobacco factory. He found that power relationships develop around those aspects of organizational functioning and personal interaction that are closely related to uncertainty about things upon which the organization depends (i.e., their central goals). Groups within an organization try to limit their dependence on others and, correspondingly, enlarge their own areas of discretion. They do this by making their own behavior unpredictable in relation to other groups.

Crozier begins the interpretation of what he found by using Robert Dahl's (1957) definition of power: "The power of a person A over a person B is the ability of A to obtain that B do something he would not otherwise have done." Systems attempt to limit power conflicts through rationally designed, highly routinized structures, norms, and tasks. Crozier found, however, that even in a highly centralized, routinized, bureaucratic, and monopolistic organization, it was impossible to eliminate uncertainties.

> In such a context, the power of A over B depends on A's ability to predict B's behavior and on the uncertainty of B about A's behavior. As long as the requirements of action create situations of uncertainty, the individuals who have to face them have power over those who are affected by the results of their choice [Crozier, 1964: 158].

The use of information as a means for manipulating and reducing uncertainty emerges clearly in Crozier's analysis. Supervisors in the clerical agency had no interest in passing information on to their superiors, the section chiefs. There were several section chiefs in the organization who competed with one another for attention from their superior, the division head. Section chiefs distorted the information they gave to the division head to enhance their own positions. Section chiefs could make such distortions partially because the lower-level supervisors were interested in keeping what they knew to themselves. The division head used the information he got to schedule production and to assign work. The division head only had available to him information that others were willing to give. His decisions were thus highly tenuous and aimed only at safe, minimal levels of achievement because he knew he lacked sufficient information to take narrow risks:

> The power of prediction stems to a major extent from the way information is distributed. The whole system of roles is so arranged that people are given information, the possibility of prediction, and therefore control, precisely because of their position within the hierarchical pattern [Crozier, 1964: 158].

The power that comes with information is most clearly illustrated in the government's complex system of documents classification: "Limited distribution," "confidential," "secret," and "top secret" are only a few of the designations used to limit the distribution of information. This system is a clear recognition of the power of information and knowledge. It also is fertile ground for political manipulation, especially as the number of U.S. government employees who have authority to classify documents is substantial: 2,491,555 (Harper's, 1985: 11).

Whereas Crozier's analysis centers on power relationships and uncertainties within organizations, James Thompson argues that a similar set of concepts can be applied at the level of the whole organization in relationship to other organizations and its larger environment. He argues that organizations are open systems that need resources and materials from outside, and that "with this conception the central problem for complex organizations is one of coping with uncertainty" (Thompson, 1967: 13). He is primarily concerned with industrial, production-oriented, profit organizations. Thompson suggests that assessment and evaluation are used by organizations as mechanisms for reducing uncertainty and enhancing their control over the multitude of contingencies with which they are faced. They evaluate themselves to assess their fitness for the future, and they evaluate the effectiveness of other organizations to increase their control over the maintenance of crucial exchange relationships.

Dornbusch and Scott (1975) have presented an empirically grounded theory that authority relations are based on the process of personnel evaluation. Evaluation is a control mechanism. To be effective, however, the evaluation mechanism must be agreed to by both subordinates and superordinates. Workers can sabotage evaluation systems. Thus, evaluations as part of authority systems work most effectively when the evaluation content and procedures are considered fair, important, and stable by workers. If the personnel evaluation information is to be used in making actual personnel decisions, this use of power must be authorized from below and above. The theory was tested in five settings—a basic research organization, a large hospital, a student newspaper, a university football team, and a factory. In all five organizations Dornbusch and Scott found that evaluation (in this case personnel evaluation) was the central process around which authority relations developed and through which organizational control mechanisms functioned. In this context, organizations use personnel evaluations to reduce uncertainty and increase predictability about worker/employee/member performance. *Information for prediction is information for control: thus the power of evaluation.*

The Political Practice of Evaluation

The Kalamazoo Accountability System evaluation with which this chapter opened is a good illustration of the political practice of evaluation. The accountability system was initiated to reduce uncertainty about teacher and student performance. The hostility of teachers to the accountability system led to uncertainty concerning management's ability to manage. The superintendent actively worked to stop the study that would establish the degree to which teacher opposition was widespread and crystallized. Once the study clearly established the failure of the accountability system in the opinion of teachers, union officials used that information to help force the superintendent's resignation, to mobilize public opinion, and to gain influence in the new administration. In particular, teachers won the right to participate in developing the system that would be used to evaluate them. The Kalamazoo evaluation was precisely the kind of political enterprise that Cohen has argued characterizes evaluation research: "To evaluate a social action program is *to establish an information system* in which the main questions involve the allocation of power, status, and other public goods" (Cohen, 1970: 232; italics added).

Limits on Knowledge as Power

There is a countering perspective to this notion of knowledge as power. A British colleague, L.J. Sharpe, cogently represents this opposing point of view. In trying to explain why social scientists of the 1960s so grossly overestimated their potential influence on government decision making, he argued that one "important cause of this overoptimism is the widespread assumption that governments are always in need of, or actively seek, information. But it seems doubtful whether this is the case. It is more likely that government has too much information, not too little—too much, that is, by it's own estimation" (Sharpe, 1977: 44). Sharpe argues that information delays and complicates government decision making. He then quotes Keynes to the effect that information avoidance is a central feature of government: "There is nothing a government hates more than to be well-informed; for it makes the process of arriving at decisions more complicated and difficult."

The perspectives of Keynes and Sharpe demonstrate the necessity of limiting the generalization that "knowledge is power." There are three qualifiers on this maxim that will take us closer to understanding how to approach evaluation with a utilization focus.

(1) Not all information is useful. To be power-laden, information must be relevant and in a form that is understandable to users. Crozier (1964: 158) introduces this qualifier in his discussion of power derived from differential control over uncertainties: "One should be precise and specify *relevant* uncertainty. . . . People and organizations will care only about what they can recognize as affecting them and, in turn, what is possibly within their control." A similar point is made by Dornbusch and Scott (1975) when they conclude that authority relations develop around personnel evaluation only to the extent that workers believe the evaluations are important, soundly based, fairly applied, and central to their work.

Evaluation is not useful just because it is information. Government may well have too much irrelevant, trivial, and useless information. One evaluator in our interviews made this point in contrasting short-term, highly focused evaluations with the long-term work of the National Center for Health Services Research.

> I mean, they don't respond quick enough, they can't bring their resources to bear on the issues of the day quickly enough, and when they do provide an answer—well, that's yesterday's question. . . . Gee, they're nice people out there looking at pretty global questions, but what have they done for me lately? And there's not a whole lot you can point to [EV81: 17].

Our study of the utilization of federal health evaluations indicates that in political practice, decision makers are anxious to have relevant information that will reduce the uncertainties they face.

(2) Not all people are information users. Social science is essentially a story of patterning and routinizing behavior. Habits, norms, rules, custom, tradition—this is the stuff of basic social science. The socialization process into society at large as well as into work organizations is aimed at limiting those things about which individuals make decisions. Individuals vary in their aptitude for handling uncertainty and their ability to exercise discretion. Socialization, education, and experience magnify such differences.

In the political practice of evaluation, this means simply that information is power only in the hands (minds) of people who know how to use it and are open to using it. The problem of utilization is one of matching: *getting the right information to the right people.*

Widespread notions about "the bureaucratic personality" and "organization man" are now part of our organizational folklore, affirming this assertion that not all people are information users. Many, perhaps most, people rely on the predispositions of their socialization and the pressure of peers to chart their daily course of action. But there are those people who can and do make information part of their decision-making frame of reference. One evaluator in our utilization of federal health evaluation interviews made this point quite succinctly. This person had had 35 years' experience in government, 20 of those years directly involved in research and evaluation. He had also worked for several years as a private evaluation research contractor, during which time he had been involved in evaluating some 80 projects. Throughout his responses to our questions on the importance of various specific factors in affecting utilization, he returned to the theme of individual variability in the ability to use information. He tied this to his idea of the good manager.

The good manager is aggressive, open, confident, anxious to interchange ideas. He's not defensive. Rather, "he's interested in finding out what your views are, not defending his. . . . You know my sample is relatively small, but I'd say probably there are a quarter (25%) of what I'd call good managers" (EV346: 15). *These, he believes, are the people who use evaluation.*

What of people who are not inclined to use information—people who are intimidated by, indifferent to, or even hostile to evaluation? The utilization-focused evaluation process includes opportunities and strategies for *creating and training information users.* In *Creative Evaluation* (Patton, 1981), the argument is made that evaluators have a responsibility to train information users. Thus, there are two parts to the utilization challenge: finding real information users and creating/supporting/training information users.

(3) Until actually used, information is only potential power, not actual power. One of the critical uncertainties of decision making and "muddling through" is the difficulty of knowing in advance precisely what information will be needed. In the battle for control over uncertainty one thing is certain—no one wants to be caught with less information than competitors

for power. A lot of information is collected "just in case." One evaluator we interviewed explained the entire function of his office in these terms:

> I wouldn't want to be quoted by name, but there was a real question as to whether we were asked for these reports because they wanted them for decision making. We felt that the five-foot shelf that we were turning out may actually have had no particular relevance to the real world. Again, that's something you don't know, you're never in a position to find out.
>
> A list of OMB questions were dealt with in here and we didn't know why we were being asked those questions. They were not questions that we would have asked about the program, for example. We all worked for Richard Nixon. We'd produce answers to questions. It's a political aspect, but it's probably the form political effects take inside a bureaucracy.
>
> This operation made it impossible for NIMH, some congressman, or someone, it made it impossible for him to say that the issue had never been studied. Therefore, it would be a fairly standard administration ploy to study the issue so that it is not possible for somebody to insist you never even looked at this issue. And one did wonder to what extent we were turning out paper for that purpose [EV152: 18].

It is possible to become quite cynical about the "just in case" approach to data gathering. The utilization-focused approach is not aimed at potential utilization but, rather, at actual utilization. It is simply impossible to collect data on every possible future contingency, so evaluators might as well attempt to study questions in which the odds favor utilization. Utilization-focused evaluation is aimed at more than producing pages of reports "just in case." One official described the "just in case" approach as follows:

> Yeah, it can be put in crude terms that evaluation studies are just to cover your ass. But that's kind of misunderstanding when it's put that crudely because they do more than that. They also give you information by which you could make changes if you want to make changes or by which you can test if you're doing things that are really wrong, and so they would exercise some controlling function even though, in fact, you never use them. They could also serve as a way of checking out options so that if contingencies come up where certain kinds of information would be useful, then that information would be there. Just because that condition doesn't come up doesn't mean that they haven't served a purpose [DM4: 13].

Utilization-focused evaluation aims at closing the gap between potential utilization and actual utilization. Lazarsfeld and Reitz (1975) call this the gap between knowledge and action. Bridging that gap, they believe, is the most important translation step in the utilization process. Bridging that gap is a creative process that generates power. The process of focusing evaluation questions on matters of real importance to stakeholders and actively involving them in all phases of an evaluation is how utilization-focused evaluation bridges that gap.

Political Viability

The Joint Committee on Standards for Educational Evaluation (1981: 56) provides explicit recognition of the political nature of evaluation and the need for evaluators to be politically sophisticated. The standard on political viability prescribes,

> The evaluation should be planned and conducted with anticipation of the different positions of various interest groups, so that their cooperation may be obtained, and so that possible attempts by any of these groups to curtail evaluation operations or to bias or misapply the results can be averted or counteracted.

Political situations vary considerably. The point is that evaluations are inherently political, therefore situational responsiveness will necessarily require attention to political considerations and their likely consequences for use, credibility, propriety, and accuracy. As the evaluator undertakes this political analysis, a corresponding analysis will be needed of organizational factors that may affect situational responsiveness and evaluation utilization. The next section discusses such factors.

ORGANIZATIONAL VARIATIONS AND EVALUATION

Understanding variations in how organizations function can help evaluators adapt evaluation processes to specific organizational conditions and climates. Studer (1978) found that staff and administrator perceptions of "organizational health" affected beliefs in the value of evaluation and subsequent evaluation use. The sections that follow suggest some ways in which organizational factors may affect evaluation, beginning with differing theoretical conceptualizations of the purpose of an organization. This theoretical discussion will lead to practical suggestions for taking the organizational context into consideration in designing useful evaluations.

Models of Organization:
From Goal Maximization to Systems Optimization

Under the classical closed-system, rational view of organizations (Weber, 1947), organizations were expected to try to maximize attainment of their major goal, e.g., profit. A central goal was assumed in this model to be the basic focus of organizational activity. In evaluation, this model is represented by the traditional question, "To what extent did the program achieve its major goal?"

The first major step away from the purely closed system, rational view of organizations represented by the goal model was systems theory. Etzioni (1964: 17), for example, proposed replacing the goal model with a systems model in which the criterion of success becomes optimization rather than maximization:

> Using a systems model we are able to see a basic distortion in the analysis of organizations that is not visible or explicable from the perspective of goal-model evaluation. . . . The systems model explicitly recognizes that the organization solves certain problems other than those directly involved in the achievement of the goal, and the excessive concern with the latter may result in insufficient attention to other necessary organizational activities, and to a lack of coordination between the inflated goal activities and the de-emphasized non-goal activities.

The systems approach to evaluation involves the measurement of a variety of indicators of effectiveness (e.g., productivity, morale, adaptiveness, growth, quality) in a comparative framework. These indicators of effectiveness are considered to be interdependent and to vary with other organizational characteristics. Price (1968) compiled an inventory of propositions concerning effectiveness using systems assumptions with particular emphasis on operative goals. The comparative framework means that "rather than comparing existing organizations to ideals of what they might be, we may assess their performances relative to one another" (Etzioni, 1964: 17).

The problem with the systems model is how to decide what is optimal. While one may agree that optimizing is a better term than maximizing for describing what really happens in program decision making, from an evaluation perspective someone still has to decide what is optimal and how "optimality" will be measured. Evaluators may be concerned with a variety of effectiveness indicators, but Becker and Neuhauser (1975: 45-46) argue that, for practical purposes, systems evaluators simply look at the degree of attainment of the *primary* goal of the governing body of a program or organization—an approach that is actually little different from the maximizing approach of the rational goal model. In other cases, systems evaluators look at attainment of a series of goals, but lack a clear method for determining the *optimal* relationship among goals.

A third view of organizations, decision making, and goals based on the open systems perspective is an alternative to the overrationalistic goal model of maximization and the overrelativistic systems model of optimization.

The Open Systems Perspective: Satisficing in the Face of Uncertainty

The emergent view among several organizational sociologists is that "the central problem for complex organizations is one of coping with uncertainty" (Thompson, 1967: 13). Both organizations and individuals within organizations are faced with numerous uncertainties. Social action programs are particularly vulnerable to environmental uncertainties. Will funding be continued? Will programs be enlarged or retrenched? Can staff be maintained? How will clients react to the program? What effects will the program have on clients? How will changes in the political climate affect the program? The degree of uncertainty varies from organization to organization, program to program, but *there is always uncertainty.*

Terreberry (1971) reviewed work in economics, business, management, sociology, and social psychology concerning the effects of uncertainty on organizations. She pulled together a substantial literature indicating that the kind, extent, and sheer rapidity of social change requires greater organizational adaptability and makes the future less predictable. Classical models of rational organizational decision making are substantially undermined by this uncertainty: "Increasingly, the rational strategies of planned innovation and long-range planning are being undermined by unpredictable changes" (Terreberry, 1971: 60). She argued that the complexity of modern society has increased the degree to which organizations face multiple uncertainties. Modern organizations have become "open systems" subject to a variety of environmental influences and contingencies.

There is a substantial literature based on the open systems approach to organizations (see Maurer, 1971). To understand the implications of open systems for evaluation, it is necessary to understand how decision making is changed in open systems programs.

When decision makers are struggling to reduce uncertainty under highly turbulent conditions, the nature of the decision-making process changes. Cyert and March (1963: 100) found in their studies of business organizations that "so long as the environment of the firm is unstable—and predictably unstable—the heart of the theory [of organizational behavior] must be the process of short-run adaptive reactions." Short-run adaptive reactions are not aimed at maximizing attainment of a central goal; nor do such reactions lead necessarily to optimal goal attainment. Short-run adaptive reactions involve *"satisficing"* (Simon, 1957) rather than maximizing or optimizing. Under the criterion of satisficing, decision makers search for *satisfactory* solutions. In situations of great complexity and multiple uncertainties, rational decision making gives way to "heuristic" problem solving (Taylor, 1965: 73, 80).

This shift in perspective is based on two crucial assumptions. First, a decision maker never has all the information needed to meet the conditions necessary for rational action. Rationality requires making the best choice from among all possible alternatives, taking into account the consequences of each alternative. In reality, all possible alternatives are seldom known and knowledge of consequences is always incomplete. Second, even if all the necessary knowledge were available, the human mind could not manage the complexity of dealing with all the possible permutations and combinations.

The capacity of the human mind for formulating and solving complex problems is very small compared with the size of the problems whose solution is
required for objectively rational behavior in the real world—or even for a reasonable approximation to such objective rationality [Simon, 1957: 198].

Despite incomplete information, great complexity, and multiple uncertainties, the decision maker is still required to act. He or she therefore sim-
plifies the situation and exhibits what Simon (1957: 204) calls "subjective
rationality" or "bounded rationality." "The key to the simplification of the
choice process . . . is the replacement of the goal of *maximizing* with the
goal of *satisficing*, of finding a course of action that is 'good enough.'"

Donald Taylor (1965: 62-63), in his extensive review of decision-making
and problem-solving literatures, describes the active-reactive nature of organizational behavior:

Administrative man, confronted with a situation in which he must make a decision, is assumed to begin by searching for possible alternative courses of
action and for information concerning the consequences of each alternative.
He is assumed to select the first alternative he encounters which meets some
minimum standard of satisfaction with respect to each of the values he is seeking to attain—in other words, he satisfices. . . . The concept of satisficing
should not be misinterpreted to imply that an individual confronted simultaneously with several alternatives will fail to pick the optimal one. . . . The concept of satisficing is closely linked to the concept of search. The essential idea
is that the individual searches until he finds an alternative that is "good
enough."

This view of decision making fits well with the data presented in Chapters
2 and 3 on how federal health evaluations were used. Evaluation is used
when decision makers try to reduce uncertainty as part of the process of
short-run adaptive reactions. Evaluations provide important information to
decision makers, but information is also sought from other sources—and is
never complete. Program development is a process of facing problems and
solving them. It is a process of "muddling through" or of "disjointed incrementalism" (Lindblom, 1959; Braybrooke and Lindblom, 1963). The incrementalist notion refers to a coping strategy for satisficing in which
decision makers consider only those activities and outcomes that differ incrementally (i.e., to a small extent) from existing highly focused issues or
"focus-elements" (Shackle, 1961: 122). In this action-reaction-adaptation
process, decision makers do not simply adjust means to ends, as would be
done under conditions of "rational" decision making; rather, "ends are
chosen that are appropriate to available or nearly available means" (Hirschman and Lindblom, 1962: 215). Reviewing contemporary work in several
fields, Hirschman and Lindblom (1962) concluded that there is considerable
convergence of evidence supporting the incrementalism view.

The incrementalist perspective does not describe an "irrational" process in the colloquial sense of the term. Rather, it is a pragmatic perspective. It is not a matter of organizational Horatio Algers struggling singlemindedly to accomplish a single goal but, rather, one of program decision makers doing their best to solve specific problems in the face of great complexity and multiple uncertainties. It is not a romantic picture, but the evidence is that for many programs it is a highly realistic one.

Situational Responsiveness and Organizational Variations

Variations in how an organization functions—or is perceived as functioning—can affect how an evaluation is undertaken when the evaluator is situationally responsive. For example, the three models of organizational decision making reviewed above (the maximizing goal attainment model, the optimizing model, and the incremental satisficing model) have implications for how an evaluator might approach the task of goals clarification. The next section describes how differing degrees of uncertainty in the environment of a program or organization can affect the utility of attempting to clarify and measure specific goals.

Organizational Dynamics and Program Goals: Theory and Practice

The power of evaluation resides in part in its potential for reducing uncertainty. Uncertainty is not, however, a dichotomous variable. The degree of uncertainty varies for different decision makers, for different parts of an organization, and for different organizations (see Thompson, 1967). Emery and Trist (1965) identify four types of environments characterized by varying degrees of uncertainty based on the degree of system connectedness that exists among the components of the environment. What is important about their work from an evaluation perspective is their presentation of evidence that the degree of uncertainty facing an organization directly affects the degree to which goals and strategies for attaining goals can be made concrete and stable. The less certain the environment, the less stable and the less concrete the organization's goals will be.

This theoretical perspective has practical implications for evaluators. It means that the more unstable and turbulent the environment of a program, the less likely it is that the evaluator will be able to generate concrete and stable goals. Second, few evaluations can investigate and assess all the many program components and special projects of an agency, organization, or program. The clarity, specificity, and measurability of goals will vary throughout a program depending upon the environmental turbulence faced by specific projects and program subparts. As the evaluator works with decision makers and information users to focus the evaluation, the degree to which it is useful to labor over writing a goals statement will vary for different parts of the program. As some parts of a program may have highly unstable goals, it may not be efficient or useful to try to force such programs into a static and rigid goals model. *The evaluation issue is what information is needed, not whether goals are clear, specific, and measurable. Clear, specific, and measurable goals are only one means to the end of conducting a useful evaluation.*

An example may help clarify the options involved. The Minnesota State Department of Education funded a "human liberation" program in the Minneapolis public schools, using federal funds. The program was an innovative high school course aimed at enhancing communication skills around the issues of sexism and racism. Initial funding was to be for three years, but a renewal application would have to be filed each year. Program staff were not at all sure how the program would fit into the local high school where it was located, much less how it would fit into the total school system. An external, out-of-state evaluator was hired to assist the program. The evaluator's idea of assistance was to force staff to articulate clear, specific, and measurable goals in behavioral terms. The staff had no previous experience in writing behavioral objectives, nor was program conceptualization sufficiently advanced to concretize goals. Virtually everything about the program was uncertain: curriculum content, student reaction, staffing, funding, relationship to the school system, public support. None of these things were known with any degree of certainty.

For an evaluator operating within a rational goals model framework such a program is chaos. How can a program operate if it does not know where it is going? How can it be evaluated if there are no operational objectives? Yet the evidence is that thousands of programs operate with highly fluid structures and changing goals. Moreover, the research literature on organizations clearly points to the "appropriateness" of dynamic goals and flexible structures under conditions of great uncertainty (see Burns and Stalker, 1961; Lawrence and Lorsch, 1967; Hage and Aiken, 1970). Evaluators who view such programs from the perspective of the rational goals model see chaos and confusion; organizational sociologists who view such programs from the perspective of organizational dynamics in open systems see adaptation and environmental-organizational interdependence. *In utilization-focused evaluation the burden rests with the evaluator to understand what kind of evaluation is appropriate for different types of programs rather than forcing all programs into a single evaluation mold.*

In the Minneapolis Human Liberation Program, the first-year evaluation based on behavioral objectives was quite negative—and disastrous. It was dismissed by program staff as irrelevant and ignored by school officials, who understood the problems of first-year programs. The program staff refused to work with the same evaluator the second year and faced the prospect of a new evaluator with suspicion and hostility. When we were asked for help during the second year, it was immediately clear that the new program staff wanted nothing to do with writing behavioral goal statements. The funders and school officials agreed to a formative evaluation with program staff as primary stakeholders. The evaluation focused on *staff information needs* for short-run, adaptive decisions aimed at immediate program improvement. This meant confidential interviews with students about strengths and weaknesses of the course, observations of classes to describe interracial dynamics and student reactions, and beginning work on trying to develop measures of racism and sexism. On this latter point, program staff were undecided as to whether they were really trying to change student attitudes and behaviors, or just make students more "aware." They needed time and information to work out satisfactory approaches to the problems of racism and sexism.

By the third year, the program had begun to take more concrete shape. Uncertainties about student reaction and school system support had been reduced by the evaluation. Initial findings indicated support for the program. Program staff were more confident and experienced. They decided that for the third year they wanted to develop more concrete, quantitative instruments to measure student changes. They were ready to deal with program outcomes, although it was clear that such goals and objectives were to be viewed as experimental and flexible. By working back and forth between specific information needs, contextual goals, and focused evaluation questions, it was possible to conduct an evaluation that was used to improve the program, which was the purpose of the evaluation agreed to by decision makers and evaluators. The key to utilization was matching the evaluation to program conditions and decision maker needs.

Being Active-Reactive-Adaptive

Several times in this chapter I have referred to the consultative interactions between evaluators and primary stakeholders as an "active-reactive-adaptive" process. What do I mean?

There is no single term that fully describes the nature of the collaborative decision-making process that jointly involves evaluators and primary intended information users in focusing an evaluation. To label this process as "active-reactive-adaptive" is meant to be both descriptive and prescriptive. It is descriptive in that it is based on empirical studies of how much real world decision making actually unfolds. It is prescriptive in that this strategy can be consciously and deliberately used by evaluators to increase their effectiveness in working with evaluation stakeholders.

Active-reactive-adaptive evaluators are situationally responsive. Utilization-focused evaluators cannot assume that every evaluation will involve the same issues, for example, measurement of goal attainment or program outcomes. A useful evaluation emerges from the special characteristics and conditions of a particular situation—a mixture of people, politics, history, context, resources, constraints, values, needs, interests, and chance. This means that evaluators must be active-reactive-adaptive in analyzing situational variations.

Utilization-focused evaluators are first active in deliberately and calculatedly identifying intended users and focusing useful questions. They are reactive in listening to intended users and responding to what they learn about the particular situation in which the evaluation unfolds. They are adaptive in altering evaluation questions and designs in light of their increased understanding of the situation and changing conditions. Active-reactive-adaptive evaluators don't impose cookbook designs. They don't do the same thing time after time. They are genuinely immersed in the challenges of each new setting and genuinely responsive to the intended users of each new evaluation.

It is not easy to be an "active-reactive-adaptive" evaluator. It is not easy to conduct what Gerald Barkdoll, associate commissioner for planning and evaluation of the U.S. Food and Drug Administration, has called "Type III Evaluations," in which the evaluator works in a consultative, consensus-building process to help policymakers and program analysts cooperatively and openly clarify their information needs and use information to improve their joint effectiveness. He contrasts this style of evaluation (Type III) to the more typical "surveillance and compliance" approach of aggressively independent and highly critical auditors committed to getting the goods on a program (Type I) or the aloof and value-free scientists (Type II) who focus only on acquiring technically impeccable data while ignoring the political, ethical, and utilization contexts of an evaluation process (Barkdoll, 1980). In being active-reactive-adaptive, and in facilitating a process whereby stakeholders can work with an evaluator to examine a particular situation in such a way that useful information can be gathered and applied to improve program effectiveness (Type III evaluations), evaluators are called on to be, among other things, creative (Patton, 1981).

The active-reactive-adaptive approach is similar to what Etzioni calls a "mixed-scanning" strategy. Under this decision-making strategy, policymakers move back and forth between "contextuating" information (which is the goals-oriented overview of policy) and "bit" information (which provides the details about immediate, incremental needs and alternatives): "Together they make for a third approach which is more realistic *and* more transforming than each of its elements" (Etzioni, 1968: 283). Etzioni's definition of mixed scanning is aimed primarily at national policymaking for the "active society." What is missing in the imagery of mixed scanning is the highly reactive-adaptive side of much decision making. Etzioni stressed the active aspects of decision making, but much of what passes for action in decision making is really reaction and adaptation—i.e., trying to make the best of things until uncertainty is sufficiently reduced or external constraints have been sufficiently removed to permit a reassertion of activism.

It is the paradox of decision making that effective action is born of reaction. Only when organizations and people take in information from the environment and react to changing conditions can they act on that same environment to reduce uncertainty and increase discretionary flexibility (see Thompson, 1967). The same is true for the individual decision maker or for a problem-solving group. Action emerges through reaction and leads to adaptation. The imagery is familiar: thesis-antithesis-synthesis, stimulus-response-change. But what does all this have to do with the utilization-focused approach to evaluation?

The active-reactive-adaptive evaluator in utilization-focused evaluation moves back and forth between overall program goals and specific evaluation questions in order to establish the relevance of various information options to stakeholders in a particular situation. For example, the evaluator need not attempt to construct a written-in-stone set of goals for an evaluation in which goals are changeable because of an uncertain environment, fluid in the face of different contingencies, and abstractions that are only semireal. This follows in part the incrementalist strategy: "One need not try to organize all possible values into a coherent scheme, but instead can evaluate only what is relevant in actual policy choices" (Lindblom, 1965: 145).

The crux of the matter is that effective evaluators trying to enhance utilization decide how to act with regard to goals by reacting and adapting to particular situations and specific stakeholders. This active-reactive-adaptive stance characterizes all phases of evaluator-stakeholder interaction in utilization-focused evaluation. Identifying intended users, focusing relevant questions, choosing methods, and analyzing results are all collaborative processes of action-reaction-adaption aimed at increasing utility.

INTERNAL AND EXTERNAL EVALUATORS

This chapter has been looking at power and organizational conditions as key situational factors to consider in evaluation practice. It is appropriate in this context to look at how the location of the evaluator vis-à-vis the program and organization affects the evaluation generally, and the extent to which it is possible to be utilization-focused from internal and external vantage points.

The early evaluation literature was aimed primarily at external evaluators. External evaluators are typically researchers who conduct evaluations under contract to funders. External evaluators come from universities, consulting firms, and research organizations, or work as independent consultants. The defining characteristic of external evaluators is that they have no long-term, ongoing position within the program or organization being evaluated. They are therefore not subordinated to someone in the organization and not directly dependent on the organization for their job and career.

External evaluators are valuable precisely because they are outside the organization. It is typically assumed that their external status permits external evaluators to be more independent, objective, and credible than internal evaluators. The problem is that external evaluators are also typically more costly than internal evaluators, less knowledgeable about the nuances and particulars of the local situation, and less able to follow through to facilitate the implementation of recommendations. When external evaluators complete their contract, they may take with them a great deal of knowledge and insight that is lost to the program. That knowledge stays "in-house" with internal evaluators. External evaluators have also been known to cause difficulties in a program through insensitivity to organizational relationships and norms, one of the reasons the work of external evaluators is sometimes called "out-house" evaluation in contrast to "in-house" work.

One of the major trends in evaluation during the 1970s was a transition from external to internal evaluation. At the beginning of the 1970s evaluation was just emerging as a profession. There were fewer distinct evaluation units within government bureaus, human service agencies, and private sector organizations than there are now. School districts had research and evaluation units, but even they contracted out much of the evaluation work mandated by the landmark 1965 Elementary and Secondary Education Act in the United States. As evaluation became more pervasive in the 1970s, as the mandate for evaluation was added to more and more legislation, and as training for evaluators became more available and widespread, internal evaluation units became more common. Now most federal, state, and local agencies have internal evaluation units. International organizations also have internal evaluation divisions.

The first edition of this book was based primarily on my experiences as an external evaluator. Since that time, I have had extensive contact with internal evaluators through training and consulting opportunities. I have worked closely with several internal evaluators over a number of years, and I interviewed ten internal evaluators for this book. I asked them specifically about the relevance of utilization-focused evaluation to internal evaluations. They all agreed that the ideas and emphases of utilization-focused evaluation were relevant and applicable. Their comments about how they have applied utilization-focused approaches include insights into the world of the internal evaluator.

Themes from Internal Evaluators

(1) Actively involving stakeholders within the organization can be difficult because evaluation is often perceived by both superiors and subordinates as the job of the evaluator. The internal evaluator is typically expected to *do* evaluations, not facilitate an evaluation process involving others. Inter-

nal evaluators who have had success involving others have had to work hard at finding special incentives to attract participation in the evaluation process. One internal evaluator commented,

> My director told me he doesn't want to spend time thinking about evaluation. That's why he hired me. He wants me to "anticipate his information needs." I've had to find ways to talk with him about his interests and information needs without explicitly telling him he's helping me focus the evaluation. I guess you could say I kinda involve him without his really knowing he's involved.

(2) Internal evaluators are often asked by superiors for public relations information rather than evaluation. The internal evaluator may be told, "I want a report for the legislature proving our program is effective." It takes clear conviction, subtle diplomacy, and an astute understanding of how to help superiors appreciate evaluation to keep internal evaluation responsibilities from degenerating into public relations. One mechanism used by several internal evaluators to increase support for real evaluation rather than public relations is establishing an evaluation advisory committee, including influential people from outside the organization, to provide independent checks on the integrity of internal evaluations.

(3) Internal evaluators get asked to do lots of little data-gathering and report-writing tasks that are quite time consuming but too minor to be considered meaningful evaluation. For example, if someone in the agency wants a quick review of what other states are doing about some problem, the internal evaluator is an easy target for assigning the task. Such assignments can become so pervasive that it's difficult to have time for longer-term, more meaningful evaluation efforts.

(4) Internal evaluators are often excluded from major decisions or so far removed from critical information networks that they don't know about new initiatives or developments in time to build in an evaluation perspective upfront. One internal evaluator explained,

> We have separate people doing planning and evaluation. I'm not included in the planning process and usually don't even see the plan until it's approved. Then they expect me to add on an evaluation. It's a real bitch to take a plan done without any thought of evaluation and add an evaluation without screwing up or changing the plan. They think evaluation is something you do at the end rather than think about from the start. It's damn hard to break through these perceptions. Besides, I don't want to do the planners' job, and they don't want to do my job, but we've got to find better ways of making the whole thing work together. That's my frustration. . . . It takes me constantly bugging them and sometimes they think I'm encroaching on their turf. Some days I think, "Who needs the hassle?" even though I know it's not as useful just to tack on the evaluation at the end.

(5) Getting evaluation used takes a lot of follow-through. One internal evaluator explained that her job was defined as data gathering and report writing without consideration of following up to see if report recommendations were adopted. That's not part of her job description, and it takes time—and some authority. She commented,

> How do I get managers to use a report if my job is just to write the report? But they're above me. I don't have the authority to ask them in 6 months what they've done. I wrote a follow-up memo once reminding managers about recommendations in an evaluation and some of them didn't like it at all, although a couple of the good ones said they were glad I reminded them.

Another internal evaluator told me he had learned how to follow up informally. He has seven years' experience as an internal human services evaluator. He said,

> At first I just wrote a report and figured my job was done. Now I tell them when we review the initial report that I'll check back in a few months to see how things are going. I find I have to keep pushing, keep reminding, or they get busy and just file the report. We're gradually getting some understanding that our job should include some follow-up. Mostly it's on a few things that we decide are really important. You can't do it all.

Internal Role Definitions

The themes from internal evaluators indicate the importance of carefully defining the job to include attention to use. When and if the internal evaluation job is defined primarily as writing a report and filling out routine reporting forms, the ability of the evaluator to influence use is quite limited. When and if the internal evaluator is organizationally separated from managers and planners, it is difficult to establish collaborative arrangements that facilitate use. Thus, a utilization-focused approach to internal evaluation will often require a redefinition of the position to include responsibility for working with intended users to develop strategies for acting on findings.

One of the most effective internal evaluation units I've encountered is in the U.S. Federal Bureau of Investigation (FBI). This unit is a direct responsibility of the Bureau's deputy director. The evaluation unit director has direct access to the director of the FBI in both problem identification and discussion of findings. The purpose of the unit is program improvement. Reports are written *only* for internal use; there is no public relations use of reports. Public relations is the function of a different unit. The internal evaluation staff is drawn from experienced FBI agents. They thus have high credibility with agents in the field. They also have the status and authority of the director's office behind them. The evaluation unit has an operations handbook that clearly delineates responsibilities and procedures. Evaluation proposals and designs are planned and reviewed with intended users. Multiple methods are used. Reports are written with use in mind. Six months after the report has been written and reviewed, follow-up is formally undertaken to find out if recommendations have been implemented. The internal evaluators have a strong commitment to improving FBI programs and clear authority to plan, conduct, and report evaluations in ways that will have an impact on the organization, including follow-up to make sure recommendations approved by the director are actually implemented.

Internal-External Evaluation Combinations

In workshops I am often asked to compare the relative advantages and disadvantages of internal versus external evaluations, or "in-house" versus "out-house" evaluators. After describing some of the differences along the lines of the preceding sections, I like to point out that the question is loaded by implying that internal and external approaches are mutually exclusive. Actually, there are a good many possible combinations of internal *and* external evaluations that may be more desirable and more cost-effective than either a purely internal *or* purely external evaluation.

Accreditation processes are a good example of an internal-external combination. The internal group collects the data and arranges them so that the external group can come in, inspect the data collected by the internal group, sometimes collect additional information on their own, and pass judgment on the program. There are many ways in which an evaluation can be set up so that some external group of respected professionals and evaluators guarantees the validity and fairness of the evaluation process while the people internal to the program actually collect and/or analyze the evaluation data. The cost savings of such an approach can be substantial while still allowing the evaluation to have basic credibility and legitimacy through the blessing of the external review committee.

I worked for several years with one of the leading chemical dependency programs in the country, the Hazelden Foundation of Minnesota. They have established a rigorous evaluation process that involves data collection at the point of entry into the program and then follow-up questionnaires six months, twelve months, and eighteen months after leaving the program. Hazelden's own research and evaluation department collects all of the data. My responsibility as an external evaluator was to monitor that data collection periodically to make sure that the established procedures were being followed correctly. I then worked with the program decision makers to identify the kind of data analysis that was desirable. They performed the data analysis with their own computer resources. They sent the data to me and I wrote the annual evaluation report. They participated in analyzing, interpreting, and making judgments about the data, but for purposes of legitimacy and credibility, the actual writing of the final report was done by me. This internal/external combination is sometimes extended one step farther by having still another layer of external professionals and evaluators pass judgment on the quality and accuracy of the final report through a *meta-evaluation* process—evaluating the evaluation.

There are limitations to this kind of process. One of the limitations is that the external group may impose unmanageable and overwhelming data collection procedures on the internal people. I saw this happening in an internal-external model with a group of school districts in Canada. The external committee was asking for a "comprehensive" data collection effort by the local schools that included data on learning outcomes, staff morale, facilities, curriculum, the school lunch program, the library, parent reactions, the perceptions of local businessmen, analysis of the school bus system, and so on. After listening to all of the things the external committee thought the internal people should do, the internal folks renamed the evaluation approach. They suggested that the model should not be called the "Internal-External Model" of evaluation but, rather, the "Internal-External-Eternal Model" of evaluation.

The point is that a variety of internal-external combinations are possible to combine the lower costs of internal data collection with the higher credibility of external review. In working out the details of internal-external combinations, care will need to be taken to achieve an appropriate and mutually rewarding balance based on a collaborative commitment to the standards of utility, feasibility, propriety, and accuracy.

SITUATIONAL EVALUATION

This chapter has emphasized situational responsiveness as a principal ingredient in utilization-focused evaluation. We have examined how variations in political factors, organizational conditions, and the location of the evaluator (internal or external) can affect evaluation design and use. It is important to understand the importance of the shift from standard scientific operating procedures to situational responsiveness in evaluation. This final section will review the nature and implications of that shift in emphasis.

Like the shift in perspective among modern philosophers from a search for universal laws to a concern with situational ethics, the scientific revolution manifested by the emergence of the new standards of evaluation represents a situational approach to the conduct of social science. This stands in stark contrast to the tradition of logical-positivism—with its search for universal truths, a carefully prescribed set of scientific rules, and operating procedures to be followed in every legitimate scientific inquiry. The driving force that gave rise to this new evaluation ideology is the recognition that *there is no one best way to conduct an evaluation*. This insight is critical. On this belief rests all the new principles, standards, and premises of the evaluation profession.

Every evaluation situation is unique. A successful evaluation (one that is practical, ethical, useful, and accurate) emerges from the special characteristics and conditions of a particular situation—a mixture of people, politics, history, context, resources, constraints, values, needs, interests, and chance. Despite the rather obvious, almost trite, and basically commonsense nature of these observations, there are a host of subtleties and nuances implicit in the shift in perspective from evaluation judged by a single, standard, and universal set of criteria (methodological rigor as defined by the previously dominant quantitative/experimental paradigm) to situational evaluation in which decision criteria are multiple, flexible, and diverse. This shift in perspective, this revolution in standards of excellence, places new demands on evaluators.

This revolution from universal procedures to situational creativity and process orientation provides an enormous challenge for evaluators. The slogan of this scientific revolution could have been Mao's "Let a hundred flowers blossom. Let all views contend!" Instead, the official slogan that won the hearts of evaluators in attendance at the 1978 Evaluation Network Meetings in Aspen was Jim Hennes's lament:

Evaluators do it under difficult circumstances.

In comparison to the traditional paradigms and practices of basic social and behavioral science research, implementation of a *utility-focused, feasibility-conscious, propriety-oriented, and accuracy-based approach to evaluation* will require

— different origins and sources for questions,
— different contract arrangements and conditions,
— different ways of conceptualizing the research process,
— different participants in the research process,
— interpersonal communication skills not previously required,
— political sensitivies and sophistication not previously required,
— group facilitation and consulting skills not previously required,
— a broader range of methodological capabilities than previously required,
— knowledge of and ability to work with a broader range of disciplines than previously required, and
— new and different ways of training potential evaluators in all of the above.

I intend this list to be merely suggestive, not exhaustive. The idea that is implicit throughout the above items is the need for evaluators to be situationally responsive rather than methodologically rigid and orthodox. What

TABLE 11.1
Examples of Situational Factors in Evaluation that
Can Affect Process, Design, and Use

one primary decision maker	1. Number of stakeholders to be dealt with	large number of stakeholders
formative (program improvement)	2. Purpose of the evaluation	summative (funding decision)
short	3. History of the program	long
enthusiasm	4. Staff attitude toward evaluation	resistance
knows virtually nothing	5. Staff knowledge of evaluation	highly knowledgeable
cooperative	6. Program interaction patterns (admin.-staff, staff-staff, staff-client)	conflict-laden
first time ever	7. Program's prior evaluation history	seemingly endless experience
high	8. Staff and client education levels	low
homogeneous groups	9. Staff and/or client characteristics (pick any 10 you want)	heterogeneous groups
one site	10. Program location	multiple sites

TABLE 11.1 (Continued)

no money to speak of	———————— 11. Resources available for evaluation	lots of money
one funding source	———————— 12. Number of sources of program funding	multiple funding sources
simple and unidimensional	———————— 13. Nature of the program treatment	complex and multidimensional
highly standardized and routine	———————— 14. Standardization of treatment	highly individualized and nonroutine
horizontal, little hierarchy, little stratification	———————— 15. Program organizational decision-making structure	hierarchical, long chain of command, stratified
well-articulated, specifically defined	———————— 16. Clarity about evaluation purpose and function	ambiguous, broadly defined
operating information system	———————— 17. Existing data on program	no existing data
external	———————— 18. Evaluator(s)' relationship to the program	internal
voluntary, self-initiated	———————— 19. Impetus for the evaluation	required, forced on program
long time line, open	———————— 20. Time available for the evaluation	short timeline, fixed deadline

follows is a look at just a few of the many situational variables an evaluator is supposed to be aware of and take into consideration in conducting a utilization-focused, feasibility-conscious, propriety-oriented, and accuracy-based evaluation.

The situational variables in Table 11.1 are presented in no particular order. Most of them could be broken down into several additional variables. I have no intention of trying to operationalize these dimensions (that is, make them clear, specific, and measurable). The point of presenting these dimensions is simply this: *Situational evaluation means that evaluators have to be prepared to deal with a lot of different people and situations*. If we conceive of just three points (or situations) on each of these dimensions—the two endpoints and a midpoint—then the combinations of these 20 dimensions represent 8,000 unique evaluation situations.

Nor are these static situations. The program you thought was new at the first session turns out to have been created out of and to be a continuation of another program; only the name has been changed to protect the guilty. You thought you were dealing with only one primary decision maker at the outset and suddenly you have stakeholders coming out your ears, or vice versa. With some programs I've felt like I've been through all 8,000 situations in the first month.

(In case 8,000 situations to analyze, be sensitive to, and design evaluations for doesn't seem challenging enough, just add two more points to each dimension—a point between each endpoint and the midpoint. Now combinations of the five points on all 20 dimensions yields 3,200,000 potentially different situations.)

Of course, one could make the same analysis for virtually any area of decision making, couldn't one? Life is complex, so what's new?

What's new is that the emergent ideology in evaluation says that we are striving to be *truly* situational—to match evaluations appropriately to unique situations. *The evidence from social and behavioral science is that in other areas of decision making, when faced with complex choices and multiple situations, we fall back on a set of rules and standard operating procedures that predetermine what we will do, that effectively short-circuit situational adaptability*. The evidence is that we are running most of the time on preprogrammed tapes. That has always been the function of scientific paradigms. Faced with a new situation, the scientist (unconsciously) turns to paradigmatic rules to find out what to do. This may help explain why so many evaluators who have genuinely embraced the ideology of situational evaluation find that the approaches in which they are trained and with which they are most comfortable *just happen* to be particularly appropriate in each new evaluation situation they are confronting—time after time after time.

Utilization-focused evaluation is a problem-solving approach that emphasizes adaptation to changed and changing conditions, as opposed to a technical approach, which attempts to mold and define conditions to fit pre-conceived models of how things should be done.

Utilization-focused evaluation involves overcoming what Brightman and Noble (1979) have identified as "the ineffective education of decision scientists." They portray the typical decision scientist (a generic term for evaluators, policy analysts, planners, and so on) as

> hopelessly naive and intellectually arrogant. Naive because they believe that problem solving begins and ends with analysis, and arrogant because they opt for mathematical rigor over results. They are products of their training. Decision science departments appear to have been more effective at training technocrats to deal with structured problems than problem solvers to deal with ill-structured ones [Brightman and Noble, 1979: 150].

Narrow technocratic approaches emphasize following rules and standard operating procedures. Creative problem-solving approaches, in contrast, focus on what works and what makes sense in the situation rather than doing it the way it's supposed to be done. Standard recipe books are not ignored. They just aren't taken as the final word. New ingredients are added to fit particular tastes. Home-grown or locally available ingredients replace the processed foods of the national supermarket chains, with the attendant risks of both greater failure and greater achievement.

Multiple Evaluator Roles and Individual Style

Chapter 10 discussed the shift away from allegiance to either the experimental/quantitative paradigm or the naturalistic/qualitative paradigm to a situationally responsive paradigm of choices. The utilization-focused paradigm of choices recognizes and employs a broad range of methods and evaluation ingredients. This chapter now broadens the notion of a paradigm of choices to include a variety of evaluator roles—collaborator, trainer, group facilitator, politician, organizational analyst, internal colleague, external expert, methodologist, information broker, communicator, change agent, diplomat, problem solver, and creative consultant. The roles played by an evaluator in any given situation will depend on the unique constellation of conditions with which the evaluator is faced—and the evaluator's own personal style.

The evaluator's personal style is also a part of situational responsiveness. Just as evaluation situations and program decision makers are unique (thus the importance of situational responsiveness and user-focused evaluation), so, too, individual evaluators are unique. Evaluators bring to evaluation situations their own style, personal history, and professional experience. The notion of being active-reactive-adaptive explicitly recognizes the importance of the individual evaluator's contribution by placing the mandate to be "active" first in this consulting trinity: active-reactive-adaptive. Situational responsiveness does not mean rolling over and playing dead (or passive) in the face of stakeholder interests or perceived needs. Just as the evaluator in utilization-focused evaluation does not unilaterally impose a focus and set of methods on a program, so, too, the stakeholders are not being set up to impose their initial perceptions unilaterally on the evaluation. It is a negotiated process that allows the individual style of the evaluator to intermingle with the host of other factors that affect an evaluation, thereby giving uniqueness and relevance to the final design and product. All of the techniques and ideas presented in this book must be adapted to the style of the individuals using them.

Evaluator personal style and individuality, then, blend with the other themes of this chapter—the power of evaluation and political sophistication, organizational variations, theory-based practices, diverse evaluator roles, being active-reactive-adaptive, and situational responsiveness. Any particular evaluation will manifest unique variations on these themes. At time there may be discord, at other times harmony. Whatever the sounds, and whatever the themes, the utilization-focused evaluator does not sing alone. Utilization-focused evaluators are part of a choir made up of stakeholders. There are solo parts, to be sure, but the climatic theme song of utilization-focused evaluation is not Frank Sinatra's "I Did It My Way." It is rather the full chorus joining in a unique, situationally specific rendition of "We Did It *Our* Way."

Going Bananas

Before closing this chapter on situational responsiveness it seems appropriate to provide a situation for situational analysis, a bit of a practice exercise, if you will. Consider, then, the evaluation relevance of the following story repeated from generation to generation by schoolchildren.

A man walking along the street notices another man on the other side with bananas in his ears. He shouts, "Hey, mister, why do you have bananas in your ears?" Receiving no response he pursues the man, calling again as he approaches, "Pardon me, but why have you got bananas in your ears?" Again there is no response.

He catches up to the man, puts his hand on his shoulder, and says "Do you realize you have bananas in your ears?"

The gentleman in question stops, looks puzzled, takes the bananas out of his ears, and says, "I'm sorry, what did you ask? I couldn't hear you because I have bananas in my ears."

*   *   *

Now for the situational analysis. Who do you assume is the evaluator and who the stakeholder in the story? Why?

What are the implications of the story for evaluation under four different conditions—that is, if

(1) the man with the bananas in his ears is a stakeholder and the man in pursuit is an evaluator;
(2) the banana man is an evaluator, and the man in pursuit is a stakeholder;
(3) both are primary stakeholders and the evaluator observes this scene; or
(4) both are evaluators observed by a stakeholder?

It is just such situational variations that make situational responsiveness so important, and so difficult.

Chapter 12

UTILIZATION-FOCUSED EVALUATION

It's easy to make judgments—that's evaluation. It's easy to ask questions about impact—that's evaluation. It's easy to disseminate reports—that's evaluation. What's hard is to put all those pieces together in a meaningful whole which tells people something they want to know and can use about a matter of importance. *That's* evaluation!

—Halcolm

A User's Perspective

This final chapter will provide an overall framework for utilization-focused evaluation based on the preceding chapters. I want to set the stage for this final chapter by presenting the perspective of a very thoughtful evaluation user, Dr. Wayne Jennings of the Saint Paul (Minnesota) Public Schools. The interview sequence that follows is an example of the kind of information we obtained in studying use of federal health evaluations. At the time of the interview, Jennings was principal of the Saint Paul Open School. His comments are indicative of the concerns I hear from administrators and stakeholders in all kinds of programs, not just educational programs. The concerns of potential evaluation users like Wayne Jennings are the reason for working at utilization-focused evaluation.

* * *

Patton: I know that federal legislation requires Title III programs to be evaluated. Were there any other reasons why this evaluation was undertaken?

Jennings: It was our hope that there would be some added benefit to the school, that is to say, the school staff itself would obtain knowledge about its own program, so we could use it to improve this program.

Initially, we were interested in a process kind of evaluation, one that might address some of the basic issues of education. The school operates on the assumption that students learn from experience, and the more varied experiences they have, the more they learn. And we hoped to learn what parts of the program made a contribution in this area and what parts maybe detracted from that.

We hoped to learn whether the program affected different groups of students differently; for instance, whether the program was highly effective for younger children or older children as a whole, whether it worked especially well for kids who already had a lot of initiative and drive and were self-motivated learners, or whether it was effective for those who do not have this kind of attitude, and so we were interested in determining what aspects of the program we should concentrate on more, or continue or discontinue. But I don't think we got information to make those kind of basic decisions about education.

We asked the research firm for an evaluation design that would help us with those kinds of information. They came up with a design that seemed far off target from what we had asked. It takes a little imagination to do an evaluation. But if I'd asked totally different questions, we'd have gotten the same design. It's as though they had a recipe or a pattern book, and whether they were evaluating us or evaluating vocational education or whether they were evaluating anything—a hospital or a prison—it would have been the same evaluation design.

Patton: Okay, to what extent was this failure caused by a lack of explicitness on your part, or perhaps even a hasty decision to accept an evaluation design that you thought would be educationally useless, from your viewpoint?

Jennings: That's a good question. Perhaps I can answer that by saying a little about our experiences with evaluation firms the preceding two years. The first year we worked with an out-of-state firm. The president came for the initial discussion in September, when we were first getting started. He said he'd like to go to the school and look around. I found him about ten minutes later sitting in the front hall in a state of what appeared to be absolute shock. He simply was not prepared for this program. He had accepted the evaluation by mail. He came and found kids were running around, the place was noisy, they weren't in straight rows, it didn't resemble school in any way, apparently. He was just not prepared to do it. That was the last we saw of him. He sent out a new researcher who didn't walk around the school—we simply met in the office and hashed it out. These people were not prepared to analyze a nonstandard school operation.

I think schools have operated pretty much in the same way for so long that all of us have a mind set of what school is. So to see something different from that tends to give one a sense of shock or culture shock. We saw that in the minds of all our evaluators we've had in here. Now, I don't know how to prepare somebody for that unless it's a participant observer, an anthropological approach, where you come in and live there for a while and find out what the hell's going on. We did have, somewhere along the line, an evaluation proposal from an out-of-state firm which does have experience with these kinds of schools. They were going to give us the kind of evaluation we were very much interested in. We accepted that evaluation and the State Department of Education said, "No, that won't provide us with enough concrete data."

Patton: When the State Department of Education did approve the design of the evaluation for the third year, did that design provide some "concrete data?" What were the findings of that study?

Jennings: We knew politically that we had to achieve a certain degree of respectability with regard to standardized testing. So we looked at the testing results, the reading scores, and all that sort of thing, and they seemed satisfactory. We didn't discover anything particularly startling to cause any serious problems with the Board of Education or the State Department of Education.

Patton: In what form did you receive the findings of the evaluation?

Jennings: In a final report. I think it would have been helpful for their staff to meet with our staff and talk us through the report, elaborate a little on it, but that didn't happen. Partly because the report came, I think, either during the summer or the following fall.

Patton: We are interested in any ways in which this evaluation may have had an impact on program operation and planning, on funding, on policy-making and decisions, and so forth. From your point of view, what would you say was the impact of this evaluation?

Jennings: It served to legitimize us. The Board of Education, the district administration, and the State Department of Education were all interested in seeing an evaluation undertaken, but I don't think a single member of the board or the administration read it. They may have glanced at the summary and the summary says that the school is okay.

Patton: Any other impacts of this study that come to mind besides the legitimization function?

Jennings: I suppose some knowledge of how difficult it is to do evaluations.

Patton: What about staff reaction to the report?

Jennings: I'm not sure how many bothered to read through it. They were looking for something worthwhile and helpful, but it's just not there. You know, I don't know what kind of evaluation would do that.

I think the staff was interested in thinking through a good evaluation. What it would have meant was that we would have all had to become thoroughly backgrounded in the subject in order to help the evaluation firm think it through and provide a proper evaluation. I think we sensed that.

As it turned out, I think the staff has something of a negative attitude about evaluation. I mean they are interested in evaluation, but then the reports seem to lack so much in terms of things that would help us on a day-to-day decision-making basis, or give us a good reflection or mirror image of what's going on in that school from an outsider's point of view, in terms of the growth and development of kids in all dimensions.

Patton: We've been focusing mainly on the study's impact on the Open School itself. Sometimes studies have a broader impact on a program, and things that go beyond immediate programs. Things like general thinking on issues that arise from the study, or position papers, or legislative authorization. Did the evaluation have an impact on any of those kinds of things?

Jennings: I'm glad you're getting into that area, because that was a major interest to me. . . . It was my hope that as the school got under way, it would become fairly clear, or would be evident to those who would be interested in finding out, that this was a highly effective educational program, and that it would make a considerable difference in the lives of most children. Well the study didn't address that; the study simply said, "The program's okay." That's all it said. *Given the limited resources and imagination that were put into the evaluation I'm not convinced they had enough knowledge to say anything about the effectiveness of the program!*

Our major job is to educate 500 students, but we're engaged in a much larger struggle, at least I am, and that is to show that in less formal kinds of education, experiential programs are highly effective forms of education that may bring students to the same level of achievement in a shorter time. We're concerned about that aspect of the thing, but also that it is a form of education that produces genuinely humane people for a complex changing world.

In terms not quite so global the evaluations we have do say something useful. When parents or other educators ask if the program has been evaluated and what the findings were, we say yes, the evaluation shows the program is effective. Now anyone worth their salt, I suspect, if they read the evaluations carefully, would decide they don't show much of anything, really, when you come right down to it. *We're left where we began, but we have the illusion of at least having evaluated the program here.*

Patton: I pulled some the recommendations out of the study, and I'd just like to have you react to how those were received and used in any way by the school. The first one that's listed in the report is that objectives as they are related to the goals of the Open School should be written in performance-specific language. What was the reaction to that recommendation?

Jennings: I know that's the current popular view in education today, but I'm not sure it could be done. It would require an enormous amount of energy. Many of our objectives are not very specific subject matter kinds of objectives. The general goals of the school are more philosophical in tone, and I guess we're just not willing to invest the time and energy to reduce those to the kinds of performance objectives that we're speaking of, and I don't know if the end results would be particularly helpful.

Patton: Did it seem to you that that recommendation followed in any way from the findings of the study?

Jennings: When I read that one, I thought, "Where did that come from?" You know, how did they arrive at that, is that just some conventional wisdom in education today, which could be plugged into any evaluation you want?

Patton: What, then, was your overall reaction to the recommendations?

Jennings: Each was too much of a simpleminded kind of statement. They lacked depth of understanding of what the program was trying to accomplish. Each recommendation could be a report in itself rather than some surface scratching and coming up with some conclusions that we recognize as not very helpful.

Patton: Thinking about the overall utilization and impact of the evaluation study, what would you identify as its single most important effect or impact?

Jennings: Legitimization. It served that function. Just the report's existence, if it had that cover on it, and it was filled with Chinese or some other language, as long as it was filled, and it had a lot of figures in it and people thought it was an evaluation, and somewhere near the end it said that the school seemed to be doing a reasonably good job, that would be satisfactory for most people.

Patton: Is there a single factor that explains that kind of impact in your mind, that people accept it that way, that the evaluation had that legitimation impact? Some factor about the evaluation itself?

Jennings: Well, I think its thickness . . . it's got numbers and statistics in it, it's authored by some Ph.D.s—I think these things all lend credibility. It was done by an outside firm.

Patton: A factor affecting utilization that's frequently mentioned has to do with the nature of contact between the evaluators and the decision makers. Are there any aspects of that that might be important here? Do any of these kinds of factors seem to you to have an effect on the outcome of this study and how it was used?

Jennings: Very definitely. I would say that to do the job right, we'd have to have people on our own staff who were free from most other responsibilities so that they could deal with designing the evaluation and work with the evaluators. Then I think that as the evaluation proceeded, there should probably have been regular sessions or talks in which we would have been able to adjust the evaluation. There just wasn't much attention given to that.

Patton: There's a side effect that comes out of evaluation studies that affects the way people like yourself, who are administrators and work in government and agencies and schools, feel about evaluations. What we'd like to get a feel for is whether or not it's true, as is speculated on in a lot of the literature, that people in administrative positions have a rather poor opinion of evaluation research in general. How would you describe your general opinion of evaluation research—positive, negative, favorable, unfavorable?

Jennings: We want careful evaluation. We want to know what we're doing and to get it from data that will help us make the decisions for improving the program. We want that. We want the best that's available and we want it to be accurate and we want the conclusions to be justified, and so on. *We just desperately want and need that information, to know if we're on the right track.* By and large my opinion is not very good. Most reports look like they were written the last week before they're published, with hastily drawn conclusions and sometimes conclusions from data that's manipulated for a given end.

Patton: Did this study affect those opinions or did you already hold those before?

Jennings: Before. I guess the reason hope springs eternal is that I have read carefully done evaluation reports, that seemed that way to me, and they've been helpful in guiding my thinking about education and brought me to my present state of beliefs. Ninety-nine percent of evaluation is done on a model of education that I think is obsolete—a presentation, subject matter, and mastery kind of mode, so it's like a factory trying to perfect its way of making wagon wheels. We went out of business making wagon wheels, and all of the evaluation and all of the research that will be done in that area isn't of much value.

(The evaluators were also interviewed, but when they read Jenning's comments they asked that their interviews not be used and that they not be named, because their business might be hurt.)

Contrasting Evaluation Approaches

Shortly after this interview, Jennings formed an evaluation task force made up of teachers, parents, students, community people, and graduate students in evaluation research from the Minnesota Center for Social Research. With very limited resources, they conducted an intensive evaluation study of Saint Paul Open School processes and outcomes. They used a variety of methods, both quantitative and qualitative. That report (Harvey and Townsend, 1976) provided useful information for incremental program development and decision making. The contrasts between the Open School

TABLE 12.1
Contrasting Evaluation Approaches

Open School Utilization-Focused Evaluation	Original Title III Evaluations Done for Open School
1. A task force was formed of identified and organized decision-makers and information users to focus evaluation questions. This group worked together to determine what information would be useful to collect both for program improvement and to maintain public accountability.	1. No clear decision makers and information users for the evaluation were identified. The evaluation was aimed vaguely at multiple audiences: federal funders, school board, State Department of Education, general public, and Open School staff. Because specific people were not identified and organized as decision makers and information users, the evaluators unilaterally determined the focus of the research based on what they thought could be done, not on what would be useful.
2. Evaluation questions focused on needed information derived from decisions of basic program direction and areas in which it would be desirable to reduce uncertainty about program operations and effects.	2. Evaluators collected data on presumed operational goals (i.e., normal scores on standardized achievement tests), framing their questions in terms of formal goals based on a rational model that fit the evaluators' but not program assumptions.
3. Evaluation collected both implementation (process) data and outcomes data (follow-up of achievements and activities of Open School graduates).	3. Evaluation was largely a pure outcomes evaluation, emphasizing operational goals important to evaluators and public officials.
4. The task force based their evaluation upon an explicit statement of educational philosophy (a theory of action).	4. Evaluators ignored the program's philosophy and conceptualized the evaluation in terms of their own implicit educational theory of action.

5. A variety of methods were used to investigate a variety of questions. Methods were selected jointly by evaluators and decision makers using multiple criteria: (a) methodological appropriateness, (b) face validity of instrumentation, (c) believability, credibility, and relevance of the design and measuring instruments to information users and decision makers; (d) scientific rigor of design as judged by the likelihood of obtaining valid, reliable, interpretable, and replicable results; and (e) available resources. The task force was involved on a continual basis in making methods and measurement decisions as circumstances changed.

6. Task force members worked together to analyze and interpret data as they were gathered. Data were discussed in rough form over a period of time before the evaluators wrote the final report. Findings and conclusions were known and being used before the final report was ready for dissemination.

7. When the final report was made public both decision makers (Jennings) and evaluators (Harvey and Townsend) made presentations to parent, staff, and school officials.

8. The evaluation was used by Open School staff and administrators for program development, program improvement, and public accountability.

5. The major measurement technique was use of standardized tests which had low face validity, low credibility, and low relevance to program staff; other audiences, especially federal funders, appeared to want such instruments, but it was unclear who the evaluation was supposed to serve. Methods were determined largely by evaluators, based on available resources, with only initial review by program staff and federal and state officials.

6. Evaluators analyzed and interpreted data by themselves. A final report was the only form in which findings were presented. No interpretation sessions with program staff or any audience were ever held.

7. The final report was mailed to responsible offices. No verbal presentations were made. No discussions of findings took place.

8. There was no specific utilization of the evaluation for actual decision making or program planning, though the evaluation may have helped legitimize the program by giving the "illusion" of outcomes evaluation.

Task Force evaluation and the earlier, required Title III evaluations highlight the critical elements of utilization-focused evaluation (see Table 12.1).

The actual money spent on the three years of original Title III evaluations at the Saint Paul Open School was under $40,000, which is not a great deal of money as research goes. But the Saint Paul Open School is one small program out of the hundreds that receive federal funding; in the aggregate, evaluations on those hundreds of programs represent millions of dollars. There are relatively few truly national evaluations compared to the thousands of small-scale evaluations done on single health, education, criminal justice, welfare, and other human service programs. There is no reason to write off such small-scale evaluations as meaningless: They constitute the major proportion of all evaluations conducted in the country. The fourth Saint Paul Open School evaluation cost less than $1,000 in real money because the labor was all volunteer and release time. Due to the success of the internal task force effort, the school has continued to use the approach outlined above. They continued doing utilization-focused evaluation using their own program funds and resources—because they found such evaluations useful.

THE FLOW OF A
UTILIZATION-FOCUSED EVALUATION PROCESS

Figure 12.1 presents a flowchart of the utilization-focused evaluation process. There is a logical flow or series of steps to the process. The basic elements are really quite simple. First, intended users of the evaluation are identified (Chapter 3). These intended users are brought together or organized in some fashion (e.g., an evaluation task force of primary stakeholders) to work with the evaluator and share in making major decisions about the evaluation.

Second, the evaluator and intended users focus the evaluation (Chapter 4). This involves reviewing critical issues and considering the relative importance of focusing on attainment of goals (Chapter 5), program implementation (Chapter 6), and/or the program's theory of action (Chapter 7). There are many different types of and foci for evaluations. (See Appendix II for a suggestive list of different evaluation questions and types.) The evaluator works with intended users in deciding what major questions are useful to answer this particular evaluation situation (Chapter 11). During this part of the process the evaluator pushes stakeholders to think clearly about the intended uses of the evaluation. Given expected uses, is the evaluation worth doing? To what extent and in what ways are intended users committed to intended use?

The third part of the process involves methods, measurement, and design decisions (Chapters 8 and 9). A variety of options are considered: qualitative and quantitative data, naturalistic, experimental, and quasi-experimental designs, purposeful and probabilistic sampling approaches,

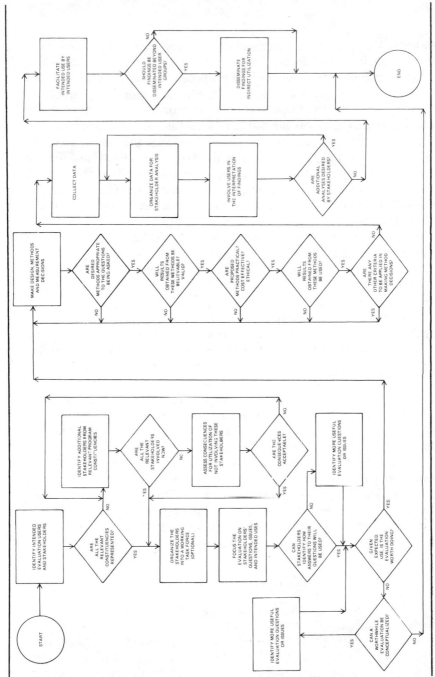

Figure 12.1 Utilization-Focused Evaluation Flowchart

greater and lesser emphasis on generalizations, and alternative ways of dealing with validity and reliability concerns. In particular, the discussion at this
point will include attention to issues of methodological appropriateness, believability of the data, understandability, accuracy, balance, practicality,
propriety, and cost. As always, the overriding concern will be utility. Will
results obtained from these methods be useful—and actually used?

Once data are collected and organized for analysis, the fourth part of the
utilization-focused process begins. Intended users are actively and directly
involved in interpreting findings, making judgments based on the data, and
generating recommendations (Chapter 10). Specific strategies for use can
then be formalized in light of actual findings, and the evaluator can facilitate
following through on actual use.

Finally, decisions about dissemination of the evaluation report can be
made beyond whatever initial commitments were made earlier in planning
for intended use. This is in keeping with the distinction between intended
use by intended users (planned utilization) are more general dissemination
for broad public accountability (where unintended uses may occur).

While there is a seemingly straightforward, one-step-at-a-time logic to
the flow of a utilization-focused evaluation, in reality it is seldom a simple
linear process. The flowchart attempts to capture the sometimes circular
and iterative nature of the process by depicting loops at the points where
intended users are identified and again where evaluation questions are focused. For the sake of diagrammatic simplicity, however, many potential
loops are missing. The active-reactive-adaptive evaluator who is situationally responsive and politically sensitive may find that new stakeholders become important or new questions emerge in the midst of methods decisions.
Nor is there a clear and clean distinction between the processes of focusing
evaluation questions and making methods decisions.

The real world of utilization-focused evaluation is considerably more
complex than the flowchart in Figure 12.1 can possibly depict. The purpose
of the flowchart is to present the basic logic of the process. The application
of the logic in any given situation will require flexibility and creativity.

The Essence of Utilization-Focused Evaluation

Utilization-focused evaluation is not a formal model or recipe for how to
conduct evaluations. Rather, it is an approach, an orientation, and a set of
options. The active-reactive-adaptive evaluator chooses from among these
options as he or she works with decision makers and information users
throughout the evaluation process. There is no formula guaranteeing success in this approach—indeed, the criteria for success are variable. Utilization means different things to different people in different settings, and is an
issue subject to negotiation between evaluators and intended users.

There are only two fundamental requirements in this approach: Everything else is a matter for negotiation, adaptation, selection, and matching. First, the intended evaluation users must be identified and "organized"—real, visible, specific, and caring human beings, not ephemeral, general, and abstract "audiences," organizations, or agencies. Second, evaluators must work actively, reactively, and adaptively with these specific stakeholders to make all other decisions about the evaluation—decisions about focus, design, methods, analysis, interpretation, and dissemination.

The essence of utilization-focused evaluation is, quite simply, the focus on utility. The standards of evaluation mandate a focus on utility (Joint Committee on Standards, 1981). The evaluation literature contains substantial evidence that focusing on use and working with intended users is important and can increase evaluation use (e.g., Alkin, 1985; Cooley and Bickel, 1985; Lawler et al., 1985; Siegel and Tuckel, 1985; Bedell et al., 1985; Dawson and D'Amico, 1985; King, 1985; Burry, 1984; Cole, 1984; Evans and Blunden, 1984; Hevey, 1984; Rafter, 1984; Glaser et al., 1983; Campbell, 1983; Bryk, 1983; Lewy and Alkin, 1983; Stalford, 1983; Saxe and Koretz, 1982; Beyer and Trice, 1982; King and Pechman, 1982; Barkdoll, 1982; Canadian Evaluation Society, 1982; Leviton and Hughes, 1981; Dickey and Hampton, 1981; Braskamp and Brown, 1980; Alkin and Law, 1980; Alkin et al., 1979; and Studer, 1978).

Having depicted the utilization-focused evaluation process, and with the essence of utilization-focused evaluation spotlighted on use and users, the next section summarizes the underpinnings of utilization-focused evaluation through presentation of ten fundamental premises.

UTILIZATION FOCUSED EVALUATION PREMISES

Ten Basic Premises of Utilization-Focused Evaluation

(1) A concern for use should be the driving force in an evaluation. At every point at which a decision about the evaluation is being made—whether the decision concerns the focus of study, design, methods, measurement, analysis, or reporting—the evaluator asks, "How would that affect the utility of this evaluation?"

(2) The concern for utilization is ongoing and continuous from the very beginning of the evaluation. Use isn't something one becomes interested in at the end of an evaluation. By the end of the evaluation, the potential for utilization has been largely determined. From the moment stakeholders and evaluators begin conceptualizing the evaluation, decisions are being made that will affect use in major ways.

(3) Evaluations should be user-oriented. This means that the evaluation is aimed at the interests and information needs of specific, identifiable peo-

ple, not vague, passive audiences. Therefore, the first step in utilization-focused evaluation is identification of primary intended information users.

(4) Once identified, these intended evaluation users should be personally and actively involved in making decisions about the evaluation. Working actively with people who have a stake in the outcomes of an evaluation (the "stakeholders") is aimed at increasing the potential for use by building a genuine commitment to and understanding of the evaluation over the course of the evaluation process. Such an approach recognizes the importance of the "personal factor" (Chapter 3) to evaluation use. People who are *personally* interested and involved in an evaluation are more likely to use evaluation findings. The best way to be sure that an evaluation is targeted at the personal concerns of stakeholders is to involve them actively at every stage of the evaluation.

(5) There are multiple and varied interests around any evaluation. Staff, administrators, clients, public officials, funders, and community leaders all have an interest in evaluation, but the degree and nature of their interests will vary. The process of identifying and organizing stakeholders to participate in an evaluation process should be done in a way that is sensitive to and respectful of these varied and multiple interests. At the same time, it must be recognized that resource, time, and staff limitations will make it impossible for any single evaluation to answer everyone's questions, or to give full attention to all possible issues. Stakeholders representing various constituencies should come together at the beginning of the evaluation to decide whose issues and questions will be given priority in the evaluation in order to maximize the utility of the evaluation. The process of focusing the content of the evaluation should not be done by evaluators acting alone or in isolation from primary users.

(6) Careful selection of stakeholders for active participation in the evaluation process will permit *high-quality participation*— and high-quality participation is the goal, not high-quantity participation. The quantity of group interaction time is often inversely related to the quality of the process. Thus, evaluators conducting utilization-focused evaluations must be skilled group facilitators and have a large repertoire of techniques available for working actively with stakeholders in the evaluation (Patton, 1981). High-quality involvement of stakeholders will result in higher-quality evaluations. Many evaluators assume that methodological rigor will inevitably be sacrificed if nonscientists collaborate in making methods decisions. This need not be the case. Decision makers want data that are useful *and* accurate (Weiss and Bucuvalas, 1980). Skilled evaluators can help nonscientists understand methodological issues so that they can judge for themselves the trade-offs involved in choosing among the strengths and weaknesses of design options and methods alternatives. Such involvement in and collaborative deliberations on methodological issues can significantly increase

stakeholders' understanding of the evaluation, while giving evaluators a better understanding of stakeholder priorities and situational constraints on the feasibility of alternative approaches. These shared decisions can thus enhance both utilization potential and methodological rigor.

(7) Evaluators committed to enhancing utilization have a responsibility *to train stakeholders* in evaluation processes and the uses of information. By training stakeholders in evaluation methods and processes, the evaluator is looking to both short-term and long-term utilization. Making decision makers more sophisticated about evaluation can contribute to greater use of evaluation data and evaluation processes over time.

(8) There are a variety of ways in which evaluation processes and findings are used. Evaluations can directly influence major, specific decisions. Evaluations can be used to make minor adjustments in programs. Decision makers can and do use evaluations to reduce uncertainty, enlarge their options, increase control over program activities, and increase their sophistication about program processes. Sometimes evaluations have more of a *conceptual impact* (i.e., they influence how stakeholders think about a program) rather than an *instrumental impact* (i.e., evaluation use manifested in concrete actions and explicit decisions). A broad view of utilization reveals multiple layers of impact over varying amounts of time. All of these kinds of utilization are important and legitimate from a utilization-focused evaluation perspective. This view of utilization also broadens the notion of evaluation impact to include use of the entire evaluation process as a stakeholder learning experience, not just use of the findings in the final report. The relative value of these different kinds of utilization can only be judged in the context of a specific evaluation. However, the highest priority is *intended use by intended users*.

(9) A variety of situational factors affect utilization. These factors include community variables, organizational characteristics, the nature of the evaluation, evaluator credibility, political considerations, and resource constraints (Alkin et al., 1979). In conducting a utilization-focused evaluation, the active-reactive-adaptive evaluator attempts to be situationally responsive. This means being sensitive to and aware of how various factors and conditions affect the potential for utilization. An analysis of the factors that may affect the usefulness of an evaluation should be undertaken jointly with stakeholders early in the evaluation process. These factors, and their actual effects on utilization, are then monitored throughout the utilization-focused evaluation process.

(10) Serious attention to utilization involves financial and staff time costs that are far from trivial. The benefits of these costs are manifested in greater utilization. These costs should be made explicit in evaluation proposals and budgets so that utilization efforts are not neglected for lack of resources.

FUTURE DIRECTIONS

If it is not already clear to the reader, let me make it absolutely clear: I believe that we already know enough about how to increase the use of evaluations that the immediate task is acting on what we know, and evaluating those actions. In so acting, and in order to be accountable, evaluators ought to document their experiences in using what we know. Appendix I presents my experiences with the Caribbean Agricultural Extension Project as case documentation and illustration of utilization-focused evaluation premises. I'm satisfied that if we use what we already know, as illustrated in the Caribbean Project, we can make a significant difference in evaluation and program practice. While we know a great deal about how to increase use, we know less about how to prevent misuse and abuse.

Misutilization

I have become increasingly concerned about problems of misutilization. The most common concern I hear about utilization-focused evaluation is that it potentially coopts evaluators. This cooptation, apparent or real, can reduce evaluation credibility, neutrality, and significance.

In our concern with and focus on ways of increasing the use of evaluation, I agree with those who worry that we have neglected misutilization. As I do workshops and travel around the country talking with people about evaluation, I hear increasingly about cases of abuse and misuse. As I've thought about this, I'd like to share some preliminary observations by way of generating additional discussion on this important issue.

(1) Misutilization is not at the opposite end of a continuum from utilization. There are really two dimensions here. One dimension is a continuum from nonutilization to utilization. A second continuum is nonmisutilization to misutilization. Studying misuse is quite different from studying use.

(2) Having conceptualized two separate dimensions, it is possible to explore the relationship between them. Therefore, permit me the following proposition: *As use increases, misuse will also increase*. It seems to me that when people ignore evaluations, they ignore their potential uses as well as abuses. As we successfully focus greater attention on evaluation data, and as we increase actual use, we can also expect there to be a corresponding increase in abuse, often within the same evaluation experience.

(3) Misuse can be either intentional or unintentional. Unintentional misuse can be corrected through the processes aimed at increasing appropriate and proper use. Intentional misuse is an entirely different matter to which, it seems to me, we have paid very little attention except to say it shouldn't happen. In terms of incidence and prevalence, I have no clear notion of whether unintentional or intentional misuse is more common.

(4) A comprehensive approach to the study of misuse might well be guided by the six honest serving men of Kipling:

I keep six honest serving men.
They taught me all I knew:
Their names are What and Why and When
And How and Where and Who.

To study evaluation misuse, Kipling's framework suggests six major questions:

(1) What is misused?
(2) Who misuses evaluation?
(3) When is evaluation misused?
(4) How is it misused?
(5) Where is it misused?
(6) Why is it misused?

What better way to approach dishonesty and misuse than by mobilizing Kipling's six honest serving men in the service of appropriate evaluation utilization? The Joint Committee Standards (1981) on propriety are a further reminder of the importance of addressing ethical issues in evaluation, with particular focus on problems of misuse and abuse.

EVALUATION AND CHANGE

In an important article on the utilization of evaluation, Davis and Salasin (1975: 652) asserted that "any change model should . . . generally *accommodate* rather than *manipulate* the views of persons involved." Utilization-focused evaluation does just that. The evaluator does not attempt to mold and manipulate decision makers and information users to accept the evaluator's preconceived notions about what constitutes useful or high-quality research, but neither is the evaluator a mere technician who does whatever decision makers want. Utilization-focused evaluation brings together evaluators and stakeholders in an interactive process in which all participants share responsibility for creatively shaping and rigorously implementing an evaluation that is both useful and of high quality. Egon Guba has described in powerful language the archetypical evaluator, who is the antithesis of the active-reactive-adaptive researcher in utilization-focused evaluation:

It is my experience that evaluators sometimes adopt a very supercilious attitude with respect to their clients; their presumptuousness and arrogance are sometimes overwhelming. We treat the client as a "child-like" person who needs to be taken in hand; as an ignoramus who cannot possibly understand the tactics and strategies that we will bring to bear; as someone who doesn't appreciate the questions he *ought* to ask until we tell him—and what we tell him often reflects our own biases and interests rather than the problems with which the client is actually beset. The phrase "Ugly American" has emerged in international settings to describe the person who enters into a new culture, immediately knows what is wrong with it, and proceeds to foist his own solutions onto the locals. In some ways I have come to think of evaluators as "Ugly Americans." And if what we are looking for are ways to manipulate clients so that they will fall in with *our* wishes and cease to resist our blandishments, I for one will have none of it [Guba, 1977: 1].

For others who "will have none of it" there is the alternative of undertaking a utilization-focused evaluation process based on mutual respect between evaluators and stakeholders. Part of this process involves defining and working toward use in a way that is meaningful and rewarding to both evaluators and stakeholders. The nature of use will depend on the purpose of the evaluation, the needs of intended information users, and the circumstances in which the evaluation is conducted.

At the same time, the hope expressed by Davis and Salasin (1975) that evaluators can be expected to play a "change consultant role" is entirely compatible with utilization-focused evaluation. The change consultant role begins in the very first step with identification and organization of stakeholders. Both the change process and the utilization process begin at step one and carry through as the evaluation takes shape and finally reaches its culmination in data analysis and interpretation. Bringing together a group of people who actively engage in discussions about what a program is doing, where it is going, how it could be improved, and what information is needed to reduce uncertainty about program implementation and effects—these processes are in themselves change producing. In my experience, the people who engage in utilization-focused evaluation come out of those processes with more penetrating perspectives, increased capabilities, and greater commitments to action than they had before the evaluation began. It is a deeply involving process for both evaluators and stakeholders.

Ultimately, generating and using information is a personal process. Therein lies the power of evaluation—*in the mobilization of individual energies for action*. As the barrier of uncertainty is attacked and as systematic information emerges to improve program effectiveness, evaluation is used.

A Final Note

Utilization-focused evaluation is an approach that combines style and substance, activism and science, personal perspective and systematic information. I have used a variety of approaches in trying to describe utilization-focused evaluation: scenarios, case examples, quotations from our federal utilization study, Sufi parables, and children's stories. In the end, this approach to evaluation must also be judged by its usefulness.

I have presented research and referenced literature that supports the premises of utilization-focused evaluation. Still, there will be skeptics, some who don't want to take the time to work with stakeholders, others who don't want to give up control of the process, and still others who are convinced that it probably works for certain kinds of evaluators (the charismatic, the personable, the confident, the human-relations types, whatever . . .), but that it won't work for them.

Certainly, there are no guarantees that the utilization-focused approach will always work. Just as decision makers live in a world of uncertainty, so too evaluators are faced with the ever-present possibility that, despite their best efforts, their work will be ignored. The challenge of producing good evaluation studies that are actually used is enormous. In many ways the odds are all against utilization, and it is quite possible to become skeptical about the futility of trying to have an impact in a world in which situation after situation seems impervious to change. Utilization-focused evaluators may be told, or may sometimes feel, that they are wasting their time. A final Sufi story perhaps provides a reply to skeptics.

> Yogurt is made by adding a small quantity of old yogurt to a larger measure of milk. The action of the bacillus bulgaricus in the seeding portion of yogurt will in time convert the whole into a mass of new yogurt.
>
> One day some friends saw Nasrudin down on his knees beside a pond. He was adding a little yogurt to the water. One of the men said, "What are you trying to do, Nasrudin?"
>
> "I am trying to make yogurt."
>
> "But you can't make yogurt in that way!"
>
> "Yes, I know; but just *supposing* it takes!" [Shah, 1964: 90].

The effort involved in working interactively with stakeholders can be considerable. Utilization-focused evaluation may, indeed, be a long shot, but the potential payoff is worth the risk. At stake is improving the effectiveness of human service programs that express and embody the highest ideals of humankind. It may be a long shot, "but just *supposing* it works!" And works for you. The only way to find out is to try it—and evaluate the results. Build the study of use into evaluations and thereby help make not only programs, but also evaluations, accountable.

APPENDIX I

A CASE EXAMPLE OF UTILIZATION-FOCUSED EVALUATION

The Caribbean Agricultural Extension Project is funded by the U.S. Agency for International Development (U.S.AID). The project is aimed at improving national agricultural extension services in eight Caribbean countries. With staff from the University of Minnesota and the University of the West Indies, the project has involved organizational development work with key officials in eight Caribbean countries,[1] providing in-service training for extension staff, and providing equipment, including vehicles, office equipment, and agricultural equipment.

The project was designed based on 18 months of needs assessment and planning. The assessment and planning included establishing an advisory committee in each country as well as a regional advisory committee made up of representatives from all eight participating countries and other organizations involved in agricultural development in the Caribbean.

The contract for implementing the project with all key participants was signed in January 1983. In April 1983, a meeting of the regional advisory committee was held with a team of external evaluators. The external evaluators were chosen to represent the major constituencies of the project, these being U.S.AID, the University of the West Indies, and the Midwest Universities Consortium for International Activities (MUCIA), for which the University of Minnesota was the primary representative. Each of these three prime constituencies named one of the evaluators. The fourth evaluator was chosen for his stature in the field of evaluation, because of his commitment to user-oriented evaluations, and because he was neutral from the point of view of the other three constituencies. The stakeholders agreed he should be chair of the evaluation team to work in collaboration with the three evaluators who had been named by specific constituencies.[2]

Prior to designing the evaluation, the evaluators met with representatives of each of these constituencies separately, including the funding source, U.S.AID. At the April meeting of the regional advisory group, the evaluators focused three days' of discussion on the criteria that could be used to determine if the project had been successful. These criteria constituted a set of questions and primary outcomes, both qualitative and quantitative indicators. Based on those discussions, the evaluators reviewed design possibilities with the 50 participants in that regional advisory meeting. The details of the design were then worked out with specific representatives of the project staff and U.S.AID.

The evaluation design included several different data collection approaches. The project staff organized all of their required reporting around the evaluation design. The work plan for project staff was based on the evaluation elements, and staff meetings routinely reviewed the elements of the evaluation as a way of directing implementation and focusing on those outcomes that were primary from the point of view of the project and the evaluation. Members of the evaluation team were sent monthly and quarterly reports based on the elements of the evaluation. For example, the first element in the evaluation design focused on the project goal that in each country a national agricultural extension planning committee be established and involved in providing direction to the extension service in the country. All staff meetings began by reviewing the progress of national planning committees and all monthly and quarterly reports included information on the activities and progress of national committees. In addition, the minutes of the national planning committees were provided to the evaluators. In the actual data collection phase, the evaluators conducted interviews to gather first-hand information about the operations and activities of the national planning committees. *The point here is that program implementation and evaluation were synchronized from the beginning of each.* As a result, the evaluation process improved program implementation from the very beginning by focusing staff program implementation efforts. The evaluation constituted a framework for program planning and reporting that provided focus to staff activities. This focus became more important as the project moved forward and staff encountered many opportunities to be diverted from those primary foci. However, having organized the project work plan, staff meetings, and reporting around the key evaluation issues, the evaluation contributed substantially to keeping staff efforts from being diffused into other areas or activities that would have taken away from the primary purposes of the project. This is an example of using the evaluation process for program improvement.

Data collection and reporting were carefully timed to provide critical information for the project's refunding decision. Working backward from the project completion date, a time schedule for data collection and reporting was developed that would make sure that needed information would be available when the decision about refunding and future project activities was to be made. The ongoing nature of the external evaluation was a major break with U.S.AID tradition. Indeed, the evaluators and project staff had some difficulty helping U.S.AID personnel understand why the evaluators needed to be involved from the very beginning and then throughout the life of the project. Traditionally, U.S.AID external evaluations occur at discrete points in the life of a project, but not on the basis of ongoing involvement from the beginning. This limits the possibility of the evaluation playing a major role in project decision making. Moreover, it was unusual for U.S.AID to get a project-funded evaluation report, at least one that was more than cursory, at the time of a funding decision. In this case, operational project funding would end in September 1985. Given the lengthy funding process of U.S.AID, a decision for additional funding and activities would have to be made by December 1984, to do the paperwork to keep the project alive. Thus, a meeting of the regional advisory group was scheduled for November 1984, to focus on the evaluation findings. This meant that the report would have to be ready by that time, so the data collection would have to take place in the summer of 1984, only 18 months into project implementation and only a year after the initial design, fully a year ahead of the operational project completion date. Clearly, such an evaluation could not be definitive about project impacts, as data collection would take place well before project completion, but a definitive data collection effort would not be available at the time the decision was to be taken. Data collection did occur in June 1984, and the evaluation report was ready for the regional advisory meeting in November 1984. Prior to that critical November regional advisory committee meeting, the evaluators met separately with project staff to provide informal feedback about evaluation findings and with U.S.AID to provide informal feedback and discussion of potential future funding. In both cases, those informal meetings were critical.

The first informal meeting occurred immediately after data collection in June 1984. The evaluators, who had been gathering data in different locations, met together to review their findings and divide the writing tasks. Following that session together, the evaluators met with the project director to review major findings. Those findings included a confirmation of the overall successes of the project, a high degree of support for project activities among the participating countries, and identification of areas of weakness. The areas of weakness included insights that had escaped the attention of project staff. The staff immediately began to correct those weaknesses, two of which required assistance from outside and one of which brought a new focus to implementation activities. A month later, one representative of the evaluation team met with the project staff in their full staff meeting and reviewed the evaluation findings. It was at that staff meeting that activities were reoriented to direct attention to identified weaknesses.

Following the staff meeting, the evaluator who had been selected by U.S.AID met the U.S.AID officials to informally report initial findings. At that meeting the question of future funding arose. The director of the funding agency in the Caribbean (U.S.AID) had been present in the initial meeting with the evaluators, at which important questions were identified. He now put those questions to the evaluator again, with special reference to future activities. The evaluator was able to directly address his questions with high credibility and with concrete data. It has subsequently been reported to me independently by several U.S.AID staff members that this informal feedback was critical, because the director of the funding agency was not predisposed to continue funding for the project. The evaluation report made it clear that the project was effective, was having an impact, but that further funding and activities would be necessary and justifiable to institutionalize short-term successes and guarantee long-term success and long-term effectiveness. With the November 1984 regional advisory meeting already scheduled, and with the informal evaluation results having been reported to the funding agency, the project director formally wrote to U.S.AID asking them to take a position on their openness to future funding. A response was needed prior to the November 1984 meeting of the regional advisory group, as the delegates to the regional advisory group would need to know AID's position as a context for their discussions of the evaluation. Prior to that meeting, U.S.AID indicated that they had reviewed the evaluation and were inclined to continue funding activities. They therefore invited project staff and the regional advisory group to submit a continuation proposal.

The published evaluation report was completed in time for the November regional advisory meeting. At that meeting the evaluators reviewed overall findings and different ways in which the report could be used for local purposes as well as regional purposes. Delegates to the meeting reviewed the executive summary and commented on its accuracy. They then adopted a resolution accepting the evaluation report as generally accurate, fair, thorough, and balanced. They suggested that project staff use the evaluation findings as a basis for future activities and a new proposal to U.S.AID. They discussed major new directions suggested by the evaluation findings. They brought to bear on those discussions other information and their own experiences, and subsequently adopted resolutions identifying the major components that should be included in continuing activities.

In the interim between the data collection, informal feedback, and the formal November review of the evaluation, project staff had made major progress in overcoming the weaknesses identified in the preliminary feedback. In addition, through the grapevine, the fact that the evaluation report would show substantial progress and major successes was communicated throughout the region. Project staff and U.S.AID had the opportunity to comment on draft copies of the report before it was published to guarantee accuracy and so as to know details of what the report would say prior to its publication.

In summary, the evaluation had a major impact on project implementation. It had a major corrective effect in reorienting the project a year and a half into implementation so as to correct weaknesses that had emerged during that time and to more directly focus on some areas that were being neglected. Finally, the evaluation had a major impact on the decision to continue project funding.

The evaluation direct costs were approximately $100,000 out of a total project budget of $5.4 million dollars. This is under 2% of the project budget.

Although the details given here of this evaluation are skimpy to preserve space, all of the premises of utilization-focused evaluation were followed in this evaluation (see Chapter 12), and the result was a high level of use. Of course, it is not possible to make causative statements about the relationship between what was done in the evaluation and what subsequently occurred in the project. However, there is no question among the nine project staff members or the U.S.AID officials that both the evaluation processes and outcomes made important differences. Likewise, the resolution adopted by the regional advisory group made it clear that they had learned from the evaluation both about the project and about how evaluations ought to be conducted. This utilization-focused evaluation was used by intended users as intended.

NOTES

1. The participating countries were Antigua, Belize, Dominica, Grenada, Montserrat, St. Kitts/Nevis, St. Lucia, and St. Vincent and the Grenadines. I was the project director on behalf of the University of Minnesota.

2. Marvin Alkin of UCLA chaired the evaluation team. Evaluation team members were Jerry West, University of Missouri, on behalf of U.S.AID; Marlene Cuthbert, University of the West Indies; and Kay Adams, Ohio State University, on behalf of MUCIA.

APPENDIX II

TYPES OF EVALUATION

Different types of evaluations ask different questions and focus on different purposes. This list is meant to be illustrative rather than exhaustive.

Accreditation evaluation	Does the program meet minimum standards for accreditation or licensing?
Cost/benefit analysis	What is the relationship between program costs and program outcomes (benefits) expressed in dollars?
Cost-effectiveness evaluation	What is the relationship between program costs and outcomes (where outcomes are *not* measured in dollars)?
Criterion-referenced evaluation	To what extent has a specific objective been attained at the desired level of attainment (the criterion)?
Decision-focused evaluation	What information is needed to make a specific decision at a precise point in time?
Descriptive evaluation	What happens in the program? (No "why" questions or cause/effect analyses.)
Effectiveness evaluation	To what extent is the program effective in attaining its goals?
Efficiency evaluation	Can inputs be reduced and still obtain the same level of output or can greater output be obtained with no increase in inputs?
Effort evaluation	What are the inputs into the program in terms of number of personnel, staff/client ratios, and other descriptors of levels of activity and effort in the program?
Evaluability assessment	What is the feasibility of various evaluation approaches and methods?

Extensiveness evaluation	To what extent is this program able to deal with the total problem? How does the present level of services compare to the needed level of services?
External evaluation	The evaluation is conducted by people outside the program in an effort to increase objectivity.
Formative evaluation	How can the program be improved?
Goals-based evaluation	To what extent have program goals been attained?
Goal-free evaluation	What are the *actual* effects of the program on clients (without regard to what staff say they want to accomplish)?
Impact evaluation	What are the direct and indirect program effects?
Internal evaluation	Program staff conduct the evaluation.
Longitudinal evaluation	What happens to the program and to participants over time?
Meta-evaluation	Was the evaluation well-done? Is it worth using?
Needs assessment	What do clients need and how can those needs be met?
Norm-referenced evaluation	How does this program population compare to some specific norm or reference group on selected variables?
Outcomes evaluation	To what extent are desired client outcomes being attained? What are the effects of the program on clients?
Performance evaluation	What are participants actually able to do as a result of participation in the program?
Personnel evaluation	How effective are staff in carrying out their assigned tasks and in accomplishing their goals?
Process evaluation	What are the strengths and weaknesses of day-to-day operations? How can these processes be improved?
Product evaluation	What are the costs, benefits, and market for a specific product?
Quality assurance	Are minimum and accepted standards of care being routinely and systematically provided

	to patients and clients? How can quality of care be monitored and demonstrated?
Social indicators	What routine social and economic data should be monitored to assess the impacts of this program?
Summative evaluation	Should the program be continued? If so, at what level?
Utilization-focused evaluation	What information is needed and wanted by decision makers, information users, and stakeholders that will actually be used for program improvement and to make decisions about the program? (Utilization-focused evaluation can include any of the other types above.)

REFERENCES

Abramson, M. A. 1978. *The Funding of Social Knowledge Production and Application: A Survey of Federal Agencies*. Washington, DC: National Academy of Sciences.

Ackerman, Bruce A. 1977. "Illusions About New Cars, Clean Air." Minneapolis *Tribune* (August 29): 4A.

Adelson, Marvin, Marvin Alkin, Charles Carey, and Olaf Helmer. 1967. "Planning Education for the Future." *American Behavioral Scientist* 10, 7 (March): 1-29.

Agarwala-Rogers, Rehka. 1977. "Why Is Evaluation Research Not Utilized?" pp. 327-333 in Marcia Guttentag (ed.) *Evaluation Studies Review Annual* (Vol. 2). Beverly Hills, CA: Sage.

Alkin, Marvin. 1985. *A Guide for Evaluation Decision Makers*. Beverly Hills, CA: Sage.

———1975a. "Evaluation: Who Needs It? Who Cares?" *Studies in Educational Evaluation* 1, 3 (Winter): 201-212.

———1975b. "Framing the Decision Context." *AERA Cassette Series in Evaluation*. Washington, DC: American Educational Research Association.

———1972. "Wider Context Goals and Goal-Based Evaluators." *Evaluation Comment: The Journal of Educational Evaluation* (Center for the Study of Evaluation, UCLA) 3, 4 (December): 10-11.

———1970. "A Review of the Evaluation of the Follow Through Program." An individual report written as a member of the USOE Review Team, May 14-15, 1970, Washington, DC Center for the Study of Evaluation, Working Paper 10. Los Angeles: Center for the Study of Evaluation, UCLA.

Alkin, Marvin C. and Fred Ellett. 1984. "Evaluation Models," *International Encyclopedia of Education*. New York: Pergamon Press.

Alkin, Marvin and Alex Law. 1980. "A Conversation on Evaluation Utilization." *Educational Evaluation and Policy Analysis* 2, 3 (May-June): 73-79.

Alkin, Marvin C. and Lewis C. Solmon (eds.) 1983. *The Costs of Evaluation*. Beverly Hills, CA: Sage.

Alkin, Marvin C., Richard Daillak, and Peter White. 1979. *Using Evaluations: Does Evaluation Make a Difference?* Beverly Hills, CA: Sage.

Alkin, Marvin C. with P. Jacobson, J. Burry, P. White, and L. Kent. 1985. *Organizing for Evaluation Use: A Handbook for Administrators*. Los Angeles: Center for the Study of Evaluation, UCLA.

Alkin, Marvin C., Jacqueline Kosecoff, Carol Fitz Gibbon, and Richard Seligman. 1974. *Evaluation and Decision-Making: The Title VII Experience*. Los Angeles: Center for the Study of Evaluation, UCLA.

Allison, Graham T. 1971. *Essence of Decision: Explaining the Cuban Missile Crisis*. Boston: Little, Brown.

American Institute for Research. 1970. *Evaluative Research Strategies and Methods*. Pittsburgh: American Institute for Research.

Anastasi, Anne. 1973. "Preface." *Assessment in a Pluralistic Society*. Proceedings of the 1972 Invitational Conference on Testing Problems. Princeton, NJ: Educational Testing Service.

Anderson, Barry F. 1980. *The Complete Thinker*. Englewood Cliffs, NJ: Prentice-Hall.

Anderson, Gary and Herbert Walberg. 1968. "Classroom Climate and Group Learning." *International Journal of the Educational Science* (September): 175-180.

Anderson, Richard B. 1977. "The Effectiveness of Follow Through: What Have We Learned?" Presented at the annual meeting of the American Educational Research Association, New York.

Anderson, Scarvia B., Samuel Bell, Richard T. Murphy, and Associates. 1976. *Encyclopedia of Educational Evaluation*. San Francisco: Jossey-Bass.

Archibald, Kathleen. 1970. "Alternative Orientations to Social Science Utilization." *Social Science Information* 9, 2: 7-34.

Argyris, Chris. 1976. *Increasing Leadership Effectiveness*. New York: John Wiley.

———1974. *Theory in Practice: Increasing Professional Effectiveness*. San Francisco: Jossey-Bass.

Attkisson, C. Clifford, W. A. Hargreaves, M. J. Horowitz, and J. E. Sorenson (eds.). 1978. *Evaluation of Human Service Programs*. New York: Academic Press.

Australian Development Assistance Bureau. 1982. *Summaries and Review of Ongoing Evaluation Studies, 1975-80*. Canberra: Australian Government Publishing Service.

Azumi, Koya and Jerald Hage (eds.). 1972. *Organizational Systems*. Lexington, MA: D.C. Heath.

Baizerman, Michael. 1974. "Evaluation Research and Evaluation: Scientific Social Reform Movement and Ideology." *Journal of Sociology and Social Welfare* (Winter): 277-288.

Barkdoll, Gerald L. 1982. "Increasing the Impact of Program Evaluation by Altering the Working Relationship Between the Program Manager and the Evaluator." Ph.D. dissertation, University of Southern California.

———1980. "Type III Evaluations: Consultation and Consensus." *Public Administration Review* (March/April): 174-179.

Becker, Howard. 1970. "Whose Side Are We On?" pp. 15-26 in William J. Filstead (ed.) *Qualitative Methodology*. Chicago: Markham.

Becker, Selwyn W. and Duncan Neuhauser. 1975. *The Efficient Organization*. New York: Elsevier.

Bedell, J. R., J. C. Ward, Jr., R. P. Archer, and M. K. Stokes. 1985. "An Empirical Evaluation of a Model of Knowledge Utilization." *Evaluation Review* 9, 2 (April): 109-126.

Bennett, Carl A. and Arthur A. Lumsdaine (ed.). 1975. *Evaluation and Experience: Some Critical Issues in Assessing Social Programs*. New York: Academic Press.

Bennett, Claude F. 1982. *Reflective Appraisal of Programs*. Ithaca, NY: Cornell University Media Services.

———1979. *Analyzing Impacts of Extension Programs*. Washington, DC: U.S. Department of Agriculture.

Bennis, Warren. 1966. *Changing Organizations*. New York: McGraw Hill.

Bennis, Warren, K. Berne, R. Chen, and K. Corey (eds.). 1976. *The Planning of Change*. New York: Holt, Rinehart & Winston.

Berger, Peter L. and Thomas Luckman. 1967. *The Social Construction of Reality*. Garden City, NY: Doubleday/Anchor.

Bernstein, Ilene and Howard E. Freeman. 1975. *Academic and Entrepreneural Research: Consequences of Diversity in Federal Evaluation Studies*. New York: Russell Sage,

Beyer, Janice M. and Harrison M. Trice. 1982. "The Utilization Process: A Conceptual Framework and Synthesis of Empirical Findings." *Administrative Science Quarterly* 27: 591-622.

Bickman, Leonard. 1985. "Improving Established Statewide Programs: A Component Theory of Evaluation." *Evaluation Review* 9, 2 (April): 189-208.

Blalock, Hubert M., Jr. 1964. *Causal Inferences in Nonexperimental Research*. Chapel Hill: University of North Carolina Press.

Blau, Peter. 1967. "Formal Organizations: Dimensions of Analysis," pp. 336-350 in Walter A. Hill and Douglas Egan (eds.) *Readings in Organizations: A Behavioral Approach*. Boston: Allyn & Bacon.

Blau, Peter and Otis D. Duncan. 1967. *The American Occupational Structure*. New York: John Wiley.

Blau, Peter and William R. Scott. 1962. *Formal Organizations*. San Francisco: Chandler.

Blumer, Herbert. 1969. *Symbolic Interactionism*. Englewood Cliffs, NJ: Prentice-Hall.

Bolles, Richard Nelson. 1982. *What Color Is Your Parachute?* Berkeley, CA: Ten Speed Press.

Boruch, Robert and David Rindskopf. 1984. "Data Analysis," pp. 121-158 in Leonard Rutman (ed.) *Evaluation Research Methods.* Beverly Hills, CA: Sage.

Boruch, R. F., A. J. Sweeney, and E. J. Soderstrom. 1978. "Randomized Field Experiments for Program Planning, Development, and Evaluation: An Illustrative Bibliography." *Evaluation Quarterly* 2 (November): 655-695.

Bracht, Glenn H. and Gene V. Glass. 1968. "The External Validity of Experiments." *American Educational Research Journal* 5: 437-474.

Braskamp, L. A. and R. D. Brown (eds.) 1980. *Utilization of Evaluative Information.* New Directions for Program Evaluation, Vol. 5. San Francisco: Jossey-Bass.

Braybrooke, David and C. E. Lindblom. 1963. *A Strategy of Decision.* New York: Free Press.

Brightman, Harvey and Carl Noble. 1979. "On the Ineffective Education of Decision Scientists." *Decision Sciences* 10: 151-157.

Brinkerhoff, R. O., D. M. Brethower, T. Hluchyj, and J. R. Nowakowski. 1983. *Program Evaluation: Sourcebook, Casebook—A Practitioner's Guide for Trainers and Educators.* Boston: Kluwer-Nijhoff.

Brock, James, Richard Schwaller, and R. L. Smith. 1985. "The Social and Local Government Impacts of the Abandonment of the Milwaukee Railroad in Montana." *Evaluation Review* 9, 2 (April): 127-143.

Broskowski, A., J. Driscoll, and H. C. Schulberg. 1978. "A Management Information and Planning System for Indirect Services," pp. 189-214 in C. Clifford Attkisson et al. (eds.) *Evaluation of Human Service Programs.* New York: Academic Press.

Brown, Lawrence A. 1981. *Innovation Diffusion.* London: Methuen.

Bruyn, Severyn. 1966. *The Human Perspective in Sociology: The Methodology of Participant Observation.* Englewood Cliffs, NJ: Prentice-Hall.

Bryk, Anthony S. (ed.). 1983. *Stakeholder-Based Evaluation.* San Francisco: Jossey-Bass.

Bunge, Mario. 1959. *Causality.* Cambridge, MA: Harvard University Press.

Burns, Tom and G. M. Stalker. 1961. *The Management of Innovations.* London: Tavistock.

Burry, James. 1985. Personal conversation at the UCLA Center for the Study of Evaluation Invited Conference on Evaluation Use, Santa Monica.

———1984. *Synthesis of the Evaluation Use Literature. NIE Grant Report.* Los Angeles: UCLA Center for the Study of Evaluation.

Bussis, Anne, Edward A. Chittenden, and Marianne Amarel. 1973. "Methodology in Educational Evaluation and Research." Princeton, NJ: Educational Testing Service. (unpublished)

Campbell, Donald T. 1974. "Qualitative Knowing in Action Research." Presented at the annual meeting of the American Psychological Association, New Orleans.

Campbell, Donald T. and Robert F. Boruch. 1975. "Making the Case for Randomized Assignment to Treatments by Considering the Alternatives: Six Ways in Which Quasi-Experimental Evaluations in Compensatory Education Tend to Underestimate Effects," pp. 195-296 in Carol A. Bennett and Arthur A. Lumsdaine (eds.) *Evaluation and Experiment.* New York: Academic Press.

Campbell, Donald T. and Julian C. Stanley. 1963. *Experimental and Quasi-Experimental Designs for Research.* Chicago: Rand McNally.

Campbell, Jeanne L. 1983. "Factors and Conditions Influencing Usefulness of Planning, Evaluation, and Reporting in Schools." Ph.D. dissertation, University of Minnesota.

Canadian Evaluation Society. 1982. *The Bottom Line: Utilization of What, by Whom?* Proceedings of the 3rd Annual Conference of the Canadian Evaluation Society. Toronto: University of Toronto.

Caplan, Nathan. 1977. "A Minimal Set of Conditions Necessary for the Utilization of Social Science Knowledge in Policy Formulation at the National Level," pp. 183-198 in Carol H. Weiss (ed.) *Using Social Research in Public Policy Making.* Lexington, MA: D.C. Heath.

Caplan, Nathan, Andrea Morrison, and Russell J. Stambough. 1975. "The Use of Social Science Knowledge in Policy Decisions at the National Level." Ann Arbor: Center for Research on Utilization of Scientific Knowledge, Institute for Social Research, University of Michigan.

Carini, Patricia F. 1975. *Observation and Description: An Alternative Methodology for the Investigation of Human Phenomena.* North Dakota Study Group on Evaluation Monograph Series. Grand Fork: University of North Dakota.

Caro, Francis G. (ed.). 1971. *Readings in Evaluation Research.* New York: Russell Sage.

Champion, Dean J. 1975. *The Sociology of Organizations.* New York: McGraw Hill.

Champion, Dean J. 1975. *The Sociology of Organizations.* New York: McGraw Hill.

Chelimsky, Eleanor. 1983. "Improving the Cost Effectiveness of Evaluation," pp. 149-170 in Marvin C. Alkin and Lewis C. Solmon (eds.) *The Costs of Evaluation.* Beverly Hills, CA: Sage.

Cherney, Paul R. (ed.). 1971. *Making Evaluation Research Useful.* Columbia, MD: American City Corporation.

Ciarlo, James A. (ed.). 1981. *Utilizing Evaluation: Concepts and Measurement Techniques.* Beverly Hills, CA: Sage.

Cicarelli, Victor. 1971. "The Impact of Head Start: Executive Summary," pp. 397-401 in Francis G. Caro (ed.) *Readings in Evaluation Research.* New York: Russell Sage.

Cohen, David K. 1970. "Politics and Research: Evaluation of Social Action Programs in Education." *Educational Evaluation.* American Educational Research Association, *Review of Educational Research* (April): 213-238.

Cohen, David K. and Michael S. Garet. 1975. "Reforming Educational Policy with Applied Social Research." *Harvard Educational Review* 45 (February): 17-41.

Cohen, David K. and Janet A. Weiss. 1977. "Social Science and Social Policy: Schools and Race," pp. 67-84 in Carol H. Weiss (ed.) *Using Social Research in Public Policy Making.* Lexington, MA: D.C. Heath.

Cole, M. B. 1984. "User-Focused Evaluation of Training Programme Effectiveness in a South African Industrial Company." National Productivity Institute of Conference. Johannesburg: University of Witwatersrand.

Coleman, James C. 1972. *Policy Research in the Social Sciences.* Morristown, NJ: General Learning Press.

Coleman, James F. 1977. "Response to Professors Pettigrew and Green," pp. 417-424 in Marcia Guttentag (ed.) *Evaluation Studies Annual Review* (Vol. 2). Beverly Hills, CA: Sage.

Combs, Arthur. 1972. *Educational Accountability: Beyond Behavioral Objectives.* Washington, DC: Association for Supervision and Curriculum Development.

Cook, T. D. and C. S. Reichardt (eds.) 1979. *Qualitative and Quantitative Methods in Evaluation Research.* Beverly Hills, CA: Sage.

Cook, T. D., F. L. Cook, and M. M. Mark. 1977. "Randomized and Quasi-Experimental Designs in Evaluation Research," pp. 101-140 in Leonard Rutman (ed.) *Evaluation Research Methods.* Beverly Hills, CA: Sage.

Cooley, William W. and William E. Bickel. 1985. *Decision-Oriented Educational Research.* Boston: Kluwer-Nijhoff.

Corwin, Ronald G. 1973. *Reform and Organizational Survival.* New York: Wiley Interscience.

Coser, Lewis. 1964. *The Functions of Social Conflict.* New York: Free Press.

Cronbach, Lee J. 1982. *Designing Evaluations of Educational and Social Programs.* San Francisco: Jossey-Bass.

———1975. "Beyond the Two Disciplines of Scientific Psychology." *American Psychologist* 30: 116-117.

———1964a. "The Logic of Experiments on Discovery," pp. 77-92 in Less S. Shulman and Evan R. Keislar (eds.) *Learning by Discovery.* Chicago: Rand McNally.

———1964b. "Evaluation for Course Improvement," pp. 231-248 in R. Heath (ed.) *New Curricula*. New York: Harper & Row.

Cronbach, Lee J. and P. Suppes (eds.). 1969. *Research for Tomorrow's Schools: Disciplined Inquiry of Education*. New York: Macmillan.

Cronbach, Lee J. and associates. 1980. *Toward Reform of Program Evaluation*. San Francisco: Jossey-Bass.

Crozier, Michel. 1964. *The Bureaucratic Phenomenon*. Chicago: University of Chicago Press.

Cyert, Richard and James G. March. 1963. *A Behavioral Theory of the Firm*. Englewood Cliffs, NJ: Prentice-Hall.

Dahl, Robert. 1957. "The Concept of Power." *Behavioral Science* 2 (July): 201-215.

Dalkey, N. C. 1969. *The Delphi Method: An Experimental Study of Group Opinion*. Santa Monica, CA: Rand Corporation.

Danziger, J. N., W. H. Dutton, R. Kling, and K. L. Kraemer. 1982. *Computers and Politics: High Technology in American Local Governments*. New York: Columbia University Press.

Datta, Lois-ellin. 1977. "Does It Work When It Has Been Tried? And Half Full or Half Empty?" pp. 301-319 in Marcia Guttentag (ed.) *Evaluation Studies Annual Review* (Vol. 2). Beverly Hills, CA: Sage.

Davis, Howard R. and Susan E. Salasin. 1975. "The Utilization of Evaluation," pp. 621-666 in Elmer L. Struening and Marcia Guttentag (eds.) *Handbook of Evaluation Research* (Vol. 1). Beverly Hills, CA: Sage.

Dawson, Judith A. and J. J. D'Amico. 1985. "Involving Program Staff in Evaluation Studies: A Strategy for Increasing Use and Enriching the Data Base." *Evaluation Review* 9, 2 (April): 173-188.

Deitchman, Seymour. 1976. *The Best-Laid Schemes: A Tale of Social Research and Bureaucracy*. Cambridge, MA: MIT Press.

Dery, D. 1981. *Computers in Welfare: The MIS-Match*. Beverly Hills, CA: Sage.

Deutscher, Irwin. 1970. "Words and Deeds: Social Science and Social Policy," pp. 27-51 in William J. Filstead (ed.) *Qualitative Methodology*. Chicago: Markham.

Devaney, Kathleen. 1977. "Surveying Teachers' Centers." *Teachers' Centers Exchange, Occasional Paper 1*. Washington, DC: National Institute of Education.

Dewey, John. 1956a. *The Child and the Curriculum*. Chicago: University of Chicago Press.

———1956b. *The School and Society*. Chicago: University of Chicago Press.

deWilde, John C. 1967. *Experiences with Agricultural Development in Tropical Africa* (Vols. 1 & 2). Baltimore: Johns Hopkins University Press.

Dickey, Barbara. 1981. "Utilization of Evaluation of Small-Scale Educational Projects." *Educational Evaluation and Policy Analysis* 2, 6: 65-77.

———1979. "Utilization of Evaluations of Small-Scale Educational Projects." Ph.D. dissertation, University of Minnesota.

Dickey, Barbara and Eber Hampton. 1981. "Effective Problem-Solving for Evaluation Utilization." *Knowledge: Creation, Diffusion, Utilization* 2, 3 (March): 361-374.

Dornbush, Sanford and Richard Scott. 1975. *Evaluation and the Exercise of Authority*. San Francisco: Jossey-Bass.

Dunagin, Ralph. 1977. *Dunagin's People*. Sentinel Star, Field Newspaper Syndicate (August 30).

Dyer, Henry S. 1973. "Recycling the Problems in Testing." Assessment in a Pluralistic Society: Proceedings of the 1972 Invitational Conference on Testing Problems. Princeton, NJ: Educational Testing Service.

Edison, Thomas. 1983. *The Diary and Observations*. New York: Philosophical Library.

Edwards, Ward and Marcia Guttentag. 1975. "Experiments and Evaluation: A Reexamination," pp. 409-463 in Carl Bennet and Arthur Lumsdaine (eds.) *Evaluation and Experiment: Some Critical Issues in Assessing Social Programs*. New York: Academic Press.

Edwards, Ward, Marcia Guttentag, and Kurt Snapper. 1975. "A Decision-Theoretic Approach to Evaluation Research," pp. 139-182 in Elmer L. Struening and Marcia Guttentag (eds.) *Handbook of Evaluation Research* (Vol. 1). Beverly Hills, CA: Sage.

Elmore, Richard F. 1976. "Follow Through Planned Variation," pp. 101-123 in Walter Williams and Richard Elmore (eds.) *Social Program Implementation*. New York: Academic Press.

Elpers, J. R. and R. L. Chapman. 1978. "Basis of the Information System Design and Implementation Process," pp. 173-188 in C. Clifford Attkisson et al. (eds.) *Evaluation of Human Service Programs*. New York: Academic Press.

Emery, F. W. and E. L. Trist. 1965. "The Causal Texture of Organizational Environment." *Human Relations* 18 (February): 21-31.

Etzioni, Amitai. 1968. *The Active Society: A Theory of Societal and Political Processes.* New York: Free Press.

———1964. *Modern Organizations.* Englewood Cliffs, NJ: Prentice-Hall.

———1961. *A Comparative Analysis of Complex Organizations.* New York: Free Press.

Etzioni, Amitai and Michael Patton. 1976. "Update on Policy Research." Videotape interview with Michael Patton, April 22. Minneapolis: Program Evaluation Resource Center.

Evaluation Research Society. 1980. *Standards for Evaluation* (draft). Washington, DC: Evaluation Research Society.

Evans, Gerry and Roger Blunden. 1984. "A Collaborative Approach to Evaluation." *Journal of Practical Approaches to Developmental Handicaps* 8, 1: 14-18.

Evans, John W. 1971. "Head Start: Comments on Criticisms," pp. 401-407 in Francis G. Caro (ed.) *Readings in Evaluation Research*. New York: Russell Sage.

Fairweather, George W. 1967. *Methods for Experimental Social Innovation.* New York: John Wiley.

Fairweather, G. W., D. Sanders, and L. Tornatzky. 1974. *Creating Change in Mental Health Organizations*. New York: Pergamon.

Feiman, Sharon. 1977. "Evaluation Teacher Centers." *Social Review* 8 (May): 395-411.

Fetterman, D. M. 1984. "Ethnography in Educational Research: The Dynamics of Diffusion," pp. 21-35 in D. M. Fetterman (ed.) *Ethnography in Educational Evaluation*. Beverly Hills, CA: Sage.

———1980. "Ethnographic Approaches in Educational Evaluation: An Illustration," *Journal of Thought* 15, 3: 31-48.

Filstead, William J. (ed.) 1970. *Qualitative Methodology.* Chicago: Markham.

Firestone, W. A. and R. E. Herriott. 1984. "Multisite Qualitative Policy Research: Some Design and Implementation Issues," pp. 63-88 in D. M. Fetterman (ed.) *Ethnography in Educational Evaluation*. Beverly Hills, CA: Sage.

Frantzich, Stephen E. 1982. *Computers in Congress: The Politics of Information.* Beverly Hills, CA: Sage.

Freeman, Howard E. 1977. "The Present Status of Evaluation Research," pp. 17-51 in Marcia Guttentag (ed.) *Evaluation Studies Review Annual* (Vol. 2). Beverly Hills, CA: Sage.

Fuller, Bruce and Tamar Rapoport. 1984. "Indigenous Evaluation: Distinguishing the Formal and Informal Structures of Youth Programs." *Evaluation Review* 8, 1 (February): 25-44.

Gardiner, Peter C. and Ward Edwards. 1975. "Public Values: Multi-Attribute-Utility Measurement for Social Decision Making," pp. 1-38 in Martin F. Kaplan and Steven Schwartz (eds.) *Human Judgment and Decision Processes*. New York: Academic Press.

General Accounting Office. 1981. *Federal Evaluations.* Washington, DC: Government Printing Office.

Gephart, William J. 1981. "Watercolor Painting," pp. 247-272 in Nick L. Smith (ed.) *Metaphors for Evaluation*. Beverly Hills, CA: Sage.

Glaser, Barney G. and Anselm L. Strauss. 1967. *Discovery of Grounded Theory: Strategies for Qualitative Research*. Chicago: AVC.

Glaser, Edward M. 1967. "Utilization of Applicable Research and Demonstration Results." Final Report to Vocational Rehabilitation Administration, HEW. Los Angeles: Human Interaction Research Institute.

Glaser, Edward M., Harold H. Abelson, and Kathalee N. Garrison. 1983. *Putting Knowledge to Use.* San Francisco: Jossey-Bass.

Glaser, Edward M. and Samuel H. Taylor. 1969. "Factors Influencing the Success of Applied Research: A Study of Ten NIMH Funded Projects." Los Angeles: Human Interaction Research Institute.

Glass, Gene V. (ed.). 1976. *Evaluation Studies Review Annual* (Vol. 1). Beverly Hills, CA: Sage.

Gouldner, Alvin. 1970. *The Coming Crisis of Western Sociology.* New York: Basic Books.

Governor's Commission on Crime Prevention and Control (GCCPC). 1976. "Residential Community Corrections Programs in Minnesota: An Evaluation Report." Saint Paul: State of Minnesota.

Grant, Donald L. (ed.) 1978. *Monitoring Ongoing Programs.* New Directions for Program Evaluation, Vol. 3. San Francisco: Jossey-Bass.

Gray, Peter J. 1984. "Microcomputers in Evaluation." *Evaluation News* (Nos. 1-5).

Gross, B. M. 1969. "The Definition of Organizational Goals." *British Journal of Sociology* 20: 227-297.

Guba, Egon G. 1981. "Investigative Reporting," pp. 67-86 in Nick L. Smith (ed.) *Metaphors for Evaluation.* Beverly Hills, CA: Sage.

——1978. *Toward a Methodology of Naturalistic Inquiry in Educational Evaluation.* Monograph Series 8. Los Angeles: UCLA Center for the Study of Evaluation.

——1977. "Overcoming Resistance to Evaluation." Presented at the Second Annual Conference on Evaluation, University of North Dakota.

——1968. "Development, Diffusion and Evaluation," pp. 37-63 in Terry L. Eidell and Joanne M. Kitchel (eds.) *Knowledge Production and Utilization in Educational Administration.* University Council for Educational Administration (Columbus, Ohio) and Center for the Advanced Study of Educational Administration (Eugene, Oregon) Career Development Seminar, October. Eugene: University of Oregon Press.

Guba, Egon G. and Yvonna S. Lincoln. 1981. *Effective Evaluation: Improving the Usefulness of Evaluation Results Through Responsive and Naturalistic Approaches.* San Francisco: Jossey-Bass.

Guttentag, Marcia and Elmer L. Struening. 1975a. *Handbook of Evaluation Research* (Vols. 1 & 2). Beverly Hills, CA: Sage.

——1975b. "The Handbook: Its Purpose and Organization," pp. 3-10 in Marcia Guttentag and Elmer L. Struening (eds.) *Handbook of Evaluation Research* (Vol. 2). Beverly Hills, CA: Sage.

Hage, Jerome. 1977. "Generalizing Particularities and Particularizing Generalities: Techniques for Constructing Multi-Variate Hypotheses." Presented at the 72nd Annual Meeting of the American Sociological Association, Chicago.

——1972. Techniques and Problems of Theory Construction in Sociology. New York: Wiley Interscience.

——1965. "An Axiomatic Theory of Organizations." *Administrative Science Quarterly* 10 (December): 289-321.

Hage, Jerald and Michael Aiken. 1970. *Social Change in Complex Organizations.* New York: Random House.

——1969. "Routine, Technology, Social Structure, and Organizational Goals." *Administrative Science Quarterly* 12: 72-92.

Halpert, Harold P. 1969. "Communications as a Basic Tool in Promoting Utilization of Research Findings," pp. 203-225 in Herbert C. Schulberg et al. (eds.) *Program Evaluation in the Mental Health Fields.* New York: Behavioral Publications.

"Harper's Statistical Index." 1985. *Harper's Magazine* (April): 11. Source: Government Accounting Office/General Services Administration.

Harvey, Leah and John Townsend. 1976. *Evaluation of the Saint Paul Open School*. Saint Paul: Saint Paul Open School.

Havelock, Ronald G. 1980. "Forward," pp. 11-14 in Jack Rothman (ed.) *Using Research in Organizations*. Beverly Hills, CA: Sage.

———1973. *The Change Agent's Guide to Innovation in Education*. Englewood Cliffs, NJ: Prentice-Hall.

———1968. "Dissemination and Translation roles," pp. 64-119 in Terry L. Eidell and Joanne M. Kitchel (eds.) *Knowledge Production and Utilization in Educational Administration*. University Council for Educational Administration (Columbus, Ohio) and Center for the Advanced Study of Educational Administration (Eugene, Oregon) Career Development Seminar, October. Eugene: University of Oregon Press.

Hayman, John L., Jr. and Rodney N. Napier. 1975. *Evaluation in the Schools: A Human Renewal Process*. Monterey, CA: Brooks/Cole.

Health and Human Services, Department of. 1983. *Compendium of HHS Evaluation Studies*. Washington, DC: HHS Evaluation Documentation Center.

Heilman, John G. 1980. "Paradigmatic Choices in Evaluation Methodology." *Evaluation Review* 4, 5: 693-712.

Helmer, Olaf. 1966. *Social Technology*. New York: Basic Books.

Hevey, Denise. 1984. "An Exercise in Utilization-Focused Evaluation: The Under-Fives Coordinators." Unpublished paper of the Preschool Evaluation Project, Bristol University.

Hirschman, Albert O. and Charles E. Lindblom. 1962. "Economic Development, Research Development, Policy Making: Some Converging Views." *Behavioral Sciences* 7: 211-222.

Hoffman, Yoel. 1975. *The Sound of One Hand*. New York: Basic Books.

Holzner, Burkart and John H. Marx. 1979. *Knowledge Application: The Knowledge System in Society*. Boston: Allyn & Bacon.

Homans, George. 1949. "The Strategy of Industrial Sociology." *American Journal of Sociology* 54: 330-337.

Hoogerwerf, Andries. 1985. "The Anatomy of Collective Failure in the Netherlands," pp. 47-60 in M. Q. Patton (ed.) *Culture and Evaluation*. San Francisco: Jossey-Bass.

House, Ernest R. 1980. *Evaluating with Validity*. Beverly Hills, CA: Sage.

———1977. "The Logic of Evaluative Argument." *CSE Monograph Lines in Evaluation 7*. Los Angeles: UCLA Center for the Study of Education.

———1974. *The Politics of Educational Innovation*. Berkeley, CA: McCutchan.

———(ed.). 1973. *School Evaluation: The Politics and Process*. Berkeley, CA: McCutchan.

———1972. "The Conscience of Educational Evaluation." *Teachers College Record* 73, 3: 405-414.

Hudson, Joe. 1977. "Problems of Measurement in Criminal Justice," pp. 73-100 in Leonard Rutman (ed.) *Evaluation Research Methods*. Beverly Hills, CA: Sage.

Johnson, George H. 1970. "The Purpose of Evaluation and the Role of the Evaluator," pp. 1-18 in *Evaluation Research: Strategies and Methods*. Pittsburgh: American Institute of Research.

Johnson, Jerome (ed.). 1984. *Evaluating the New Information Technologies*. San Francisco: Jossey-Bass.

Joint Committee on Standards for Educational Evaluation. 1981. *Standards for Evaluations of Educational Programs, Projects, and Materials*. New York: McGraw-Hill.

Kagan, Jerome. 1966. "Learning, Attention and the Issue of Discovery," pp. 151-161 in Lee S. Shulman and Evan R. Keislar (eds.) *Learning by Discovery: A Critical Appraisal*. Chicago: Rand McNally.

Kantor, Rosabeth Moss. 1983. *The Change Masters*. New York: Simon & Schuster.

King, Jean. 1985. "Existing Research on Evaluation Use and Its Implications for the Improvement of Evaluation Research and Practice." Invited conference on evaluation use. Los Angeles: UCLA Center for the Study of Evaluation.

King, Jean A. and Ellen Pechman. 1982. *Improving Evaluation Use in Local Schools*. Washington, DC: National Institute of Education.

King, Jean A., Bruce Thompson, and Ellen Pechman. 1985. "Optimizing Evaluation Use: An Evaluation Utilization Bibliography." New Orleans: Tulane University, University of New Orleans, and Orleans Parish Public Schools. (mimeo)

Kirk, Stuart A. 1977. "Understanding the Utilization of Research in Social Work and Other Applied Professions." Presented at the Conference on Research Utilization in Social Work Education, New Orleans.

Kneller, George F. 1972. "Goal-Free Evaluation." *Evaluation Comment: The Journal of Educational Evaluation* (Center for the Study of Evaluation, UCLA) 3, 4 (December): 13-15.

Kochen, Manfred. 1975. "Applications of Fuzzy Sets in Psychology," pp. 395-407 in Lofti A. Zadeh et al. (eds.) *Fuzzy Sets and Their Applications to Cognitive and Decision Processes*. New York: Academic Press.

Kourilsky, Marilyn. 1974. "An Adversary Model for Educational Evaluation." *Evaluation Comment* 4, 2.

Kuhn, Thomas. 1970. *The Structure of Scientific Revolutions*. Chicago: University of Chicago Press.

Laundergan, J. Clark. 1983. *Easy Does It*. Center City, MN: Hazelden Foundation.

Lawler, E. E., III, A. M. Mohrman, Jr., S. A. Mohrman, G. E. Ledford, Jr., T. G. Cummings, and associates. 1985. *Doing Research that Is Useful for Theory and Practice*. San Francisco: Jossey-Bass.

Lawrence, Paul R. and Jay W. Lorsch. 1972. "Differentiation and Integration in Complex Organizations," pp. 334-358 in Koya Azumi and Jerald Hage (eds.) *Organizational Systems*. Lexington, MA: D.C. Heath.

———1967. *Organization and Environment*. Boston: Graduate School of Business Administration, Harvard University.

Lazarsfeld, Paul F. and Jeffrey G. Reitz. 1975. *An Introduction to Applied Sociology*. New York: Elsevier.

Levine, Adaline and Murray Levine. 1977. "The Social Context of Evaluative Research." *Evaluation Quarterly* 1, 4 (November): 515-542.

Levine, Harold G., R. Gallimore, T. S. Weisner, and J. L. Turner. 1980. "Teaching Participant-Observation Research Methods: A Skills-Building Approach." *Anthropology and Education Quarterly* 9, 1: 38-54.

Levine, Murray. 1974. "Scientific Method and the Adversary." *American Psychologist* (September): 666-677.

Leviton, L. A. and E.F.X. Hughes. 1981. "Research on Utilization of Evaluations: A Review and Synthesis." *Evaluation Review* 5, 4: 525-548.

Lewy, Arieh and Marvin Alkin. 1983. *The Impact of a Major National Evaluation Study: Israel's Van Leer Report*. Los Angeles: UCLA Center for the Study of Evaluation.

Lincoln, Yvonna S. and Egon G. Guba. 1985. *Naturalistic Inquiry*. Beverly Hills, CA: Sage.

Lindblom, Charles E. 1959. "The Science of Muddling Through. Public Administration." *Public Administration Review* 19: 79-99.

———1965. *The Intelligence of Democracy*. New York: Free Press.

Lofland, John. 1971. *Analyzing Social Settings*. Belmont, CA: Wadsworth.

Lucas, H. C. 1975. *Why Information Systems Fail*. New York: Columbia University Press.

Lynn, Lawrence E., Jr. 1980. *Designing Public Policies: A Casework on the Role of Policy Analysis*. Santa Monica, CA: Goodyear.

Lynn, Lawrence E., Jr. and Susan Salasin. 1974. "Human Services: Should We, Can We Make Them Available to Everyone?" *Evaluation* (Spring Special Issue): 4-5.

MacKenzie, R. A. 1972. *The Time Trap*. New York: AMACOM.

MacRae, Duncan, Jr. 1976. *The Social Function of Social Science*. New Haven, CT: Yale University Press.

Mann, Floyd C. and F. W. Neff. 1961. *Managing Major Change in Organizations*. Ann Arbor, MI: Foundation for Research on Human Behavior.

March, James G. (ed.). 1965. *Handbook of Organizations*. Chicago: Rand McNally.

March, James G. and Herbert Simon. 1958. *Organizations*. New York: John Wiley.

Mark, M. M. and T. D. Cook. 1984. "Design of Randomized Experiments and Quasi-Experiments," pp. 65-120 in Leonard Rutman (ed.) *Evaluation Research Methods*. Beverly Hills, CA: Sage.

Maurer, John (ed.). 1971. *Open-System Approaches in Organizational Theory*. New York: Random House.

Maxwell, J. A., Bashook, P. G., and L. J. Sandlow. 1985. "Combining Ethnographic and Experimental Methods in Educational Research: A Case Study," in D. M. Fetterman and M. A. Pitman (eds.), *Beyond the Status Quo: Theory, Politics and Practice in Ethnographic Evaluation*. Washington, DC: Cato Institute.

Mayntz, Renate. 1977. "Sociology, Value Freedom, and the Problems of Political Counseling," pp. 55-66 in Carol H. Weiss (ed.) *Using Social Research in Public Policy Making*. Lexington, MA: D.C. Heath.

McIntyre, Ken. 1976. "Evaluating Educational Programs." *Review* (University Council for Educational Administration) 18, 1 (September): 39.

McLaughlin, Milbrey. 1976. "Implementation as Mutual Adaptation," pp. 167-180 in Walter Williams and Richard F. Elmore (eds.) *Social Program Implementation*. New York: Academic Press.

McTavish, Donald, E. Brent, J. Cleary, and K. R. Knudsen. 1975. "The Systematic Assessment and Prediction of Research Methodology, Vol. 1: Advisory Report." Final Report on Grant OEO 005-P-20-2-74, Minnesota Continuing Program for the Assessment and Improvement of Research. Minneapolis: University of Minnesota.

Merton, Robert K. 1957. *Social Theory and Social Structure*. New York: Free Press.

Meyers, William R. 1981. *The Evaluation Enterprise*. San Francisco: Jossey-Bass.

Mills, C. Wright. 1961. *The Sociological Imagination*. New York: Grove Press.

Mills, C. Wright. 1959. *The Sociological Imagination*. New York: Oxford University Press.

Moos, Rudolf H. 1979. *Evaluating Educational Environments*. San Francisco: Jossey-Bass.

Moos, Rudolf. 1975. *Evaluating Correctional and Community Settings*. New York: Wiley Interscience.

———1974. *Evaluating Treatment Environments*. New York: Wiley Interscience.

Morris, Lynn Lyons and Carol Taylor Fitz-Gibbon. 1978. *How to Deal with Goals and Objectives*. Beverly Hills, CA: Sage.

Murphy, Jerome T. 1976. "Title V of ESEA: The Impact of Discretionary Funds on State Education Bureaucracies," pp. 77-100 in Walter Williams and Richard Elmore (eds.) *Social Program Implementation*. New York: Academic Press.

Mushkin, S. 1973. "Evaluations: Use with Caution." *Evaluation* 1, 2: 31-35.

Nagel, Ernest. 1961. *The Structure of Science*. New York: Harcourt Brace Jovanovich.

National Academy of Sciences. 1968. *The Behavioral Sciences and the Federal Government*. Washington, DC: Government Printing Office.

Newman, D., R. Brown, L. Rivers, and R. Glock. 1983. "School Boards' and Administrators' Use of Evaluation Information: Influencing Factors." *Evaluation Review* 7, 1: 110-125.

Northwest Regional Educational Laboratory (NWREL). 1977. *3-on-2 Evaluation Report, 1976-1977* (Vols. 1-3). Portland, OR: NWREL.

Nunnally, Jim C., Jr. 1970. *Introduction to Psychological Measurement*. New York: McGraw-Hill.

Odiorne, George S. 1984. *Strategic Management of Human Resources*. San Francisco: Jossey-Bass.

Office of Program Analysis, General Accounting Office. 1976. *Federal Program Evaluations: A Directory for the Congress*. Washington, DC: Government Printing Office.

Owens, Thomas. 1973. "Education Evaluation by Adversary Proceeding," in Ernest R. House (ed.) *School Evaluation: The Politics and Process*. Berkeley, CA: McCutchan.

Palumbo, D. J., S. Maynard-Moody, and P. Wright. 1984. "Measuring Degrees of Successful Implementation." *Evaluation Review* 8, 1 (February): 45-74.

Palumbo, D. J., M. Musheno, and S. Maynard-Moody. 1985. *An Evaluation of the Implementation of Community Corrections in Oregon, Colorado and Connecticut*. Final Report prepared for Grant 82-15-CUK015. Washington, DC: National Institute of Justice.

Parlett, Malcolm and David Hamilton. 1976. "Evaluation as Illumination: A New Approach to the Study of Innovatory Programs," pp. 140-157 in Gene V. Glass (ed.) *Evaluation Studies Review Annual* (Vol. 1). Beverly Hills, CA: Sage.

————1972. "Evaluation as Illumination: A New Approach to the Study of Innovative Programs." Occasional Paper 9. Edinburgh: University of Edinburgh Center for Research in the Educational Sciences.

Parsons, Talcott. 1960. *Structure and Process in Modern Society*. New York: Free Press.

Patton, Michael Q. (ed.). 1985. *Culture and Evaluation*. San Francisco: Jossey-Bass.

————1983. "Similarities of Extension and Evaluation." *Journal of Extension* 21 (September-October): 14-21.

————1982a. *Practical Evaluation*. Beverly Hills, CA: Sage.

————1982b. "Managing Management Information Systems," pp. 227-239 in M. Q. Patton (ed.) *Practical Evaluation*. Beverly Hills, CA: Sage.

————1981. *Creative Evaluation*. Beverly Hills, CA: Sage.

————1980a. *Qualitative Evaluation Methods*. Beverly Hills, CA: Sage.

————1980b. *The Processes and Outcomes of Chemical Dependency*. Center City, MN: Hazelden Foundation.

————1978. *Utilization-Focused Evaluation*. Beverly Hills, CA: Sage.

————1975a. *Alternative Evaluation Research Paradigm*. Grand Fork: University of North Dakota.

————1975b. "Understanding the Gobble-dy-Gook: A People's Guide to Standardized Test Results and Statistics," *Testing and Evaluation: New Views*. Washington, DC: Association for Childhood Education International.

————1973. *Structure and Diffusion of Open Education*. Report on the Trainers of Teacher Trainer Program, New School of Behavioral Studies in Education. Grand Forks: University of North Dakota.

Patton, Michael Q., Patricia S. Grimes, Kathryn M. Guthrie, Nancy J. Brennan, Barbara D. French, and Dale A. Blyth. 1977. "In Search of Impact: An Analysis of the Utilization of Federal Health Evaluation Research," pp. 141-164 in Carol Weiss (ed.) *Using Social Research in Public Policy Making*. Lexington, MA: D.C. Heath.

Patton, Michael Q., Kathy Guthrie, Steven Gray, Carl Hearle, Rich Wiseman, and Neala Yount. 1977. *Environments that Make a Difference: An Evaluation of Ramsey County Corrections Foster Group Homes*. Minneapolis: Minnesota Center for Social Research, University of Minnesota.

Pederson, Clara A. (ed.). 1977. *Informal Education: Evaluation and Record Keeping*. Grand Forks: University of North Dakota.

Perrone, Vito. 1977. *The Abuses of Standardized Testing*. Bloomington, IN: Phi Delta Kappa Educational Foundation.

Perrone, Vito, Michael Q. Patton, and Barbara French. 1976. *Does Accountability Count Without Teacher Support?* Minneapolis: Minnesota Center for Social Research, University of Minnesota.

Perrow, Charles. 1970. *Organizational Analysis: A Sociological View*. Belmont, CA: Wadsworth.

———1968. "Organizational Goals," pp. 305-311 in *International Encyclopedia of Social Sciences*. New York: Macmillan.

———1961. "The Analysis of Goals in Complex Organizations." *American Sociological Review* 6 (December): 854-866.

Peters, Thomas and Robert Waterman. 1982. *In Search of Excellence*. New York: Harper & Row.

Petrie, Hugh G. 1972. "Theories Are Tested by Observing the Facts: Or Are They?" pp. 47-73 in Lawrence G. Thomas (ed.) *Philosophical Redirection of Educational Research: The Seventy-First Yearbook of the National Society for the Study of Education*. Chicago: University of Chicago Press.

Pettigrew, Thomas F. and Robert L. Green. 1977. "School Desegregation in Large Cities: A Critique of the Coleman 'White Flight' Thesis," pp. 363-416 in Marcia Guttentag (ed.) *Evaluation Studies Review Annual* (Vol. 2). Beverly Hills, CA: Sage.

Policy Analysis Source Book for Social Programs. 1976. Washington, DC: Government Printing Office.

Popham, James W. 1972. "Results Rather than Rhetoric." *Evaluation Comment: The Journal of Educational Evaluation* (Center for the Study of Evaluation, UCLA) 3, 4 (December): 12-13.

———1969. *Instructional Objectives*. Chicago: Rand McNally.

Popham, James W. and Dale Carlson. 1977. "Deep Dark Deficits of the Adversary Evaluation Model." *Educational Researcher* (June): 3-6.

Pressman, Jeffrey L. and Aaron Wildavsky. 1984. *Implementation*. Berkeley: University of California Press.

Price, James. 1968. *Organizational Effectiveness*. Homewood, IL: Irwin.

Provus, Malcolm. 1971. *Discrepancy Evaluation for Educational Program Improvement and Assessment*. Berkeley, CA: McCutchan.

Rafter, David O. 1984. "Three Approaches to Evaluation Research." *Knowledge: Creation, Diffusion, Utilization* 6, 2 (December): 165-185.

Raskin, A. H. 1977. "Major Impact of the New Consumer Price Index." *New York Times Service, Minneapolis Tribune* (July 21): 11A.

Reichardt, Charles S. and Thomas D. Cook. 1979. "Beyond Qualitative Versus Quantitative Methods," in T. Cook and C. S. Reichardt (eds.) *Qualitative and Quantitative Methods*. Beverly Hills, CA: Sage.

Reicken, Henry W. and Robert F. Boruch. 1974. *Social Experimentation: A Method for Planning and Evaluating Social Intervention*. New York: Academic Press.

Resnick, Michael. 1984. "Teen Sex: How Girls Decide." *Update-Research Briefs* (University of Minnesota) 11, 5 (October): 15.

Rist, Raymond. 1977. "On the Relations Among Educational Research Paradigms: From Disdain to Detente." *Anthropology and Education* 8: 42-49.

Rivlin, Alice M. 1971. *Systematic Thinking for Social Action*. Washington, DC: Brookings Institution.

Rogers, Everett. 1962. *Diffusion of Innovation*. New York: Free Press.

Rogers, Everett M. and Lynne Svenning. 1969. *Managing Change*. San Mateo, CA: Operation PEP.

Rogers, Everett M. and Floyd F. Shoemaker. 1971. *Communication of Innovation*. New York: Free Press.

Rosenthal, Elsa J. 1976. "Delphi Technique," pp. 121-122 in S. Anderson et al. (eds.) *Encyclopedia of Educational Evaluation*. San Francisco: Jossey-Bass.

Rosenthal, Elsa J. and Ann Z. Smith. 1976. "Goals and Objectives," pp. 179-184 in Scarvia B. Anderson et al. (eds.) *Encyclopedia of Educational Evaluation*. San Francisco: Jossey-Bass.

Rossi, Peter H. 1972. "Testing for Success and Failure in Social Action," pp. 11-65 in Peter H. Rossi and Walter Williams (eds.), *Evaluating Social Programs*. New York: Seminar Press.

Rossi, Peter H. and H. E. Freeman. 1982. *Evaluation: A Systematic Approach*. Beverly Hills, CA: Sage.

Rossi, Peter H. and Walter Williams (eds.). 1972. *Evaluating Social Programs: Theory, Practice, and Politics*. New York: Seminar Press.

Rossi, Peter H., Howard E. Freeman, and Sonia R. Wright. 1979. *Evaluation: A Systematic Approach*. Beverly Hills, CA: Sage.

Rothman, Jack. 1980. *Using Research in Organizations*. Beverly Hills, CA: Sage.

Rutman, Leonard. 1984. "Evaluability Assessment," pp. 27-38 in L. Rutman (ed.) *Evaluation Research Methods: A Basic Guide*. Beverly Hills, CA: Sage.

————1980. *Planning Useful Evaluations: Evaluability Assessment*. Beverly Hills, CA: Sage.

————1977. "Barriers to the Utilization of Evaluation Research." Presented at the 27th Annual Meeting of the Society for the Study of Social Problems, Chicago.

Rutman, Leonard and John Mayne. 1985. "Institutionalization of Program Evaluation in Canada: The Federal Level," pp. 61-68 in M. Q. Patton (ed.) *Culture and Evaluation*. San Francisco: Jossey-Bass.

Salasin, Susan (ed.). 1974. "The Human Services Shortfall." *Evaluation: A Forum for Human Service Decision-Makers* (Spring). Minneapolis: Minneapolis Medical Research Foundation.

Sax, Gilbert. 1974. "The Use of Standardized Tests in Evaluation," pp. 243-307 in W. James Popham (ed.) *Evaluation in Education: Current Applications*. Berkeley, CA: McCutchan.

Saxe, Leonard and Daniel Koretz (eds.) 1982. *Making Evaluation Research Useful to Congress*. San Francisco: Jossey-Bass.

Schutz, Alfred. 1967. *The Phenomenology of the Social World*. Evanston, IL: Washington University Press.

Scriven, Michael. 1972a. "Objectivity and Subjectivity in Educational Research," pp. 94-142 in Lawrence G. Thomas (ed.) *Philosophical Redirection of Educational Research: The Seventy-First Yearbook of the National Society for the Study of Education*. Chicago: University of Chicago Press.

————1972b. "Pros and Cons About Goal-Free Evaluation." *Evaluation Comment: The Journal of Educational Evaluation* (Center for the Study of Evaluation, UCLA) 3, 4 (December): 1-7.

————1967. "The Methodology of Evaluation," pp. 39-83 in Ralph W. Tyler et al. (eds.) *Perspectives of Curriculum Evaluation*. AERA Monograph Series on Curriculum Evaluation, 1. Chicago: Rand McNally.

Scriven, Michael and Michael Patton. 1976. "A Perspective on Evaluation." Videotape interview. Minneapolis: Program Evaluation Resource Center.

Shackle, G.L.S. 1961. *Decision, Order, and Time in Human Affairs*. Cambridge, MA: Harvard University Press.

Shah, I. 1964. *The Sufis*. Garden City, NY: Doubleday.

Shapiro, Edna. 1973. "Educational Evaluation: Rethinking the Criteria of Competence." *School Review* (November): 523-549.

Sharpe, L. J. 1977. "The Social Scientist and Policymaking: Some Cautionary Thoughts and Transatlantic Reflections," pp. 37-54 in Carol Weiss (ed.) *Using Social Research for Public Policy Making*. Lexington, MA: D.C. Heath.

Siegel, Karolynn and Peter Tuckel. 1985. "The Utilization of Evaluation Research: A Case Analysis." *Evaluation Review* 9, 3 (June): 307-328.

Silberman, Charles E. 1970. *Crisis in the Classroom: The Remaking of American Education*. New York: Random House.

Silverman, David. 1971. *The Theory of Organizations*. New York: Basic Books.

Simon, Herbert A. 1957. *Administrative Behavior*. New York: Macmillan.

Sjoberg, Gideon. 1975. "Politics, Ethics, and Evaluation Research," pp. 29-51 in Marcia Guttentag and Elmer L. Struening (eds.) *Handbook of Evaluation Research* (Vol. 2). Beverly Hills, CA: Sage.

Sjoberg, Gideon and R. Nett. 1968. *A Methodology for Social Research*. New York: Harper & Row.

Smelser, Neil. 1959. *Social Change in the Industrial Revolution*. Chicago: University of Chicago Press.

Smith, Nick L. 1980. "Studying Evaluation Assumptions." *Evaluation Network Newsletter* (Winter): 39-40.

Social Science Research Council, National Academy of Sciences. 1969. *The Behavioral and Social Sciences: Outlook and Need*. Englewood Cliffs, NJ: Prentice-Hall.

Sorenson, J. E. and J. R. Elpers. 1978. "Developing Information Systems for Human Service Organizations," pp. 127-172 in C. C. Attkisson et al. (eds.) *Evaluation of Human Service Programs*. New York: Academic Press.

Special Commission on the Social Sciences, National Science Foundation. 1968. *Knowledge into Action: Improving the Nation's Use of the Social Sciences*. Washington, DC: Government Printing Office.

Stake, Robert E. 1981. "Case Study Methodology: An Epistemological Advocacy," pp. 31-40 in W. W. Welch (ed.) *Case Study Methodology in Educational Evaluation*. Minneapolis: Minnesota Research and Evaluation Center.

———1978. "Should Educational Evaluation Be More Objective or More Subjective?" Presented at the annual meeting of the American Educational Research Association, Toronto.

———1975. *Evaluating the Arts in Education: A Responsive Approach*. Columbus, OH: Charles E. Merrill.

———1973. "Evaluation Design, Instrumentation, Data Collection, and Analysis of Data," pp. 303-316 in Blaine R. Worthen and James R. Sanders (eds.) *Educational Evaluation: Theory and Practice*. Worthington, OH: Charles A. Jones.

———1967. "The Countenance of Educational Evaluation." *Teachers College Record* 68 (April): 523-540.

Stalford, Charles B. 1983. "School Board Use of Evaluation Information." Presented at the joint meeting of the Evaluation Network and the Evaluation Research Society, Chicago.

Statewide Study of Education. 1967. *Educational Development for North Dakota, 1967-1975*. Grand Forks: University of North Dakota.

Stephens, John. 1967. *The Process of Schooling*. New York: Holt, Rinehart & Winston.

Stevens, William F. and Louis G. Tornatsky. 1980. "The Dissemination of Evaluation: An Experiment." *Evaluation Review* 4, 3: 339-354.

Stinchcombe, Arthur. 1965. "Social Structure and Organizations," pp. 142-193 in James G. March (ed.) *Handbook of Organizations*. Chicago: Rand McNally.

Stolurow, Lawrence M. 1965. "Model the Master Teacher or Master the Teaching Model?" pp. 223-247 in John D. Krumboltz (ed.) *Learning and the Educational Process*. Chicago: Rand McNally.

Stone, Clarence N. 1985. "Efficiency Versus Social Learning: A Reconsideration of the Implementation Process." *Policy Studies Review* 4, 3 (February): 484-496.

Stufflebeam, Daniel. 1980. "An Interview with Daniel L. Stufflebeam." *Educational Evaluation and Policy Analysis* 2, 4.

Strike, Kenneth. 1972. "Explaining and Understanding the Impact of Science on Our Concept of Man," pp. 26-46 in Lawrence G. Thomas (ed.) *Philosophical Redirection of Educational Research: The Seventy-First Yearbook of the National Society for the Study of Education*. Chicago: University of Chicago Press.

Studer, Sharon L. 1978. "A Validity Study of a Measure of 'Readiness to Accept Program Evaluation.'" Ph.D. dissertation, University of Minnesota.

Stufflebeam, Daniel L. 1972. "Should or Can Evaluation Be Goal-Free?" *Evaluation Comment: The Journal of Educational Evaluation* (Center for the Study of Evaluation, UCLA) 3, 4 (December): 7-9.

Stufflebeam, Daniel L. and Egon Guba. 1970. "Strategies for the Institutionalization of the CIPP Evaluation Model." Presented at the 11th Annual PDK Symposium on Education Research, Columbus, Ohio.

Stufflebeam, Daniel L., W. J. Foley, W. J. Gephart, L. R. Hammond, H. O. Merriman, and M. M. Provus. 1971. *Educational Evaluation and Decision-Making in Education*. Itasca, IL: Peacock.

Suchman, Edward A. 1972. "Action for What? A Critique of Evaluative Research," pp. 42-84 in Carol H. Weiss (ed.) *Evaluating Action Programs*. Boston: Allyn & Bacon.

———1967. *Evaluative Research: Principles and Practice in Public Service and Social Action Programs*. New York: Russell Sage.

Taylor, Donald W. 1965. "Decision Making and Problem Solving," pp. 48-86 in James G. March (ed.) *Handbook of Organizations*. Chicago: Rand McNally.

Terreberry, Shirley. 1971. "The Evaluation of Organizational Environments," pp. 58-73 in John G. Maurer (ed.) *Open-System Approaches to Organization Theory*. New York: Random House.

Thomas, Jo. 1977. "Consultant Costs Concern Carter, Congress." *New York Times Service, Minneapolis Tribune* (December 12): 17A.

Thompson, James D. 1967. *Organizations in Action*. New York: McGraw-Hill.

Thompson, Mark. 1975. *Evaluation for Decision in Social Programmes*. Lexington, MA: D.C. Heath.

Thoreau, Henry D. 1838. *Journal*, March 14.

Trend, M. G. 1978. "On Reconciliation of Qualitative and Quantitative Analysis." *Human Organization* 37: 345-354.

Tripodi, Tony, Phillip Felin, and Irwin Epstein. 1971. *Social Program Evaluation Guidelines for Health, Education, and Welfare Administration*. Itasca, IL: Peacock.

Tucker, Eugene. 1977. "The Follow Through Planned Variation Experiment: What Is the Pay-Off?" Presented at the annual meeting of the American Educational Research Association, April.

Tyler, Ralph W. (ed.). 1969. *Educational Evaluation: New Roles, New Means*. Chicago: University of Chicago Press.

———1950. *Basic Principles of Curriculum and Instruction*. Chicago: University of Chicago Press.

U.S. House of Representatives, Committee on Government Operations, Research and Technical Programs Subcommittee. 1967. *The Use of Social Research in Federal Domestic Programs*. Washington, DC: Government Printing Office.

Ward, David , Gene Kassebaum, and Daniel Wilner. 1971. *Prison Treatment and Parole Survival: An Empirical Assessment*. New York: John Wiley.

Weber, Max. 1947. *The Theory of Social and Economic Organizations*. New York: Oxford University Press.

Weidman, Donald R., Pamela Horst, Grace Taher, and Joseph S. Wholey. 1973. "Design of an Evaluation System for NIMH." *Contract Report 962-7*. Washington, DC: Urban Institute.

Weiss, C. H. 1982. "Measuring the Use of Evaluations," pp. 129-146 in E. House (ed.) *Evaluation Studies Review Annual* (Vol. 7). Beverly Hills, CA: Sage.

———1977. "Introduction," pp. 1-22 in Carol H. Weiss (ed.) *Using Social Research in Public Policy Making*. Lexington, MA: D.C. Heath.

———1975. "Evaluation Research in the Political Context," pp. 13-26 in Marcia Guttentag and Elmer L. Struening (eds.) *Handbook of Evaluation Research* (Vol. 1). Beverly Hills, CA: Sage.

————(ed.) 1972a. *Evaluating Action Programs*. Boston: Allyn & Bacon.
————1972b. *Evaluation Research: Methods of Assessing Program Effectiveness*. Englewood Cliffs, NJ: Prentice-Hall.
————1970. "The Politicization of Evaluation Research." *Journal of Social Issues* 26, 4: 57-68.
Weiss, Carol H. and Michael Bucuvalas. 1980. "Truth Test and Utility Test: Decision Makers' Frame of Reference for Social Science Research." *American Sociological Review* (April): 302-313.
Weiss, Robert S. and Martin Rein. 1969. "The Evaluation of Broad-Aim Programs: A Cautionary Case and a Moral." *Annals of the American Academy of Political and Social Science* 385 (September): 118-132.
Westinghouse Learning Corporation. 1969. *The Impact of Head Start: An Evaluation of the Effects of Head Start on Children's Cognitive and Affective Development*. Bladensburg, MD: Westinghouse Learning Corporation.
Wholey, Joseph. 1979. *Evaluation: Promise and Performance*. Washington, DC: Urban Institute.
Wholey, Joseph S., John W. Scanlon, Hugh G. Duffy, James S. Fukumotu, and Leona M. Vogt. 1970. *Federal Evaluation Policy: Analyzing the Effects of Public Programs*. Washington, DC: Urban Institute.
Willems, E. P. and H. L. Raush. 1969. *Naturalistic Viewpoint in Psychological Research*. New York: Holt, Rinehart & Winston.
Williams, Jay. 1976. *Everyone Knows What a Dragon Looks Like*. New York: Four Winds Press.
Williams, Walter. 1976. "Implementation Analysis and Assessment," pp. 267-292 in W. Williams and R. F. Elmore (eds.) *Social Program Implementation*. New York: Academic Press.
Williams, Walter and Richard F. Elmore. 1976. *Social Program Implementation*. New York: Academic Press.
Williams, Walter and John W. Evans. 1969. "The Politics of Evaluation: The Case of Head Start." *Annals of the American Academy of Political and Social Science* 385 (September): 118-132.
Windle, Charles. n.d. "Factors in the Success of NIMH's Community Mental Health Centers Program Evaluation Studies." Unpublished mimeograph.
Wolf, Robert L. 1975. "Trial by Jury: A New Evaluation Method." *Phi Delta Kappan* (November).
Wolf, Robert L. and Barbara Tymitz. 1976. Whatever Happened to the Giant Wombat. An investigation of the impact of the Ice Age Mammals and Emergence of Man Exhibit, National Museum of Natural History, Smithsonian Institutes. (mimeo)
Worley, D. R. 1960. "Amount and Generality of Information-Seeking Behavior in Sequential Decision Making as Dependent on Level of Incentive," pp. 1-11 in D. W. Taylor (ed.) *Experiments on Decision Making*. Technical Report 6. New Haven, CT: Yale University, Department of Industrial Administration and Psychology.
Worthen, Blaine R. and James R. Sanders (eds.). 1973. *Educational Evaluation: Theory and Practice*. Worthington, OH: Charles A. Jones.
Young, Carlotta J. and Joseph Comtois. 1979. "Increasing Congressional Utilization of Evaluation," in Franklin M. Zweig (ed.) *Evaluation in Legislation*. Beverly Hills, CA: Sage.
Zadeh, Lofti A. 1965. "Fuzzy Sets." *Inform and Control* 8: 338-353.
Zadeh, Lofti A., King-Sun Fu, Kokichi Tanaka, and Masamichi Shimura (eds.). 1975. *Fuzzy Sets and Their Applications to Cognitive and Decision Processes*. New York: Academic Press.

INDEX

accuracy, 24-26, 222, 235, 279
action, 14, 26, 50-51, 270, 293, 300, 308-309, 320, 338
active-reactive-adaptive, 106, 111, 205, 304, 307-309, 319-320, 332-323, 335, 337
advocacy-adversary model, 62-64
Alice in Wonderland, 92
alligators, 134
American Evaluation Association, 12
analysis, 244-280
appropriateness, 180, 204-205, 209, 211, 213-217, 220
assumptions, 154-155, 198
audience, 52, 276-8

backpacking, 122-123
balance, 195-8, 256-258, 279
bear hunt, 83-85
believability, 222, 224-227, 279
black box, 129-131, 142
bullseye, 117
bureaucratic model, 118-119

Canada, 21, 75, 79
Canadian Evaluation Society, 21
Caribbean Project, 6, 99, 340-344
case studies, 205-209
causality, 150, 151, 154-164, 172, 174, 192, 234-235

central issues, 106-107, 109-110
chain of objectives, 153-154, 169-171
change, 202-204, 337-338
Change Agent Study, 137
charity orientation, 15-17
CIPP model, 140
closeness to a program, 198-200
communicating, 93-94
comparative evaluation, 67
comparisons, 143-144, 167-169, 190-191, 260-263, 279, 302
compliance research, 13
component evaluation, 140-141
comprehensive approach, 26-27
conclusion-oriented inquiry, 14
conflict, 87-88, 132
context, 74, 220, 286
creativity, 25, 51, 205, 213, 221, 235, 243, 272, 280, 319, 338
credibility, 180, 220, 222, 224-227, 257, 335, 336

decision context, 74
decision-oriented research, 14, 53, 56, 66, 67, 345
decision-theoretic evaluation, 103
deductive approach, 152, 193-194
definitions, 179, 258-260, 279
    program evaluation, 14

alternative definitions, 67-68
utilization-focused evaluation, 68
stakeholders' definitions, 68-69
cautions about, 69
use, utilization, 30-31, 37-39
personal factor, 45
paradigms, 181-182
Delphi Technique, 87-88
Desiderata, 59
differential evaluation, 117, 166-167
direction, 151
discrepancy evaluation, 135-136
disordinal interactions, 207-208
dissemination, 276-278, 279, 322, 332
distance from a program, 198-200
diverstiy, 207-209

effort evaluation, 138, 345
empirical perspective, 18-20, 69, 70
Epilepsy Program, 100-104, 152-153
epitaph, 38-39
error, 151, 214, 228-230, 262
Evaluation Network, 12
Evaluation Research Society, 12
experimental designs, 142-145, 182-185,
    192-193, 200-213, 241
extension, 6, 13
external evaluation, 164, 240, 309-310, 346
extrapolations, 206, 235

fairness, 197-198
feasibility standards, 25-26
FBI, 312-313
feedback, 80
findings, 235, 238, 250-267, 293, 331, 332
flexibility, 25, 176, 181, 191, 211, 246, 314-
    321
focus, 51, 61-82, 126-130, 148-149, 154,
    165-166, 172-173, 207, 231-234, 253,
    270, 330-331, 333
Follow Through Evaluation, 134-135, 190-
    191, 199
formative evaluation, 65-66, 179, 203, 231,
    307, 346
Frontier School Division, 75-77
funders, 54
future orientation, 53, 74-75, 79-80, 118,
    164
fuzzy goals, 92-93, 95, 113
fuzzy set theory, 93

generalizations, 14-15, 205-208, 234-235
Gestalt, 118
goal-free evaluation, 112-117, 179, 346
goals, 10, 67, 83-121, 153-164, 167, 169-
    171, 179, 194, 203, 248, 301-303, 305-
    309, 330, 346
group home study, 142-145, 263-267, 271
guarantees, 82
guessing, 250-251

Halcolm, 9, 10, 29, 40, 59, 61, 72, 175-176,
    177, 209, 244, 281-282, 283, 322
hand exercise for focus, 81-82
hard data, 188, 221
Hawaii, 61
Head Start Evaluation, 87
health evaluation utilization study, 30-39,
    106-110, 124, 189-190, 195, 199, 235-
    240, 271, 273-278, 286-295, 298-300
holistic perspective, 200-202, 204
human services shortfall, 125

ideal plans, 131-132, 135-136, 165
ideology, 196
illuminative evaluation, 186
impacts, 169-171, 249, 346
implementation evaluation, 122-149, 151,
    156-158, 179, 203, 239, 330
improvement, 65-66, 70-71, 163-164, 172-
    173, 203, 280, 338
incremental decisions, 36-37, 106, 133,
    158, 236, 304-305
indecision, 59, 60
inductive approach, 152-153, 193-194
information age, 12-13
information-seeking endurance, 111
innovations adoption, 132-133, 137
inputs, 169-171
interdisciplinary, 210
internal evaluation, 164, 240, 309-314, 346
internal-external, 79, 313-314
international evaluation, 21, 125
interpretation, 244-280, 293, 332
involving intended users, 56-57, 220-222,
    238-244, 247-253, 278, 307-309, 310,
    330-333, 334

jargon, 66
judgments, 252, 261-263, 279, 322, 332

Kalamazoo evaluation, 283-285, 297
Koan, 24-26

labels, misleading, 142-145
levels of evidence, 169-171

management information systems, 138-139
manipulable variables, 75, 270
maximizing, 301-302, 304
means-ends hierarchy, 153-154, 169-171
measurement of goals, 94-96, 171
merit, 67
meta-evaluation, 314, 346
methodological quality, 235-239
mission statements, 99-102
misutilization, 336-337
models of evaluation, 67-68
monitoring, 66, 138-139
multiattribute utility measurement, 103
multiple methods, 181, 191-192, 193, 212-213, 246, 279

naturalistic inquiry, 185, 192-193, 200-213, 241
needs assessment, 17, 114, 346
negative thinking, 275-6
New School case, 158-160

objectivity, 195-200
open systems, 302-307
optimization, 301-322
organizational models, 301-307
outcomes, 96-98, 126-130, 151, 153, 169-171, 179, 203-204, 223-224, 241, 247, 260-261, 346

parachute story, 122-123
paradox, 120
paradigms debate, 177-217, 316, 319
Patton's Law, 244
peripheral-defined issues, 45, 106-107
personal factor, 40-58, 109-111
personal interest criterion, 73
personal evaluation, 71-72, 74, 297, 346
planned use, 80
political sophistication, 25, 270
politics, 45, 52, 91, 181, 222, 243, 261, 270, 283-321, 335
pork barrel orientation, 15, 17-18
positive thinking, 275-276
power, 283, 293-294, 295-300, 305, 338

practicality, 119-120, 220
presentations, 253-256, 277-278
priorities, 103-106
problem-solving, 67-68
process evaluation, 139-140, 204, 346
program design, 160-164
program improvement, 65-66, 163-164, 172-173, 203, 280, 338
propriety standards, 25-26
public issues, definition of, 11

qualitative data, 179, 181-182, 185-191, 233, 241
quality assurance, 346-347
quantitative measurement, 179-185, 186-191, 233, 241
questions, 246, 281-282, 315, 322, 337, 345-347
    alternative kinds of questions, 67-68, 191
    criteria for, 69-71
    empirical, 70-71
    generating, 75-77
    hierarchy of, 173
    identifying and focusing, 64-68, 158
    value, 70-71

ratings, 103
rationality, 52, 53, 118-120, 131, 133, 292, 294, 301-307
reality-testing, 156, 197
recidivism, 224, 249, 259
recommendations, 252, 263, 268-271, 274, 279, 324-325, 332
reification of goals, 118-120
reliability, 220, 228-230, 241-243
reporting, 244-280, 271-274, 278-280, 327
request-for-proposal, 51
responsive evaluation, 185-186
Robin Hood approach, 78
roles, multiple, 25, 312-313, 319-321
rule of thumb (20-80), 80

sampling, 205-207, 227
satisficing, 106, 302-305
scenarios, 79-80, 247-248
simplicity, 253-256, 279
simplifying reality, 165
situational responsiveness, 25, 181, 189, 191, 220, 283, 286, 305-310, 314-321, 330-331

social ecological approach, 146-18
sociology, 54, 119, 152, 199, 225
soft data, 95, 188, 221
stakeholders, 43-45, 51-53, 57, 68-69, 109-
    110, 147, 149, 152-153, 154, 156, 172,
    174, 180, 220-227, 235-244, 246-250,
    272-275, 278-279, 295, 299, 307-309,
    320
standards, 6, 24-26, 180, 197-198, 209-210,
    211, 219-220, 243-244, 301, 314-316,
    333, 334, 337
standards of desirability, 248-252, 278
student achievement, 95
subjectivity, 195-200
Sufi stories, 5, 27-28, 37, 83-84, 121, 150,
    174, 177-179, 259-260, 276, 280, 320-
    321, 339
summative evaluations, 65-66, 165, 179,
    203, 347
surprises, 272-273
systems analysis, 68, 163-164, 302-303

targeting audiences, 52-55
targets of opportunity, 158
teenage pregnancies, 13
test scores, 95, 105, 127, 190-191, 228-230
theory, 147-148, 150, 194
theory of action, 150-176, 330
timing, 164-167, 203, 235, 271
trade-offs, 231-238
training, 181, 211-212, 247, 255, 299, 315,
    316, 335
treatments, 129, 141-148, 168-169, 200-
    204
truth, 14, 15, 197, 222, 235-238, 243
20-80 rule, 80
types of evaluation, 14-20, 67-68, 137-142,
    179, 185-186, 308, 328-329, 345-347

uncertainty reduction, 35-36, 151, 293,
    295-297, 299, 302-307, 338
uniformity, 207-209
universal evaluation, 281-282
user-oriented, 57, 333
utility standards, 25-26, 220
utility tests, 222, 235-238, 242, 243
utilization
    continuum, 336
    crisis, 10, 21-22, 221
    definition of, 30-31, 51, 80, 278

evaluation vs. research, 14-15
factors affecting, 45-50, 55-56
first step, 43, 52, 57
issue, the, 6, 7, 11-13
premises, 57-58
related to methods, 235-244
second step, 65
strategies for reducing, 52-55
study of, 30-38
types of, 335
utilization-focused evaluation
alternatives to, 78-79
analysis and interpretation, 247, 263-
    267
causal linkages in, 150-155, 172-174
compared to Zen, 245-246
comprehensive nature, 26-27
consulting style, 307-309, 314-321, 337-
    9
essence, 332-333, 347
examples of, 107-109, 263-267, 336,
    340-344
face validity, 226
first step, 43, 52, 57, 246-247, 278, 330-
    331, 334, 338
flowchart, 330-333
fourth step, 332
goals in, 85, 91, 103-106, 109-111, 120
implementation focus in, 148-149
methods decisions, 180-183, 185, 195,
    202, 205, 214-217, 219-227, 238-
    244, 314-321, 330-333
outcome of, 80, 278, 300-301, 315, 335,
    337-339
practicality of, 197
premises, 57-58, 333-335
process, the, 314-321, 330-333, 337-
    339
reporting, 271, 274, 278-280
sampling, 207
second step, 65, 330-331
theory of action in, 150-155, 172-174
third step, 180-181, 220-221, 330-331

validity assumptions, 154-164
valuation, 67
variables, 200-202
verstehen, 185
vital facts, 80

worth, 67

ABOUT THE AUTHOR

MICHAEL QUINN PATTON is on the faculty of the University of Minnesota, where he has been Director of the Minnesota Center for Social Research (1975-1980) and where he was named outstanding teacher of the year in 1976 for his innovative evaluation teaching. His Ph.D. in Sociology is from the University of Wisconsin. He has worked on a broad range of evaluation projects spanning the human services spectrum, including evaluation of programs in agricultural extension, education, criminal justice, health, energy conservation, community development, welfare, commercial banks, manpower planning, mental health, charitable services, youth development, wilderness experiences, and private businesses. He has done evaluations at local, county, state, national, and international levels, including a ten-year project in the Caribbean in collaboration with colleagues at the University of the West Indies. He is the author of numerous articles on evaluation, as well as three other Sage books: *Qualitative Evaluation Methods* (1980); *Creative Evaluation* (1981); and *Practical Evaluation* (1982). He is editor of *Culture and Evaluation* (1985). He was awarded the Alva and Gunnar Myrdal Award for "Outstanding Contributions to Evaluation Practice and Use" at the 1984 Evaluation Research Society meeting in San Francisco. He is in great demand as a speaker and trainer. Readers of this book will not be surprised to learn that he won the 1985 Storytelling Competition at the University of Minnesota.